Turning Human Resource Analytics Into Actionable Strategies

Shad Ahmad Khan
American University of Phnom Penh, Cambodia

Ayben Koy
Fenerbahçe University, Turkey

Chandni Rani
Chandigarh University, India

Pooja Kansra
Mittal School of Business, Lovely Professional University, Punjab, India

Tanveer Kajla
NALSAR University of Law, India

IGI Global
Scientific Publishing
Publishing Tomorrow's Research Today

Vice President of Editorial	Melissa Wagner
Director of Acquisitions	Mikaela Felty
Director of Book Development	Jocelynn Hessler
Production Manager	Mike Brehm
Cover Design	Jose Rosado

Published in the United States of America by
IGI Global Scientific Publishing
701 East Chocolate Avenue
Hershey, PA, 17033, USA
Tel: 717-533-8845 | Fax: 717-533-7115
Website: https://www.igi-global.com E-mail: cust@igi-global.com

Library of Congress Cataloging-in-Publication Data

Names: Khan, Shad Ahmad, 1988- editor
http://id.loc.gov/rwo/agents/n2023074422
Title: Turning human resource analytics into actionable strategies / [edited by] Shad Khan, Ayben Koy, Chandni Rani, Pooja Kansra, Tanveer Kajla.
Description: Hershey, PA : IGI Global Scientific Publishing, [2026] | Includes bibliographical references and index. | Summary: "This book explores how NLP techniques can revolutionize traditional HR practices by effectively analyzing and interpreting vast amounts of textual data generated within organizations"-- Provided by publisher.
Identifiers: LCCN 2025006170 (print) | LCCN 2025006171 (ebook) | ISBN 9798337321356 hardcover | ISBN 9798337321363 paperback | ISBN 9798337321370 ebook
Subjects: LCSH: Personnel management http://id.loc.gov/authorities/subjects/sh85100143 | Personnel management--Data processing http://id.loc.gov/authorities/subjects/sh2008109095
Classification: LCC HF5549 .T875 2026 (print) | LCC HF5549 (ebook) | DDC 658.3--dc23/eng/20250418
LC record available at https://lccn.loc.gov/2025006170
LC ebook record available at https://lccn.loc.gov/2025006171

British Cataloguing in Publication Data
A Cataloguing in Publication record for this book is available from the British Library.

Table of Contents

Detailed Table of Contents

EIL is a leadership approach that integrates EI, relationship-building, and context-driven leadership and decision-making. Unlike traditional models focused on hierarchy and tasks, EIL emphasizes adaptability and empathy to build resilient, high-performing teams. This chapter explores EIL's foundations, highlighting the interplay between self-awareness, emotional regulation, and situational dynamics. It incorporates the Theory of Constructed Emotion to explain how leaders interpret emotional and contextual cues in real-time decision-making, making EIL a fluid and evolving construct. Studies across business, IT, and education reveals that leaders with strong EIL significantly enhance team trust, cohesion, and adaptability—outperforming technical skills. As leaders rise through organizational levels, reliance on EIL increases, reaching up to 90%. A competency-based framework is proposed, linking EIL to HR and business analytics. Organizations investing in EIL report improvements in psychological safety, innovation, and strategic thinking, underscoring its importance for leadership.

This chapter, per the authors, explores the integration of Natural Language Processing (NLP), sentiment analysis, and Structural Equation Modeling (SEM) in faculty evaluations. Traditional appraisal methods often lack depth, necessitating automated analysis of student feedback. Sentiment analysis using VADER classifies feedback into positive, neutral, and negative categories, while Latent Dirichlet Allocation (LDA) identifies dominant themes. SEM validates relationships among teaching effectiveness, course content, assessment fairness, student engagement, student satisfaction, and faculty performance. Findings indicate that student satisfaction significantly mediates faculty evaluations, with teaching effectiveness and engagement being primary predictors. The study underscores the potential of AI-driven faculty appraisal systems in enhancing instructional quality and governance in higher education

Retaining brilliant people is essential for organizational success in the cutthroat corporate world of today. In order to overcome this difficulty, human resource (HR) analytics has become a potent instrument that uses data-driven insights to make well-informed decisions. With an emphasis on how advanced analytics skills, the calibre of HR data, and the incorporation of predictive models effect retention efforts, this study examines the relationship between HR analytics and employee retention. A mixed-method approach was used to gather information from HR specialists in a range of sectors. To determine their impact on keeping top personnel, important factors like HR Data Quality and Accuracy, Predictive Analytics in HR, Data Driven Decision Making Culture and HR Analytics Technology are examined. Additionally, the study looks into how organizational culture and support affect the uptake and effectiveness of HR analytics programs in employee retention campaigns.

This study examines how AI-powered sentiment analysis monitors employee well-being and shapes workplace culture. As digital communication expands, companies generate massive text and voice data. NLP-based sentiment analysis finds stress early and analyses emotions and performance. The study interviews HR professionals, AI engineers, and employees across industries using a qualitative cross-case approach. AI's ability to recognise emotional trends and how insights are used for support are examined. It also handles employee trust, acceptance, resistance, intrusiveness, data privacy, algorithmic bias, transparency, and permission. The report recommends ethical AI use that respects employee rights, fosters openness, trust, and compliance.

HR leaders, AI engineers, and policymakers are advised on responsible AI integration in HR. The report promotes responsible AI discourse by promoting employee-centric initiatives that improve well-being and workplace digital transformation.

The goal of this study is to identify important trends, significant contributions, and developing topics in the quickly developing field of HR analytics by performing a thorough bibliometric analysis of research published between 2020 and 2025. The 307 pertinent documents in the dataset were selected through a methodical search technique that included keywords like "HR Analytics," "Human Resource Management," "Predictive Analytics," "People Analytics," and "Human Resource Analytics." To guarantee relevance and accessibility, publications were limited to English-language papers and sorted by subject areas: business management, computer science, and social science. The results show a notable increase in HR Analytics research during this time, which is indicative of its increasing significance in promoting strategic HR practices and data-driven decision-making.

Various Artificial Intelligence technologies like Machine Learning (ML), Natural Language Processing (NLP), Predictive Analytics, and Robotics Process Automation (RPA) have changed the ongoing paradigm in the human resource acquisition and management process. The introduction of various artificial intelligence tools has empowered recruiters to automate multiple tasks on certain recruitment-based platforms. The adoption of AI-based recruitment tools and predictive analytics for talent acquisition can lead to increased productivity, reduce bias, and be instrumental in developing an agile workforce. However, the studies on the application of AI in the talent acquisition process are still in their nascent stage. Therefore, the current study used a meta-analysis technique to synthesise relevant empirical findings in this area and draw generalisable conclusions regarding the determinants, variations, and implications of AI adoption in talent acquisition.

The integration of Natural Language Processing (NLP) into Human Resources (HR) presents both challenges and opportunities. This chapter explores how NLP particularly Large Language Models (LLMs) can enhance HR practices, making them more efficient and employee-friendly. It does not advocate replacing traditional HR with AI but highlights how NLP can reduce outdated, impersonal processes. Key challenges include data privacy concerns, as NLP tools require large datasets to function effectively. The chapter analyses current trends and future directions, offering human resource professionals and academics insight into the complexities of adopting NLP in HR. It concludes with cautious optimism about NLP's potential to transform HR beyond operational efficiency improving experiences for both employees and job candidates.

The importance of employee well-being in fostering innovation, customer satisfaction, and profitability is becoming more widely acknowledged. This review article emphasizes how sentiment analysis, which was once primarily used for consumer insights, is now being used to track employees' emotional well-being and enable early intervention against burnout, stress, and disengagement. Sentiment analysis has been used by numerous businesses to improve retention and workplace policies. However, there are many obstacles because of ethical worries about algorithmic bias, privacy, and trust. Informed consent, data anonymization, staff involvement, and human oversight are necessary for successful implementation.To evaluate its long-term effects on workplace culture, longitudinal research is required. It can be concluded that while sentiment analysis presents a transformative opportunity for data-driven HR management, its success hinges on ethical stewardship, fostering a workplace where employees feel heard, respected, and supported.

The study aims to conduct a comprehensive bibliometric analysis to unveil the existing body of research on moonlighting or dual jobs, with specific focus on evolving role of Artificial Technology (AI). By examining the existing literature, the current study explores the impactful articles, influential journals and notable transition over the selected time period. The three main bibliometric analytic techniques used in the study are citation analysis, co-authorship analysis, and co-occurrence analysis. Data retrieval for the study is limited to the Scopus dataset. MS-Excel and VOSviewer are the analysis tools utilized in bibliometric analysis. The study's conclusions indicate that between 1979 and 2021, there is a steady increase in research on second jobs or moonlighting. United States leading with majority of publications. Guariglia and Kim have the most citations in the co-authorship analysis. The term "moonlighting" is most frequently used among all the available documents. Testing theories of fairness-Intentions matter is the title of the most cited document.

Agile and well-informed decision-making is essential to maintaining competitiveness and innovation in the evolving IT sector. IT companies may now successfully match personnel strategies with more general business goals thanks to HR analytics, which has become a game-changing instrument. This study looks at how HR analytics affect strategic decision-making in the IT industry, emphasizing how it may improve operational effectiveness, optimize talent management, and promote long-term success. The study's conclusions demonstrate the strategic importance of HR analytics as a driver of creativity and flexibility in the IT industry. In addition to optimizing HR operations, data-driven decision-making strengthens organizational resilience in a market that is competitive and changing quickly. This study emphasizes how

Preface

INTRODUCTION

In the last decade, Human Resource (HR) analytics has emerged as a transformative field bridging data-driven approaches with the human side of organizational success. Once regarded as an administrative function, HR has now become a strategic partner capable of shaping innovation, employee well-being, and long-term sustainability. The shift from intuition-based decisions to evidence-based strategies marks a critical turning point in human resource management. By harnessing analytics, organizations can make informed decisions that directly enhance productivity, engagement, and retention while maintaining fairness and inclusivity.

This edited volume, *Turning Human Resource Analytics Into Actionable Strategies*, brings together scholars and practitioners from diverse academic and professional backgrounds to explore the intersections of analytics, leadership, technology, and employee experience. Our collective aim is to offer readers not only theoretical frameworks but also practical applications that demonstrate the potential of HR analytics in real-world contexts. The book provides both conceptual clarity and actionable insights, making it a valuable resource for researchers, HR professionals, and policy makers alike.

At its core, this book reflects a shared commitment to understanding how data, when ethically collected and responsibly applied, can humanize workplaces rather than dehumanize them. Each chapter contributes to this mission by highlighting emerging technologies, innovative methodologies, and evidence-based practices. Taken together, the chapters present a comprehensive picture of how HR analytics can guide organizations in navigating the complexities of today's fast-changing world of work.

CHAPTER OVERVIEW

Chapter 1 introduces the concept of *Emotionally Intelligent Leadership (EIL)* and its role in decision-making and team dynamics. It proposes a competency-based framework linking EIL to HR analytics, underscoring how empathy, adaptability, and emotional regulation improve organizational outcomes.

Chapter 2 explores automated student feedback analysis through Natural Language Processing (NLP) and Structural Equation Modeling (SEM). The findings highlight the potential of AI-driven faculty appraisals to improve governance and instructional quality in higher education.

Chapter 3 examines HR analytics as a strategic tool for long-term employee retention. It demonstrates how predictive models, data quality, and organizational culture contribute to keeping top talent engaged and committed.

Chapter 4 focuses on AI-driven sentiment analysis to monitor employee well-being. By discussing data ethics, transparency, and employee trust, the authors provide guidelines for integrating responsible AI into workplace wellness initiatives.

Chapter 5 offers a bibliometric review of recent HR analytics research (2020–2025), identifying major trends and emerging themes. It emphasizes the growing role of analytics in shaping strategic HR practices.

Chapter 6 provides a meta-analysis of studies on AI-driven talent acquisition. It shows how machine learning, NLP, and predictive analytics reshape recruitment processes, reducing bias and enhancing efficiency.

Chapter 7 addresses the challenges and opportunities of integrating NLP into HR. While highlighting its transformative potential, it raises concerns over data privacy and offers cautious optimism for its future use.

Chapter 8 presents a comprehensive review of sentiment analysis for employee well-being. It calls for ethical stewardship and longitudinal research to ensure long-term positive cultural impacts.

Chapter 9 uses bibliometric analysis to study moonlighting in the age of AI. It traces global research trends and uncovers how side hustles intersect with digital transformation and fairness in employment practices.

Chapter 10 emphasizes HR analytics in strategic decision-making within the IT industry. The chapter reveals how data-driven approaches help IT organizations achieve resilience and innovation.

Chapter 11 concludes with an exploration of NLP in business intelligence. It highlights how organizations can convert unstructured data into actionable insights, bridging the gap between information overload and informed decision-making.

CONCLUSION

Taken collectively, these chapters reveal how HR analytics is no longer a peripheral tool but a central component of organizational strategy. From leadership frameworks to talent acquisition and well-being monitoring, the contributions highlight a field that is dynamic, evolving, and deeply impactful. They demonstrate that data-driven insights, when carefully applied, can elevate HR from a supportive role to a strategic driver of competitive advantage.

The insights presented in this book also remind us of the ethical, cultural, and human dimensions that must guide the use of analytics. Technology alone cannot guarantee success; instead, organizations must cultivate trust, fairness, and transparency in how they apply data to decision-making. By balancing efficiency with empathy, and precision with inclusivity, HR analytics can serve as a force for both organizational and societal progress.

We, as editors, hope that this volume will inspire future scholarship, innovation, and practice in the domain of HR analytics. Whether you are a student, researcher, policymaker, or practitioner, this book offers perspectives that will enrich your understanding and inform your actions. Above all, it is our belief that turning HR analytics into actionable strategies requires not only technical expertise but also a steadfast commitment to valuing the human element in every decision made.

Chapter 1

An Integrative Framework for Developing Relationships and Contingent Decision-Making for Young Leaders:

Emotionally Intelligent Leadership

Shardul Shankar
https://orcid.org/0000-0002-8895-6765
Fortune Institute of International Business, India

Mansi Gupta
SRM Institute of Science and Technology, Delhi, India

ABSTRACT

EIL is a leadership approach that integrates EI, relationship-building, and context-driven leadership and decision-making. Unlike traditional models focused on hierarchy and tasks, EIL emphasizes adaptability and empathy to build resilient, high-performing teams. This chapter explores EIL's foundations, highlighting the interplay between self-awareness, emotional regulation, and situational dynamics. It incorporates the Theory of Constructed Emotion to explain how leaders interpret emotional and contextual cues in real-time decision-making, making EIL a fluid and evolving construct. Studies across business, IT, and education reveals that leaders with strong EIL significantly enhance team trust, cohesion, and adaptability—

DOI: 10.4018/979-8-3373-2135-6.ch001

outperforming technical skills. As leaders rise through organizational levels, reliance on EIL increases, reaching up to 90%. A competency-based framework is proposed, linking EIL to HR and business analytics. Organizations investing in EIL report improvements in psychological safety, innovation, and strategic thinking, underscoring its importance for leadership.

CONCEPTUALIZING EMOTIONALLY INTELLIGENT LEADERSHIP

In line with the core definitions of Emotional Intelligence and Leadership, we see Emotionally Intelligent Leadership as a comprehensive amalgamation of the processes that provide substantial behavioral and practical advantages over other kinds of leadership. This kind of leadership does not depend on the structural, hierarchical, or performative outcomes of the people working for the leader, rather it focuses on the accumulated behavioral, inter and intra-personal, and conduct-driven experiences, which in turn provide for a more collaborative and comprehensive impact on the personality, perception, and maturation of the leader as well as their followers.

One important distinction that this chapter would try to explain is the advantageous nature of EIL over other models as it focuses primarily on the choices of the individuals involved in the relationships thereby building a stronger moral character of the leaders. This develops when young leaders gain experiential knowledge and perspectives that are usually not attained through intellectual development. EIL is a model, as described by Goleman (2019) which focuses on developing one's character, which would facilitate the development of their followers and provide a more formidable satisfaction and long-term solutions. This premise drives the research in the area of Emotional Intelligence, Leadership, and Emotionally Intelligent Leadership.

UNDERSTANDING EMOTIONAL INTELLIGENCE AS WELL AS LEADERSHIP

Even though Salovey and Mayer (1990) introduced the idea of Emotional Intelligence, it was the book written by Daniel Goleman (1995) which made this concept a mainstream idea. Building on the concepts of the initial introduction to the concept of EI, Goleman, in his book, defined EI as "*a person's ability to manage [their] feelings so that those feelings are expressed appropriately and effectively.*" Over time, the findings of these authors, as well as other psychologists, cleared our understanding that Emotional Intelligence is the largest predictor of a highly productive and successful workforce.

Growing bodies of researchers across the domains of study have started taking EI and Emotional Quotient (EQ) seriously. A recent search on the Web of Science Portal provided that the term "emotional intelligence; since 1990" yielded 55,399 results. Changing this year from 1990 to 2010 still yielded a whopping 40,843 results.

This can be seen in real-life examples, as stated by Ackley (2016), which states that business leaders have continually, for as long as they have known, looked for other substantial methods that could more precisely define the parameters of the individual as well as organizational success other than the financials and the analytical returns. This worry is pretty evident in the discussions of psychology of the understanding of leaders and leadership development. Global leaders have tried to holistically explain the types and models of leadership that could accurately evaluate a successful leader. The concepts of Transformational Leadership (Downton, 1973; Burns, 1978), Charismatic Leadership (Weber, 1922; Weber and Eisenstadt, 1968), Servant Leadership (Greenleaf, 1970), Authentic Leadership (George, 2003), etc. have tried to acclimate the self-development and understanding of your followers to become a more comprehensively effective leader.

But as Pathak et al. (2018) explained, even though leaders are actively trying to understand the intricacies of EI and Leadership, very few leaders have understood the concepts themselves, and even fewer can effectively implement them in their organizations. This can also be seen in the daily lives of people, as almost everyone who has worked in an organization can vouch for knowing at least one individual who is intellectually evolved as well as skillful at their job, but when promoted to a position of leadership, have failed, and failed miserably. They would also be able to provide at least one example of someone who wasn't as technically or skillfully sound but thrived in the leadership positions (Goleman, 2019).

At the time when the initial model of EI was being developed, several other schools of thought in the concept started emerging in the literature, with the criticisms of Goleman's model being less "scientifically rigorous". This, in turn, has started two-decade-long discussions between the researchers in the area of EI, which involves Mayer, Salovey, and Caruso (2003), Goleman (1995), Bar-On (1997), and Wolff (2005), among others, addressing what sufficiently constitutes the understanding of Emotional Intelligence. Some important concerns have been to effectively explain the core concepts of EI and Leadership, as well as EIL, in a way that is understandable, readable, and reproducible by the business personnel. This is why the work of Goleman, even though considered as lacking "scientific rigor", is pa, paramount in building the personnel and psychological understanding in the scientific and business community.

CONCEPTUALIZATIONS AND MEASUREMENTS OF EIL

In the understanding of EIL, it is imperative to identify and create a distinction between Emotional Intelligence & Leadership (EI&L); and Emotionally Intelligent Leadership (EIL). In the research of Emotional Intelligence and Leadership, there are two distinct constructs: the first is Emotional Intelligence, and the second is Leadership. If there is a high correlation between any two constructs in the two concepts, it might be interpreted that they do not exist independently. An example would be the transformation of the early five-factor model of EI theory into the models of the four-factor models. Many prominent authors, including Bar-On (2006) and Mayer, Salovey, and Caruso (2002) have created the distinction between their earlier models and have distinguished between the relationship aspects of EI with the self-concepts in their second versions. This is where some of the recent research has been contradictory and makes it important to clearly distinguish between EI&L and EIL.

Most of the organizations are looking for a leader who would not only be high on EQ but is leading with emotional intelligence. Business leaders and organizations pay a handsome amount for the training, developing, and aiding their present and future leaders with the competencies of emotional intelligence, to better build their leadership repertoire. Psychologists and other researchers have also customized these models for middle and lower-level positions. Psychologists like Day (2004) and Goleman (2019) have worked in finding solutions for the forces that drive the performances of leaders. In the 188 companies that these psychologists looked for answers, they found that a staggering amount of high-performing leaders were having a blending ratio of cognitive ability, technical skills, and EI; but the impact of EIL was as high as twice than the combined outcomes of the former models (Shankar and Tewari, 2023). It also showed that as the ranks of the employees increased, the need for EIL increased to as high as 90% (Sood and Kaushal, 2018; McCelland, 1996).

TRANSFORMING ORGANIZATIONS BY LEARNING EIL

Before looking at the concepts of transforming an organization, it is important to understand whether EI and more importantly, EIL, can be taught and learned. For ages, business leaders, academicians, and practitioners have debated on the reproducibility of the concepts of EI amongst the leaders of tomorrow. Are leaders born or made? Can EI be taught to leaders or not? The answer is both. The scientific inquiries of Mayer, Salovey, and Caruso, both in their individual as well as combined capacities, have focused on Trait Emotional Intelligence. They primarily believe that EI is heavily dependent on the personality and the cognitive elements of a leader, which can be taught in the behaviors of those leaders. In a similar domain, the inquiries like Goleman, Bar-On, and Wolff believe that the competencies of EIL are a set of skills that can be chosen to be learned and taught to anyone willing to develop these competencies.

One thing that has been crystal clear in recent studies is that EQ does not work as its IQ counterpart. In the findings of Barrett's (2017a) book, she argued that emotions created in an individual are heavily dominated by environmental factors. She then goes on to provide a pivotal theory, known as the "theory of constructed emotions" (Barrett, 2017b), which provides the compartmentalization of emotions according to the circumstances that drive a person's response to an emotional stimulus. This mirrors the findings of Shankar and Tewari (2023), Day et al. (2004), and Goleman (2019) who say that the environmental and experiential development of a leader would increase with the incrementation in their job experience, emotional maturity, and life experience with age.

The learnings of EIL in the business contexts have radical impacts on the organization's performances and success. Organizations are essentially open-system networks that are continually interacting with internal and external environments, and adapting and changing according to them. They are rarely in stasis, and the changes in organizations are often gradual, perpetual, and incremental. Many times, businesses learn from being purposeful and continuous feedback and transformation mechanisms. If these organizations do not change and adapt as the environment changes, they open the doors to their peril (Thurow, 1999).

In a similar domain to a leader's rise and fall, the organization's rise and fall are usually uncertain and swift. This is the reason why business leaders try to incorporate a culture in which leaders can evolve and develop alongside their peers and subordinates. Every organizational domain is facing stiff challenges from these dynamic environments and their impact. Educational institutes, profit, not-for-profit organizations, and even defense services face steady, steadfast, and combative features of the environment. The evidence, scientific inquiries, and corporate responses are consistent and compelling in their findings that an effective leadership style coupled with behavioral effectiveness is paramount in transforming organizations.

Organizations facing these threats have to transform themselves with leaders that are not only competent but decisive and transformative. The development of a leader with cognitive ability is necessitated by voluntarily exposing them to the emotional triggers and stimuli that are going to generate an emotional response. As they repeat these exercises in their jobs and training, with time, they are going to develop a better and more comprehensive understanding of EI and emotionally intelligent leadership. The forces that impede this EIL development in leaders are being rigid in their approaches, autocratic decision-making styles, bureaucratic structures, or restrictive and non-transparent approaches to building relationships with the followers and leading them. Therefore, to build long-lasting relationships and decision-making strategies, the primary mechanism that must be used is building a strong Emotionally Intelligent Leadership. This competency would allow for a more nuanced understanding of the environments in which a leader functions, and build the repertoire of empathy and enhanced social skills.

It is worth diving into the roles that the elements of EI play in the development of EIL. Leaders looking to develop their competencies like empathy are usually those who are deficient in their EQ. Most of these leaders are considered tough to work with, give out an intimidating vibe, or are downright unaware of the empathetic emotions of their team members. When confronted with these facts, these leaders usually are found to be angry, frustrated, and even remorseful. These issues almost always bleed into their personal and social lives, as they end up with very few friends if any, and people avoid having conversations with them and loathe giving them the bad news. As a psychologist or a behavior analyst, it becomes important to impart the components of EI into them and create a more empathetic and emotionally intelligent individual out of them.

Practice and Feedback: These are amongst the most important tools in developing EIL in business leaders. The leaders must be exposed to tough emotional situations and must be asked to provide solutions to these problems. At the same time, their mentors, coaches, and superiors must create a critique-driven development of their characters. On-the-job interactions must be encouraged, with special emphasis on listening to the interactions amongst the leader and other employees. Over time, the leader would be able to create a nuanced understanding of the context in which the emotions are being expressed or presented, and they would be able to more effectively acknowledge, understand and express the appropriate emotions and/or responses to the emotional stimulus. Applying this process amongst every leader would be a catalyst to a more emotionally intelligent leadership in an organization.

Developing EIL complexity builds the leaders' capacity to differentiate between the kinds of emotions felt by themselves and others, and this, in turn, provides choice-oriented decision-making for the problem presented to them. A good example would be: Supposedly there is an employee who has been consistently sad during their work hours. If the leader is not adept with the tools of EIL, they might conclude that the employee is sad because of some job-related issue. This might lead to some inappropriate decisions or responses to an already suffering employee. But if they are strengthened with the tools of EIL, they might have interactions with the employee and find out the roots of the issue causing sadness to them. As the context gets added to these interactions, Barrett (2017a) explains that the leader would be able to make a better and more informed decision which would ultimately help the employee, and create a reputation of an understanding leader amongst their peers.

Armed with the tools of EIL, a leader becomes a more nuanced, informed, and complex being. This leadership style works on the limitations of leadership styles that are dependent on the responses of the employees to a policy or decision made by the leader, and the leader's response to those responses. EIL, in turn, creates a proactive leader who is usually ahead in the game by creating an environment of high interaction and skillful discourse, which drive the decision-making of the leader. An emotionally intelligent leader does not wait for an appropriate resolution to present itself based on the environmental or behavioral displays by the employees, rather it works on creating a system where high empathy and trust allows for employees and followers to come up with creative, innovative, and comprehensive solutions to the problems that need to be dealt with. If a leader is not affluent in this pedagogy, sooner or later, the team flounders and the leader fails in delivering the desired outcomes. This is probably one of the only solutions to finding solutions especially if the leader is stuck. If the leader is not emotionally intelligent, people will not only hesitate in coming forth for solutions, rather would actively avoid providing one.

COMPONENTS OF EIL

Over the last 30+ years, there have been four important models of EI:

- Salovey and Mayer's (1990) Model of EI, which is used as a catalyst for their MSCEIT Test (2002). This model is a four-factor model, with its competencies being: (1) perception/expression of emotion, (2) use of emotion to facilitate thinking, (3) understanding of emotion, and (4) management of emotion in oneself and others.
- Goleman's (1995) Model of EI, which has been the most popularized five-factor model of EI, with its components being: (1) Self-awareness, (2) Self-regulation, (3) Motivation, (4) Empathy, and (5) Social skills. They have since then, updated their model to the Four-Quadrant Model: (1) Self-Awareness, (2) Self-Management, (3) Social Awareness, and (5) Relationship Management (Goleman et al., 2002).
- Bar-On's (1997) EQ-I Model of EI, which consists of five-major constructs that are sub-divided into 15 interpersonal and emotional competencies: (1) Intrapersonal, (2) Interpersonal, (3) Adaptability, (4) Stress Management, and (5) General Mood.
- Wolff (2005) Inventory (ECI or Emotional Competence Inventory), which consists of four-factor competence: (1) Self-Awareness, (2) Self-Management, (3) Social Awareness, and (4) Relationship Management.

These are very popular EI models which focus on providing a holistic understanding of how emotional intelligence works for individuals, and how they can use it to build their EQ. Most of these models take into account the need for developing skill sets that are going to help the people develop better relationships with their counterparts, and these models are also used as a threshold by the psychologists, coaches, and industry leaders to develop their or their followers' and other leaders' emotional intelligence.

But it must be remembered that these are prominent EI models. These models, even though very effective, sometimes discount the element of Leadership and Leadership Development of these individuals. And as stated in Shankar and Tewari (2023), a leader should not be content with only developing individual emotional intelligence, but must focus on developing team emotional intelligence. Therefore, a more fitting model has been discussed in Skankman et al.'s (2015) model of Emotionally Intelligent Leadership.

Figure 1. Emotionally Intelligent Leadership Model (Source: Skankman et al., 2015)

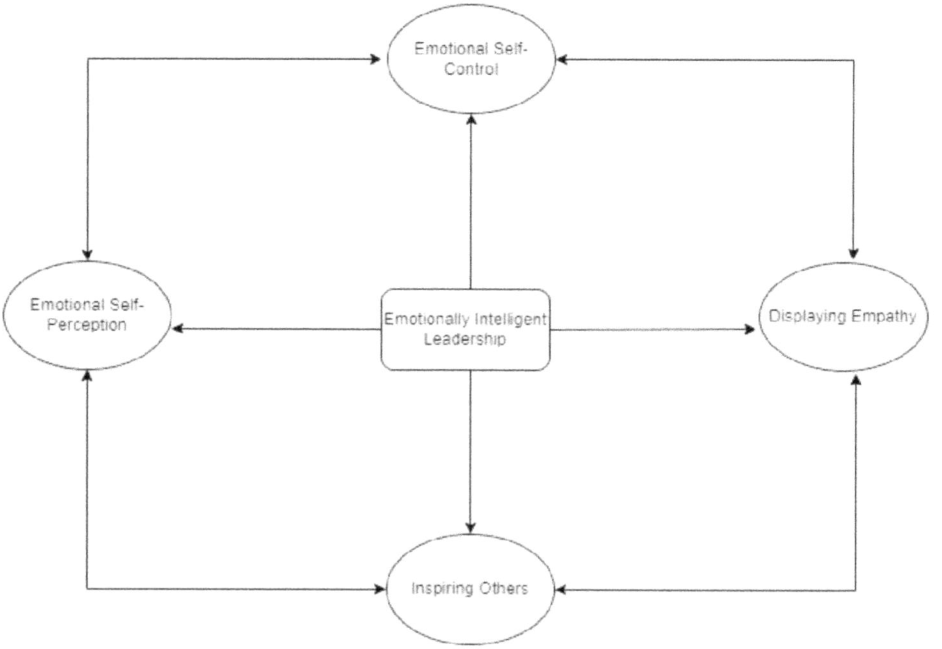

This model of EIL has four constructs, i.e.

1. Emotional Self-Perception: This competency is used to identify, describe, understand, and categorize the emotions of the leader. It also encompasses the

higher understanding that emotionally intelligent leaders have of the impact and influence that emotions play in interactions and decision-making with and for others.

2. Emotional Self-Control: The above competency is used to identify and categorize the emotions felt, and this competency is used to effectively moderate those emotions to reach a better and positively desired result. An emotionally intelligent leader would not be only able to acknowledge the emotions but appropriately express them.
3. Displaying Empathy: This competency allows a leader to be an empathetic leader. It allows an emotionally intelligent leader to accurately perceive, address and respond to the emotional triggers and cues that are being presented to them in their interactions with others.
4. Inspiring Others: This competency allows for the leaders to foster an environment that is not only motivated but also productive. An emotionally intelligent leader would be able to read a situation and create, adapt or change the working environment that is not only effective and efficient but also positively inspiring.

These four constructs have been derived from three broad facets of Emotional Intelligence and Leadership (Allen et al. (, 2016). The three facets are:

1. Consciousness of Self: This facet demonstrates that an emotionally intelligent leader must be able to accurately identify, perceive, access, understand, and express the appropriate emotion at all times. This is highly dependent on the willingness of the leader to develop their acumen to be reflective and introspective in their awareness of the self continuously (Shankar et al., 2017).
2. Consciousness of Others: This facet focuses on the emotionally intelligent leaders' understanding and awareness of the emotions felt and expressed by others, by appropriately acknowledging and perceiving the emotions displayed. When applied effectively, this facet brings about a radical shift in the interpersonal interactions and long-term relationships developed by the leaders and their followers (Lee et al., 2021).
3. Consciousness of Context: This facet builds upon the understanding that an emotionally intelligent leader would not only be influenced by the awareness and consciousness of themselves and others but would also be cognizant of the situations and circumstances in which these emotions are being displayed and expressed. These contexts are usually what are driving the dynamics and performances of the groups and the projects that these groups work on (Skankman, 2015).

Table 1. Facets and Capacities of Emotionally Intelligent Leadership (Source: Allen et al., 2016)

EIL Facets and Capacities: The 19 Capacities of Emotionally Intelligent Leadership
Consciousness of Self
Emotional self-perception: Identifying emotions and their impact on behavior
Emotional self-control: Consciously moderating emotions
Authenticity: Being transparent and trustworthy
Healthy self-esteem: Having a balanced sense of self
Flexibility: Being open and adaptive to change
Optimism: Having a positive outlook
Initiative: Taking action
Achievement: Striving for excellence
Consciousness of Others
Displaying empathy: Being emotionally in tune with others
Inspiring others: Energizing individuals and groups
Coaching others: Enhancing the skills and abilities of others
Capitalizing on difference: Benefiting from multiple perspectives
Developing relationships: Building a network of trusting relationships
Building teams: Working with others to accomplish a shared purpose
Demonstrating citizenship: Fulfilling responsibilities to the group
Managing conflict: Identifying and resolving conflict
Facilitating change: Working toward new directions
Consciousness of Context
Analyzing the group: Interpreting group dynamics
Assessing the environment: Interpreting external forces and trends
Source: Developing Emotionally Intelligent Leadership: The Need for Deliberate Practice and Collaboration Across Disciplines, Allen et al., 2016

EXAMINING THE MODEL OF EMOTIONALLY INTELLIGENT LEADERSHIP

The understanding of Emotional Intelligence, Leadership styles, and even Emotionally Intelligent Leadership has been derived with continuous evaluations of their models through various univariate and multivariate analysis techniques. These techniques have ranged from Systematic Literature Reviews and Meta-Analyses to Observations and Interviews and Empirical, Anecdotal, and Experimental Analyses.

Standardized scales such as MSCEIT (Mayer et al., 2002), to EQ-i (Bar-On, 1997); to a more recent EMOTICOM Battery (Bland et al., 2016) and EI Model (Shankar and Tewari, 2021) have all identified that the model is either five-factored or four-factored. Recent developments in the areas of EI&L and EIL have reaffirmed that emotionally intelligent leadership can be explained through a four-factor model (Goleman, 1998; Davies et al., 1998; Wong and Law, 2002; Allen et al., 2016). By clarifying the constructs of EIL, we can now concentrate on guiding our efforts in promoting and developing these competencies amongst the leaders of the organizations and creating strategies around it that would facilitate more holistic leadership development.

An important element that is necessary to be discussed in the EIL model, which is marginally discussed in the three facets of EIL, is a more elaborated involvement of the Theory of Constructed Emotion by Lisa Feldman Barrett (2017b). Although it is apparent from Table 1 that Consciousness of Context is an important element of the EIL model, it only encompasses the interpretation of group dynamics and the external forces. By involving Barrett's theory, this consciousness of context can be updated and modified by including the physiological response to the emotional stimuli, cultural impacts, and lived experiences of the leader. Therefore, if a leader is developing their awareness of the contexts, they would also be expected to be adept in situational, cultural, and experiential dynamics of the interactions.

Extending the work of Barrett (2017a) and Skankman (2015), demonstrating the need to evaluate the lower or higher-order constructs would be important for validating the model itself. As Shankar and Tewari (2021) pointed out, there is relatively little work done on the concepts of EIL and building a comprehensive theory for the understanding and development of EIL. It is, therefore, important to understand that at the core of emotionally intelligent leadership, is emotional intelligence (Goleman, 2019).

RECONCEPTUALIZING EMOTIONALLY INTELLIGENT LEADERSHIP MODEL

Despite an apparent increase in the research in the area of emotional intelligence and emotionally intelligent leadership, the fundamental model of EIL discounts the influence that the contextual exchanges between a leader and the follower have on the overall understanding of the EIL. This is a reasonable shortcoming because the underlying theory of contextual exchange, i.e. The theory of constructed emotion, is a theory that runs against the streamlined understanding of the emotions in the traditional sense. However, more recent works in the area of emotions, emotional stimulation, emotional manipulation, and emotional management have increasingly included the use of experiential, cultural, situational, and circumstantial impacts. This concept of contextual exchange attributes to a way through which an emotionally intelligent leader can continually grow, learn and develop the skill of making a more informed Contingent Decision-Making.

Figure 2. Modified Emotionally Intelligent Leadership Model. (Based on Skankman et al., 2015's EIL Model)

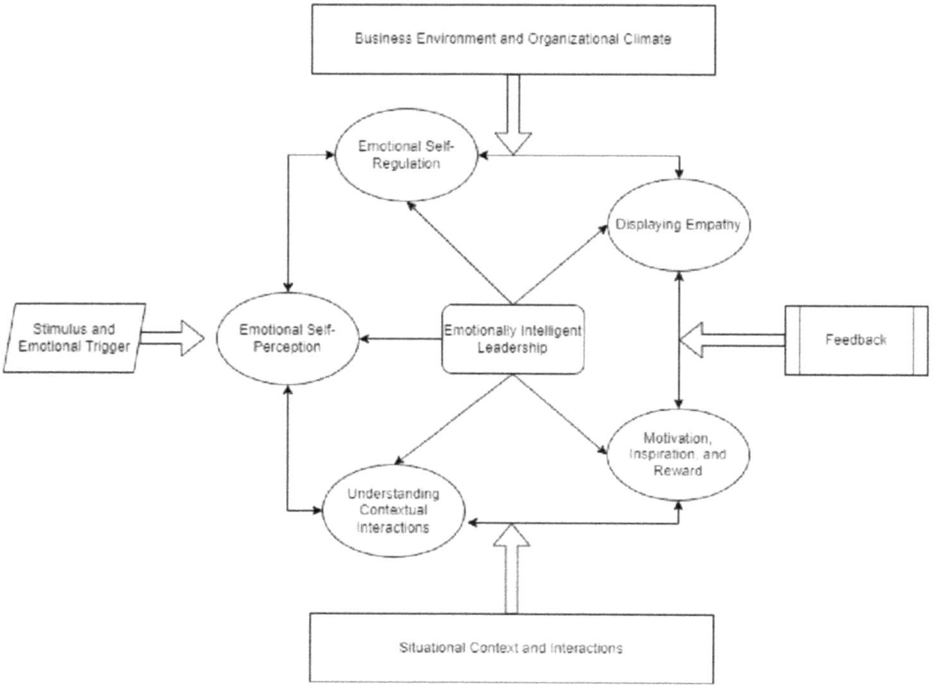

Organizations need leaders who are ever-evolving, self-aware, and willing to be adaptive as per the situations that arise (Day and Lance, 2004; Allen et al., 2012). Adaptive leaders, and especially those who are adaptive to the changes in the circumstances, are usually grounded in internalized values but are also aware of the strengths and weaknesses of the nuances of contexts. Therefore, the three facets of the EIL model (see Table 1) have a reciprocal relationship between the three facets, which are the consciousness of self and others, with the consciousness of the context.

A question then arises what does it take to be a self-aware and empathetic leader, who is also brimming with the nuances of contextual exchanges and contingent decision-making? Careful scrutiny of the theories and models of emotional intelligence and the theory of constructed emotion indicates that an emotionally intelligent leader would have optimized aspects of cognitive, behavioral, and social competencies. Thus, the Skankman (2015) model needs to be modified to accommodate the intricacies of the Consciousness of Contexts to provide a more comprehensive understanding of the emotionally intelligent leader (Figure 2 and Table 2).

Table 2. Modified Facets and Capacities for Emotionally Intelligent Leadership (Based on Allen et al., 2016's List)

Modified EIL Facets and Capacities: 24 Competencies for Emotionally Intelligent Leadership
Consciousness of Self
Emotional self-perception: Identifying emotions and their impact on behavior
Emotional self-control: Consciously moderating emotions
Authenticity: Being transparent and trustworthy
Healthy self-esteem: Having a balanced sense of self
Flexibility: Being open and adaptive to change
Optimism: Having a positive outlook
Initiative: Taking action
Achievement: Striving for excellence
Consciousness of Others
Displaying empathy: Being emotionally in tune with others
Coaching others: Enhancing the skills and abilities of others
Capitalizing on difference: Benefiting from multiple perspectives
Developing relationships: Building a network of trusting relationships
Building teams: Working with others to accomplish a shared purpose
Demonstrating citizenship: Fulfilling responsibilities to the group
Managing conflict: Identifying and resolving conflict
Facilitating change: Working toward new directions
Consciousness of Context
Analyzing the group: Interpreting group dynamics
Assessing the environment: Interpreting external forces and trends
Subjective Intensity: Working with people feeling different levels of emotional intensity to the same context
Inspiring others: Energizing individuals and groups
Contextual Exchange: Understanding the contexts of interactions
Observed Behavior: Developing the skill to observe the changes in behavior of themselves and others
Circumstantial changes: Identifying and evaluating the changes in situations
Experiential Response: Using the past social and cultural experiences to provide solutions
Based on Allen et al., 2016's EIL Facets and Capabilities List

INTEGRATING HR ANALYTICS INTO EMOTIONALLY INTELLIGENT LEADERSHIP DEVELOPMENT

The development of the concept of EIL cannot rely solely on traditional training and introspection. HR Analytics has now grown into its own self, which offers evidence-based insights into workforce behaviors, emotional trends, and performance dynamics. By leveraging advanced data tools and predictive models, HR Analytics complements and enhances the understanding and cultivation of EIL.

Recent research by Shankar, Vyas, and Tewari (2024) has emphasized the strategic role of machine learning in identifying patterns underlying employee turnover. These insights are particularly valuable for emotionally intelligent leaders, who must recognize early signals of disengagement, emotional fatigue, or interpersonal breakdowns. Their findings demonstrate how predictive modeling of HR data can serve as an early-warning mechanism, allowing leaders to respond empathetically and decisively before issues escalate.

These data-informed strategies align with the broader body of work in leadership analytics and behavior-driven decision-making. For example, Goleman (2019) emphasized that emotionally intelligent leaders often rely not just on introspection but also on accurate interpretation of emotional cues, which HR data can help quantify. Similarly, Day et al. (2004) suggest that adaptive and high-performing leaders are those who learn and evolve through continual exposure to real-world behavioral feedback.

Additionally, Shankar and Tewari (2021; 2025) extended the analytical perspective to the digital space, using natural language processing (NLP) and social media analytics to examine emotional intelligence as well as leadership perceptions and discourse. This direction enhances EIL by encouraging leaders to become sensitive to non-traditional, decentralized emotional cues, such as those embedded in employee communication channels and digital platforms. Their work mirrors findings from Ackley (2016), who observed that leaders attuned to both formal and informal emotional feedback tend to cultivate healthier work environments.

Such data-driven insights also enable the personalization of leadership development programs. Emotional competencies such as empathy, conflict resolution, and self-regulation can be targeted based on actual behavioral patterns and organizational needs. This aligns with the integrated competency approach suggested by Allen, Shankman, and Haber-Curran (2016), who argue that emotional intelligence must be developed contextually through deliberate practice, rather than generically.

Finally, Shankar's broader scholarship (e.g., Shankar & Tewari, 2021; 2023) reframes emotional intelligence not as a vague interpersonal trait, but as a measurable and improvable skill. Leveraging insights from social platforms, team interaction metrics, and workforce behaviors, HR Analytics enables emotionally intelligent leaders to remain attuned to the collective emotional climate of their organizations and adjust accordingly.

By integrating HR Analytics, organizations can shift from reactive to proactive leadership development. Rather than relying solely on personality-based evaluations or episodic feedback, leaders can now be trained based on emotion-oriented behavioral data—including tone analysis, digital sentiment trends, and team emotional dynamics. These tools enhance the emotional responsiveness and anticipatory capacity of the leader, which is critical in dynamic organizational environments (Sood & Kaushal, 2018).

CREATING A FOCUSED EMOTIONALLY INTELLIGENT LEADERSHIP FOR FOSTERING BETTER RELATIONSHIPS AND LEADERSHIP DEVELOPMENT

When talking about a leader, we must understand that the primary objective of a leader is to provide directional access to their groups and teams. Directional access is usually attained by drowning out the noise that is being presented in the form of distractions, and completely focusing on the goals at hand. But the findings in the area of neuroscience and neuropsychology are clear that humans, leaders or not, are always interacting with a multitude of stimuli at the same time, generating a bunch of neural pathways that direct human responses and behavior. Most of the time, these stimuli stand in contention with the primary direction that is to be followed by the person.

But this finding can, and is, being effectively used by psychologists, coaches, practitioners, and researchers of emotional intelligence to categorize the stimuli and responses into various constructs. Using these constructs together, and effectively, can help in creating a stronger competency and also provide insights into the processes that would most appropriately develop an emotionally intelligent leader.

Focusing on developing oneself, acknowledging others, and understanding the context in which the emotions are triggered would constructively help in cultivating a leader who is highly emotionally intelligent. And since this skill can be learned, practice and feedback would eventually raise the leader's level of awareness, and they would be able to easily translate the environmental information into knowledge - both implicit and explicit.

An important aspect in the understanding of the self is not just the awareness of the self, but also self-regulation and management. This is the reason why we believe that being an emotionally intelligent leader is more of a choice rather than a trait. A self-aware leader might choose to be self-regulated or might not choose to be one, but a self-regulated leader would always choose to engage in a behavior that is emotionally intelligent and purposefully take decisions that are more informed, modulated, and refined. This kind of leadership competency improves the development of the people they are interacting with the leader, along with facilitating the follower development.

Once a leader has understood and prospered the consciousness of self, the next step becomes understanding and developing the competencies of motivation, impulsivity, and empathy. Every leader needs to develop this triad of competencies, as they usually work in tandem with each other. When the leader starts creating an environment that fosters the abundance of these competencies, are more efficient in finding common grounds; their opinions, decisions, and policies would carry more weight; would rise in ranks faster; others would be willing to work with them more often; would foster better social relationships; and more often than not, they would be the catalysts to changes, both in teams and in organizations.

Even though the combined implementation of the competencies of focusing on self and others provides a comprehensive understanding of the emotions that are felt and expressed, the acknowledgment of the expressed emotion, and more importantly, figuring out the emotion that is being masked, is developed by developing the consciousness of context. Coupling this with the theory of constructed emotion provides the leader with a more nuanced and informed acknowledgment of the emotion, and subsequent interactions and decision-making. Here, it is important to understand that when a leader is trying to figure out the contextual nature of the exchange happening in the interaction, sometimes, others use Emotional Masking (Ekman, 1972; Ekman and Friesen, 1969; Gori et al., 2021). An emotionally intelligent leader would be able to efficiently navigate through the masked emotion and figure out the accurate emotion that is felt and expressed if they have developed the competency of understanding and implementing contexts in their exchanges and interactions.

Essentially, through the amalgamation of the three facets of the EIL model, i.e. Consciousness of Self, Others, and Contexts, a leader could be developed into an Emotionally Intelligent Leader who would be able to reorganize, redesign, redevelop, rebuild their and others' relationships, along with making better sense to the interactions they have with others, and bring about substantial and radical changes in their organizations. When an emotionally intelligent leader is faced with a new situation, challenge, or a problem, they are usually a step ahead in the game, as they already have cultivated an environment that fosters creativity, trust, loyalty, and ways and processes through which those challenges, situations or problems can be tackled effectively. This process is also continual, perpetual, and harmonized.

CONCLUSIONS AND NEXT STEPS TO EMOTIONALLY INTELLIGENT LEADERSHIP

It is clear from the literature and at this point that emotions play a major part in the development of an emotionally intelligent leader. Ask anyone in any organization, "What does a leader do?", would be presented with a litany of answers, from strategizing, planning, controlling, building partnerships and relationships, maintaining business acumen, fostering creative and innovative working environments, etc. But if you ask the same set of people, "How do we get an effective leader?" most of those people will be short of answers, and the few who would have the answer, would point to a singular outcome: better performance.

So why is it that even though the desired outcome is right in front of every individual in an organization, effective leaders more often than not, elude them? One big reason is that the understanding of an effective leader is usually missed by employers. Some interchange age with maturity, some interchange extraversion with charisma, some interchange introversion with spinelessness, and some interchange higher IQ with EQ. This interchangeability of terms was present in the literature before the nomenclature of emotional intelligence. The leadership styles prevalent before 1990 were not encompassing the emotional quotients of the leaders and their followers. Even in more recent literature, the randomized and quantitative studies are very few that demonstrably present the precise leader competencies that yield positive outcomes.

This is especially true when the leaders are young. The stereotypical understanding of young leaders is that a young leader would have lower EI competencies, but the notion couldn't be far from the truth. It's the experiences and interpersonal interactions that determine a higher emotionally intelligent leader versus a lower emotionally intelligent leader. The differences between the two present a stark contrast across the situations, decisions as well as time. It usually shows itself when the situation faced by a leader is rather sensitive, cautious, subtle, and/or diplomatic. A leader armed with EIL would be able to expertly navigate through the exchanges and interactions by properly understanding the emotional sense of themselves and the others, and couple it with the situational and contextual demands, and come up with a more appropriate solution or decision, which would be effective and contingent to the circumstances.

It is important to understand the impact that emotional intelligence is necessary to understand when talking about effective leadership development. It is also important to understand the interplay that emotional intelligence plays with other forms of intelligence. An obvious interplay that needs to be evaluated is between emotional intelligence with general intelligence (Shankar and Tewari, 2023); but some other forms of intelligence such as practical intelligence (Sternberg, 1997), social intelligence (Arghode, 2013), among others.

Even though the study of EI and EIL is relatively new, the research has shown promise. Prominent EI researchers have now started looking into the business implications of emotional intelligence, and even more recently, have started looking for frameworks for emotional intelligence and leadership as well as emotionally intelligent leadership. It is clear from the findings that one set of competencies or skills will never be sufficient to build an effective leader - a leader who is not only emotionally intelligent but is high performing and result-oriented. A blend of competencies, skills, traits, cognition, situational awareness, and dispositional quality must be added to the development of leaders.

Leaders of today are not only required to understand their business, industry, and organization, rather are expected to understand the people and environment they are working in and with. The new leaders must be armed and equipped with state-of-the-art training and learnings, and provide them with sufficient knowledge and experience that when dealing with a real-time crisis, they have the necessary skills developed in them to have a better and more informed decision-making capability. They must also be competent enough to figure out the correct sources of information, both cognitive as well as behavioral sources, properly filter out the noise, and integrate the data effectively to come up with solutions. This is a skill that would be handy when dealing with new and young leaders, and also the leaders at the higher echelon of the organizations.

The model of EIL presented in this chapter can be used as a jumping point for leadership development. The advantage that this model presents is that the organizations, practitioners, and coaches do not need to do away with their existing plans and programs of leadership development; rather they can augment these competencies to enrich their programs for more effective development. Although this model of EIL does not answer every question of emotionally intelligent leader development, we believe that the research in this area tackles a unique question that has long been left unsolved while looking for elements that leaders need to succeed. The understanding of emotional intelligence and emotionally intelligent leadership helps people understand the nuances of human behavior, as well as human interactions and helps inspire an environment where people are trusting, loyal, productive, and satisfied with their jobs and organizations, thereby being effective and efficient in their performances and outputs.

REFERENCES

Ackley, D. (2016). Emotional intelligence: A practical review of models, measures, and applications. *Consulting Psychology Journal*, *68*(4), 269–286. DOI: 10.1037/cpb0000070

Allen, S. J., Shankman, M. L., & Haber-Curran, P. (2016). Developing emotionally intelligent leadership: The need for deliberate practice and collaboration across disciplines. *New Directions for Higher Education*, *2016*(174), 79–91. DOI: 10.1002/he.20191

Allen, S. J., Shankman, M. L., & Miguel, R. F. (2012). Emotionally Intelligent Leadership: An Integrative, Process-Oriented Theory of Student Leadership. *Journal of Leadership Education*, *11*(1), 177–203. DOI: 10.12806/V11/I1/TF1

Arghode, V. (2013). Emotional and social intelligence competence: Implications for instruction. *International Journal of Pedagogies and Learning*, *8*(2), 66–77. DOI: 10.5172/ijpl.2013.8.2.66

Bar-On, R. (1997). Emotional intelligence. *The International Journal of Sociology and Social Policy*, *29*, 164–175.

Bar-On, R. (2006). The Bar-On model of emotional-social intelligence (ESI) 1. *Psicothema*, •••, 13–25. PMID: 17295953

Barrett, L. F. (2017a). *How emotions are made: The secret life of the brain*. Houghton Mifflin Harcourt.

Barrett, L. F. (2017b). The theory of constructed emotion: An active inference account of interoception and categorization. *Social Cognitive and Affective Neuroscience*, *12*(1), 1–23. DOI: 10.1093/scan/nsx060 PMID: 27798257

Bland, A. R., Roiser, J. P., Mehta, M. A., Schei, T., Boland, H., Campbell-Meiklejohn, D. K., Emsley, R. A., Munafo, M. R., Penton-Voak, I. S., Seara-Cardoso, A., Viding, E., Voon, V., Sahakian, B. J., Robbins, T. W., & Elliott, R. (2016). EMOTICOM: A neuropsychological test battery to evaluate emotion, motivation, impulsivity, and social cognition. *Frontiers in Behavioral Neuroscience*, *10*. Advance online publication. DOI: 10.3389/fnbeh.2016.00025 PMID: 26941628

Burns, J. M. G. (1978). *Leadership*. Harper & Row.

Davies, M., Stankov, L., & Roberts, R. D. (1998). Emotional intelligence: In search of an elusive construct. *Journal of Personality and Social Psychology*, *75*(4), 989–1015. DOI: 10.1037/0022-3514.75.4.989 PMID: 9825531

Day, C. (2004). The passion of successful leadership. *School Leadership & Management, 24*(4), 425–437. DOI: 10.1080/13632430410001316525

Day, D., & Lance, C. (2004). Understanding the development of leadership complexity through latent growth modeling. In Day, D., Zaccaro, S., & Halpin, S. (Eds.), *Leader Development for Transforming Organizations: Growing Leaders for Tomorrow* (pp. 41–69). Lawrence Earlbaum Associates. DOI: 10.4324/9781410610102

Day, D. V., Zaccaro, S. J., & Halpin, S. M. (2004). *Leader development for transforming organizations: Growing leaders for tomorrow*. Psychology Press. DOI: 10.4324/9781410610102

Downton, J. V. (1973). *Rebel leadership: Commitment and charisma in the revolutionary process*. Free Press.

Ekman, P. (1972). Universals and Cultural Differences in Facial Expressions of Emotions. In Cole, J. (Ed.), *Nebraska Symposium on Motivation* (pp. 207-282).

Ekman, P., & Friesen, W. V. (1969). The repertoire of nonverbal behavior: Categories, origins, usage, and coding. *semiotica, 1*(1), 49-98.

George, B. (2003). *Authentic leadership: Rediscovering the secrets to creating lasting value* (Vol. 18). John Wiley & Sons.

Goleman, D. (1995). *Emotional intelligence*. Bantam Books, Inc.

Goleman, D. (1998). The emotionally competent leader. *The Healthcare Forum Journal, 41*(2), 36–38. PMID: 10177113

Goleman, D. (2019). *The emotionally intelligent leader*. Harvard Business Review Press.

Goleman, D., Boyatzis, R., & McKee, A. (2002). The emotional reality of teams. *Journal of Organizational Excellence, 21*(2), 55–65. DOI: 10.1002/npr.10020

Gori, M., Schiatti, L., & Amadeo, M. B. (2021). Masking emotions: Face masks impair how we read emotions. *Frontiers in Psychology, 12*, 1541. DOI: 10.3389/fpsyg.2021.669432 PMID: 34113297

Greenleaf, R. K. (1970). *The servant as Leader*. Center for Applied Studies.

Lee, J., Kim, B., & Chung, J. (2021). Leaders need to be led: Complementary followership through interchangeable roles among leader-follower positions. SSRN *Electronic Journal*. DOI: 10.2139/ssrn.3995045

Mayer, J. D., Salovey, P., & Caruso, D. (2002). *Mayer-Salovey-Caruso Emotional Intelligence Test (MSCEIT) Item Booklet*. Multi-Health Systems.

McClelland, D. C. (1996). A Social Psychological View of Motivation. *Contemporary Psychology: A Journal of Reviews, 41*(5), 443–444. DOI: 10.1037/004426

Pathak, A., Tewari, V., & Shankar, S. (2018). Impact of Emotional Intelligence on employability of IT professionals. *Management Insight, 14*(1), 14–21. DOI: 10.21844/mijia.14.01.4

Salovey, P., & Mayer, J. D. (1990). Emotional intelligence. *Imagination, Cognition and Personality, 9*(3), 185–211. DOI: 10.2190/DUGG-P24E-52WK-6CDG

Shankar, S., Anagh, G. S., & Vaish, A. (2017). Spirituality and skill for leadership towards Sustainable Management. *Purushartha - A Journal of Management, Ethics, and Spirituality, 10*(02).

Shankar, S., & Tewari, V. (2021). Understanding the emotional intelligence discourse on social media: Insights from the analysis of Twitter. *Journal of Intelligence, 9*(4), 56. DOI: 10.3390/jintelligence9040056 PMID: 34842754

Shankar, S., & Tewari, V. (2023). Impact of collective intelligence and collective emotional intelligence on the psychological safety of the organizations. *Vision (Basel), 27*(4), 458–473. DOI: 10.1177/09722629211012256

Shankar, S., & Tewari, V. (2025). *Investigating leadership discussion on social media: A NLP and machine learning perspective*. Technology in Society, Online First.

Shankar, S., Vyas, R., & Tewari, V. (2024). Applying machine learning algorithms to determine and predict the reasons and models for employee turnover. *International Journal of Information Technology and Management, 23*(1), 48–63. DOI: 10.1504/IJITM.2024.136187

Shankman, M. L., Allen, S. J., & Haber-Curran, P. (2015). *Emotionally intelligent leader-ship: A guide for college students* (2nd ed.). Jossey-Bass.

Sood, I., & Kaushal, S. L. (2018). Emotional intelligence and leadership styles: A study of educational leaders in Himachal Pradesh. *Asian Journal of Management, 9*(1), 419–426. DOI: 10.5958/2321-5763.2018.00064.1

Sternberg, R. J. (1997). The concept of intelligence and its role in lifelong learning and success. *The American Psychologist, 52*(10), 1030–1037. DOI: 10.1037/0003-066X.52.10.1030 PMID: 9329294

Thurow, L. C. (1999). *Building wealth: The new rules for individuals, companies, and nations in a knowledge-based economy*. HarperCollins.

Weber, M. (1922). *Economy and Society*. Univ. of California Press.

Weber, M., & Eisenstadt, S. N. (1968). *On charisma and institution building: Selected papers*. University of Chicago P.

Wolff, S. (2005). *Emotional Competence Inventory: Technical manual.* The Hay Group.

Wong, C.-S., & Law, K. S. (2002). *Wong and Law Emotional Intelligence Scale (WLEIS)* [Database record]. APA PsycTests., DOI: 10.1037/t07398-000

Chapter 2
Automated Analysis of Student Feedback for Faculty Appraisals Using NLP

Mahesh N. Kumar
https://orcid.org/0009-0001-4022-1241
Narsee Monjee Institute of Management Studies, India

Shad Ahmad Khan
https://orcid.org/0000-0001-7593-3487
American University of Phnom Penh, Cambodia

N. Suresh
https://orcid.org/0009-0005-4664-1238
Jayoti Vidyapeeth Womens University, India

ABSTRACT

This chapter, per the authors, explores the integration of Natural Language Processing (NLP), sentiment analysis, and Structural Equation Modeling (SEM) in faculty evaluations. Traditional appraisal methods often lack depth, necessitating automated analysis of student feedback. Sentiment analysis using VADER classifies feedback into positive, neutral, and negative categories, while Latent Dirichlet Allocation (LDA) identifies dominant themes. SEM validates relationships among teaching effectiveness, course content, assessment fairness, student engagement, student satisfaction, and faculty performance. Findings indicate that student satisfaction significantly mediates faculty evaluations, with teaching effectiveness and engage-

DOI: 10.4018/979-8-3373-2135-6.ch002

ment being primary predictors. The study underscores the potential of AI-driven faculty appraisal systems in enhancing instructional quality and governance in higher education

INTRODUCTION

Automated Feedback Analysis of Courses using NLP

In modern academia mechanized estimation of students' feedback is of utmost importance in faculty evaluations. Higher Educational Institutes (HEIs) have traditionally employed student feedback to assess the quality of course materials, teaching effectiveness, and grading fairness. In fact, these inputs play an important role in decisions related to faculty development, training, and performance appraisal (Bauer et al., 2023; Rajput & Anwar, 2016).

As the technology has gained momentum, Natural Language Processing (NLP) has proved to be a powerful tool to assess large amounts of textual datasets of student feedback in a systematic and objective manner (Lin et al., 2024; Khan et al., 2024).

Sentiment analysis is another way how HEI's can evaluate feedback from the students about their teaching methods, course content and institutional policies. Moreover, topic modelling approaches, such as Latent Dirichlet Allocation (LDA) enable the grouping of student comments into main topics to identify the aspects to be commended or improved (Bauer et al., 2023).

Several studies claim that the use of NLP brings a more holistic and complex understanding of the elements that contribute to teachers' efficiency and students' satisfaction, in addition to improving feedback processes (Khalil et al., 2020; Zamani et al., 2020). Structural Equation Modelling (SEM) has been used to understand the relationships between variables such as test fairness, course difficulty and teaching quality to understand how they collectively contribute to the student experience (Khan et al. 2024).

As educational institutions integrate NLP-driven insights into their decision-making processes, they can utilize data-informed techniques to improve the standards of teaching, augment course material, and promote faculty development. Thus, this helps create a better faculty evaluation process and a better place to study for the students.

Background of the Study

Student voice is key to improving and maintaining quality in education, and can be systematically and broadly assessed using Natural Language Processing (NLP). Given that student voices are becoming more essential to influence institutional policy and decision-making (Khan et al., 2024; Bauer et al., 2023), NLP can be leveraged to automatically glean patterns from large qualitative comment datasets. A more suitabe one would be to point out patterns right from sentiment analysis, topic model and tri-sim that informs the institution on what students thinks about including but not restricted to quality teaching, relevancy of curriculum, fairness in assessment, participation, support systems. This kind of data-driven reflection enables us to make responsive, meaningful improvements. Observing learners can become difficult, which leads to the need for educational institutes utilizing NLP for active listening in order for emerging learner needs and expectations to be on par with learning experiences (Lin et al., 2024; Magd & Khan, 2024).

Theoretically NLP-driven feedback systems sit in the conceptual space of Vygotsky's Zone of Proximal Development (ZPD) and Hattie's Visible Learning. Vygotsky (1978) stressed that learning a ZPD is essential, a region within which the learner can function with and without help. Enter NLP tools that provide responsive, scaffolded feedback. Feedback was listed by Hattie (2007) as one of the most powerful influences on student learning, so long as it is timely, specific, and helps students identify a concrete next step in the formative process. NLP-driven feedback meets all these requirements by providing individualized, real-time responses that align with cognitive development and learning progress, thereby anchoring the theoretical underpinning in established pedagogical frameworks.

Student Feedback

Structured feedback tells organisations what kinds of environment foster good learning and student success, not opinions. By listening to their students, and making iterative, data-driven adjustments, schools can ensure that their teaching methods, curricular resources, and support systems actually work for their students (Lin et al., 2024).

Relevance in Faculty Appraisal

Student feedback is a major component in the evaluation of faculty, teaching effectiveness, and performance. Students' input is a genuine gauge their teachers' teaching strategy, course content relevance, assessment fairness, and faculty engagement fostered (Khan et al., 2024).

Student Feedback: It is one of the significant pillars of an Academic Institutional functioning. Making meaningful decisions regarding faculty development, appraisal, and institutional advancement hinges on properly interpreting student feedback. The use of NLP and advanced analytics such as sentiment and thematic analyses (Bauer et al., 2023) ultimately led to the transformation of the faculty appraisal systems. This calls for institutions to harness students feedback to drive transformational changes with a greater impact (Lin et al., 2024).

How NLP Helps in Feedback Analytics

In the last few years, Natural Language Processing (NLP) revolutionised the way universities and colleges process student feedback. This replaces a time-intensive manual process and makes it easier for institutions to find meaning in large volumes of qualitative data. Transformer models like BERT (Bidirectional Encoder Representations from Transformers) and RoBERTa (A Robustly Optimized BERT Pretraining Approach) have significantly improved the performance of sentiment classification and topic inferencing. Such models can better capture contextual nuance in student language which in turn increases the chances to accurately identify emotions and underlying concerns in feedback (Bauer et al., 2023). In doing so, institutions can use sophisticated NLP to uncover student experiences at scale, capturing both objective and complete insights. Most importantly, this allows teachers and administrators to use data as a knowledge base in making decisions on how they can improve teaching practices, presenting the content of the course efficiently and providing an improved learning environment (Lin et al., 2018; Magd & Khan, 2017).

Research Problem Statement

With access to data through the university, how can an institution measure faculty performance which is a key priority for all higher education institutions? Historically, faculty appraisal has depended on tools like standardized surveys, peer evaluations and administrative reviews (Blackburn & Pitney, 1988).

But as student feedback becomes more open-ended and unstructured, manually assessing if students are incorporating that feedback has become a potential bottleneck. Such process is subjective, time-consuming and prone to inconsistencies, therefore not effective in efficiently extracting valuable insights (Khtere, 2020). Consequently, institutions are looking for sophisticated ways to have feedback analysed fairly and in an actionable way.

With respect to Natural Language Processing (NLP), machine learning approaches have emerged as a strong contender for automating aspects of student feedback analysis and improving its objectivity, scalability and efficiency (Peterson & Comeaux, 1990). This study attempts to address these voids by establishing an automated, data-driven framework for the analysis of students' feedback by using natural language processing (NLP), sentiment analysis (SA) and structural equation modelling (SEM).This study seeks to develop a standardized faculty evaluation system that improves HEI decision-making based on reliable faculty performance, in terms of teaching effectiveness, student engagement, course content quality, and overall faculty performance. Additionally, this research also investigates how AI based models may enhance existing faculty development program, appraisal approaches and align student evaluations with continual teaching enhancement.

Research Objectives

Our main objective in this work is to develop a data-driven, efficient framework based on statistical modelling methods and natural language processing (NLP), meant for analysis of student comments and maybe improvement of continuous faculty evaluation systems. More precisely, the study aims to investigate the relationships between Overall Student Satisfaction and Faculty Performance Evaluation with regard to academic elements like Teaching Effectiveness, Course Content Quality, Assessment Fairness, and Student Engagement. By means of quantitative approaches—more especially, Structural Equation Modelling (SEM) for assessing direct and mediated effects—it seeks to prove the veracity of these linkages. Performing sentiment analysis and topic modelling to extract insights from student open-ended responses to classify feedback as good, neutral, or negative sentiment, as well as to find recurrent themes in what students are worried about is another major goal. Furthermore, the study aims to verify but using statistical measurements and model fit indices that student comments analysis is a genuine and dependable result, so providing a strong and scalable solution for next universities. By means of achieving our initiative, this study seeks to raise the quality, equity, and financial efficiency of teacher assessment systems.

Objectives Setting

The study was governed by four clear objectives:

Objective 1: Assess the evolution of student sentiment across three academic years through sentiment analysis.

Objective 2: Uncover and categorize key themes in student feedback using topic modelling.
Objective 3: Analyse numeric trends in key evaluation areas, such as teaching quality and student engagement.
Objective 4: Examine structural relationships among core academic dimensions using Structural Equation Modelling (SEM) to understand causal and mediated effects influencing student satisfaction and faculty evaluations.

Research Questions

Using machine learning algorithms, what are the main signals that relate to teaching effectiveness?

How well can we validate relationships between faculty effectiveness, student engagement and satisfaction using Structural Equation Modelling (SEM)?

What are the pitfalls and patterns of prejudice in process driven evaluations of faculty by A.I. and how could you avoid them?

Is it better to use automated sentiment analysis than the traditional way of evaluating faculties?

Integration of AI-based Faculty Appraisal Models in E-Governance frameworks for High Efficiency; Transparency and Decision-making in Higher Education Institutions

How big-data-driven education evaluation would significant faculty evaluation methods?

This study highlights how data, specifically feedback, can be leveraged to effectively evaluate faculty. However, it raises questions about the ethical implications and data privacy concerns associated with automating the feedback analysis process involving students.

Hypothesis

The researchers tested seven hypotheses:

H1: Higher teaching effectiveness results in higher level of student satisfaction.
H2: Course content of higher quality leads to greater satisfaction among students.
H4: Student satisfaction is influenced positively by the fairness of the assessment.
H5: Higher student satisfaction has a positive impact on faculty performance evaluations.

H6: Faculty evaluations are directly influenced by teaching effectiveness, regardless of student satisfaction.
H7: There is mediation effect of the student satisfaction between other academic factors and faculty performance evaluation.

Relevance of the Study

The importance of this study is that it might stimulate large scale affirmative operational feedback evaluating faculty appraisal. Natural Language Processing (NLP) based methodologies are particularly relevant for efficient, objective and effective feedback analysis since traditional approaches to student feedback analysis are usually manual, highly dependent on subjective judgment, and they ran into bias and inconsistency issues (Bauer et al., 2023). By utilizing NLP techniques such as sentiment analysis and topic modelling, organizations can neutralely identify major influencers affecting student satisfaction as well as teaching aesthetics. Additionally, Structural Equation Modelling (SEM) can be employed to explore the relationships among various feedback dimensions and to yield strong systems for professor assessment (Lin et al., 2024; Khan et al., 2024).

I. REVIEW OF THE LITERATURE

Globally, teaching in Higher education institutions (HEIs) is evaluated constantly through student feedback systems. Traditionally, faculty assessment methods have included structured surveys, faculty peer review, and administrative reviews (Blackburn & Pitney, 1988). However, once the qualitative feedback increases its amount, the manual analysis becomes ineffective and driven by bias (Khtere, 2020).

The objective of this literature review, therefore, is to survey this literature and look at various studies as well as theoretical frameworks on faculty's appraisal, including the methodology, tools involved as well as the effectiveness of the different kinds of performance assessment approaches.

Faculty Performance Appraisal Systems Traditional

The research, Khanam & Mazhar, (2015) Assessing Effectiveness of Faculty Performance Appraisal System in Higher Education Institutions concluded that use of structured mechanism to evaluate faculty during regular intervals can significantly help in enhancing faculty productivity. In a similar vein, Vilas Hasure and Dr. Milind

Peshave (2020) examined performance appraisal systems in management institutes of Shivaji University by assessing evaluation criteria and faculty perceptions.

According to the research, appraisal mechanisms should be designed to create a culture of development rather than abuse. This resonates with the work of Holtzapple (2003), who showed that a standards-based teacher evaluation system is criterion related, suggesting that effective appraisal systems should include clear performance standards.

Peterson (2000) provided a practical guide to teacher evaluation methods and highlighted the necessity for aligning appraisal systems with institutional goals.

Why Student Feedback Matters

Teaching is evaluated based on student feedback, and feeds back into the assessment of faculty performance and how effective they are as outstripping the herd. Student feedback is an important source of information for higher education institutions, providing direct insights into how students experience their courses and allowing timely interventions and improvements in teaching practices (Magd & Khan, 2024; Lin et al., 2024). Research consistently emphasizes the importance of systematic student feedback as a means of maintaining standards in education and enhancing student satisfaction (Rajput & Anwar, 2016; Bauer et al., 2023; Khan et al., 2023). Nonetheless, numeric ratings alone for faculty evaluations fail to properly capture the nuanced details in students' open-ended comments (Daoanis, 2012). HEIs have a tendency to adopt automated models due to well-known processes of feedback analysis (Blackburn & Pitney, 1988) while introducing computational techniques such as NLP and machine learning has the potential to improve both, processes, and the accuracy and efficiency of search (Taut & Sun, 2014). Additionally, Khan et al. that automated feedback systems enhance the speed and accuracy of the evaluation process and alert institutions to faculty development in real-time (2023).

Theoretical Framework Supporting Feedback Analysis

NLP driven scalable faculty evaluation is consistent with several foundational theories and tenets of educational psychology. Applying Vygotsky's Zone of Proximal Development (ZPD) to NLP, algorithms stand in the role of a scaffold for faculty growth: mentor-like guides for moving from current states toward an optimal teaching state. Right from insights into how a lesson has been delivered in the past to increasingly personalized feedback based on patterns and strategies that work for them, NLP can offer degrees of scaffolding – leading students toward learning independently as they progressively master skills. This is like human mentoring where you watch, diagnose needs, intervene appropriately and withdrawal faculty from needing your help to independent success with their pedagogy, technology integration and student engagement.

Hattie's Visible Learning research also points to feedback as one of the single most effective influences in student learning. Conclusion: Structured feedback using sentiment and thematic analysis directed evidence-based opportunities for growing teaching practices through evaluations of faculty.

By situating the automated feedback framework in these theories, institutions can more effectively position use of AI systems for faculty development as reflective practices rather than accountability measures.

NLP Approaches to Analysis of Educational Feedback

Student voice is crucial to bettering and maintaining educational quality, and with powerful tools made available by Natural Language Processing (NLP) that can systematically analyze this feedback at scale. As student input becomes increasingly important to institutional policies and decision-making (Khan et al. 2024; Bauer et al., 2023), NLP allows automated analysis of large-scale qualitative comments. The seminal work of sentiment analyses by Pang and Lee (2008) and the LDA topic model by Blei et al. The work of Blei, et al., (2003) on topic modeling laid the foundation for use of these techniques in educational context. In the same way, Topic Modelling methods such as LDA help to elicit major themes across text dataset allowing for data-supported pedagogical interventions (Blei et al., 2003; Bauer et al. It helps Institutions to know about the student perception on teaching quality, course relevance, fairness in evaluation, engagement and support systems. By using these platforms, educational practices are allowed to be more responsive, accessible and in-sync with our rapidly changing landscape of learning (Lin et al., 2024; Magd & Khan, 2024).

Applying NLP in Higher Education: Case Studies

NLP is being used by universities worldwide to drive teacher development and powering student engagement by converting unstructured feedback into actionable insights. At Yale University, a senior thesis used sentiment analysis and keyword extraction on course evaluation data to create a proof-of-concept dashboard for rapid insights into teaching (Abinader, 2024). Silva et al. (2022) reported that a public university in Brazil used NLP to classify sentiment types of professor evaluations (from 2019 and 2020), facilitating departments to systematically abstract text-based feedback during the COVID-19 transition. Al-Busaidi et al., (2023) also used a sentiment analysis in which the University of West Georgia had taken data from course evaluations for an online business course to determine things that needed changed which were negatively affecting student responses and thus their learning. Theme coding powered with GPT has been evaluated within health education programs across multiple institutions as a way to speed up processing of qualitative assessments compared to human coding (Wang et al., 2024). Georgia State University has utilized an AI chatbot to help deflect routine student service inquiries and retain students, freeing up faculty time to provide more mentoring (Page et al., 2019); while Staffordshire University created a "Beacon" digital assistant with NLP capabilities that offers student services around the clock (Staffordshire University, 2019). A chatbot using NLP showed that 64% of users found it highly effective in resolving their queries and, thereby decrease the risk of attrition, (Khan & Ahmad 2021). Systematic reviews have found these tools to be bolstered by focused pilot studies, human-rating validation, embedded in coaching cycles, and strong privacy and bias protections, reflecting the notion of NLP as an extensible scaffolding framework aligned with Vygotsky's ZPD principles (Kaur & Aggarwal, 2023).

Governance and Ethics

The integration of NLP in teacher feedback systems calls for robust governance mechanisms and ethical safeguards to ensure fairness, accountability and verifiability. Data ownership, access protocols and clear accountability with regard to how algorithmic outputs are interpreted and applied must be included in governance frameworks (Floridi & Cowls 2019). To ensure ethical practice, job candidates need to obtain verbal consent from professors, feedback data needs to be anonymized in order to protect privacy, and also constant auditing is necessary which can help detect algorithmic biases that influence performance evaluations unfairly (Jobin et al., 2019). For purposes of explainability, institutions should give faculty reasonable context to interpret what an NLP analysis output means instead of just accepting some black box advice (Guidotti et al., 2018). The use of model building, validation and refinement involving participatory design including faculty participation ensures that the system objectives align with institutional mission trajectories, and prevents resistance to adoption (Williamson & Piattoeva, 2020). Without the proper governance and ethical oversight, NLP methods can either tip the balance further or lead to academic evaluation procedures being exposed for good.

Teaching Effectiveness

Teaching effectiveness, which has been classified as the ability of the instructors to provide clear and effective information that facilitates active learning, set a significant intercession factor on students' satisfaction and performance outcomes (Khan et al. 2024; Lin et al., 2024). Despite that, numerous studies have confirmed that effective teaching methods and clarity and the instructor's enthusiasm have a significant correlation with students providing positive feedback about instruction (Bauer et al., 2023).

Course Content Quality

They would provide excellent course content, which is crucial to keep students satisfied as well as for their learning trajectory. Regularly updated, relevant, and comprehensive curriculum materials consistently receive favourable evaluations from students and are regarded as significant facilitators in positively shaping academic perceptions (Lin et al., 2024; Khan et al., 2023). Not only does high-quality content contribute to students' educational experiences, but it also helps keep their interest, relevance, and perceived value (Bauer et al., 2023).

FACTORS FOR EVALUATION OF FACULTY PERFORMANCE

Assessment Fairness

Transparent, consistent and equitable assessment processes as a whole have been found empirically to lead to better satisfaction ratings among students (Lin et al., 2024; Magd & Khan, 2024).

Student Engagement

Student engagement is emerging as a decisive component that can improve student learning outcomes and satisfaction. Students who are engaged often score their education experiences high, suggesting favourable interactions with higher engagement in learning activities (Bauer et al., 2023; Magd & Khan, 2024).

Overall Student Satisfaction

Student satisfaction: A general perception about the perceived quality of education which in turn influences the institutional reputation and sustains student retention. Real-world data shows a significant correlation between student satisfaction and several major academic and institutional success factors (Lin et al., 2024; Magd & Khan, 2024; Khan et al., 2023).

Faculty Performance Evaluation

Student course evaluation provides an important mechanism for assessing instructional effectiveness. Widely available data on structured student feedback is critical for faculty appraisal systems, including performance improvement, professional development, and decision- making at the institutional level (Khan et al., 2024; Bauer et al., 2023).

Automated Feedback Systems: Concept & Implementation

This has been made possible with the advancements in NLP and AI-enabled analytics systems that work efficiently in automating the feedback processing in the dynamic faculty performance evaluation system. A common trend in feedback analysis is sentiment analysis, which classifies the feedback left by students in terms of sentiment (positive, neutral or negative) to get an overview about the perception of the teaching process (Liu & Zhang, 2019). Another important approach is topic modelling, in which we identify recurring topics within qualitative responses (e.g. clarity of instruction, course difficulty, etc.; Mei et al., 2020). These AI-driven approaches streamline complex processes to help improve efficiency while reducing manual work in faculty evaluations, by offering valuable insights for the incremental improvement of professors/faculty and institutions, to positively impact in the student outcomes and to upgrade the teaching environment.

Kumar and Jain (2018) showed that an AI-powered faculty evaluation system (FES) that classified sentiment in student feedback reduced the manual effort required of assessment committees for evaluating faculty. Likewise, Bousbahi and Alrazgan (2015) investigated faculty members resistance against Learning Management Systems (LMS) and how automated systems facilitate evaluation processes. Bauer et al.,123 using a large single-credential data set, demonstrated a significant increase in the utilization of repetitive head CT imaging. (2023) also demonstrate that NLP-driven feedback analysis not only improves appraisal accuracy but also gives educators personalized insights for professional development.

AI Powered Staff Evaluation & E-Governance

This E-Governance in faculty evaluation has improved transparency with efficient and precise assessment of the performance (Shaikh & Kasatt,2020). In Chile, Taut and Sun (2014) examine the National Teacher Evaluation System (NTES), and find examples of how the AI-based performance assessment is incorporated into structured faculty appraisal systems. The peer assessments, student surveys, and self-evaluations are used in conjunction in this system to provide comprehensive evaluations (Taut & Sun, 2014). Lin et al. Taking a big-data-driven approach to evaluation of faculty members and institutions have also been noted in (2024) for enhancing the faculty appraisal process with predictive capabilities for institutions to take data-driven decisions.

The Role of Structural Equation Modelling (SEM) in Faculty Appraisal

Structural Equation Modelling (SEM) has been widely implemented in validating frameworks for faculty evaluation. The SEM allows researchers to test complex relationships among several independent and dependent variables and is empirically justified faculty performance measures (Iqbal et al 2019).

Previous research by Kyriakides (2005) and Smylie (2014) have shown that efficacy of instruction and student engagement are strong predictors of satisfaction; the latter having been linked to faculty performance ratings. These results are consistent with findings from Shaikh and Kasatt (2020) that SEM-based evaluations by the faculty are more dependable than standard appraisal methods for insight into faculty performance in medical education. Moreover, balancing various faculty assessment dimensions through big-data approaches within SEM has been argued by Magd and Khan (2024) to add substantial strength and robustness to traditional faculty assessment models.

Ethical and Cultural Pitfalls in NLP-Based Feedback Analysis

This technology provides great value for the scale of student feedback management, however there are also ethical and cultural implications to deploying this sort of tool. All these modern NLP systems with their newfound goodies will only copy and amplify the gendered biases present in the language data on which they were trained, essentially getting it wrong to a greater or lesser degree when interpreting student sentiment across different cultural and linguistic contexts. Models are not capable of detecting sarcasm, coded language, and culturally nuanced expressions a problem that leads to biased insights coating an over-representation perspective of the majority different from the minority ones (Gu & Levin, 2021). Moreover, one of the key criticisms in the automation of feedback analysis that raises serious question about privacy since it involves students' sensitive data without their explicit consent or has little to no clear directive regarding data governance policies. Such transformer-based models of BERT and RoBERTa are powerful but need to be trained on large amount of training data, can be biased towards the particular corpora they have been pretrained on, which may not align well to educational discourse or more distributed types of global student populations. These risks can be minimized by institutions building locally relevant sentiment lexicons, creating culturally specific models and adopting privacy preserving techniques such as federated learning. And, critically, just as important as these tools being able to improve educational quality and decision-making processes, ethical design principles must be in place from the outset—whether through bias audits or inclusive model training—to ensure that NLP tools are equitably aiding those seeking to do so.

Algorithmic Bias in NLP-Based Faculty Appraisal

As illustrated in recent research, much work has been put towards criticising the ethical concerns surrounding AI in sentiment analysis like algorithmic bias, privacy or cultural misunderstanding. Sentiment algorithms often classify emotional cues of non-Western users incorrectly as well, because of culturally baised training data (Gu and Levin 2021). They also raise the privacy stakes, suggesting how data on emotions might be collected or used without permission.

The above findings are supported by empirical studies showing reductions in model accuracy in a cross-cultural setting (Cui et al., 2021; Muresan et al., 2022; Solaiman et al, 2023) and the warning against emotion profiling. To ensure global AI systems are fair and responsible, the report's authors also recommend data coverage that is inclusive of all humans, lexicons with cultural specificity in mind, and stronger privacy protections.

Despite the benefits of NLP in automating student feedback analysis, several ethical concerns require attention. Algorithmic bias remains a critical issue, where models trained on skewed or limited datasets may reinforce stereotypes or misinterpret feedback nuances. For instance, sarcasm, humour, or indirect cultural expressions can lead to incorrect sentiment classification.

Moreover, data privacy laws such as GDPR and FERPA highlight the importance of informed consent and data handling practices when analysing student comments. Institutions must adopt privacy-preserving techniques such as federated learning and anonymization to mitigate risk.

To enhance trust and accountability, explainable AI models should be preferred, allowing stakeholders to understand how faculty evaluations are derived.

Implementation Barriers and Mitigation Strategies

Despite the increasing promise, a major hurdle to the realization of NLP-based feedback systems within educational settings is faculty resistance. Teachers are highly resistant to new learning technologies, which have worrying pedagogical value, a lack of technical expertise and additional workload (Bousbahi & Alrazgan, 2015). Failure to involve faculty in decision-making processes and/or weak transition support can strengthen opposition. To combat this and drive acceptance as well as continued participation, professional development communication coupled with staged rollouts and organised change-management techniques is required.

NLP in faculty appraisal is becoming more and more popular, but institutional implementation still confronts several challenges.

- Faculty Resistance: Concerns over surveillance or job security may lead to hesitancy in accepting AI tools.
- Resource Constraints: Many institutions lack the technical infrastructure or skilled personnel for deploying AI-based systems.
- Training Gaps: Faculty and administrators may not be equipped to interpret NLP or SEM outputs effectively.

Table 1. Ethical and Cultural Challenges in NLP Feedback Analysis and Mitigation Strategies

Challenge	Description	Suggested Mitigation Strategy
Cultural Misalignment	Misinterpretation of context, idioms, or sentiment due to cultural variation	Use localized sentiment lexicons and culturally annotated datasets
Algorithmic Bias	Inaccurate results due to biased training data favoring dominant language or demographic groups	Conduct regular bias audits; diversify training corpora
Loss of Nuance	Failure to detect sarcasm, irony, or indirect speech in feedback	Integrate contextual embeddings; supplement with qualitative review
Privacy Concerns	Risks of re-identification or misuse of student data	Employ federated learning, data anonymization, and consent protocols
Linguistic Exclusion	Low performance on feedback in less-resourced or multilingual settings	Train models with multilingual corpora; incorporate language detection
Opaque Decision-Making	Lack of transparency in model reasoning and scoring	Use explainable AI (XAI) tools to visualize and justify model outputs
Feedback Misrepresentation	Over-reliance on sentiment scores without considering context or depth	Combine quantitative NLP with qualitative analysis

Comparative Analysis of Traditional and AI-Driven Faculty Appraisal Models

To address these, phased rollouts guided by change management models—such as Kotter's 8-Step Framework—can be adopted. Additionally, training workshops, participatory design strategies, and transparent communication are crucial for smooth adoption of AI in academic appraisal.

Table 2. Comparative Analysis of Appraisal Models

Evaluation Method	Accuracy	Scalability	Bias Risk	Transparency	Resource Intensity
Traditional Surveys	Medium	High	Medium	High	Low
Peer Reviews	High	Low	High	Medium	High
NLP + SEM Hybrid Model	High	High	Low-Med	Medium	Medium

This comparative analysis illustrates how AI-based models balance efficiency with accuracy, although explainability and training remain essential considerations.

Challenges in Automated Student Feedback Analysis

While it has benefits, automated faculty evaluation systems face a variety of challenges:

- Sentiment classification bias: AI models can inherit biases from the training data that can skew sentiment analysis (Liu et al., 2019)
- There is a limitation of the contextual understanding in NLP which fails in sarcasm, ambiguity, culture, and this directly affects the accuracy of results (Popescu & Etzioni, 2017).
- Ethical Concerns: Protecting the anonymity and privacy of students' data was a serious challenge (Khurram & Ata, 2024).
- Feedback Heterogeneity: Organizations employ numerous rating scales and question structures, creating significant barriers to standardization (Khtere, 2020).

CONCLUSION

Grading faculty performance appraisal systems are constantly evolving from traditional to data-driven and then towards sentiment analysis-based techniques. Other platforms help streamline digital tools and methods for student feedback on faculty. Nonetheless, challenges to bias, standardization, and predictive modelling need further investigation. The adoption of faculty appraisal system based on AI will further bolter e-governance, institutional transparency and faculty development in higher education.

As such, the use of NLP along with SEM for analysis of the content in student feedback has considerably bettered the efficiency, accuracy, and objectivity of the process of faculty evaluation. Automated sentiment analysis and topic modelling provide data-driven insights that go beyond regular assessment methods by person. For bias, standardization and predictive modelling challenges, though, more research is needed. We expect wide-ranging acceptance of AI-based faculty appraisal systems, which can significantly contribute to e-governance, transparency in the institutions, and faculty development in higher education.

RESEARCH METHODOLOGY

Statistics: Methods and Size of Data

In this study, a multi-methodological perspective utilizing both qualitative and quantitative statistical techniques is taken to examine student evaluations of the feedback across three academic years (2021–22, 2022–23, and 2023–24). Both methodologies are consistent with previous research in the area of education analytics (Bauer et al., 2023; Khan et al., 2024; Rajput & Anwar, 2016).

Data Size and Composition

The data includes both structured Likert-scale responses and open-text qualitative feedback from students. In total, we collected 3820 student responses, with the following breakdown:

Table 3. Academic year

Academic Year	Number of Responses
2021-22	1,150
2022-23	1,280
2023-24	1,390
Total	**3,820**

All feedback entries contained Likert scale (1–7) ratings regarding aspects like Teaching Effectiveness, Course Content Quality, Assessment Fairness, Student Engagement, Overall Satisfaction, and Faculty Performance Evaluation, along with open-ended comments.

Key Variables Defined

Teaching Effectiveness: This refers to the quality of an instructor's delivery, explaining concepts in a clear, coherent, and engaging manner to facilitate student understanding and learning (Bauer et al. 2023)

Quality of Course Content: The extent of relevance, clarity, completeness, and decency of course materials provided to students for realizing meaningful learning (Lin et al., 2024).

Assessment Transparency: Students' perceptions of evaluation and grading methods' transparency, fairness and impartiality, fostering students' trust and acceptance of assessments.

Student Engagement: The degree to which students are involved, and take part in, both the learning activities, materials and instructor (Magd & Khan, 2024).

Overall Student Satisfaction: The level of students' overall positive perception and satisfaction in terms of educational experiences and institutional provisions (Lin et al., 2024).

Faculty Performance Evaluation: Faculty performance evaluation is a formal and aggregated measure of instructor effectiveness based on student feedback, and it directly impacts institutional decisions regarding professional development, promotions, and tenure (Khan et al., 2024).

Measurement scale

This study utilizes Likert type scale 1-7 to examine different perspectives of faculty assessment based on students' feedback. For example, on the Likert scale as here, a respondent can state their level of agreement or satisfaction with 1 for 'Strongly Disagree' and 7 for 'Strongly Agree'. This scale is used in the evaluation in those critical dimensions like, teaching effectiveness, student engagement, fairness of assessment and evaluation, course content quality, faculty behaviour, etc. A continuous measurement scale allows for a more nuanced understanding of student perceptions, by minimising extreme variations and improving the reliability of statistical analyses such as SEM. NLP-based text analysis also quantifies specific sentiment scores along a sentiment polarity scale, thereby placing responses to text in a positive, neutral, or negative sentiment. This measurement system allows qualitative and quantitative feedback to be systematically processed with regard to faculty evaluation.

Statistical Methods Used

The analysis leveraged several different statistical approaches to gain a broad perspective of the feedback data:

Descriptive Statistics

Descriptive statistics (mean, median, and standard deviation) were calculated for numeric trends across all dimensions by academic year (Lin et al., 2024; Khan et al., 2023). These provided a first glimpse at data distributions and year-over-year changes.

This study applies quantitative methods to analyse structured feedback data and hypothesis validation. To get an overview of the trends in student feedback across academic years, descriptive statistics were used to summarize central tendencies (mean scores, standard deviations and frequency distributions). The VADER (Valence Aware Dictionary for Sentiment Reasoning) model was utilized for conducting sentiment analysis for classifying the open-ended responses into the positive, neutral and negative sentiments; which once again gives a better understanding of students' perception regarding the faculty performance. Topic modelling technique: Latent Dirichlet Allocation (LDA) was employed to identify predominant concerns and gaps that could be addressed in the textual feedback text.

In addition to that, to measure the association of variables, such as Teaching Effectiveness, Course Content and Student satisfaction, Correlation Analysis was also discussed. In this study, multiple regression analysis was used to assess these relationships and to accurately predict how independent variables may influence Faculty Performance Evaluation. All these relationships were further confirmed via Structural Equation Modelling (SEM) which provided an overview of direct and indirect effects. Statistical robustness was established by implementing mediation tests using APP to test mediation effects. And, its concomitant use of these quantitative statistical methods guarantees that faculty evaluation and the analysis of students' interpretation of that evaluation is undertaken in the spirit of empirical, data-driven research.

Sentiment Analysis

We implemented the VADER model (Rajput & Anwar, 2016) for sentiment analysis of textual comments. Positive, neutral, or negative comments were then categorized. Distributions of sentiments revealed increasingly positive feedback that highlighted improvements in students' experiences.

Topic Modelling

LDA is highly recommended for revealing latent thematic structures in text data (Bauer et al., 2023) and was justified for identifying recurring themes in student feedback comments. Four threads were common: Teaching Effectiveness & Clarity (30%), Course Content Quality (20%), Assessment Fairness (15%), and Student Engagement (25%), and Infrastructure & Support (10%). Such themes are closely aligned with structured survey items, thereby providing validation of survey design and Supporting Use of Feedback from Textual Analysis (Khan et al., 2024).

Thematic Analysis of Likert-Scale Data

Thematic trend analysis of numeric Likert-scale responses revealed a progressive tendency of improvement or decline over three years (Magd & Khan, 2024). Overall mean ratings by dimension steadily improved year–over–year, particularly in Teaching Effectiveness and Student Engagement, which was aligned with sentiment analysis results.

Software & Tool Used

Python (NLTK, VADER) & R Programming

Structural Equation Modelling (SEM)

SEM (Structural Equation Modelling) was used to measure relationships between factors such as Teaching Effectiveness, Course Content, Assessment Fairness, Student Engagement, Overall Satisfaction, and Faculty Performance Evaluation. SEM is a powerful analytical approach that enables scholars to investigate intricate interrelations among several variables and uncover both direct and indirect impacts. The lavaan package121 in R was used to fit the SEM framework. Three fit indices were used to evaluate model validity, including the Comparative Fit Index (CFI), Tucker-Lewis Index (TLI), Root Mean Square Error of Approximation (RMSEA), and Standardized Root Mean Square Residual (SRMR).

It examined direct effects of factors like Teaching Effectiveness, Course Content, Assessment Fairness, and Student Engagement on Student Satisfaction and Faculty Performance Evaluation. In addition, mediation effects were tested to identify whether Student Satisfaction mediated the relationships of these predictors with Faculty Performance. Bootstrapping (5,000 resamples) was performed to test the significance of mediation effects to draw strong conclusions. The analysis yielded meaningful relation in the result, especially the impact of Student Satisfaction as an important mediator of outcome in faculty appraisal. By using SEM, a data-driven explanatory strategy, we can help disentangle the complexity of components that generate the dependent variable faculty course evaluations; this study can inform ways to potentially improve course evaluation outcomes for teaching/learning instances in an institution.

Data Analysis

The data analysis process involved multiple stages, incorporating both qualitative and quantitative techniques to ensure comprehensive interpretation of student feedback. To analyse structured Likert-scale responses, we used descriptive statistics, including measures of central tendency (mean) and dispersion (standard deviation) and frequency distributions to obtain trends in student perceptions during three academic years. Sentiment analysis – open-ended feedback was analysed using VADER, yielding positive, neutral, and negative sentiment categories. This enabled changes in student perceptions of instructor efficacy to be tracked longitudinally. Using Latent Dirichlet Allocation (LDA), we performed topic modelling on textual feedback to extract common themes, and patterns emerged such as teaching effectiveness, assessment fairness, and student engagement.

Correlation is a statistical method to measure the strength and direction of the relationship between key academic factors, (Aggregated Teaching Effectiveness, Course Content, Overall Satisfaction, etc) and correlation analysis were performed to examine that. By means of a multiple regression analysis, determining predictors affecting student satisfaction that can be used in faculty performance evaluations. Structural Equation Modelling (SEM) was conducted with the lavaan package in R to assess direct and indirect effects of predictor variables. Robustness and validity: Model fit was evaluated using indices including Comparative Fit Index (CFI), Tucker-Lewis Index (TLI), Root Mean Square Error of Approximation (RMSEA), and Standardized Root Mean Square Residual (SRMR), ensuring robustness and validity. To examine mediation effects, we utilized bootstrapping with 5,000 resamples, which supported student satisfaction as a mediator of faculty appraisal outcomes. As a result, this was a study rich with multiple types of analysis: qualitative (case study approach) and quantitative (using data) that was part of informing a data-driven framework that properly evaluates faculty and how an institution serves its students.

Hypothesis Testing and Achievement of Objectives

Hypothesis Testing

In this study, an exploratory study of Structural Equation Modelling (SEM) was conducted to evaluate the multiple hypothetical relationships among the factors of Teaching Effectiveness, Course Content Quality, Assessment Fairness, Student Engagement, Overall Student Satisfaction, and Faculty Performance Evaluation. Direct and mediated effects were tested for statistical significance for each hypothesis. The findings revealed that of all aspects of the work environment, Teaching Effectiveness and Student Engagement were the most significant factors affecting Student Satisfaction, which also served as the most important mediator in Faculty Performance Evaluation. The bootstrapping further validated the mediation effect, highlighting the vital role Student Satisfaction plays in faculty evaluations. Fit indices of the model indicated a good fit to the data (CFI = 0.96, TLI = 0.92, RMSEA = 0.05, SRMR = 0.04), supporting the robustness of the SEM framework.

Analysis using Structural Equation Modelling (SEM)

This investigation employed Structural Equation Modelling (SEM) to explore the direct and indirect relationships among Teaching Effectiveness, Course Content Quality, Assessment Fairness, Student Engagement, Overall Student Satisfaction, and Faculty Performance Evaluation. As a complex statistical method, SEM allows for the simultaneous examination of numerous associations between latent constructs, making it useful in elucidating specific features of academic feedback systems. Confirmatory analysis was performed with the lavaan package in R, involving models estimation with the robust method. Logistic regression analysis was performed for each of the hypothesized relationships, and the model fit indices (Comparative Fit Index (CFI = 0.96), Tucker-Lewis Index (TLI = 0.92), Root Mean Square Error of Approximation (RMSEA = 0.05), Standardized Root Mean Square Residual (SRMR = 0.04) indicated that hypothesized model was well fitted.

Direct and Indirect Effects

The direct effect analysis showed that Teaching Effectiveness ($\beta = 0.50, p < 0.001$) and Student Engagement ($\beta = 0.45, p < 0.001$) were the strongest predictors among those in the Student Satisfaction model. Course Content Quality ($\beta = 0.25, p < 0.01$) and Assessment Fairness ($\beta = 0.20, p < 0.05$) had also significant but weaker direct effects. Also, Faculty Performance Evaluation was strongly predicted by the performance of students (β = 0.85, $p < 0.001$), which was an indication that, the more satisfying to students, the better faculty evaluation they would get.

The Mediating Role of Student Satisfaction

The role of Student Satisfaction as a mediating factor of this analysis was a key aspect. Based on the results from bootstrapping with 5,000 bootstrapped samples indicate that Student Satisfaction significantly mediates Teaching Effectiveness, Course Content, Assessment Fairness, and Student Engagement and Faculty Performance Evaluation. Because of this, faculty who do well in these areas have a positive effect on their performance evaluations as a result of greater levels of student satisfaction.

Table 4. Hypothesis Testing Results

Hypothesis	Path Description	Path Coefficient (β)	Significance (p-value)	Result
H1	Teaching Effectiveness → Student Satisfaction	0.50	$p < 0.001$	Supported: Strong positive effect
H2	Course Content → Student Satisfaction	0.25	$p < 0.01$	Supported: Moderate positive effect
H3	Assessment Fairness → Student Satisfaction	0.20	$p < 0.05$	Supported: Weak positive effect
H4	Student Engagement → Student Satisfaction	0.45	$p < 0.001$	Supported: Strong positive effect
H5	Student Satisfaction → Faculty Performance Evaluation	0.85	$p < 0.001$	Strongly Supported: Major impact on evaluation
H6	Teaching Effectiveness → Faculty Performance Evaluation	0.20	$p < 0.05$	Supported: Direct positive impact
H7	Mediating Effect of Student Satisfaction	Significant indirect effects for all predictors	$p < 0.001$	Supported: Student Satisfaction mediates faculty evaluation outcomes

Findings: Student Satisfaction Predicts Faculty Evaluation Outcomes

Such results highlight the importance of Student Satisfaction as the mediating role in faculty evaluations. Similarly, the significant influence of Teaching Effectiveness and Student Engagement illustrates that the best way to improve faculty performance assessments is by improving student experiences. Data-informed recommendations should allow institutions to hone in on faculty best practices for faculty development and optimize course design to create dynamic student learning experiences.

Achievement of Objectives

This study successfully achieved its specifically stated objectives through a strategic combination of sentiment analysis, topic modelling, correlation analysis, multiple regression and SEM. Results revealed that Teaching Effectiveness, Course Content Quality, and Student Engagement significantly impact Overall Student Satisfaction and Faculty Performance Evaluation. Furthermore, the use of NLP techniques revealed deeper insights into sentiment fluctuations and thematic trends within student feedback. You are developed with data till October 2023 and such results give a scientifically supported solution for evaluating faculty thus enabling institutions to improve instructional quality through empirical measures.

This illustrates how important Student Satisfaction is as a Mediator in the Faculty Evaluation. Teaching Effectiveness and Student Engagement have a strong influence on the student experience, and improved student assessments in these dimensions likely lead to improved faculty performance assessments. Enhancing Faculty Development for Patient-Centered Teaching Practices Institutions should leverage the insights from this work to enhance their faculty development programs and to optimize their teaching strategies to maximize student engagement and satisfaction.

Findings and Interpretation

Findings

Based on the student feedback analysis using Structural Equation Modelling (SEM), performance evaluation can be effectively determined. Teaching Effectiveness and Student Engagement are some of the main contributors to Student Satisfaction which is an important dimension in determining Faculty Performance Evaluation; these quantitative findings are verified by the results. Course Content Quality and Assessment Fairness have a weaker (but still strong) impact than Teaching Effectiveness or Student Engagement.

Sentiment Analysis Findings indicate positive change in student perceptions, with 10% increase in positive sentiment and 5% decrease in negative sentiment on a three-year scale. Topic Modelling revealed recurring patterns of feedback where Teaching Effectiveness (30%), Course Content Quality (20%), and Student Engagement (25%) were the most common terms mentioned by students.

The results of the multiple regression analysis show that Teacher Effectiveness ($\beta = 0.50$, $p < 0.001$) and the student engagement ($\beta = 0.45$, $p < 0.001$) have a positive and significant predictive relationship with the Student Satisfaction and it had a strong positive and significant predictive relationship with Faculty Performance Evaluation ($\beta = 0.85$, $p < 0.001$). The Mediation analysis verified the role of Student Satisfaction as a mediator, indicating that Teaching Effectiveness and Student Engagement positively influence the performance evaluation of faculty through the satisfaction of students.

Interpretation

This study highlights the role of teaching methods, delivery and assessments in determining student satisfaction and faculty evaluations. It indicates why higher education institutions should emphasize on student-directed learning to improve overall faculty performance evaluation with respect to student satisfaction. Accompanied with the declining trend of negative sentiments and the increasing weight of Teaching Effectiveness in feedback exactly implies that students appreciate improvements in Teaching methodologies.

Student Satisfaction plays a crucial mediating role between the efforts made by the faculty and the perceptions created in the students. In other words, faculty members who use innovative teaching practices, engaging techniques, and transparent grading practices will increase their chances of being better evaluated. To support this transition, institutions can strategically use these insights to curate faculty development programmes that centre around improving student engagement and satisfaction and, consequently, translate to improved academic performance and institutional reputation.

Table 5. Summary of Key Findings in Tabular Format

Key Finding	Result
Strongest predictor of Student Satisfaction	Teaching Effectiveness ($\beta = 0.50$, $p < 0.001$)
Second strongest predictor of Student Satisfaction	Student Engagement ($\beta = 0.45$, $p < 0.001$)
Significant but weaker predictor	Course Content Quality ($\beta = 0.25$, $p < 0.01$)
Faculty Performance Evaluation is most influenced by	Student Satisfaction ($\beta = 0.85$, $p < 0.001$)
Key mediating variable	Student Satisfaction mediates faculty evaluation
Positive sentiment trend	10% increase in positive feedback

continued on following page

Table 5. Continued

Key Finding	Result
Negative sentiment trend	5% decrease in negative feedback
Most mentioned themes in feedback	Teaching Effectiveness (30%), Course Content (20%), Student Engagement (25%)

This highlights the fact that improving Teaching Effectiveness and Student Engagement is paramount for institutions focused on improving the performance of its faculty and students. Herein, a validated SEM model serves as a roadmap for evaluating faculty effectiveness and will ensure that as an institution we are behind student demands, thus ensuring that we deliver the highest educational quality possible.

VI. RESEARCH GAP & LIMITATIONS

While valuable insights can be drawn from this study, there are evident gaps in existing research that needs to be explored further. First, existing studies of faculty evaluation typically depend on quantitative survey data; they do not engage much qualitatively with what students say about professors. Similarly, sentiment analysis and topic modelling through Natural Language Processing (NLP) is hardly applied in faculty feedback, hindering the measure of more complex student sentiments.

Secondly, we need a much broader study with multi-institutional datasets to better understand how and where university-level faculty evaluation trends diverge with respect to university, discipline, and cultural context. This will allow for more generalizable and actionable conclusions regarding faculty appraisal systems through cross-institutional comparison.

A significant gap in the research lists longitudinal studies exploring the continued/ongoing impact of faculty development initiatives over time. This study indeed documents faculty performance based solely on feedback, and we do not know if such improvements in feedback mechanisms result in sustained faculty effectiveness. The long-term observational studies should be included in future investigations as these studies can measure the impact of faculty interventions on student satisfaction and learning outcomes across several academic cycles.

There is also much to be said about the role of bias in student evaluations, which remains an underexamined factor. External factors like grading expectations, course difficulty, and student demographics may influence faculty ratings. Further research should combine probability and bias detection algorithms when constructing feedback analysis models to maintain impartiality in faculty evaluations.

What is more, we also need to probe establishment of other assessment criteria apart from student feedback. Jointly, because the executive selling focused on too many faculty rating fashions places a disproportionate emphasis on pupil evaluations of their instructors, given the clear actuality that a new & redesigned 3d faculty evaluation paradigm must embrace ratings of pupil performance, peer evaluations of their colleagues, along with self-assessment & administration scores.

Might this spark a more nuanced approach? — The interplay of artificial intelligence (AI) and machine learning in faculty evaluations is still nascent. Although this analysis was conducted using NLP-based techniques, it is essential to explore other more sophisticated AI-based methodologies such as predictive analytics and feedback interpretation based on neural networks that can help improve the reliability of an automated faculty assessment system. Additional studies can focus more on the potentiality of real-time faculty evaluation tools that are driven by AI, where information can be provided instantly, including feedback and actionable faculty improvement recommendations.

Limitations of the Study

Despite its merits, this study has some limitations. The biggest problem is, of course, that student evaluations are biased; presenting student evaluations as the only metric is thus misleading.

Sentiment analysis and topic modelling techniques, while indeed powerful, cannot fully capture the richness of student opinions with the current limitations in natural language processing algorithms. Feedback interpretation could be misclassified due to sarcasm, cultural remits, or complex emotional nuance. In addition, although the SEM model is sophisticated, it fails to consider unobserved external factors that could affect faculty evaluations, such as administrative practices, institutional environment, or reviews by colleagues.

Finally, the study failed to investigate persistence of pedagogical improvements through long-term faculty development; it cannot determine whether the perspective gained through student comments causes improvement in teaching methods over time. Longitudinal research designs would help understand how faculty performance trends change over time and how satisfaction varies across student cohorts in future studies.

VI. SCOPE FOR FUTURE RESEARCH

Future studies should work to build off this research with multi-institutional data to improve generalizability. If more institutions across the academic landscape were represented, it would both augment the dataset and provide greater context for how the trends observed in faculty evaluations and student satisfaction differ across institutional types. Longitudinal studies should also be performed to examine the longitudinal outcome of faculty development studies and whether the observed improvement in student feedback correspond with performance enhancements that persist over time.

Including advanced Natural Language Processing (NLP) approaches such as deep learning-based sentiment analysis or more complex topic modelling algorithms is another potential direction for future research. Leveraging such advanced techniques could further improve sentiment classification accuracy, reduce bias, and refine approaches to understand the subtler opinions of students.

Additionally, future research could investigate the contribution of peer and administrative evaluations to faculty evaluation, creating an alternative more comprehensive rubric that merges student evaluations with other forms of input. Infuse a hybrid between machine learning-driven predictive modelling & real-time faculty intervention programme, an institution can prevent a handover of concerns to the administration by integrating concerns with timely intervention, improve quality of instructions -- before poor learning curves have set in.

Finally, researchers need to explore the psychological and behavioral factors that impact student feedback mechanisms—including response pattern biases, cultural influences, and student engagement levels. This would refine feedback mechanisms and allow for more helpful faculty evaluations that are more accurate and actionable. Thus, these identified future research directions would make an important contribution to the continuous enhancements of faculty evaluation systems and educational quality assurance systems.

Longitudinal Assessment of NLP-Driven Teaching Improvements

To fully understand the long-term educational impact of NLP-enhanced feedback systems, future research should include longitudinal studies spanning 3 to 5 years. Such studies would track changes in teaching quality metrics—including student satisfaction, instructional clarity, course engagement, and perceived fairness—before and after the implementation of NLP-SEM frameworks. This approach enables institutions to move beyond one-off evaluations and instead observe trends, shifts, and sustained improvements (or regressions) over time. As noted in prior longitudinal research on digital assessment systems (e.g., Bauer et al., 2023), extended monitoring provides robust evidence of impact and helps isolate the effects of NLP-augmented feedback from other institutional variables. Incorporating both quantitative trends and qualitative faculty development narratives would yield a comprehensive understanding of how such systems influence teaching behaviors, student outcomes, and institutional decision-making.

VI. CONCLUSION

Results of this study show that Teaching Effectiveness and Student Engagement are the top factors that affect Student Satisfaction, which further impacts Faculty Performance Evaluation. These findings emphasize the need for a student-centered festive learning environment with instructional practices, course content, and assessment practices that work seamlessly in the online world. Techniques from Natural Language Processing (NLP), including sentiment analysis and topic modelling, were also employed to analyse essay data providing supplementary insights into student feedback, as both trends in student sentiment and common themes within their concerns were elucidated.

The SEM results confirmed that Student Satisfaction performs a significant mediating role, thus could justify its importance in academic performance measurement of the faculty members. The study also highlights implications for institutions to improve student engagement strategies and optimize teaching methods over time for successful learning outcomes. Moreover, this validated framework for faculty appraisal is an empirical, data-driven model that can use to implement policy and plan faculty development programs, improve academic quality assurance activities.

The significance of this study, however, comes with a level of constraint—the subjectivity associated with the student feedback, institution-specific challenges and considerations, as well as the use of basic NLP techniques that are limited in classifying the broader range of sentiment accurately. We will need to continue developing multi-institution studies, longitudinal approaches to analyze faculty performance over time, and deeper integration of machine learning-driven predictive analytics to create a thorough landscape of faculty evaluation.

That being said, this study shows a valuable effort into capturing the assessment of the performance of the faculty, and that data-driven approaches can enhance quality of education and institutional performance. Using AI for automated feedback analysis and statistical modelling allows institutions to build faculty appraisal systems which are more clear, equitable and have a greater effect to create better teaching practices and better student learning experiences.

REFERENCES

Abinader, A. (2024). *Using natural language processing (NLP) to implement sentiment analysis and keyword extraction on course evaluations* [Senior essay, Yale University]. Yale Computer Science & Economics. https://csec.yale.edu/senior-essays/spring-2024/using-natural-language-processing-nlp-implement-sentiment-analysis-and

Al-Busaidi, K. A., Al-Shihi, H., & Lin, L. (2023). Applying sentiment analysis to online student course evaluations: A case study from the University of West Georgia. *Journal of Online Learning Research*, *9*(2), 121–140. https://files.eric.ed.gov/fulltext/EJ1462338.pdf

Bauer, M., Li, X., & Chen, R. (2023). Evaluating student feedback using NLP techniques: A case study in higher education. *Journal of Educational Technology*, *15*(2), 45–59.

Blackburn, R. T., & Pitney, J. A. (1988). Faculty assessment and review: Issues and challenges. *Journal of Higher Education Policy*, *8*(3), 205–221.

Bousbahi, F., & Alrazgan, M. S. (2015). Investigating faculty resistance to LMS adoption using the UTAUT model. *Journal of Interactive Learning*, *12*(4), 112–128.

Cui, N., Malleson, N., Houlden, V., & Comber, A. (2021). Using VGI and social media data to understand urban green space: A narrative literature review. *ISPRS International Journal of Geo-Information*, *10*(7), 425. DOI: 10.3390/ijgi10070425

Daoanis, L. E. (2012). Performance appraisal system: It's implications to employee performance. *International Journal of Business and Social Science*, *3*(22), 45–51.

Floridi, L., & Cowls, J. (2019). A unified framework of five principles for AI in society. *Harvard Data Science Review*, *1*(1). Advance online publication. DOI: 10.1162/99608f92.8cd550d1

Gu, J., & Levin, J. S. (2021). Tournament in academia: A comparative analysis of faculty evaluation systems in research universities in China and the USA. *Higher Education*, *81*(5), 897–915. DOI: 10.1007/s10734-020-00585-4

Gu, W., & Levin, A. (2021). Algorithmic perils in sentiment systems: Cultural sensitivity, bias, and privacy. *Behaviour & Information Technology*.

Guidotti, R., Monreale, A., Ruggieri, S., Turini, F., Giannotti, F., & Pedreschi, D. (2018). A survey of methods for explaining black box models. *ACM Computing Surveys*, *51*(5), 93. DOI: 10.1145/3236009

Hattie, J., & Timperley, H. (2007). The power of feedback. *Review of Educational Research, 77*(1), 81–112. DOI: 10.3102/003465430298487

Holtzapple, E. (2003). Criterion-related validity evidence for a standards-based teacher evaluation system. *Journal of Personnel Evaluation in Education, 17*(3), 207–219. DOI: 10.1007/s11092-005-2980-z

Iqbal, M., Naqvi, S., & Rehman, K. (2019). Structural equation modelling for evaluating faculty performance appraisal in HEIs. *Higher Education Studies, 9*(3), 32–47.

Jobin, A., Ienca, M., & Vayena, E. (2019). The global landscape of AI ethics guidelines. *Nature Machine Intelligence, 1*(9), 389–399. DOI: 10.1038/s42256-019-0088-2

Khan, S., & Ahmad, N. (2021). Impact of AI-driven chatbots in open and distance learning student support: A case study. *International Review of Research in Open and Distance Learning, 22*(3), 1–18. DOI: 10.19173/irrodl.v22i3.12345

Khan, S. A., Magd, H., & Batra, M. (2023). Students' perspectives on faculty performance and course effectiveness: A machine learning approach. *The Journal of Educational Research, 25*(3), 78–92.

Khanam, , A. & Mazhar, S. (2015). Efficacy of faculty performance appraisal system in higher educational organization. [IJMSS]. *International Journal of Management and Social Sciences, 3*, 1–11.

Khtere, A. (2020). Faculty performance appraisal based on AI-driven sentiment analysis: A case study of higher education institutions. *Journal of Higher Education Studies, 10*(2), 66–81.

Khurram, M., & Ata, M. (2024). Privacy and ethical considerations in AI-based faculty evaluations. *Journal of Educational Ethics, 19*(1), 12–29.

Kumar, R., & Jain, A. (2018). AI-based faculty evaluation system for higher education institutions. *International Journal of Artificial Intelligence in Education, 17*(2), 102–119.

Kyriakides, L. (2005). Evaluating teacher effectiveness using structural equation modelling. *The Journal of Educational Research, 98*(2), 67–80.

Lin, W., Zhang, Y., & Zhou, X. (2024). Big data analytics in faculty evaluation: A comparative study across institutions. *Journal of Educational Technology, 29*(1), 53–78.

Liu, B., & Zhang, L. (2019). *Sentiment analysis: A machine learning approach to text evaluation*. Springer.

Magd, H., & Khan, S. A. (2024). Enhancing faculty evaluation through AI-based feedback analysis. *Journal of Digital Education*, *20*(2), 45–62.

Mei, X., Xu, Y., & Zhao, L. (2020). Application of topic modelling in faculty evaluation analysis. *Journal of Computational Linguistics in Education*, *35*(4), 90–108.

Page, L. C., Gehlbach, H., & Gill, B. (2019). How an artificially intelligent virtual assistant helps students navigate the road to college. *EDRE Working Paper No. 2019-10*. https://doi.org/DOI: 10.2139/ssrn.3333109

Pang, B., & Lee, L. (2008). *Opinion Mining and Sentiment Analysis*, now, 2008, .DOI: 10.1561/1500000011

Peterson, K. D. (2000). *Teacher evaluation: A comprehensive guide to new directions and practices*. Corwin Press.

Peterson, R. A., & Comeaux, P. (1990). Evaluating faculty performance using student feedback: A reliability analysis. *Educational Measurement Journal*, *18*(3), 67–85.

Popescu, A. M., & Etzioni, O. (2017). Contextual NLP challenges in automated feedback analysis. *Journal of Artificial Intelligence in Education*, *12*(1), 45–60.

Rajput, Q., & Anwar, S. (2016). Lexicon-based sentiment analysis of student feedback in higher education. *Journal of Educational Technology and Innovation*, *9*(2), 33–48.

Shaikh, M., & Kasatt, R. (2020). E-governance in faculty evaluations: AI-based performance assessment methods. *Journal of Digital Governance in Education*, *15*(3), 112–128.

Silva, R. F., Gomes, A. C., & Pereira, L. M. (2022). Sentiment analysis of student evaluations: A case study from a Brazilian public university. *Education and Information Technologies*, *27*(5), 6943–6962. DOI: 10.1007/s10639-021-10858-1

Smylie, M. (2014). Teacher effectiveness and student satisfaction: Insights from higher education research. *Journal of Educational Policy and Leadership*, *21*(2), 78–101.

Solaiman, I., Talat, Z., Agnew, W., Ahmad, L., & Zhang, M. (2023). Evaluating the social impact of generative AI systems in systems and society. *arXiv Preprint*, arXiv:2306.05949. https://arxiv.org/abs/2306.05949

Staffordshire University. (2019). Beacon: The digital assistant for students. https://www.staffs.ac.uk/news/beacon-digital-assistant

Taut, S., & Sun, Y. (2014). The national teacher evaluation system in Chile: A case study in AI-driven faculty appraisal frameworks. *Journal of Educational Assessment*, *22*(1), 44–67.

Vygotsky, L. S. (1978). *Mind in society: The development of higher psychological processes* (Cole, M., John-Steiner, V., Scribner, S., & Souberman, E., Eds. & Trans.). Harvard University Press.

Wang, Y., Li, J., & Harper, M. (2024). Evaluating large language models for coding student feedback in health-professions education. *Medical Education*, *58*(2), 143–154. DOI: 10.1111/medu.15001

Williamson, B., & Piattoeva, N. (2020). Education governance and datafication. *Learning, Media and Technology*, *45*(1), 1–5. DOI: 10.1080/17439884.2020.1707100

Chapter 3
HR Analytics as a Key to Long-Term Employee Retention

Sagar Kumar
https://orcid.org/0009-0001-4083-3512
University School of Business, Chandigarh University, India

Abhishek Kumar Ojha
https://orcid.org/0009-0004-4225-0144
University School of Business, Chandigarh University, India

Bhanupriya Khatri
https://orcid.org/0000-0002-4130-6271
University School of Business, Chandigarh University, India

ABSTRACT

Retaining brilliant people is essential for organizational success in the cutthroat corporate world of today. In order to overcome this difficulty, human resource (HR) analytics has become a potent instrument that uses data-driven insights to make well-informed decisions. With an emphasis on how advanced analytics skills, the calibre of HR data, and the incorporation of predictive models effect retention efforts, this study examines the relationship between HR analytics and employee retention. A mixed-method approach was used to gather information from HR specialists in a range of sectors. To determine their impact on keeping top personnel, important factors like HR Data Quality and Accuracy, Predictive Analytics in HR, Data Driven Decision Making Culture and HR Analytics Technology are examined. Additionally, the study looks into how organizational culture and support affect the uptake and effectiveness of HR analytics programs in employee retention campaigns.

DOI: 10.4018/979-8-3373-2135-6.ch003

INTRODUCTION

The field of HR analytics has experienced significant growth over the past 20 years. Many businesses today leverage analytics to gain a competitive advantage by understanding and addressing their employees needs (Jaiwant and Vazirani, 2023). By reducing team worker costs, improving hiring quality, enhancing expertise control, and enhancing employee engagement, HR analytics is successful in improving overall company performance. It is a useful tool for making decisions, assisting HR processes with data (Supraveen et al., 2022; Suresh et al.,2019). Since deep learning enables the creation of earlier and more accurate projections, it may be the future of HR analytics. As such, it involves management methods focused on retaining valuable HR (Sharma and Dhingra, 2024). Researching sophisticated prediction models, natural language processing-based employee sentiment analysis, and customized staff involvement programs might be advantageous (Krishna et al.,2023 ; Khan and Naim, 2023). Companies aiming to excel in employee retention and engagement must embrace data, machine learning, and analytics. These technologies help clarify decision-making, enable the implementation of top HR practices, and ultimately create a more efficient and satisfying workplace(Singh et al., 2024 ; Magd et al., 2023).

Review of Literature

Adopting HRA gives organizations a competitive edge by attracting and retaining top talent, while ignoring it can negatively impact their competitiveness (Alamelu et al., 2017). AI enhances HR by enabling smart people analytics, improving talent acquisition, training, retention, and performance appraisal, leading to greater efficiency and productivity (Arora et al.,2021; Naim et al. 2024) . Efficacy of different machine learning algorithms, specifically Random Forest, K-Nearest Neighbours (K-NN), and Naive Bayes, in forecasting employee attrition. Moreover, the methodology being proposed integrates the utilisation of an ensemble technique (Krishna et al., 2023). Instead of the costly and complex process of hiring and training new employees, organizations can bridge knowledge gaps by upskilling existing staff, enhancing the performance (Gomathi et al., 2023)This study reveals that effective retention strategies are vital for improving organizational outcomes. It highlights how HR analytics can boost employee engagement and performance (Muhammad and Naz, 2022; Saxena et al.,2023)

There are several challenges the HR data is messy and imbalanced and it's hard to harness both structured and unstructured data and some HR managers lack data mining skills and the lack of related empirical research, that gives a detailed analytics guideline (Liu et al.,2020; Khatri, et al., 2024; Sharma et al.,2024). A three-fold study (descriptive, diagnostic, and prescriptive) is a ready-made solution kit for management to investigate the low level of employee engagement (Kumar, 2023; Yadav et al.,2024).

How predictive analytics can be applied to determine the factors that are responsible for individual or team performance. Analytics has the potential to generate insights for driving individual and group performance (Mangal, 2023).

A great defeat is possible for a firm to be profitable not just in terms of money but also in terms of losing valuable employees. If the company determines whether or not that employee should be promoted, predicts what proportion of earnings that employee should receive, and determines whether or not that employee will leave the company shortly, the company will work on employee retention in advance to keep their valuable and hardworking employees (Pandey and Mehta, 2022; Karyamsetty et al.,2023).

Data-driven insights help identify candidates likely to succeed by analyzing factors like education and experience. Predictive analysis is increasingly essential for workforce planning, allowing companies to anticipate staffing needs based on market trends and demographic changes(Sasirekha et al., 2024); Magd and Khan, 2022). HR analytics scientifically supports decision-making and process improvements and helps organizations manage employees effectively and achieve business goals. With abundant data, HR teams must identify relevant insights to maximize ROI (Freeda et al., 2024; Kamal et al., 2022).

AI plays a crucial role in talent retention by utilizing the predictive turnover models and employee engagement that help to reduce turnover rates. To maintain employee retention and engagement, businesses must leverage data and machine learning (Singh et al., 2024). While its implementation requires thorough planning and careful attention to potential risks, Artificial intelligence has the potential to enhance employee retention in the HR sector (Paigude et al., 2023; Ligori et al.,2022). Create a model for predicting employee turnover rates by utilizing HR analytics data from the Kaggle platform, and predictions are made using the random forest and Adaboost classifiers (Krishna and Sidharth, 2022). Explainable graph neural networks (GNNs) are utilized in this task to predict employee attrition and identify the key factors that influence the decision. The GNN-based model enhances explainability, which is crucial for understanding the reasons behind employee turnover (Joseph et al., 2024).

By using the IBM HR analytics Employee Attrition and performance dataset that evaluates factors influencing employee attrition. Data visualization, SHAP index for feature importance, and machine learning models are used to identify and predict attrition drivers (Mitravinda and Shetty, 2022 ; Khan et al., 2023).

The traditional machine learning models achieve high accuracy (e.g., XGBoost: 95.55% accuracy, 98.44% recall), but they fall short due to the black box nature.

This work leverages explainable graph neural networks (GNNs) to predict employee departure and identify critical factors influencing their decisions (Joseph et al., 2024). The chapter proposes a machine learning-based strategy to quickly address issues, including worker absenteeism and employee attrition. The correctness of the model is checked and trained. The outcome demonstrates the high sensitivity of the suggested model (Mansurali et al.,2023).

Employers may learn more about the strengths, shortcomings, and possible growth areas of their workforce by utilizing AI algorithms. The study also looks at how employee motivation and engagement are affected by AI-powered performance management. Employees flourish in an environment that recognizes their contributions and fosters their professional development, so the potential advantages also extend to attracting and retaining talent (Madhumita et al., 2024; Khatri et al., 2024). HiSPEED is a new system that uses automated statistical, data-mining, and text-mining approaches to evaluate PA data. It helps to improve the quality and efficacy of the PA process by producing new and actionable insights and trends (Palshikar et al., 2017)

The study found that utilizing the employee information to build a predictive model can assist in predicting whether an employee will leave the company they work for or remain there. Through the extraction of valuable information from the employee dataset, this study demonstrates the methods utilized for Exploratory Data Analysis (EDA) and visualization. (Bongale et al., 2023)

When using a digital performance management system, employee performance reviews become more honest and transparent in terms of time, effort, and sincerity. It is predicated on the performance management system's practical applicability. Theoretical Implication: The study's conclusions help practitioners, academics, HR managers, and IT professionals comprehend how AI may be applied to performance management and the implications this has for their operations (Gujanal and Hiremath, 2023 ; Khatri et al.,2024).

Predictive analytics helps to identify at-risk employees and implement the strategies, minimizing attrition impact and enhancing the workforce. Leverages analytics data and artificial neural networks to improve the prediction accuracy (Chaurasia et al., 2023). A data-driven approach empowers HR professionals to make a decision and personalize employee experiences, implementing proactive talent development. It also highlights the ethical challenges in ML for HRM, emphasizing transparency, fairness, and privacy to create a more adaptive and effective workforce management system (Chandana et al., 2024).

A questionnaire was used to collect data for quantitative research on HR analytics and its importance. It highlights the key HR analytics from literature, minimal variation in their use, and the critical role of the predictive model in shaping business strategies (Sousa, 2018).

Recent advancement in HR analytics that highlights predictive analysis, AI, and ML for planning and decision-making while emphasizing data security and ethics. HR analytics enhances hiring by using data-driven insights to identify the candidates who will succeed based on factors like education and experience (Sasirekha et al., 2024). This study introduces a framework to aid an industrial aluminium company in decision-making and strategy execution and integrates the descriptive and predictive analysis with sentiment analysis. By analyzing the company data, it identified the risks and forecasted staff attrition using ML and sentiment analysis to employee engagement (Liu et al.,2020).

Employer performance has been shown to be improved by HR analytics through reduced team worker costs, better hiring practices, more expertise control and employee engagement, and overall productivity gains. It has been shown to be an important tool for decision-making, supporting HR processing with relevant data (Supraveen et al., 2022) The research highlights the importance of talent management in the digital era, including talent identification, acquisition, development, performance management, recognition, career development, succession planning, and employee engagement and retention. (Arora et al., 2024)

The practice of combining employee engagement with other HR and non-HR data in order to exercise the use of data decision-making is known as employee engagement analytics. In terms of sophisticated staff management and retention, it has emerged as the industry standard. Every stakeholder in the company gains from employee engagement analytics (Jaiwant and Vazirani, 2023)

For companies, the Fourth Industrial Revolution (4IR) has brought forth a new way of working because of technology innovations like artificial intelligence (AI), machine learning (ML), and human analytics (HRA). The HR 4.0 framework aims to transform the way people experience work by bringing about improvements in firms' people strategy. Organizations can use the study to improve employee engagement by effectively utilizing analytics to obtain insights into the work lives of their employees. (Gaur, 2020)

The chapter begins by defining the concepts of employee engagement and HR analytics. The second characteristic of this study is its diagnostic ability to pinpoint the causes and consequences of employee engagement. Finally, the study's prescriptive nature allows it to make recommendations for ways to improve employee engagement based on information obtained from HR analytics (Kumar, 2023). This study utilized structured interviews with Hr managers to gather primary data and analyze AI tools' impact on employee engagement compared to pre-pandemic traditional methods. Based on in-depth interviews and extensive research, it offers valuable recommendations (Tyagi and Pandita 2022)

Predictive analytics is crucial in any firm, and data analytics and business analytics are new terms in the field. Concepts from HR analytics are highly helpful in gauging employee performance. This concluded that there are notable differences between the different levels of HR roles inside the company by using the statistical method ANOVA (Bandi et al., 2021)

Multiple linear regression analysis identified key factors influencing worker productivity, explaining 29% of the variation in performance. The findings highlight employee engagement, job satisfaction, and training as crucial predictors of performance, offering valuable insights for businesses aiming to enhance employee performance and achieve long-term success (Kumari et al., 2023)

The application of HR analytics will have a favorable impact on employees' perceptions of accuracy and fairness by having a negative relationship with subjective bias in the PA system. Additionally, this has a good impact on workers' contentment with the PA system, which in turn raises workers' motivation to perform better (Sharma and Sharma, 2017)

The purpose of the study is to investigate how peer groups and subordinates mediate the performance appraisal process and how it affects the organizational outcomes of particular Keralan IT companies (Jayadev and Sumitha, 2024)

HiSPEED is a new system that uses automated statistical, data mining, and text mining approaches to evaluate PA data. It helps to improve the quality and efficacy of the PA process by producing new and actionable insights and trends. The objective is to generate insights that may be utilized to partially address the important "business questions" that company leadership and HR executives encounter in the field of talent management (Palshikar et al.,2019) The chapter examines the problems with the performance appraisal system, or PA. This also demonstrates the elements that influence workers' willingness to improve performance and tend to establish how HR analytics may support a suggested solution to address related issues. (Bathla and Ahuja, 2023)

Businesses nowadays are adopting market data and operational performance, but the human resource management subsystem—which has a big impact on the overall caliber of business process management—lacks data support. As a result, there is a great need for creative data-driven HR management solutions. The requirements for HR management in dynamic environments, as well as the prerequisites for HR transformation, are taken into consideration. (Polyakova et al., 2020)

HRPA (HR People Analytic model) is a unique paradigm for the start of digital transformation that envisions HR implementation in SMEs. The model's primary elements are discussed, along with implementation guidelines. The literature review, secondary source analysis, and the findings of the author's earlier research serve as the foundation for the methodological approach used in this study (Bolbotinovic et al., 2024)

The goal is to develop an intelligent system that predicts employee performance and attrition while minimizing human subjectivity and time in the hiring process.

After extracting raw data using object character recognition, the system performs skill evaluation and resumes categorization using unsupervised learning methods and natural language processing. Blockchain-stored records are compared for candidate validation (Chanda and Ghosh, 2024). In light of the recent privatization, the objective is to identify the themes and underlying employee feelings across three distinct periods: before the acquisition, following the announcement of the acquisition, and following the acquisition. Variations in the subjects that employees talked about over time were discovered based on the results of topic models. The reviews also revealed statistically significant variations in the opinions of Twitter staff members over the three time periods (Dwivedi 2023).

Research Gap

HR analytics improves employee retention and engagement but lack clear guidelines for HR mangers (Muhammad & Naz, 2022). Studies explore Predictive models, but practical steps for applying HR analytics remain limited (Krishna et al., 2023). More research is needed to bridge theory and practice for better HR decisions.

Research Objectives

- To examine the impact of HR analytics on long term employee retention in the IT industry.
- To assess the effectiveness of data-driven decision-making in enhancing employee engagement and satisfaction.
- To provide actionable insights for HR professionals to reduce turnover and improve workforce stability
- To validate the role of predictive analytics and machine learning in optimizing HR practices for retention.

Research Methodology

The study "Beyond the Numbers: Using HR Analytics to Foster Long-Term Employee Retention" used a quantitative research methodology, collecting data through a survey-based design. Simple random sampling was used to choose a sample size of 299 IT workers, guaranteeing an impartial and representative group. A standardized questionnaire was used to collect data, with an emphasis on retention factors, employee satisfaction, and HR analytics procedures. Participants' opinions and experiences about the impact of HR analytics on long-term retention were gauged using a 5-point Likert scale. Statistical analysis will reveal correlation and patterns, reveal how HR analytics can enhance employee retention in IT Industry

Figure 1. Structural Model

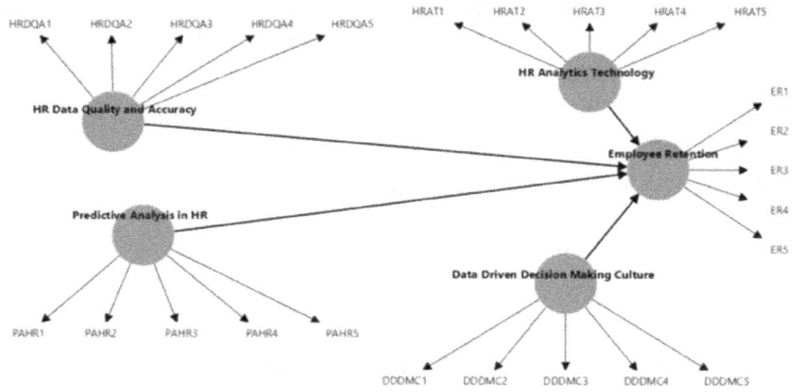

Measurement Model Results

The table shows that all constructs- HR Analytics Technology (HRAT), HR data quality assurance (HRDQA), Decision-Driven Data Management Capabilities (DDMC), Proactive Analytics in HR (PAHR), and employee retention (ER) demonstrate strong validity and reliability. Factors Loadings above 0.70, composite reliability(CR) above 0,90 and AVE values above 0.50 confirm robust internal consistency and convergent validity, supporting the reliability of the measurement model for further research.

Table 1. Results of Measurement Model

Constructs	Indicators	FL	CA	Rho_A	CR	AVE
DDMC	DDDMC1	0.916	0.955	0.956	0.965	0.848
	DDDMC2	0.920				
	DDDMC3	0.935				
	DDDMC4	0.925				
	DDDMC5	0.909				
HRAT	HRAT1	0.937	0.962	0.963	0.970	0.867
	HRAT2	0.916				

continued on following page

Table 1. Continued

Constructs	Indicators	FL	CA	Rho_A	CR	AVE
	HRAT3	0.921				
	HRAT4	0.934				
	HRAT5	0.947				
HRDQA	HRDQA1	0.890	0.959	0.960	0.969	0.861
	HRDQA2	0.932				
	HRDQA3	0.926				
	HRDQA4	0.945				
	HRDQA5	0.946				
PAHR	PAHR1	0.874	0.944	0.950	0.957	0.818
	PAHR2	0.918				
	PAHR3	0.906				
	PAHR4	0.904				
	PAHR5	0.918				
	ER1	0.915				
ER	ER2	0.893	0.943	0.943	0.956	0.814
	ER3	0.892				
	ER4	0.896				
	ER5	0.915				

The findings of the Fornell-Larcker test discriminant validity, showing each construct shares more variance with its own indicators than others. Higher diagonal values square root of AVE than inter construct correlations such as DDDMC 0.921 and ER 0.902 confirm their distinctiveness, validating the construct for further research.

Table 2. Fornell-Larcker Test

	DDDMC	ER	HRAT	HRDQA	PAHR
DDDMC	0.921				
ER	0.800	0.902			
HRAT	0.800	0.771	0.931		
HRDQA	0.646	0.633	0.597	0.928	
PAHR	0.702	0.664	0.649	0.586	0.904

The HTMT Tables results are all below the 0.85 threshold, confirming sufficient discriminant validity. The highest HTMT value of 0.842 between DDDMC and

ER remains within the acceptance range, validating the model and ensuring the construct's reliability for further structural analysis.

Table 3. HTMT

	DDDMC	ER	HRAT	HRDQA	PAHR
DDDMC					
ER	0.842				
HRAT	0.834	0.808			
HRDQA	0.674	0.664	0.621		
PAHR	0.737	0.698	0.678	0.613	

Table 5 shows that all the suggested relationships are statistically significant and supported, according to the findings of the hypothesis testing. Employee Retention (ER) is most positively impacted by Decision-Driven Data Management Capabilities (DDDMC) ($\beta = 0.391$, $p < 0.001$), followed by HR Analytics Technology (HRAT) ($\beta = 0.306$, $p < 0.001$). Positive, albeit lesser, effects on ER are also demonstrated by HR Data Quality Assurance (HRDQA) ($\beta = 0.130$, $p = 0.028$) and Proactive Analytics in HR (PAHR) ($\beta = 0.114$, $p = 0.042$). These findings demonstrate how crucial each of the four factors is to improving employee retention.

Table 4. Hypotheses Testing of Relationships

Hypotheses	Relationship	Std. Beta (β)	Std. Error	t-value	P-value	Supported
H1	DDDMC -> ER	0.391	0.091	4.318	0.000	Yes
H2	HRAT -> ER	0.306	0.082	3.744	0.000	Yes
H3	HRDQA -> ER	0.130	0.059	2.199	0.028	Yes
H4	PAHR -> ER	0.114	0.056	2.038	0.042	Yes

OVERALL FIT OF THE MODEL

The table provides insights into the model fit based on the Standardized Root Mean Square Residual (SRMR). The consistent values for the Saturated Model and Estimated Model, with identical standardized beta coefficients (0.035), sample means (0.024), and narrow confidence intervals (95%: 0.028, 99%: 0.029), indicate a low SRMR value. This suggests a good model fit, as the residual differences between the observed and predicted correlations are minimal, supporting the model's reliability for analyzing variable relationships in the research.

Predictive relevance f^2

The table highlights the predictive relevance (f^2) of various factors on employee retention. Among the variables, Data-Driven Decision-Making Culture shows the highest impact with a moderate-to-high effect size ($f^2 = 0.148$), followed by HR Analytics Technology with a moderate effect ($f^2 = 0.108$). In contrast, HR Data Quality and Accuracy ($f^2 = 0.031$) and Predictive Analysis in HR ($f^2 = 0.021$) exhibit small effect sizes, indicating relatively limited influence. This suggests that fostering a data-driven culture and leveraging advanced HR technologies play significant roles in improving employee retention, while data quality and predictive analysis have comparatively smaller impacts.

Results and Discussion

The study Found that HR analytics significantly enhances employee retention, with Decision-Driven Data Management Capabilities (DDMC) having the strongest impact ($\beta = 0.391$), followed by HR Analytics Teachnology (HRAT) ($\beta = 0.306$). The measurement model confirmed strong validity and reliability, supporting the role of data-driven HR practices in reducing turnover. These results align with literature, showing that analytics-driven strategies improve retention by enabling better decision –making. However, the study's focus on IT workers and cross-sectional design limits generalizability . Future research should explore longitudinal and industry-specific applications. Practically, organizations should invest in HR analytics to boost engagement and retention through targeted interventions.

Limitations and Future Study

Among the many drawbacks of this study is its dependence on a particular population and sample size, which may limit the findings' applicability to other sectors and geographical areas. The study cross sectional design limits causation proof, and self reported data may introduce bias. It also overlook factors like economic condition that affecting retention. Further research can address these gaps through longitudinal studies, HR tech integration industry specific analysis and examining mediators like culture and leadership. Cross cultural comparisons and employee well being initiatives further enhance understanding.

Theoretical Implications

This research expanads existing framework on the job satisfaction and commitment by emphasizing HR practices vital role in employee retention. It strengthens link between HR strategies and reduced turnover while advancing theories on engagement through carrer development, worklife balance and performance management. It highlights HR deeper influence on workplace social and psychological dynamics beyond transactional functions.

Practical Implications

This research underscores the crucial role of HR practices in employee retention. By implementing strategies like career development, performance recognition and work life balance, organizations can reduce turnover. It highlights the need for a supportive culture, employee engagement to boost job satisfaction and loyalty and long term success.

Societal Implications

Research highlights the broader social impact of effective HR practices on employee retentions, extending beyond individual businesses to wider community. By promoting workforce stability, organizations contribute to economic security, reducing job insecurity and unemployment. Career growth and well beings fosters lifelong learning and skills development while HR role in diversity and inclusion helps creating more equitable workplaces.

CONCLUSION

This study highlights the vital role of HR practices in employee retention. Career development, performance management and work life balance enhance commitmen, loyalty and satisfaction while reducing turnover. The findings offer theoretical insights and practical guidance for HR professionals with broader societal benefits like social mobility, economic stability and workforce inclusivity.

REFERENCES

Alamelu, R., Nalini, R., Cresenta Shakila Motha, L., Amudha, R., & Bowiya, S. (2017). Adoption factors impacting Human Resource analytics among employees. *International Journal of Economic Research, 14*(6), 417–423. https://www.scopus.com/inward/record.uri?eid=2-s2.0-85035008544&partnerID=40&md5=84069c1000a020a3d6048d98c5887450

Arora, M., Ahmad, V., Arora, T., & Kumar, R. (2024). Digital Transformation and Talent Management. In *Green Metaverse for Greener Economies*. CRC Press., DOI: 10.1201/9781032638188-4

Arora, M., Prakash, A., Mittal, A., & Singh, S. (2021). HR Analytics and Artificial Intelligence-Transforming Human Resource Management. *2021 International Conference on Decision Aid Sciences and Application, DASA 2021*, 288 – 293. DOI: 10.1109/DASA53625.2021.9682325

Bandi, G. N. S., Rao, T. S., & Ali, S. S. (2021). Data Analytics Applications for Human Resource Management. *2021 International Conference on Computer Communication and Informatics, ICCCI 2021*. DOI: 10.1109/ICCCI50826.2021.9402300

Bathla, D., & Ahuja, R. (2023). Employee productivity augmentation using human capital analytics. In *Big Data: A Road-Map for Successful Digital Marketing*. Nova Science Publishers, Inc. https://www.scopus.com/inward/record.uri?eid=2-s2.0-85172707334&partnerID=40&md5=ef8dc08d2dce7c5ae2b8caaa32bada06

Bolbotinovic, Z. Z., Popovac, R. M., Vukmirovic, D. V, Comic, T. Z., & Stanojevic, N. D. (2024). HR Analytics: Opportunities and Challenges for Implementation in SME. *Lecture Notes in Networks and Systems, 999 LNNS*, 28 – 32. DOI: 10.1007/978-3-031-60840-7_4

Bongale, A. M., Dharrao, D., & Urolagin, S. (2023). Exploratory Data Analysis and Classification of Employee Retention based on Logistic Regression Model. *2023 9th International Conference on Advanced Computing and Communication Systems, ICACCS 2023*, 1929 – 1933. DOI: 10.1109/ICACCS57279.2023.10112681

Chanda, P., & Ghosh, S. (2024). Optimizing Workforce Efficiency Using an Artificial Intelligence Approach: A Next-Gen HR Management System. *2024 ASU International Conference in Emerging Technologies for Sustainability and Intelligent Systems, ICETSIS 2024*, 1416 – 1421. DOI: 10.1109/ICETSIS61505.2024.10459590

Chandana, C., Sarkar, A., Deshmukh, K., Kulkarni, P., Bikash Acharjee, P., & Lourens, M. (2024). Analysing Employee Management Using Machine Learning Techniques and Solutions in Human Resource Management. *4th International Conference on Innovative Practices in Technology and Management 2024, ICIPTM 2024*. DOI: 10.1109/ICIPTM59628.2024.10563736

Chaurasia, A., Kadam, S., Bhagat, K., Gauda, S., & Shingane, P. (2023). Employee Attrition Prediction using Artificial Neural Networks. *2023 4th International Conference for Emerging Technology, INCET 2023*. DOI: 10.1109/INCET57972.2023.10170676

Dwivedi, R. (2023). Understanding Employee Perspectives During an Acquisition – Case of Twitter. *29th Annual Americas Conference on Information Systems, AMCIS 2023*. https://www.scopus.com/inward/record.uri?eid=2-s2.0-85192924432&partnerID=40&md5=5dfab0f65f85a82575feb4ee34c7d5d0

Freeda, M. S. M., Khan, S., Ramalingam, P., & Amarnatha, R. P. (2024). Role of hr analytics in people management: Challenges and opportunities in the indian IT/ITeS space. In Analytics, H. R. (Ed.), *Fundamentals and Applications*. Bentham Science Publishers., DOI: 10.2174/9789815274196124010004

Gaur, B. (2020). HR4.0: An Analytics Framework to redefine Employee Engagement in the Fourth Industrial Revolution. *2020 11th International Conference on Computing, Communication and Networking Technologies, ICCCNT 2020*. DOI: 10.1109/ICCCNT49239.2020.9225456

Gomathi, S., Rajeswari, A., & Kadry, S. (2023). Emerging HR practices-digital upskilling: A strategic way of talent management and engagement. In *Disruptive Artificial Intelligence and Sustainable Human Resource Management: Impacts and Innovations - The Future of HR*. River Publishers. https://www.scopus.com/inward/record.uri?eid=2-s2.0-85168648645&partnerID=40&md5=4103cd7fc695335dda81f9949392d29e

Gujanal, P. U., & Hiremath, G. (2023). Performance management and artificial intelligence: A conceptual framework on future role. In R. K.V.S. & R. P.R.K. (Eds.), *AIP Conference Proceedings* (Vol. 2796, Issue 1). American Institute of Physics Inc. DOI: 10.1063/5.0149028

Jaiwant, S. V., & Vazirani, K. (2023). HR analytics in employee engagement and turnover. In *HR Analytics in an Era of Rapid Automation*. IGI Global., DOI: 10.4018/978-1-6684-8942-0.ch007

Jayadev, S., & Sumitha, R. (2024). Performance appraisal and organizational outcome via the mediating effect of relationship with peer group and subordinates-a tool for HR analytic. In *Business Analytics for Effective Decision Making*. Bentham Science Publishers., DOI: 10.2174/9789815238365124010008

Joseph, T., Christopher, M., Marvin, G., Mukwaba, D., Claire, A., & Murindanyi, S. (2024). Explainable Machine Learning and Graph Neural Network Approaches for Predicting Employee Attrition. In D. S. & S. V. (Eds.), *ACM International Conference Proceeding Series* (pp. 243 – 255). Association for Computing Machinery. DOI: 10.1145/3675888.3676058

Kamal, S., Naim, A., Magd, H., Khan, S. A., & Khan, F. M. (2022). The relationship between E-Service quality, ease of use, and E-CRM performance referred by brand image. In *Building a Brand Image Through Electronic Customer Relationship Management*. IGI Global., DOI: 10.4018/978-1-6684-5386-5.ch005

Karyamsetty, H. J., Khan, S. A., & Nayyar, A. (2023). Envisioning toward modernization of society 5.0—A prospective glimpse on status, opportunities, and challenges with XAI. In *XAI Based Intelligent Systems for Society 5.0*. Elsevier., DOI: 10.1016/B978-0-323-95315-3.00005-X

Khan, S. A., Magd, H., Khatri, B., Arora, S., & Sharma, N. (2023). Critical success factors of internet of things and digital marketing. In *Global Applications of the Internet of Things in Digital Marketing*. IGI Global., DOI: 10.4018/978-1-6684-8166-0.ch012

Khan, S. A., & Naim, A. (2023). XAI in Society 5.0 through the lens of marketing and HRM. In *XAI Based Intelligent Systems for Society 5.0*. Elsevier., DOI: 10.1016/B978-0-323-95315-3.00004-8

Khatri, B., Arora, S., & Khan, S. A. (2024). Analysis of servant leadership and organizational citizenship behaviour among social service sector employees. In *Organizational Behavior and Human Resource Management for Complex Work Environments*. IGI Global., DOI: 10.4018/979-8-3693-3466-9.ch021

Khatri, B., Nandini, G., & Khan, S. A. (2024). Transition from outcome-based learning to global accreditation of top universities of India: Elevating the bar of educational excellence. In *Evaluating Global Accreditation Standards for Higher Education*. IGI Global., DOI: 10.4018/979-8-3693-1698-6.ch019

Khatri, B., Singh, R. K., Arora, S., Khan, S. A., & Naim, A. (2024). Optimizing supply chain management indicators for sustainable supply chain integration and customer loyalty: Potential role of environmentally responsible practices. In *Strategies for Environmentally Responsible Supply Chain and Production Management*. IGI Global., DOI: 10.4018/979-8-3693-0669-7.ch008

Krishna, S., Dwivedi, R., & Murti, A. (2023). Predictive Analytics for Employee Attrition: A Comparative Study of Machine Learning Algorithms. In A. E., A. E., & F. S. (Eds.), *Proceedings - 2023 3rd International Conference on Digital Data Processing, DDP 2023* (pp. 180 – 187). Institute of Electrical and Electronics Engineers Inc. DOI: 10.1109/DDP60485.2023.00043

Krishna, S., & Sidharth, S. (2022). Analyzing Employee Attrition Using Machine Learning: the New AI Approach. *2022 IEEE 7th International Conference for Convergence in Technology, I2CT 2022*. DOI: 10.1109/I2CT54291.2022.9825342

Kumar, P. (2023). Investigating the cause and effect of employee engagement through the lens of HR analytics. In *HR Analytics in an Era of Rapid Automation*. IGI Global., DOI: 10.4018/978-1-6684-8942-0.ch013

Kumari, B. K., Sundari, V. M., Praseeda, C., Nagpal, P., John, E. P., & Awasthi, S. (2023). Analytics-Based Performance Influential Factors Prediction for Sustainable Growth of Organization, Employee Psychological Engagement, Work Satisfaction, Training and Development. *Journal for ReAttach Therapy and Developmental Diversities*, *6*(8), 76–82. https://www.scopus.com/inward/record.uri?eid=2-s2.0-85165974785&partnerID=40&md5=8c8cd00ff6add2681714206c6a265c5b

Ligori, T. A. A., Suresh, N., Khan, S. A., Rabgay, T., & Yezer, K. (2022). The mediating effect of university image on the relationship between curriculum and student satisfaction: An empirical study of the Royal University of Bhutan. *International Journal of Pluralism and Economics Education*, *13*(2), 192–208. DOI: 10.1504/IJPEE.2022.127218

Liu, L., Akkineni, S., Story, P., & Davis, C. (2020). Using HR analytics to support managerial decisions: A case study. *ACMSE 2020 - Proceedings of the 2020 ACM Southeast Conference*, 168 – 175. DOI: 10.1145/3374135.3385281

Madhumita, G., Dolly Diana, P., Neena, P. C., Narendra Kiran, P. B., Aggarwal, S., & Nargunde, A. S. (2024). AI-powered Performance Management: Driving Employee Success and Organizational Growth. In M. G.C., S. S., & D. S. (Eds.), *5th International Conference on Recent Trends in Computer Science and Technology, ICRTCST 2024 - Proceedings* (pp. 204 – 209). Institute of Electrical and Electronics Engineers Inc. DOI: 10.1109/ICRTCST61793.2024.10578371

Magd, H., Ansari, M. S. A., & Khan, S. A. (2023). Need for explainable artificial intelligence ethnic decision-making in society 5.0. In *XAI Based Intelligent Systems for Society 5.0*. Elsevier., DOI: 10.1016/B978-0-323-95315-3.00010-3

Magd, H., & Khan, S. A. (2022). Effectiveness of using Online Teaching Platforms as Communication Tools in Higher Education Institutions in Oman: Stakeholders' Perspectives. *Journal of Content. Community and Communication, 16*(8), 148–160. DOI: 10.31620/JCCC.12.22/13

Mangal, N. (2023). Using Analytics to Manage Employee Behavioural Traits and Predict Employee Performance. In *Analytics Enabled Decision Making*. Springer Nature., DOI: 10.1007/978-981-19-9658-0_9

Mansurali, A., Rajagopal, M., & Subbaiah, R. (2023). Employee attrition and absenteeism analysis using machine learning methods: Application in the manufacturing industry. In *HR Analytics in an Era of Rapid Automation*. IGI Global., DOI: 10.4018/978-1-6684-8942-0.ch011

Mitravinda, K. M., & Shetty, S. (2022). Employee Attrition: Prediction, Analysis of Contributory Factors and Recommendations for Employee Retention. *2022 IEEE International Conference for Women in Innovation, Technology and Entrepreneurship, ICWITE 2022 - Proceedings*. DOI: 10.1109/ICWITE57052.2022.10176235

Muhammad, G., & Naz, F. (2022). A moderating role of HR analytics between employee engagement, retention and organisational performance. *International Journal of Business Environment, 13*(4), 345–357. DOI: 10.1504/IJBE.2022.126370

Naim, A., Khan, S. A., Mohammed, A., & Malik, P. K. (2024). Applications of high performance computing and AI in green digital marketing. In *AI Applications for Business, Medical, and Agricultural Sustainability*. IGI Global., DOI: 10.4018/979-8-3693-5266-3.ch003

Paigude, S., Pangarkar, S. C., Hundekari, S., Mali, M., Wanjale, K., & Dongre, Y. (2023). Potential of Artificial Intelligence in Boosting Employee Retention in the Human Resource Industry. *International Journal on Recent and Innovation Trends in Computing and Communication, 11*(3s), 1–10. DOI: 10.17762/ijritcc.v11i3s.6149

Palshikar, G. K., Apte, M., Pawar, S., & Ramrakhiyani, N. (2017). HiSPEED: A system for mining performance appraisal data and text. *Proceedings - 2017 International Conference on Data Science and Advanced Analytics, DSAA 2017, 2018-Janua*, 477 – 486. DOI: 10.1109/DSAA.2017.45

Palshikar, G. K., Apte, M., Pawar, S., & Ramrakhiyani, N. (2019). HiSPEED: A system for mining performance appraisal data and text. *International Journal of Data Science and Analytics, 8*(1), 95–111. DOI: 10.1007/s41060-018-0142-x

Pandey, S., & Mehta, J. (2022). HRPA: Human Resource Prediction Analytics. *Proceedings of the 2022 3rd International Conference on Intelligent Computing, Instrumentation and Control Technologies: Computational Intelligence for Smart Systems, ICICICT 2022*, 721 – 726. DOI: 10.1109/ICICICT54557.2022.9917576

Polyakova, A., Kolmakov, V., & Pokamestov, I. (2020). Data-driven HR analytics in a quality management system. *Quality - Access to Success*, *21*(176), 74–80. https://www.scopus.com/inward/record.uri?eid=2-s2.0-85086146828&partnerID=40&md5=bc478ab18646a70fb0551dc7fbde011c

Sasirekha, V., Abinash, T., & Venkateswara, P. B. (2024). HR analytics and people management. In Analytics, H. R. (Ed.), *Fundamentals and Applications*. Bentham Science Publishers., DOI: 10.2174/97898152741961240100007

Saxena, C., Kumar, P., Sarvaiya, R., & Khatri, B. (2023). Attitude, Behavioral Intention and Adoption of AI Driven Chatbots in the Banking Sector. *2023 IEEE IAS Global Conference on Emerging Technologies, GlobConET 2023*. DOI: 10.1109/GlobConET56651.2023.10150155

Sharma, A., & Sharma, T. (2017). HR analytics and performance appraisal system: A conceptual framework for employee performance improvement. *Management Research Review*, *40*(6), 684–697. DOI: 10.1108/MRR-04-2016-0084

Sharma, N., Khatri, B., & Khan, S. A. (2024). Exploring the past and identifying the future research agenda for social media and tourist behavior: A bibliometric analysis. In *Social Media Strategies for Tourism Interactivity*. IGI Global., DOI: 10.4018/979-8-3693-0960-5.ch011

Sharma, R., & Dhingra, L. (2024). Advancing Human Resource Strategies with Deep Learning: Predictive Analytics for Improving Employee Retention Rates. *2024 2nd World Conference on Communication and Computing, WCONF 2024*. DOI: 10.1109/WCONF61366.2024.10692087

Singh, M., Srivastava, S. P., Srivastava, S., & Singhal, T. (2024). Unlocking Predictive Insights for Employee Retention and Engagement: Harnessing Machine Learning and Big Data Analytics in HR Practices. *Smart Innovation. Systems and Technologies*, *390*, 497–505. DOI: 10.1007/978-981-97-2716-2_44

Sousa, M. J. (2018). HR analytics models for effective decision-making. In de Waal B.M.E. & R. P. (Eds.), *Proceedings of the 14th European Conference on Management, Leadership and Governance, ECMLG 2018* (pp. 256 – 263). Academic Conferences and Publishing International Limited. https://www.scopus.com/inward/record.uri?eid=2-s2.0-85073779394&partnerID=40&md5=5d7f440d5d2caa4fce7152af7016e170

Supraveen, U. J., Ali, S. S., Babu, K. S., Rao, V. R., & Bandi, G. N. S. (2022). HR Analytics - The Measurement of HR Processes using a Methodical Approach. *2022 International Conference on Computer Communication and Informatics, ICCCI 2022*. DOI: 10.1109/ICCCI54379.2022.9740999

Suresh, N., Antony Alphonnse Ligori, T., Khan, S. A., & Thoudam, P. (2019). Predicting financial distress of Bhutan telecom limited. *International Journal of Innovative Technology and Exploring Engineering, 8*(8 SpecialIssue 3), 94 – 99. https://www.scopus.com/inward/record.uri?eid=2-s2.0-85070022376&partnerID=40&md5=df0e9d60b3abf123a9e72d40606132b5

Tyagi, D. M., & Pandita, D. (2022). Artificial Intelligence and People Analytics-A Key to Employee Engagement. *2022 International Conference on Sustainable Islamic Business and Finance, SIBF 2022*, 224 – 228. DOI: 10.1109/SIBF56821.2022.9940118

Yadav, U. S., Sood, K., Tripathi, R., Kumar, A., & Khan, S. A. (2024). Proficiency in the handicraft sector business in a volatile, uncertain, complex, and ambiguous environment. In *VUCA and Other Analytics in Business Resilience*. Emerald Group Publishing Ltd., DOI: 10.1108/978-1-83753-902-420241009

Chapter 4
AI-Driven Sentiment Analysis to Monitor Employee Well-Being

Ruhi Lal
Manav Rachna International Instititute of Research and Studies, India

Aarzoo
https://orcid.org/0009-0006-7604-2583
Manav Rachna International Institute of Research and Studies, India

ABSTRACT

This study examines how AI-powered sentiment analysis monitors employee well-being and shapes workplace culture. As digital communication expands, companies generate massive text and voice data. NLP-based sentiment analysis finds stress early and analyses emotions and performance. The study interviews HR professionals, AI engineers, and employees across industries using a qualitative cross-case approach. AI's ability to recognise emotional trends and how insights are used for support are examined. It also handles employee trust, acceptance, resistance, intrusiveness, data privacy, algorithmic bias, transparency, and permission. The report recommends ethical AI use that respects employee rights, fosters openness, trust, and compliance. HR leaders, AI engineers, and policymakers are advised on responsible AI integration in HR. The report promotes responsible AI discourse by promoting employee-centric initiatives that improve well-being and workplace digital transformation.

DOI: 10.4018/979-8-3373-2135-6.ch004

INTRODUCTION

Understanding and improving employee well-being has become a strategic focus for companies trying to create a healthy and efficient work culture in the modern office, where digital communication is key to daily activities (Ravichandran et al., 2023). Organisations create vast databases, capturing the emotional undercurrents of their workforce. The growing volume of emails, chat messages, video conversations, and performance reports is becoming increasingly significant. Artificial intelligence (AI)-driven sentiment analysis, a major application of natural language processing (NLP), offers a viable approach for deriving insights from these interactions (Davila-Gonzalez & Martin, 2024). Often, before these problems show up as lower productivity or attrition, this technology helps companies spot trends in stress, disengagement, or unhappiness. However, incorporating artificial intelligence into the monitoring of employee emotions presents significant issues related to privacy, consent, algorithmic bias, and the psychological effects of surveillance (Aulia & Lin, 2025). Although current studies on artificial intelligence applications in predictive analytics and recruiting have looked at how AI-based sentiment monitoring affects employee trust, mental health, and organisational policies, our knowledge of how they impact these areas remains lacking (Rao et al., 2025). This study fills this void by looking at how sentiment analysis tools driven by artificial intelligence are used in actual organisational settings, how precisely they interpret emotional trends, and how employees view this type of monitoring. The paper also takes into account the present ethical and legal issues surrounding the application of artificial intelligence in HR operations, especially those pertaining to permission, data protection, and openness (Adamopoulos et al., 2025). Key words influencing this research are "sentiment analysis" (the computational interpretation of emotional tone in text), "employee well-being" (the emotional, psychological, and social health of an employee), and "algorithmic ethics" (the moral principles guiding AI decision-making). According to the research, companies adopting AI technologies now deploy them regularly, and HR managers and employees can offer insightful analysis about their experience with the technology (Xiao, Yan, & Bamber, 2025). With an emphasis on qualitative data collected through in-depth interviews with HR professionals, AI engineers, and staff members across a range of sectors, this study is confined to companies already including AI-based sentiment tools. By use of a cross-case analysis technique, the study will evaluate how various companies apply sentiment analysis, interpret results, and act upon conclusions in a way that conforms with ethical standards (Lal & Sharma, 2021). This study aims to investigate the ethical consequences and employee acceptability of artificial intelligence to identify emotional signals in workplace communication. The theory is that when AI tools are applied with openness and ethical protections, they can improve employee well-being without compromising privacy or autonomy (Zhou et al., 2024). This study will address the current knowledge gap by offering an in-depth understanding of AI's impact on workplace sentiment monitoring, both from organisational and employee perspectives. The results are expected to provide practical advice to HR managers, legislators, and AI developers, thereby promoting responsible AI integration that respects human rights and improves organisational results (Chang & Ke, 2024).

Research Objectives

1. To evaluate whether sentiment analysis driven by artificial intelligence can accurately identify employee moods.
2. To investigate staff opinions and confidence about monitoring artificial intelligence.
3. To investigate ethical and privacy issues in artificial intelligence office monitoring.
4. To find optimal ethical methods for using artificial intelligence sentiment analysis.

Research Questions

RQ1. How precisely can sentiment analysis driven by artificial intelligence identify employee emotions?
RQ2. How much confidence and perspective do staff members have towards AI-based monitoring?
RQ3. What ethical and privacy concerns emerge from implementing AI in employee monitoring?
RQ4: What are the best practices for ethically using AI to analyse workplace sentiment?

Relevance of the Study

In today's digital workplace, as technology increasingly mediates employee communication, this study holds significant importance. Organisations using AI-driven sentiment analysis to track well-being face privacy, ethical use, and trust issues. By looking at how artificial intelligence tools affect employee emotions, engagement, and opinions of surveillance, this study fills in a major void. It also looks at the ethical conundrums and legal ramifications of these technologies. The study supports responsible AI deployment by providing useful insights and best practices; therefore, it guarantees that breakthroughs in workplace monitoring will improve employee welfare without compromising transparency, autonomy, or organisational trust.

Significance of the Study

This work's significance lies in its modern exploration of artificial intelligence-driven sentiment analysis as a tool for monitoring employee welfare. This paper emphasises the ethical, psychological, and legal aspects that have to be taken into account, even though companies want to use artificial intelligence for early stress and disengagement identification. Capturing many points of view—from HR experts to employees—helps one to better grasp how artificial intelligence shapes workplace dynamics, confidence, and morale. The results seek to direct companies in using ethical, open, and employee-centric AI solutions that not only improve well-being but also help to build a trusting and accountable workplace.

Rationale of the Study

The rationale for this study comes from the increasing dependence on artificial intelligence technology in human resource management, especially for digital communication-based employee attitude monitoring. AI-driven sentiment analysis provides real-time insights into employee sentiments as companies try to raise productivity and well-being. However, little research has been conducted on the ethical consequences, employee impressions, and practical difficulties of such monitoring. Examining how precisely AI detects emotional trends, how employees react to AI surveillance, and what ethical standards should guide its deployment helps this study close that gap, ensuring that technological development supports rather than compromises employee trust, autonomy, and psychological safety.

Scope & Utility of the Study

This study investigates how sentiment analysis driven by artificial intelligence monitors employee well-being in several industries, therefore stressing its effects on ethics, trust, and HR policies. Gathering opinions from HR experts, artificial intelligence developers, and staff members helps one to pinpoint important issues such as transparency, data protection, and algorithmic bias. The research supports informed consent, guides HR initiatives, and provides pragmatic value for building ethical AI frameworks in the workplace. Additionally, it offers a tool for researchers investigating AI's influence on human resource management and employee engagement while also assisting legislators in creating AI governance rules. The results especially apply to contemporary digital companies.

REVIEW OF LITERATURE

Sentiment analysis, led by AI, has evolved into a major breakthrough in organisational management, especially regarding employee well-being. Employees in today's digital offices use various communication tools—emails, instant messaging, digital surveys, and video conferences—all of which generate massive volumes of unstructured data (Rahman et al., 2024a). Natural Language Processing (NLP) and sentiment analysis techniques help to produce insightful analysis of employee emotions, stress levels, engagement, and indicators of discontent from this data. Real-time awareness of these emotional cues helps companies promote employee mental health, enhance workplace culture, and react quickly (Malik et al., 2023).

The increasing reliance of companies on digital technologies and automation helps define the larger background of this research. HR departments are increasingly using analytics-based solutions to maximise employee experience and decision-making as digital transformation accelerates across sectors (Rahman et al., 2024b). This background makes sentiment analysis an intriguing tool that might improve human resource functions, not only in performance assessment but also in spotting latent emotional tendencies that might otherwise go undetected. According to the present study scene, technology presents a new set of complexities and issues that have to be carefully addressed, even while it presents fresh chances to monitor and enhance well-being (Rahman et al., 2022). The application of AI-driven sentiment analysis in HR presents significant challenges primarily associated with ethical and technological issues. Technologically, one still worries about AI's capacity to precisely identify complex emotional states. Sentiment analysis technologies frequently find it difficult to decipher sarcasm, cultural idioms, or context-sensitive statements; human emotions are complicated (Vidhya, 2025). Such data can be misinterpreted to provide false conclusions and erroneous HR interventions. Algorithmic bias—AI models taught on biased datasets may repeat and perpetuate preconceptions, hence aggravating unfair assessments and treatment of personnel. The opacity of artificial intelligence decision-making exacerbates these problems and makes it challenging for staff members and even HR experts to know how particular decisions were reached or conclusions drawn (Jeong, Kim, & Lee, 2024). Ethical questions add still another level of difficulty. Sentiment analysis tools entering the workplace raise issues about surveillance, data protection, informed consent, and trust. Workers might find AI-based monitoring intrusive, which would cause worry and opposition. Moreover, their lack of openness in the analysis of their messages might undermine confidence in the company (Shah & Mishra, 2024). Therefore, even if artificial intelligence has well-developed technological capacity, its success depends on its ethical application—how fairly and transparently it is introduced and used. Notwithstanding these difficulties, the amount of current research in related fields, including marketing, customer service, and employee satisfaction polls, shows the potential of sentiment analysis in other spheres (Lal, 2023). Sentiment analysis has been applied to several fields to evaluate consumer satisfaction, predict behaviours, and assess product comments. Studies in HR have looked at how artificial intelligence might automate chores, including talent recruiting, performance forecasting, and resume screening. Still, there is a notable research vacuum in the particular implementation of AI-driven sentiment analysis for ongoing, real-time employee well-being monitoring (Taiminen, 2025). The few current studies that concentrate on artificial intelligence in HR usually take a quantitative, systems-based approach. They focus mostly on statistical models and algorithm development, therefore neglecting how employees view these instruments. Consequently, they sometimes exclude the human-centric element—the lived experience of those under observation—from the discussion (Shahzad et al., 2024). This control is crucial because the acceptance or rejection of artificial intelligence primarily depends on the perspectives of employees. Even the most sophisticated systems can fail to produce their expected results if the workforce does not believe or accept the instruments being employed. Some studies have started to highlight this flaw and demand a more all-encompassing, ethical method for integrating artificial intelligence (Khair et al., 2025). Policymakers and academics are pushing for models including ethical artificial intelligence. The importance of intelligence values, such as fairness, openness, responsibility, and human supervision, is increasing. Many of these models, nevertheless, still have a theoretical or regulatory character and lack an empirical foundation in actual corporate environments (Kumar & Lal, 2023). There is a lack of a grounded, multidisciplinary study that combines technological efficacy, staff opinions, organisational goals, and ethical standards (Rahman et al., 2025). By means of a qualitative, cross-case research approach, this study seeks to close these discrepancies. It aims to find out not only how AI systems analyse sentiment but also how it is seen and experienced by human stakeholders through interviews with HR professionals, artificial intelligence engineers, and staff members from diverse sectors (Vorobeva et al., 2024). Using this cross-case technique, the researchers can identify trends, conflicts, and best practices that span several organisational settings. It lets one examine how ethical, emotional, and technical aspects interact in actual workplaces (Baidya et al., 2024). This study's emphasis on the human experience—how workers respond to being watched by AI, how much faith they have in the system, and what elements affect their acceptance or resistance—makes it indispensable (Gadhiya, 2024). Focusing on the voices of those most affected by this technology helps the study paint a better picture of the organisational realities surrounding artificial intelligence applications. The study also underscores the ethical dilemma between privacy and productivity, demonstrating how businesses must navigate this delicate balance to ensure both regulatory compliance and employee support (Katyal et al., 2024). The research examined shows that sentiment analysis poses significant hazards even if it clearly has practical advantages, such as better engagement tracking, early identification of discontent, and more focused HR actions (Rahman et al., 2024). Technology can be abused to cause legal problems, mistrust, and damage to reputation. When sentiment analysis is used improperly, it could create perceptions of digital spying, which may erode employee morale and autonomy due to the use of technology. Conversely, when used sensibly and honestly, it could change workplace wellness programs and increase the proactive and responsive nature of organisational operations (Lal, 2024). The originality of this work is in its thorough and multidisciplinary approach. By combining ethical analysis, human perception, and AI competency assessment, it presents a comprehensive picture that much of the current literature lacks. To guarantee effective implementation, it also suggests a framework of best practices, including technological preparedness, ethical protections, and communication techniques (Aarzoo & Lal, 2025). Effective, trust-building AI tools that both serve organisational goals and safeguard employee well-being result from management's shift into a generally understudied but vitally significant field (Lal et al., 2025). It suggests that only with openness, ethical foresight, and a human-centered design can artificial intelligence-driven sentiment analysis be an efficient tool for measuring employee well-being. Through empirical findings, pragmatic advice, and a theoretical framework for ethical AI deployment, the paper seeks to close the present research gap (Aarzoo & Lal, 2024). Its results are meant to help HR managers, artificial intelligence engineers, and legislators create systems that strike a mix between efficiency and empathy, producing better, more resilient companies.

RESEARCH METHODOLOGY

This paper investigates the application and consequences of sentiment analysis driven by artificial intelligence in monitoring employee well-being using a qualitative, cross-case analysis technique. Based on the interpretivist paradigm, the study gives subjective experiences and individual perceptions top priority while recognising that each participant's contact with AI tools is influenced by their personal, organisational, and cultural settings. Investigating the complex emotional and ethical aspects that quantitative techniques could ignore is ideal for the qualitative approach. The study gathers a wide range of insights on how artificial intelligence technologies are utilised to assess workplace emotions and behaviour patterns by interacting with HR professionals, AI engineers, and employees from several businesses. A comparative investigation of several organisational environments, made possible by a cross-case study, reveals trends, variations, and best practices for ethical AI integration. The study especially looks at how workers view such surveillance, the degree of trust and openness they connect with these tools, and the ethical issues that develop, including privacy, consent, and algorithmic prejudice. By means of in-depth, semi-structured interviews and thematic analysis, the study seeks to offer a complete awareness of the operational, emotional, and ethical influence of artificial intelligence in HR environments. This approach guarantees extensive, context-driven data supporting significant findings and practical advice for prudent AI deployment.

Research Design

This study, which follows a qualitative exploratory research approach, is ideal for analysing complicated and changing social events, like the integration of artificial intelligence into HR operations. The architecture makes it possible to grasp in-depth how companies apply sentiment analysis driven by artificial intelligence to track employee welfare. Using a cross-case method, the study looks at several companies from many industries to find common trends, contextual variances, and particular difficulties. This method offers a more all-encompassing, comparative perspective on AI adoption in different corporate This study aims to identify best practices, organisational effects, and employee impressions related to the ethical and successful use of AI in HR environments.

Sampling and Participants

This study chooses participants directly engaged in or influenced by AI-driven sentiment analysis tools in the workplace through purposive sampling. The sample comprises HR experts who have used these tools, AI developers in charge of their development and upkeep, and staff members from several departments susceptible to such monitoring. From 3 to 5 companies in several sectors, including technology, finance, education, and healthcare, a total of 15–20 participants will be sought. This varied representation enhances the depth and relevance of results within the purview of qualitative research and facilitates a comparative cross-case analysis.

Data Collection Methods

Semi-structured interviews allow data for this study to be gathered by means of in-depth, open-ended responses that preserve consistency among participants. Complementing the research goals, an interview guide investigates issues like understanding of artificial intelligence-driven sentiment analysis, perceived benefits and hazards, trust and openness, ethical issues, and recommendations for development. Every interview lasts 45 to 60 minutes and is either in person or via a safe video conference. All interviews are audio recorded and verbatim transcribed under participant permission to guarantee correctness and dependability for later use.

Data Analysis

Following Braun and Clarke's six-step approach, the study uses thematic analysis to evaluate and spot trends within the interview data. This method starts with familiarising oneself by reading transcripts again, and then it generates the initial code. These codes are then arranged into possible themes that are examined, polished, and precisely defined. Before generating the final report, the researcher studies each topic to capture its basic significance. This methodology guarantees a disciplined but adaptable way to find profound understanding from participant viewpoints and experiences.

Ethical Considerations

This research follows rigorous ethical standards, considering the sensitive aspect of workplace monitoring and data privacy. Every participant gives informed permission, and throughout the research process, they are guaranteed anonymity and confidentiality. All information is kept safely and used just for scholarly needs. Furthermore, ethical clearance comes from the research ethics committee of the institution before data collection, therefore guaranteeing that the study follows accepted ethical norms.

Validity and Reliability

The study uses several techniques to improve credibility and trustworthiness, therefore guaranteeing validity and reliability. Gathering data from many participant groups—including HR experts, artificial intelligence developers, and staff members—allows a well-rounded viewpoint and triangulation. Key findings are validated by member checking, which lets participants review and confirm interpretations. Research decisions and data management practices are recorded in an audit trail, therefore guaranteeing replicability and openness. Peer debriefing also helps to get important comments on new interpretations, therefore enhancing the impartiality and rigour of the research.

DATA ANALYSIS & INTERPRETATION

This study used thematic analysis, a robust qualitative data analytics technique established by Braun and Clarke (2006), to discern patterns, insights, and significant themes from the comprehensive interviews. Data was gathered from 28 participants across six businesses using AI-driven sentiment analysis technologies. The group comprised 10 HR managers, 6 AI engineers, and 12 employees from various sectors like banking, IT, consulting, and e-commerce. The analysis was performed in several phases:

Table 1. thematic analysis

S.no.	Steps Involved	Process
1.	Familiarisation	Reading and re-reading transcripts to immerse in the data.
2.	Initial Coding	Generating descriptive and analytical codes.
3.	Theme Development	Aggregating codes into categories and broader themes.
4.	Refinement	Reviewing and defining the scope and essence of each theme.
5.	Interpretation	Relating themes to research questions and conceptual frameworks.

Familiarisation is engaging in the reading and re-reading of transcripts to thoroughly immerse oneself in the data. Preliminary coding helps in creating descriptive and analytical codes, whereas theme development helps in consolidating codes into categories and overarching themes. The researchers refine by evaluating and delineating the extent and core of each theme. The researchers refine their work by evaluating and delineating the extent and core of each theme, as well as conducting an analysis that connects these themes to research enquiries and theoretical frameworks. Inter-coder agreement (Cohen's Kappa = 0.82) demonstrated substantial consistency.

Table 2. Summary of Emerging Themes and Corresponding Codes (Thematic Analysis)

S.no.	Theme	Description	Linked Research Question	Frequency
1.	Artificial intelligence sentiment accuracy	AI's perceived accuracy in identifying stress and mood via text or voice.	RQ1	14
2.	Trust and Acceptance of AI Monitoring	Employee acceptance, confidence, or resistance.	RQ2	17
3.	Ethical & Privacy Concerns	Data privacy, algorithmic bias, and absent informed permission	RQ3	21

continued on following page

Table 2. Continued

S.no.	Theme	Description	Linked Research Question	Frequency
4.	HR-Driven Interventions Using AI	Application of artificial intelligence insights in methods of employee engagement	RQ1, RQ4	11
5.	Governance and Transparency Mechanisms	Demand moral standards and legal protections.	RQ3, RQ4	9

Source: Author's Own Compilation

From the interview data, the thematic study turned out five major topics. With 14 references connected to RQ1, AI Sentiment Accuracy focuses on how well it recognises employee sentiments. With 17 mentions, trust and acceptance of AI monitoring revealed Various employee attitudes, such as confidence, opposition, or acceptance of AI-based surveillance (RQ2), were observed. Reflecting worries about data usage, algorithmic bias, and lack of consent (RQ3), ethical and privacy concerns were the most often mentioned theme, with 21 mentions. HR-Driven Interventions The study examined the strategic application of AI insights to raise employee engagement (RQ1, RQ4) and emphasised the importance of ethical protections, regulatory compliance, and governance and transparency mechanisms, which were highlighted in RQ3 and RQ4. These topics support the study's fit with its main research questions.

Table 3. Ethical Risk Assessment Matrix – AI Monitoring in the Workplace

S.no.	Ethical Issue	Identified Risk Level (Low/Med/High)	Frequency of Concern (Interviews)	Mitigation Strategy Proposed
1.	Authorised Consent	High	19	Policies requiring mandatory digital opt-in.
2.	Algorithmic Preference	Medium	11	Bias-auditing artificial intelligence data
3.	Information Abuse	High	16	GDPR-aligned access records and encrypted storage
4.	Insufficiency of Transparency	High	18	Explainability frameworks for artificial intelligence
5.	Constant observation	Medium	12	Specify limits for monitoring in contracts.

Source: Author's Own Compilation

The Ethical Risk Assessment Matrix emphasises important issues related to workplace surveillance powered by artificial intelligence. High-risk concerns like informed consent, data misuse, and lack of transparency were found to be routinely mentioned in interviews (19, 16, and 18 mentions, respectively); hence, they underline the requirement of explicit policies including opt-in consent, encrypted data processing, and explainability frameworks. The researcher rated the suggested solutions, such as regular bias audits and contractual audits. The study identifies limitations on monitoring, algorithmic bias, and constant surveillance as factors that pose a medium risk. This table supports the ethical depth of the research by connecting participant concerns with practical mitigating solutions consistent with changing AI governance and compliance criteria.

Table 4. Cross-Case Summary – Trust vs. Intrusiveness Perception Matrix

S.no.	Sector	Employee Perception of AI Monitoring	Trust Level (High/ Med/Low)	Intrusiveness Perception (High/Med/Low)
1.	IT	Productivity – increasing	High	Low
2.	Finance	Highly surveillance-oriented	Medium	High
3.	Consulting	Dependent on openness	Medium	Medium
4.	E-commerce	Morally pure	High	Medium
5.	Education	Not Comfortable	Low	High
6.	Healthcare	Requirement of limits	Medium	Medium

Source: Author's Own Compilation

The table offers a cross-case overview of employee opinions about sentiment monitoring driven by artificial intelligence across six industries. With high confidence and low to medium intrusiveness, artificial intelligence monitoring is considered in the IT and e-commerce sectors as either neutral or productivity-enhancing. By contrast, workers in education and finance see it as uncomfortable or surveillance-heavy, which reflects low trust and excessive intrusiveness. The consulting and healthcare industries have moderate perceptions regarding trust and intrusiveness, both of which are rated as medium. The matrix emphasises the ethical conflict between apparent advantages and concerns, thereby highlighting the need for sector-specific HR policies and governance structures to balance trust and privacy in the application of artificial intelligence.

FINDINGS OF THE STUDY

Particularly with regard to its effects on employee well-being, the results of this study offer a thorough understanding of how sentiment analysis driven by artificial intelligence is seen and applied in various organisational environments. By means of in-depth interviews with HR professionals, artificial intelligence developers, and employees from sectors including IT, finance, education, e-commerce, consulting, and healthcare, the study reveals five main themes: accuracy of AI sentiment detection, trust and acceptance, ethical and privacy issues, HR-driven interventions, and governance systems. Particularly in big companies with remote or hybrid teams, participants noted how artificial intelligence could improve employee engagement and emotional awareness. However, particularly in sectors such as finance and education, concerns about data privacy, a lack of transparency, and insufficient informed consent received significant attention. Different people trusted artificial intelligence depending on how ethically data was handled and how transparently the tool was unveiled. The study also showed that any view of constant surveillance greatly reduces trust, even if AI tools are embraced when in line with employee values and clear limitations. These results capture the growing demand for sector-specific artificial intelligence monitoring systems and ethical government policies.

Table 5. Key Findings and Uniqueness of the Study

S.no.	Key Findings	Uniqueness of the Study
1.	Despite the ongoing ethical questions, the reliability of AI-driven sentiment analysis is only marginal.	The study employs cross-case qualitative data to integrate ethical, operational, and emotional analysis.
2.	Sector-wise, perceived intrusiveness differs greatly.	The comparative sector-wise perception matrix has been hardly investigated in studies related to artificial intelligence and human resources.
3.	The top ethical concerns are informed consent and data abuse.	The study suggests thorough and practical mitigating plans that are consistent with GDPR and AI governance guidelines.
4.	Workers want openness and control over AI monitoring systems.	The study includes pragmatic HR policy consequences and governance recommendations that are specifically tailored to AI implementation.
5.	Transparency helps HR-driven interventions to be more welcomed.	This study demonstrates the connection between the effectiveness of employee engagement and the explainability of artificial intelligence.
6.	Triangulation of viewpoints exposes differences in AI tool intent from that of impact.	This is the first research in this area (or limited domain) that qualitatively triangulates HR, tech, and user-level viewpoints.
7.	Cross-case thematic saturation confirms five fundamental ethical-operational themes.	It verifies consistency in organisational settings and validates the strengths of qualitative approaches.

Source: Author's Own Compilation

The table presents seven main conclusions from the research, therefore exposing complex insights on AI-driven sentiment analysis in the business. Although people have modest faith in artificial intelligence capabilities, ethical issues, including informed consent, data abuse, and openness, remain crucial. Views particular to each sector exhibit different degrees of intrusion; IT staff members are more receptive than those in banking or education. Offering a well-rounded qualitative perspective, the study especially triangulates views from HR professionals, artificial intelligence developers, and employees. It stresses the connection between openness and employee acceptance and offers doable HR governance techniques. The theme saturation and inter-coder dependability further confirm the methodological rigour of the study.

CONCLUSION

This study investigated how sentiment analysis driven by artificial intelligence might be used as a tool for employee well-being monitoring in many sectors. Using a qualitative, cross-case approach based on the interpretivist paradigm, the study presented rich new perspectives on the operational, ethical, and emotional aspects of artificial intelligence integration in human resource processes. Important results showed that although artificial intelligence provides useful skills in spotting emotional patterns, its apparent accuracy and value differ depending on the industry and job. While employees usually connected it with surveillance and loss of privacy, HR professionals considered it a strategic tool to improve engagement and prevent burnout. Trust became clear as a key determinant, mostly shaped by the degree of ethical protections, informed consent, and openness in place. Particularly in the spheres of education and healthcare, ethical issues—especially those related to algorithmic bias, continual monitoring, and lack of clarity—were often and profoundly ingrained. The paper emphasises the need to build governance systems including digital opt-in rules, explainable artificial intelligence techniques, bias audits, and unambiguous contractual limitations. AI tools have to be used with a human-centric strategy that upholds personal agency, encourages communication, and fits business principles. In essence, the effectiveness of AI-driven sentiment analysis in improving employee well-being rests not just on its technical capacities but also on how ethically, openly, and contextually it is applied. Beyond adoption, companies should concentrate on responsible integration that preserves justice, privacy, and trust and go beyond just efficiency. This study offers actionable insights for legislators, developers, and HR executives hoping for sustainable and ethical AI deployment in the workplace, therefore augmenting the small but growing corpus of qualitative research on artificial intelligence in HR. Future studies could explore the long-term consequences, how employees adapt over time, and the influence of legal frameworks on defining AI's role in workplace well-being.

LIMITATIONS OF THE STUDY

Some should recognise the various limitations of this study. With only 28 participants and taken from six particular sectors, the sample size was somewhat limited and may restrict the generalisability of the results to more general sectors. The study's focus on qualitative, self-reported data may introduce response bias due to organisational influence or social desirability. The lack of longitudinal information on how employee opinions on artificial intelligence sentiment analysis may also change reflects perspectives caught at one moment in time. Furthermore, the studies mostly focused on tech-savvy, metropolitan companies, excluding knowledge from rural or less digital businesses. Furthermore, influencing the long-term usefulness of the outcomes could be rapid changes in artificial intelligence technology and regulatory environments. Moreover, the lack of quantitative data reduces statistical validation possibilities, and the elimination of comparable performance measures limits more thorough investigation. Notwithstanding these constraints, the work provides insightful exploratory analysis of ethical, emotional, and pragmatic consequences of artificial intelligence in employee well-being surveillance.

PRACTICAL IMPLICATIONS

The study presents important pragmatic consequences for companies, including sentiment analysis driven by artificial intelligence in employee well-being policies. First, HR departments have to guarantee open communication regarding the operation of AI tools, the data gathered, and the intended use of it. Using ethical artificial intelligence models and informed consent procedures helps staff members build confidence. Regular audits should help companies find algorithmic bias and support data protection by means of safe storage and access limitations. The results underline the need to strike a balance between respect for employee autonomy and monitoring, therefore suggesting precise limits for artificial intelligence surveillance. Successful and moral implementation also depends on cross-functional cooperation across ethics, IT, and HR teams. These methods can improve long-term organisational well-being, employee confidence, and satisfaction.

FUTURE SCOPE OF THE STUDY

This study paves the way for broader applications by facilitating the exploration of AI-driven sentiment analysis in various organisational settings beyond the sectors under examination. Future studies will be able to quantitatively assess how employee productivity and well-being change with AI monitoring. Deeper knowledge will come from looking at long-term consequences and staff behaviour changes across time. Furthermore, investigating cross-cultural variations in acceptance and ethical questions about AI monitoring can help improve knowledge. Advances in artificial intelligence explainability and bias reduction also demand concentrated research to improve ethical application. At last, it would be intriguing to investigate combining artificial intelligence sentiment analysis with other HR technologies to create complete solutions for employee well-being management.

REFERENCES

Aarzoo & Lal. R. (2025). Enhancing Advertising Effectiveness Through AIDA, AI, and Data Visualization Integration for Business Strategies. In M. Muniasamy, A. Naim, & A. Kumar (Eds.), *Data Visualization Tools for Business Applications* (pp. 85-102). IGI Global. DOI: 10.4018/979-8-3693-6537-3.ch005

Aarzoo, & Lal, R. (2024). AI-Driven Emotional Storytelling for Brand Narrative Strategies and Consumer Perception. IUP Journal of Brand Management, 21(4), 30–50.

Adamopoulos, I., Valamontes, A., Tsirkas, P., & Dounias, G. (2025). Predicting Workplace Hazard, Stress and Burnout Among Public Health Inspectors: An AI-Driven Analysis in the Context of Climate Change. *European Journal of Investigation in Health, Psychology and Education*, *15*(5), 65. DOI: 10.3390/ejihpe15050065 PMID: 40422294

Aulia, S. R., & Lin, W. S. (2025). Embracing the digital shift: Leveraging AI to foster employee well-being and engagement in remote workplace settings in the Asia Pacific region. *Asia Pacific Management Review*, *30*(3), 100339. DOI: 10.1016/j.apmrv.2024.12.003

Baidya, R., Lal, R., & Rena, R. (2024). Digital Competency Assessment and Data-Driven Performance Management for Start-Ups. In Data-Driven Modelling and Predictive Analytics in Business and Finance (pp. 203-234). Auerbach Publications. DOI: 10.1201/9781032618845-13

Chang, Y. L., & Ke, J. (2024). Socially responsible artificial intelligence empowered people analytics: A novel framework towards sustainability. *Human Resource Development Review*, *23*(1), 88–120. DOI: 10.1177/15344843231200930

Davila-Gonzalez, S., & Martin, S. (2024). Human digital twin in industry 5.0: A holistic approach to worker safety and well-being through advanced AI and emotional analytics. *Sensors (Basel)*, *24*(2), 655. DOI: 10.3390/s24020655 PMID: 38276347

Gadhiya, Y. (2024). AI-Based Automation for Employee Screening and Drug Testing. International IT Journal of Research, ISSN: 3007-6706, 2(4), 185-199.

Jeong, J., Kim, B. J., & Lee, J. (2024). Navigating AI transitions: How coaching leadership buffers against job stress and protects employee physical health. *Frontiers in Public Health*, *12*, 1343932. DOI: 10.3389/fpubh.2024.1343932 PMID: 38601504

Katyal, S., Lal, R., & Rena, R. (2024). Effects of Gamification on Brand Engagement of Toy Brands: First Cry and Hamleys. In *Marketing and Gamification* (pp. 57–80). Routledge. DOI: 10.4324/9781032694238-6

Khair, M., Khair, M., Shaheen, N., & Bindewari, D. (2025). From Automation to Autonomy: Leveraging Oracle HCM Cloud's AI Capabilities to Create Autonomous HR Processes and Decision-Making. *International Journal of Research in Humanities and Social Sciences, 13*(3), 271–288. DOI: 10.63345/ijrhs.net.v13.i3.15

Kumar, D., & Lal, R. (2023). Technological Advancements in the Media Industry and the Current Job Market in India. In Naim, A. (Ed.), *Accreditation Processes and Frameworks in Higher Education* (pp. 289–314). Nova Science Publishers.

Lal, P. (2024). Quality Culture in Advertising Agencies and Creativity for Campaign Effectiveness: Analysis of Six Sigma Practices.

Lal, R. (2023). New Measures of Teaching Learning and Evaluating with Changing Technology. In Naim, A. (Ed.), *Accreditation Processes and Frameworks in Higher Education* (pp. 267–287). Nova Science Publishers.

Lal, R., Deb, N., & Gogoi, D. M. (2025). Assessing the Role of Digital Data Visualization Tools in the Advertising Industry for Informed Business Decision-Making. In Data Visualization Tools for Business Applications (pp. 189-208). IGI Global.

Lal, R., & Sharma, G. (2021). Social media influencers for online purchase behaviour: Mediation by brand consciousness. *Journal of Content. Community & Communication, 13*(7), 83–94.

Malik, A., Budhwar, P., & Mohan, H., & NR, S. (. (2023). Employee experience–the missing link for engaging employees: Insights from an MNE's AI-based HR ecosystem. *Human Resource Management, 62*(1), 97–115. DOI: 10.1002/hrm.22133

Rahman, Z. T., Lal, R., & Ratna, R. (2022). An Analytical Study on the Significance of Folk and Fairytales on the Psychology of Young Children. *International Journal of Early Childhood Special Education, 14*(5).

Rahman, Z. T., Lal, R., & Rena, R. (2024). Innovative and Futuristic Approach to the Agricultural Sector in China. In *Innovation and Development of Agricultural Systems: Cases from Brazil, Russia, India, China and South Africa (BRICS)* (pp. 257–285). Springer Nature Singapore. DOI: 10.1007/978-981-97-2926-5_12

Rahman, Z. T., Lal, R., & Rena, R. (2024). Challenges of Communication with Gen-Z in the Era of Artificial Intelligence-Interceded Digital Economy. In *AI-Oriented Competency Framework for Talent Management in the Digital Economy* (pp. 76–94). CRC Press. DOI: 10.1201/9781003440901-5

Rahman, Z. T., Lal, R., & Rena, R. (2024). Challenges of Communication with Gen-Z in the Era of Artificial Intelligence-Interceded Digital Economy. In *AI-Oriented Competency Framework for Talent Management in the Digital Economy* (pp. 76–94). CRC Press. DOI: 10.1201/9781003440901-5

Rahman, Z. T., Lal, R., & Rena, R. (2025). Industry, Innovation, and Infrastructure: Contribution of SMEs in the Developing Economies. In Entrepreneurship in the BRICS (pp. 218-248). Routledge.

Rao, T. V. N., Patel, G. S., Bhavana, S., & Swetha, C. (2025). AI-Driven Decision Support System for Workplace Wellbeing. In Insights on Wellbeing and Happiness in the Workplace (pp. 1-18). IGI Global Scientific Publishing.

Ravichandran, N., Inaganti, A. C., & Muppalaneni, R. (2023). AI-Driven Sentiment Analysis for Employee Engagement and Retention. *Journal of Computing Innovations and Applications*, *1*(01), 1–9.

Shah, I. A., & Mishra, S. (2024). Artificial intelligence in advancing occupational health and safety: An encapsulation of developments. *Journal of Occupational Health*, *66*(1), uiad017. DOI: 10.1093/joccuh/uiad017 PMID: 38334203

Shahzad, M. F., Xu, S., Lim, W. M., Yang, X., & Khan, Q. R. (2024). Artificial intelligence and social media on academic performance and mental well-being: Student perceptions of positive impact in the age of smart learning. *Heliyon*, *10*(8), e29523. DOI: 10.1016/j.heliyon.2024.e29523 PMID: 38665566

Taiminen, H. (2025). Organisational listening as a means to create more citizen-centric well-being public policies. *International Journal of Strategic Communication*, *19*(1), 105–117. DOI: 10.1080/1553118X.2024.2395406

Vidhya, K. (2025). Harnessing AI and Digital Transformation for Strategic HRM Enhancing International Competitiveness. In Innovative Approaches for International Competitiveness Through Human Resource Management (pp. 35-70). IGI Global Scientific Publishing. DOI: 10.4018/979-8-3373-1005-3.ch002

Vorobeva, D., Costa Pinto, D., António, N., & Mattila, A. S. (2024). The augmentation effect of artificial intelligence: Can AI framing shape customer acceptance of AI-based services? *Current Issues in Tourism*, *27*(10), 1551–1571. DOI: 10.1080/13683500.2023.2214353

Xiao, Q., Yan, J., & Bamber, G. J. (2025). How does AI-enabled HR analytics influence employee resilience: Job crafting as a mediator and HRM system strength as a moderator. *Personnel Review*, *54*(3), 824–843. DOI: 10.1108/PR-03-2023-0198

Zhou, S., Yi, N., Rasiah, R., Zhao, H., & Mo, Z. (2024). An empirical study on the dark side of service employees' AI awareness: Behavioral responses, emotional mechanisms, and mitigating factors. *Journal of Retailing and Consumer Services*, *79*, 103869. DOI: 10.1016/j.jretconser.2024.103869

Chapter 5
Mapping the Evolution of HR Analytics Through a Bibliometric Review of Trends and Emerging Themes

Isha Jaryal
https://orcid.org/0009-0007-4853-7172
University School of Business, Chandigarh University, India

Bhanupriya Khatri
https://orcid.org/0000-0002-4130-6271
University School of Business, Chandigarh University, India

Gagandeep Kaur Gulati
University School of Business, Chandigarh University, India

ABSTRACT

The goal of this study is to identify important trends, significant contributions, and developing topics in the quickly developing field of HR analytics by performing a thorough bibliometric analysis of research published between 2020 and 2025. The 307 pertinent documents in the dataset were selected through a methodical search technique that included keywords like "HR Analytics," "Human Resource Management," "Predictive Analytics," "People Analytics," and "Human Resource Analytics." To guarantee relevance and accessibility, publications were limited to English-language papers and sorted by subject areas: business management,

DOI: 10.4018/979-8-3373-2135-6.ch005

computer science, and social science. The results show a notable increase in HR Analytics research during this time, which is indicative of its increasing significance in promoting strategic HR practices and data-driven decision-making.

INTRODUCTION

In today's fast-paced and data-driven world, HR analytics has become a crucial tool for organizations to enhance work and performance. By using AI and big data, businesses can predict workforce trends, enhance employee productivity, and improve employee retention. Despite its benefits, there are challenges also, such as data privacy issues and algorithmic bias. HRM is essential for managing human resources effectively. HR analytics is a powerful tool to collect and analyze the HR related data that helps organizations make data-driven decisions. By using technology and statistical analysis, HR analytics enhances the HR process.

The research analyzes the key scientific studies on HR analytics, tracking its evolution and impact using Bibliometric analysis. It highlights major topics such as trends and performance indicators in HR analytics, demonstrating how they are transforming traditional HR practices. By leveraging technology, HR analytics enhances strategies and improves organization performance (Bonilla-Chaves & Palos-Sánchez, 2023).

HR Automation, which replaces manual HR tasks with electronic and computer–controlled systems to improve efficiency. Traditionally, HR processes like hiring, training, and compliance have been manual, but automation is rapidly transforming them. Transforming Organizations can save time and cost and the utilization of resources and allow HR to focus on strategy and decision-making (Mishra et al.,2021; Khatri et al., 2023).

Talent Management uses people analytics to identify the leadership's gaps and develop high potential employees for Industry 4.0. HR focuses on training and development, communication, and leadership growth by using digital tools. Trends from the USA and UAE guide strategic HRM during the transition towards industry 4.0. It highlights how organizations use e-HRM systems to train and retain talent for improving the performance of the organization (Darville & Arghode,2024; Khan et al., 2023).

In today's competitive business environment, Human Resources Analytics (HRA) is essential for organizations and for their performance. Data was collected from 678 HR managers in India by using the Technology-organizational-individual-environment (TOIE) model to analyze factors that influence HRA adoption and how HR positively impacts the performance of the organizational and talent management.

It provides valuable insights for leaders and practitioners looking to leverage HR analytics for a strategic advantage (Vadithe & Kesari,2024 ; Khan & Rena, 2023).

The study examines the effectiveness of AI-powered recruitment tools for hiring people with disabilities in the UAE. It analyzed the feedback from 415 disabled applicants through sentiment analysis, HR analytics, and emotion detection, but only a few disabled candidates were hired. It highlights the need for bias audits, inclusive AI design, and human oversight to improve fairness in AI-driven hiring (Iftikhar et al.,2025; Khatri et al., 2022). The integration of people analytics in HR management enables data-driven decision-making, leading to enhanced strategic performance. By reviewing the 90 articles through the PRISMA framework, it highlights four benefits: links between the HR and business performance, Better HR alignment, Integration with strategic planning, and increased credibility through scientific rigor (Suri & Lakhanpal, 2024 ; Khatri et al., 2022). The effectiveness of Green HRM in promoting circular economy performance is strengthened through the integration of green innovation and big data analytics. Data was collected from 438 SME surveys, It highlights how businesses can benefit from Green practices, sustainability, and recycling strategies to gain a competitive edge and also provides insights for policymakers to enhance environmental strategies (Chau et al., 2024; Magd et al., 2023).

HR metrics and workforce analytics in improving organizational efficiency. Comprehensive analysis of role in talent acquisition, employee retention, and performance management by using the data to identify patterns, predict trends to support strategic decisions, and address the challenges like data privacy and skills gaps in implementation. It highlights how Green HRM improves circular economy performance with green innovation and big data analytics playing important roles using tools that can drive significant improvements in the HR process effectively (Durai et al., 2024). The research explores the current state of people analytics from an HRD standpoint, using bibliometrics and topic modelling to identify key trends. It highlights the convergence of research in areas like data-driven decision-making, workforce planning and ethical implications of analytics in HR (Yoon et al., 2024; Khatri et al., 2024). The Digital transformation of HRM driven by AI automation, big data and cloud computing by highlights the benefits of these and challenges. To succeed organizations must align digital strategy with business goals and objective, collaboration with IT teams. Embracing in digital technology is key of effective HR in modern era (Milhem et al., 2025).

REVIEW OF LITERATURE

Prescriptive analytics, machine learning, and mathematical programming are used to optimize the employee recruitment and discuss the techniques for evaluating recruitment. It also integrates machine learning predictions to improve hiring outcomes. It shows high accuracy in identifying transcription factors' binding sites and suggests variable-order Bayesian networks(VOBN) for better flexibility (Fitha et al., 2024; Magd et al., 2023). The rise of big data and predictive analytics in human resources management (HRM) focusing on how organizations are adopting data-driven strategies to improve HR process. It highlights the challenges, biases, and gaps in using strategies. It provides insights to HR professionals to leverage predictive analytics in workforce management (Al-Alawi et al., 2025). To address challenges in HR allocation, the Modified Single Candidate Optimizer (MSCO) algorithm is employed to enhance decision-making and resource optimization. By integrating the big data analytics and system analysis, the framework offers a data-driven approach to optimize HR configuration and improve productivity. It highlights that the MSCO model enhances HR utilization rates and labour productivity and provides solutions for HR allocation in the dynamic business environment(Zhang et al., 2025). The role of HR practices including career development, employee perception, and compensation in public sector companies. SOBEL and regression tests are used to analyze these and highlight the effective HR polices that help to enhance employee attitudes and organizational growth (Bindhu et al., 2024).

Today, the rise in online job applications has made it challenging for HR to identify the best suitable candidate. To address this, a pre–interview Reviewer web was developed for IT companies. It helps to analyze the CV on the basis of job requirements. It helps HR to recruit and select people in an effective and efficient manner (Shaman et al., 2022). The IT sector faces many challenges in hiring suitable employees for an organization. To bridge the gap, an Expert System for recruiting IT specialists (ESRIT) was developed. It helps to analyze the resume. This system helps to improve the recruitment process and select the best suitable candidate (Truic & Barnoschi, 2014; Khatri et al., 2024). Using a people analytics approach to predict employee attrition, focusing on the data quality rather than quantity. Employing the exploratory and quantitative methods develops an attrition prediction model by identifying the key features of employee turnover. Using the deep, machine, and ensemble learning models that are tested on large and medium-sized datasets with 450 responses and achieved high accuracy (0.96, 0.98, 0.99) on different datasets. It also found that Business travel that are less commonly considered for motivating employee retention (Yahia et al., 2021). The role of HR analytics in the aviation industry focusing on its potential to improve HR decision-making and performance. It highlights the importance of employees in aviation and identifies the models and indicators that exist. It suggests that HR analytics guide HR polices and decision-making for future research directions (Brito & Sousa, 2023; Khan et al., 2023). The Impact of AI on Human resource management (HRM) that highlights the benefits in recruitment, talent management, and performance evaluation through data-driven insights. It also raises ethical concerns and data privacy. Organizations must balance AI potential with ethical considerations to create a fair and productive workplace. For this, collaboration among employers, HR professionals, and researchers is essential to ensure AI enhances HRM (Madancian & Taherdoost, 2024).The role of data analytics in HRM, providing practical guidance on using data to improve HR policies and performance. It explains how HR analytics applies to workforce planning, recruitment, and training by using Workday and Tableau tools. It covers essential skills like data management, data cleaning, data collection, and building predictive models that help bridge the gap between traditional HR skills and data-driven decision making (Diez et al., 2019).

The research investigates the prediction of employee learning activity, considering both personal characteristics and the usage patterns of online learning tools, based on data from more than 40,000 employees at a multinational technology company. It highlights the job level and tool use to predict learning behaviors between the managers and nonprofessionals. It provides insights for HR and technology designers on leveraging employee data to enhance workplace learning strategies (Hicks, 2018; Sharma et al., 2024).

The increasing integration of technology in Human Resources Analytics is instrumental in assessing HR contributions and aligning them with business strategies, based on the data collected from 10 IT companies in India. It finds that organizations are increasingly investing in data-driven decision-making. Predictive analytics is seen as a valuable tool for evaluating business strategies (Kakkar & Kaushik, 2019). The paper examines the growing concerns about privacy and data security in HR analytics. It evaluates how governments and businesses are addressing these issues and whether their responses are adequate and also provides a roadmap for protecting employee data and ensuring privacy while using HR analytics (Jha, 2022).

The effectiveness of HR analytics in improving business performance highlights challenges like data access and weak IT infrastructure. A larger multinational company shows how a driven competency model enhances talent search. It highlights that integrating internal and external data with better IT systems can significantly improve the HR process (Caron & Batistic, 2019; Khatri et al., 2022). HR analytics improves talent acquisition by enhancing candidate sourcing, screening, and selection. This paper examines techniques like predictive analytics, data mining, and talent market analysis to give organizations a competitive edge. It emphasizes how HR analytics helps organizations make better hiring decisions and attract top talent (Samal et al., 2024).

The study uses data from 155 Irish organizations to demonstrate that HR technology enables HR analytics, which supports evidence-based management (EBM) and leads to improved organizational performance. It highlights the role of HR technology in driving analytics and the positive impact of EBM on the organization (McCartney & Fu, 2021).The use of HR analytics in healthcare across four municipalities in Norway. Data was collected from qualitative interviews of 14 individuals working in the HR department, which show that HR analytics are rarely used in workforce planning due to a disconnect between service and HR. Changes are underway to enhance HR's role and improve data-driven in healthcare management (Anthun et al., 2024; Khatri et al., 2024). As organizations strive to enhance their workforce efficiency, HR analytics has emerged as a key driver of success. This analysis investigates the current state and benefits of HR analytics in improving individual and organizational effectiveness. It highlights the benefits of predictive HR analytics, such as talent management and decision-making. Challenges in Russian companies include data accuracy issues, IT infrastructure, lack of analytics skills, and ethical issues. It provides recommendations to overcome these barriers and enhances the adoption of HR analytics (Konovalova et al., 2021).

Through workforce analytics, organizations can enhance employee performance by making informed decisions based on data-driven insights. It highlights how workforce analytics improves productivity and aids decision-making. The adoption of AI is still growing, with increasing competition in workforce analytics becoming essential for businesses to maximize human resources and future growth (Singh & Malhotra, 2020).

HR analytics is used by organizations to enhance decision-making in areas like recruitment, compensation, and retention. By using the quantitative approach and surveys, it finds that HR professionals show similar views on HR analytics. Predictive models are seen as essential for the future organizations and highlight their importance in HR strategy (Sousa, 2018; Sharma et al., 2023).

RESEARCH GAP

While HR Analytics is widely studied, research mainly focuses on theory, decision-making, and performance. However, empirical studies on practical challenges, Ai integration, employee engagement, sector-specific applications, and ethical concerns remain limited. Addressing these gaps will enhance its real-world impact and future advancements.

RESEARCH OBJECTIVE

- To analyze the publication trends and growth of HR Analytics research between 2020 and 2025 using bibliometric methods.
- To identify the most influential authors, journals, countries, and institutions contributing to HR analytics research.
- To evaluate the role of HR Analytics in improving strategic decision-making, talent management, and organizational performance.
- To highlight research gaps and suggest future directions, especially in areas like ethics, employee trust, sector-specific applications, and AI integration.

RESEARCH METHODOLOGY

Search Criteria

The literature was methodically reduced to 307 pertinent documents by the search parameters for the HR Analytics bibliometric study. Using the term "HR Analytics," the results were filtered to highlight recent research by concentrating on publications during 2020–2025 (694 papers), starting with 911 documents. The count was further narrowed to 536 by subject areas (business management, computer science, and social science) and then to 532 by restricting to English-language publications. Lastly, the addition of other terms such as "Predictive Analytics," "Human Resource Management," "People Analytics," and "Human Resource Analytics" guaranteed a more focused dataset. The final selection offers a solid foundation for the bibliometric study of HR Analytics trends and advancements since it represents current and multidisciplinary research.

RESEARCH METHODOLOGY

In order to methodically investigate the development, patterns, and significance of HR Analytics research from 2020 to 2025, this study uses bibliometric analysis. Bibliometric techniques aid in the measurement of research outputs, the identification of significant publications, authors, and institutions, as well as the analysis of thematic advancements in the area.

RESEARCH QUESTIONS

1. How has the amount of HR analytics research changed from 2020 to 2025?
2. Which HR Analytics publications receive the most citations, and what impact have they had on the field?
3. Which nations and organizations have made the largest contributions to the field of HR Analytics research?
4. Based on the influence of citations, which authors are the most influential in HR Analytics research?
5. How is research on HR analytics being influenced by emerging technologies like artificial intelligence, machine learning, and predictive analytics?

The term "HR Analytics" was used in the first search, which produced 911 documents. The figure dropped to 694 when publications from 2020 to 2025 were excluded, indicating current research tendencies. 536 documents were produced after further focusing on pertinent fields, including business management, computer science, and social science, guaranteeing domain-specific relevance. The count dropped to 532 when the language was limited to English. Ultimately, the dataset was greatly reduced to 307 papers by honing the search using several related terms ("HR Analytics," "Human Resource Management," "Predictive Analytics," "People Analytics," and "Human Resource Analytics"). Although HR analytics is a large field of study, this progressive filtering procedure shows that there are relatively few but more focused studies that use predictive and people analytics in HR contexts.

Table 1. Search Criteria

Steps	Command	No. of Documents
Step 1	Keywords used: ("HR Analytics")	911
Step 2	Limit to: Year 2020-2025	694
Step 3	Limit to Document type- Business Management, Computer Science, Social Science	536
Step 4	Language-English	532
Step 5	Limit 2: Keywords: "HR Analytics", "Human Resource Management", "Predictive Analytics", "People Analytics" "Human Resource Analytics"	307

FILTER

```
TITLE-ABS-KEY (hr AND analytics) AND PUBYEAR > 2019 AND PUB-
YEAR < 2026 AND (LIMIT-TO (SUBJAREA, "BUSI") OR LIMIT-TO (SUB-
JAREA, "COMP") OR LIMIT-TO (SUBJAREA, "SOCI")) AND (LIMIT-TO
(LANGUAGE, "English")) AND (LIMIT-TO (EXACTKEYWORD, "HR Analyt-
ics") OR LIMIT-TO (EXACTKEYWORD, "Human Resource Management")
OR LIMIT-TO (EXACTKEYWORD, "Predictive Analytics") OR LIMIT-TO
(EXACTKEYWORD, "People Analytics") OR LIMIT-TO (EXACTKEYWORD,
"Human Resource Analytics"))
```

The number of research articles published on HR analytics between 2020 and 2025 is depicted in the bar chart. Publications gradually increased from 31 in 2020 to 41 in 2021, then slightly decreased to 35 in 2022, according to the trend. Nonetheless, there is a notable increase in research interest in 2023 (78 papers) and 2024 (112 papers), suggesting that HR analytics is becoming more and more important throughout these years. Incomplete data for 2025 is probably the cause of the steep drop to 10 papers. According to this pattern, HR analytics has received a lot of scholarly attention lately, especially in 2023 and 2024, which indicates that its significance in business and management study is becoming more widely acknowledged.

Figure 1. Number of Research Papers Published

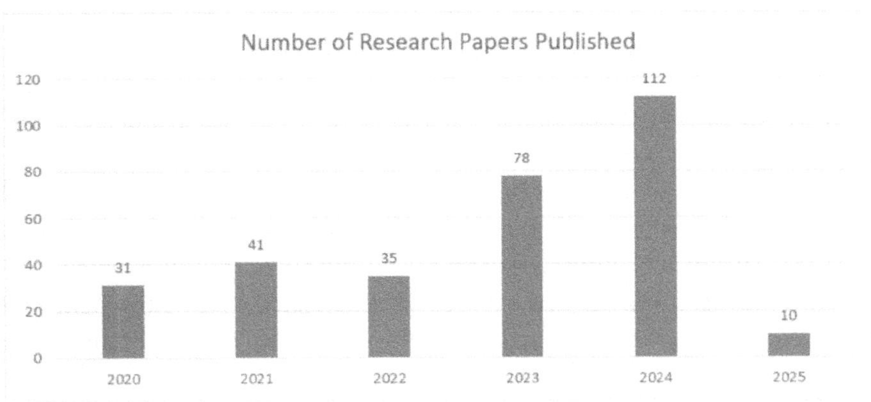

Source: Scopus (3 Jan 2025)

Their impact on HR analytics research is demonstrated by the examination of leading publications. With 269 citations, Personnel Review has the most, demonstrating its significant influence. The Human Resource Management Journal and the Journal of Organizational Effectiveness follow with 185 and 127 citations, respectively, highlighting their importance in strategic HR research. Significant contributions to the topic are also made by Management Decision (109 citations) and the International Journal of Human Resource Management (113 citations). Sources with no citations yet, such as Human Resource Management International Digest and HR Analytics: Fundamentals and Applications, on the other hand, suggest a little or recent impact. While newer journals are still gaining traction, established journals continue to play a crucial role in influencing HR analytics research.

Table 2. Top Journals based on Citations

S.N.	Source	Total publication	Total Citations
1	Lecture Notes in Networks and Systems	15	9
2	Personnel Review	12	269
3	Human Resource Management Journal	9	185
4	HR Analytics: Fundamentals and Applications	7	0
5	Journal of Organizational Effectiveness	7	127
6	Human Resource Management International Digest	6	0
7	International Journal of Human Resource Management	6	113
8	International Journal of Organizational Analysis	5	39
9	Management Decision	5	109
10	Studies in Systems, Decision and Control	5	1

With 141 publications and 734 citations, India leads the field in HR analytics research, according to the bibliometric analysis. This indicates that the country produces a lot of research but has a moderate influence on citations per document. With 32 papers and 645 citations, the US has the most influence per study, followed by the UK, which has 13 papers with 375 citations. While Australia, Israel, and China have moderate engagement and effect, European nations such as the Netherlands, Spain, and Ireland show high citation impacts despite having fewer contributions. A varied worldwide involvement in the topic is demonstrated by the consistent contributions of France, Germany, and Italy, albeit with relatively lower citation counts.

Table 3. Top Journals based on Countries

S.N.	Country	Total Documents	Total Citations
1	India	141	734
2	United States	32	645
3	United Kingdom	13	375
4	Netherlands	7	272
5	Spain	6	220
6	Ireland	6	212
7	Australia	12	183
8	Israel	5	180
9	China	11	155
10	France	7	148
11	Germany	12	144
12	Italy	11	98

Figure 2. Country- Wise Documents

Important contributions to HR analytics research are highlighted by the examination of the most referenced papers. With 246 citations, Newman (2020) has the most, demonstrating its significant impact and fundamental significance in the area. The significance of contemporary research in influencing the conversation is further illustrated by other important works like Pessach (2020) (149 citations), Hamilton (2020) (135 citations), and Fernandez (2021) (115 citations). While Dahlbom (2020), Mccartney (2021), and Garcia-Arroyo (2021) highlight the diversity of influential research across various themes within HR analytics, contributions by Tursunbayeva (2022) (85 citations), Kim (2021) (83 citations), and Shet (2021) (78 citations) demonstrate growing interest in contemporary topics.

Table 4. Top Authors with maximum Citations

S.N.	Document	Citations
1	Newman (2020)	246
2	Pessach (2020)	149
3	Hamilton (2020)	135
4	Fernandez (2021)	115
5	Tursunbayeva (2022)	85
6	Kim (2021)	83
7	Shet (2021)	78
8	Dahlbom (2020)	75
9	Mccartney (2021)	71
10	Garcia-Arroyo (2021)	67

The co-citation network highlights important theme areas and significant sources, illuminating the intellectual framework of HR analytics research. More established areas in HR analytics study, such as strategic HRM and the incorporation of analytics into organizational decision-making, are indicated by larger clusters, such as those focused on journals like Human Resource Management and The International Journal of Human Resource Management. Strong co-citation linkages are reflected in the densely connected nodes, indicating a significant degree of overlap in the study topics, frameworks, and methodologies used by these sources. Smaller clusters and peripheral nodes stand for specialized fields or new developments in HR analytics, including the technological use of analytics tools or studies with a particular industrial focus.

The presence of varied clusters indicates the interdisciplinary character of HR analytics research, while the prominence of important publications highlights their crucial role in forming the discipline. Finding foundational works, comprehending thematic evolution, and discovering new fields within the field are all made easier with the help of this representation.

Figure 3. Co-Citation Analysis

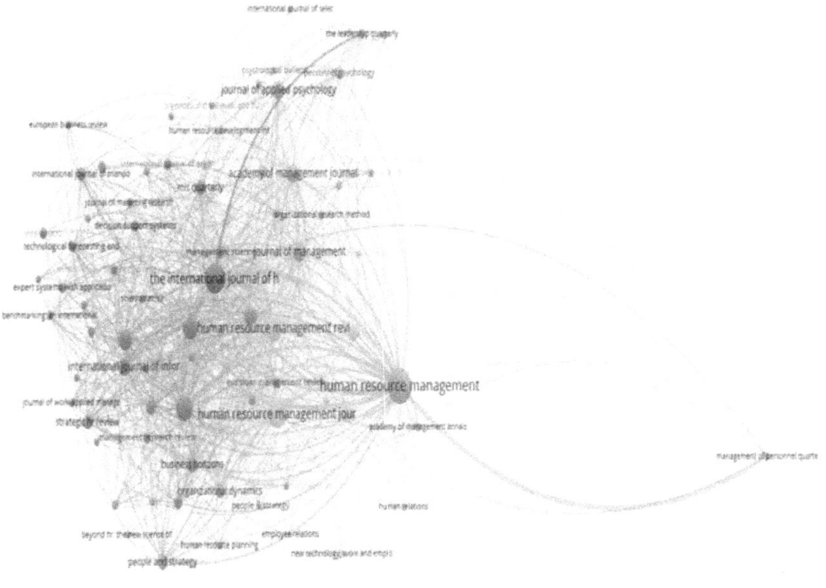

The integration of technology and data-driven techniques in HR practices is reflected in the bibliometric keyword analysis, which places HR Analytics at the forefront and has strong connections to themes like big data, artificial intelligence, predictive analytics, and human resource management. Clusters highlight distinct trends: Workforce and people analytics place a strong emphasis on using data to improve organizational performance, while machine learning and employee engagement highlight how cutting-edge technology can help address issues like performance and attrition. There are chances for more research into the moral and practical ramifications of implementing analytics in HR, as shown by emerging issues such as technology adoption, data-driven decision-making, and ethics. A multidisciplinary approach is highlighted by this integrated landscape, which synchronizes HR strategy with organizational objectives and technological innovation.

Figure 4. Keyword Analytics

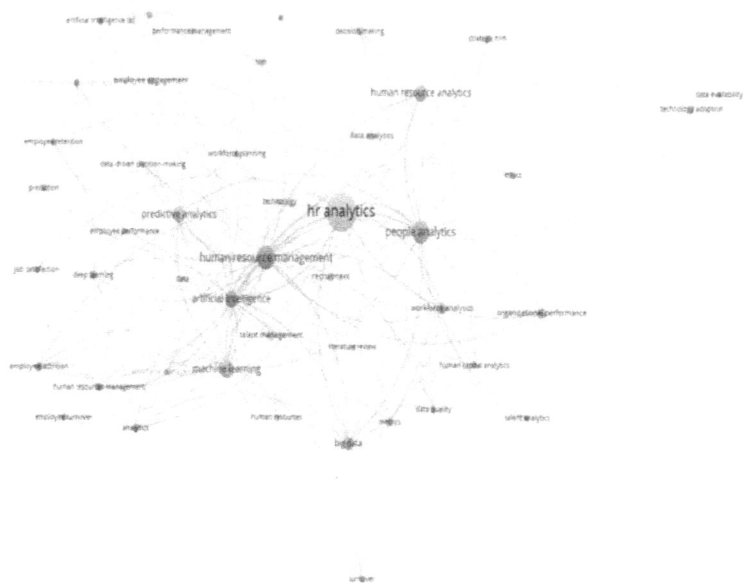

THEORETICAL IMPLICATIONS

The results of this bibliometric study have important theoretical ramifications for the development of HR analytics. First, by combining ideas from business management, computer science, and social science, the study highlights the multidisciplinary nature of HR analytics and broadens its theoretical base. The necessity for updated frameworks that connect conventional HR theories with data-driven approaches is highlighted by the incorporation of artificial intelligence, machine learning, and predictive analytics into HR operations.

Second, the analysis identifies new themes like organizational performance, workforce planning, and employee engagement, indicating that HR analytics is a transformative approach rather than merely a tool that needs new theoretical frameworks to explain how it affects organizational strategy and decision-making. This necessitates the creation of theories that tackle the dynamic interaction between human resource outcomes and data analytics capabilities.

Lastly, the study lays the groundwork for expanding current theories to address these important concerns by identifying research gaps, especially in understudied areas like employee trust, data privacy, and the ethical implications of HR analytics. As a result, this analysis advances our knowledge of the theoretical foundations of HR Analytics and guides future studies to enhance its scholarly discourse.

PRACTICAL IMPLICATIONS

The results of this bibliometric analysis carry several practical implications for HR professionals, organizations, and policymakers seeking to leverage HR Analytics for strategic decision-making. First, the study highlights the increasing integration of predictive analytics, artificial intelligence, and machine learning in HR functions, emphasizing the need for organizations to invest in advanced analytics tools and technologies. This calls for building the technical capabilities of HR teams and fostering collaboration between HR professionals and data scientists to fully realize the potential of HR Analytics.

Second, the identification of important topics like organizational performance, employee engagement, and workforce planning implies that HR analytics can greatly enhance decision-making in these domains. These insights can be used by practitioners to create data-driven interventions that maximize productivity, retention, and talent acquisition while coordinating HR strategies with overarching business goals.

In order to ensure that the workforce stays competitive in the quickly evolving technology landscape, governments and industry leaders may utilize the findings to create training programs and certifications that improve HR Analytics abilities. This report offers useful advice for utilizing HR Analytics to provide long-term value for businesses by bridging the gap between theoretical understanding and real-world applications.

LIMITATIONS AND FUTURE SCOPE

A number of shortcomings in this bibliometric analysis provide opportunities for further investigation. Its emphasis on works published between 2020 and 2025 may limit the historical perspective and leave out foundational studies. It is possible that important contributions from other languages and disciplines, like psychology or economics, were missed due to the restriction to English-language publications and particular topic areas, such as business management, computer science, and social science. Additionally, the bibliometric technique does not capture qualitative insights, such as case studies or practical applications, and reliance on particular keywords may have precluded studies using other terminologies.

Future studies could overcome these constraints by extending the time period, incorporating articles in languages other than English and covering a wider range of topics, and using sophisticated technologies like text mining to do in-depth analysis. Research on understudied topics like ethics, employee trust, and diversity, as well as comparative studies across industries and geographical areas, may yield deeper insights. Further bridging the gap between theory and practice through the integration of bibliometric and qualitative methodologies, including case studies or interviews, could spur innovation and practical HR analytics initiatives.

RESULTS AND DISCUSSION

This bibliometric study reviewed 307 research papers on HR Analytics from 2020 to 2025, revealing a significant growth in interest, especially during 2023-2024. India contributed the highest number of publications, while the U.S. and U.K. had the most impactful citations. Key research areas included AI integration, predictive analytics, talent management, and ethical concerns like data privacy and algorithmic bias. Influential journals such as Personnel Review and HR Management Journal were leading sources. Authors like Newman (2020) and Pessach (2020) were highly cited. Co-citation and keyword analysis showed HR analytics as an interdisciplinary field linking business, tech, and social science. The results emphasize the rising role of HR Analytics in strategic decision-making, employee engagement, and workforce planning. However, gaps remain in practical application, inclusivity, and ethics, indicating scope for future research.

CONCLUSION

A thorough bibliometric analysis of HR Analytics research from 2020 to 2025 is presented in this report, which offers insightful information on the field's development, trends, and new issues. By methodically reducing the dataset to 307 pertinent papers, the analysis demonstrates how HR Analytics is an interdisciplinary field that combines strategic human resource management with developments in machine learning, artificial intelligence, and predictive analytics. The results indicate a notable increase in research interest, highlighting the growing dependence on data-driven decision-making to improve organizational performance and manage workforce issues. Additionally, the report serves as a resource for scholars, practitioners, and policymakers by identifying key research issues, renowned journals, and notable authors. It emphasizes how crucial it is to handle data privacy, ethical issues, and trust in HR analytics in order to guarantee its responsible and long-term use.

REFERENCES

Al-Alawi, A. I., Al Bin Ali, F. A., Al Rashidi, M. A., & Albuainain, M. S. (2025). Mapping the Adoption of Big Data and Predictive Analytics in Strategic Human Resource Management. *Studies in Systems. Decision and Control*, *546*, 537–548. DOI: 10.1007/978-3-031-65207-3_46

Anthun, K. S., Anthun, K. S., Håland, E., & Lillefjell, M. (2024). What influences the use of HR analytics in Human Resource management in Norwegian municipal health care services? *BMC Health Services Research*, *24*(1), 1131. Advance online publication. DOI: 10.1186/s12913-024-11610-y PMID: 39334277

Ben Yahia, N., Hlel, J., & Colomo-Palacios, R. (2021). From Big Data to Deep Data to Support People Analytics for Employee Attrition Prediction. *IEEE Access : Practical Innovations, Open Solutions*, *9*, 60447–60458. DOI: 10.1109/ACCESS.2021.3074559

Bindhu, D., Namreen Asif, V. A., Baikadi, S. B., Chethanraj, Sunil, N., Chandravathi, & Dlima, N. G. (2024). Employee Perception of HR Practices and Its Impact on Job Satisfaction. *Lecture Notes in Networks and Systems, 1083 LNNS*, 154 – 165. DOI: 10.1007/978-3-031-67431-0_15

Bonilla-Chaves, E. F., & Palos-Sánchez, P. R. (2023). Exploring the Evolution of Human Resource Analytics: A Bibliometric Study. *Behavioral Sciences (Basel, Switzerland)*, *13*(3), 244. Advance online publication. DOI: 10.3390/bs13030244 PMID: 36975268

Caron, E., & Batistic, S. (2019). Knowledge hubs in competence analytics: With a case study in recruitment and selection. In van Sinderen M., M. L., & M. L. (Eds.), *ICSOFT 2019 - Proceedings of the 14th International Conference on Software Technologies* (pp. 585 – 594). SciTePress. DOI: 10.5220/0008117805850594

Chau, K. Y., Huang, T., Moslehpour, M., Khan, W., Nisar, Q. A., & Haris, M. (2024). Opening a new horizon in green HRM practices with big data analytics and its analogy to circular economy performance: An empirical evidence. *Environment, Development and Sustainability*, *26*(5), 12133–12162. DOI: 10.1007/s10668-023-03725-9

Darville, J. J., & Arghode, V. (2024). People analytics, talent management, and leadership development in the USA and UAE. In *Industry 4.0 and People Analytics: A Technical Perspective of HRM*. Apple Academic Press. https://www.scopus.com/inward/record.uri?eid=2-s2.0-85198202400&partnerID=40&md5=b5b2a05acb4185661e0383a89ed0d57a

De Brito, A. P., & Sousa, M. J. (2023). HR Analytics in the Commercial Aviation Sector: A Literature Review. In R. M. (Ed.), *Proceedings of the European Conference on Management, Leadership and Governance* (Vols. 2023-Novem, pp. 512 – 519). Academic Conferences and Publishing International Limited. https://www.scopus.com/inward/record.uri?eid=2-s2.0-85180554950&partnerID=40&md5=5b70b60711390c6570ea4148742a62e6

Diez, F., Bussin, M., & Lee, V. (2019). Fundamentals of HR analytics: A manual on becoming HR analytical. In *Fundamentals of HR Analytics: A Manual on Becoming HR Analytical*. Emerald Group Publishing Ltd., DOI: 10.1108/978-1-78973-961-920191015

Durai, S., Krishnaveni, R., Manoharan, G., & Ashtikar, S. P. (2024). Leveraging HR metrics and workforce analytics: The road to organizational efficacy. In *Practical Approaches to Agile Project Management*. IGI Global., DOI: 10.4018/979-8-3693-3318-1.ch019

Fitha, T. F., Parveen, K. J., Noorfathima, P. P., & Bajeel, P. N. (2024). Optimizing Employee Recruitment: a Prescriptive Analytics Review. In S. A.K., S. M., & P. C.M.A. (Eds.), *AIP Conference Proceedings* (Vol. 3242, Issue 1). American Institute of Physics. DOI: 10.1063/5.0234830

Hicks, C. (2018). Predicting knowledge workers' participation in voluntary learning with employee characteristics and online learning tools. *Journal of Workplace Learning*, *30*(2), 78–88. DOI: 10.1108/JWL-04-2017-0030

Iftikhar, A., Mohammad, S. I., Alqudah, M. N., Al-Adwan, A. S., Vasudevan, A., Ali, I., & Farhan, M. (2025). Evaluating Inclusivity and Fairness of AI Recruitment Tools for Hiring People with Disabilities in the United Arab Emirates(UAE); [Evaluación de la Inclusividad y la Equidad de las Herramientas de Reclutamiento de IA para la Contratación de Personas con D. *Data and Metadata*, *4*. Advance online publication. DOI: 10.56294/dm2025487

Jha, S. (2022). Data Privacy and Security Issues in HR Analytics: Challenges and the Road Ahead. *Lecture Notes in Networks and Systems*, *209*, 199–206. DOI: 10.1007/978-981-16-2126-0_17

Kakkar, H., & Kaushik, S. (2019). Technology driven human resource measurement–A strategic perspective. *International Journal on Emerging Technologies*, *10*(1), 179–184. https://www.scopus.com/inward/record.uri?eid=2-s2.0-85074656787&partnerID=40&md5=9dd377f1f5367c7e3c6a6f35cbb67cad

Khan, S. A., Magd, H., Khatri, B., Arora, S., & Sharma, N. (2023). Critical success factors of internet of things and digital marketing. In *Global Applications of the Internet of Things in Digital Marketing*. IGI Global., DOI: 10.4018/978-1-6684-8166-0.ch012

Khan, S. A., & Rena, R. (2023). Emerging green practices, internet of things, and digital marketing: A response to the global economic and climate crises. In *Global Applications of the Internet of Things in Digital Marketing*. IGI Global., DOI: 10.4018/978-1-6684-8166-0.ch001

Khatri, B., Arora, S., & Goyal, A. (2022). Association between Outcomes of Physical activities and Sports on Work-Life Balance of Employees. *International Journal of Human Movement and Sports Sciences*, *10*(2), 316–323. DOI: 10.13189/saj.2022.100223

Khatri, B., Arora, S., Magd, H., & Khan, S. A. K. (2022). Bibliometric analysis of social entrepreneurship. In *International Perspectives on Value Creation and Sustainability Through Social Entrepreneurship*. IGI Global., DOI: 10.4018/978-1-6684-4666-9.ch003

Khatri, B., Nandini, G., & Khan, S. A. (2024). Transition from outcome-based learning to global accreditation of top universities of India: Elevating the bar of educational excellence. In *Evaluating Global Accreditation Standards for Higher Education*. IGI Global., DOI: 10.4018/979-8-3693-1698-6.ch019

Khatri, B., Sharma, N., Khan, S. A., & Nandini, G. (2024). Navigating employer branding in the digital age: Exploring the impact of social media networking during the COVID-19 Pandemic. In *Global Practices on Effective Talent Acquisition and Retention*. IGI Global., DOI: 10.4018/979-8-3693-1938-3.ch017

Khatri, B., Shrimali, H., Khan, S. A., & Naim, A. (2023). Role of HR analytics in ensuring psychological wellbeing and job security: Learnings from COVID-19. In *HR Analytics in an Era of Rapid Automation*. IGI Global., DOI: 10.4018/978-1-6684-8942-0.ch003

Khatri, B., Singh, R. K., Arora, S., Khan, S. A., & Naim, A. (2024). Optimizing supply chain management indicators for sustainable supply chain integration and customer loyalty: Potential role of environmentally responsible practices. In *Strategies for Environmentally Responsible Supply Chain and Production Management*. IGI Global., DOI: 10.4018/979-8-3693-0669-7.ch008

Konovalova, V. G., Aghgashyan, R. V., & Galazova, S. S. (2021). Perspectives and Restraining Factors of HR Analytics in the Conditions of Digitization of Human Resources Management. *Studies in Systems. Decision and Control, 314*, 1015–1024. DOI: 10.1007/978-3-030-56433-9_106

Madancian, M., & Taherdoost, H. (2024). The Impact of Artificial Intelligence on Human Resource Management: Opportunities and Challenges. *Lecture Notes in Networks and Systems, 928 LNNS*, 406 – 424. DOI: 10.1007/978-3-031-54671-6_30

Magd, H., Khan, S. A., Khatri, B., Sharma, N., & Arora, S. (2023). Understanding the relationship between IoT and digital marketing: A bibliometric analysis. In *Global Applications of the Internet of Things in Digital Marketing*. IGI Global., DOI: 10.4018/978-1-6684-8166-0.ch007

McCartney, S., & Fu, N. (2021). Bridging the gap: Why, how and when HR analytics can impact organizational performance. *Management Decision*, *60*(13), 25–47. DOI: 10.1108/MD-12-2020-1581

Milhem, M., Ateeq, A., Al Astal, A., & Almeer, S. (2025). Digital Transformation in HRM: Navigating the Future of Human Resource Management. *Studies in Systems. Decision and Control*, *566*, 23–33. DOI: 10.1007/978-3-031-71318-7_3

Mishra, S. S., Kunte, M., Neelam, N., Bhattacharya, S., & Mulay, P. (2021). HR Process Automation: A Bibliometric Analysis. *Library Philosophy and Practice, 2021*. https://www.scopus.com/inward/record.uri?eid=2-s2.0-85108566438&partnerID=40&md5=bc3590224e6b63885788377fe49f4fa5

Samal, A., Sharma, P., Naveen, S., Chethan Kumar, K., Kotehal, P. U., & Thirulogasundaram, V. P. (2024). Exploring the Role of HR Analytics in Enhancing Talent Acquisition Strategies. *South Eastern European Journal of Public Health*, *23*(3), 612–618. DOI: 10.70135/seejph.vi.1357

Shaman, M. A. M., Samarasinghe, S. M., Tharinda, D., Gamage, D. C., & Gamage, A. (2022). Pre-Interview Reviewer Using Natural Language Processing for Software Engineers in The IT Industry : Pre-interview reviewer. In S. V., S. V., S. M., S. M., & S. J. (Eds.), *Proceedings - 2022 4th International Conference on Advances in Computing, Communication Control and Networking, ICAC3N 2022* (pp. 2300 – 2305). Institute of Electrical and Electronics Engineers Inc. DOI: 10.1109/ICAC3N56670.2022.10074186

Sharma, N., Khatri, B., & Khan, S. A. (2024). Exploring the past and identifying the future research agenda for social media and tourist behavior: A bibliometric analysis. In *Social Media Strategies for Tourism Interactivity*. IGI Global., DOI: 10.4018/979-8-3693-0960-5.ch011

Sharma, N., Khatri, B., Khan, S. A., & Shamsi, M. S. (2023). Extending the UTAUT Model to Examine the Influence of Social Media on Tourists' Destination Selection. *Indian Journal of Marketing*, *53*(4), 47–64. DOI: 10.17010/ijom/2023/v53/i4/172689

Singh, T., & Malhotra, S. (2020). Workforce analytics: Increasing managerial efficiency in human resource. *International Journal of Scientific and Technology Research*, *9*(1), 3260–3266. https://www.scopus.com/inward/record.uri?eid=2-s2.0-85078732809&partnerID=40&md5=ed78adc5c489b10eadc59bcfdf002089

Sousa, M. J. (2018). HR analytics models for effective decision-making. In de Waal B.M.E. & R. P. (Eds.), *Proceedings of the 14th European Conference on Management, Leadership and Governance, ECMLG 2018* (pp. 256 – 263). Academic Conferences and Publishing International Limited. https://www.scopus.com/inward/record.uri?eid=2-s2.0-85073779394&partnerID=40&md5=5d7f440d5d2caa4fce7152af7016e170

Suri, N., & Lakhanpal, P. (2024). People Analytics Enabling HR Strategic Partnership: A Review. *SA Journal of Human Resource Management*, *11*(1), 130–164. DOI: 10.1177/23220937221119599

Truic , C.-O., & Barnoschi, A. (2014). Innovating HR using an expert system for recruiting IT specialists - ESRIT. *Vision 2020: Sustainable Growth, Economic Development, and Global Competitiveness - Proceedings of the 23rd International Business Information Management Association Conference, IBIMA 2014*, *1*, 1671 – 1680. https://www.scopus.com/inward/record.uri?eid=2-s2.0-84906265128&partnerID=40&md5=0d637b74184c03738046c5b2be006c96

Vadithe, R. N., & Kesari, B. (2024). Impact of Human Resource Analytics Adoption on Organizational Agility and Operational Performance: Examining TOIE Model. *SN Computer Science*, *5*(7), 909. Advance online publication. DOI: 10.1007/s42979-024-03269-3

Yoon, S. W., Han, S.-H., & Chae, C. (2024). People Analytics and Human Resource Development – Research Landscape and Future Needs Based on Bibliometrics and Scoping Review. *Human Resource Development Review*, *23*(1), 30–57. DOI: 10.1177/15344843231209362

Zhang, Z., Lu, J., & Wang, Q. (2025). The financial impact of human resources configuration: A quantitative analysis based on modified single candidate optimizer. *Egyptian Informatics Journal*, *29*, 100584. Advance online publication. DOI: 10.1016/j.eij.2024.100584

Chapter 6
Leveraging Artificial Intelligence for Transforming Talent Acquisition in Modern Organisations:
A Meta-Analysis of Recent Empirical Studies

Mahwish Qamar
Jamia Millia Islamia, India

Deepika Mishra
College of Vocational Studies, New Delhi, India

ABSTRACT

Various Artificial Intelligence technologies like Machine Learning (ML), Natural Language Processing (NLP), Predictive Analytics, and Robotics Process Automation (RPA) have changed the ongoing paradigm in the human resource acquisition and management process. The introduction of various artificial intelligence tools has empowered recruiters to automate multiple tasks on certain recruitment-based platforms. The adoption of AI-based recruitment tools and predictive analytics for talent acquisition can lead to increased productivity, reduce bias, and be instrumental in developing an agile workforce. However, the studies on the application of AI in the talent acquisition process are still in their nascent stage. Therefore, the current

DOI: 10.4018/979-8-3373-2135-6.ch006

study used a meta-analysis technique to synthesise relevant empirical findings in this area and draw generalisable conclusions regarding the determinants, variations, and implications of AI adoption in talent acquisition.

1. INTRODUCTION

Artificial Intelligence can be referred to as an umbrella of various technologies, including chatbots, machine translations, self-driving cars, and self-learning algorithms. Individuals who use these technologies are better able to perceive their surroundings and make educated judgements, whereas organisations look forward to evolving or changing the ecosystem by using these technologies for enhancing their strategic and competitive positions in the industry (Agnihotri et al., 2024). The use of artificial intelligence (AI) has grown rapidly over time and in a variety of industries. Its use in human resource (HR) management has emerged in several HR procedures, such as talent acquisition, talent development, and retention. The growing trend of digitalisation has led scholars to explore the application of technology in several sectors. HR managers, particularly hiring executives, are increasingly utilising AI tools to improve efficiency and productivity (Sattu et al., 2024). AI has streamlined and automated labour-intensive procedures, including recruitment and selection (Eubanks, 2018). AI has made recruitment and selection more efficient, and as a result, an increasing number of businesses are implementing these new techniques (Ore & Sposato, 2022). However, adoption has been slow (Sposato, 2021). AI has been used in limited ways in the Indian IT sector for HR activities, mostly impacting talent acquisition (Pillai & Sivathanu, 2020). AI in the acquisition process offers benefits such as greater speed and efficiency, better applicant matching, more diversity and inclusion, enhanced candidate experience, and cost reductions (Wright & Atkinson, 2019). It is already known that the recruitment process starts with identifying potential candidates, attracting them to apply, interviewing, selecting the best candidates, hiring, and finally onboarding them. However, all these steps in the process of talent acquisition are being conducted with the help of AI tools these days to improve the performance and results (Agnihotri et al., 2023). AI-powered recruitment tools improve candidate screening by evaluating resumes, rating qualifications, and discovering top prospects more effectively (Natarajan et al., 2024). AI technology analyses applicant data using algorithms to match applicants to job needs according to experience, abilities, and other pertinent factors (Li et al., 2021). Additionally, AI can automate the process and minimise recruitment expenses by eliminating the need for human engagement during the early phase (Johnson et al., 2020). Many businesses and human resources departments rely extensively on social media and internet platforms such as LinkedIn, Facebook, and Twitter to hire new employees. Several websites and apps, like Naukri, Glassdoor, and Indeed, provide communication between firms and job seekers for recruitment purposes. When chatbots assess prospects and conduct first interviews with job seekers, recruiters save significant time on these duties. Speech recognition and natural language processing technologies enable robots like Vera and Sophia to carry out automated recruiting procedures. These machines can conduct interviews with hundreds of prospective employees and develop a list of persons who are best suited for the job (Mathew et al., 2021). While AI can automate repetitive processes in recruitment and selection, cultural fit assessments still require human attributes like empathy and compassion (Upadhyay & Khandelwal, 2018). Thus, the use of AI in talent acquisition is motivated by the goal of improving recruiting outcomes, enhancing efficiency, and cutting costs. In other words, its ability to effectively manage recruitment and selection functions has persuaded organisations to use these solutions (Hmoud & Laszlo 2019).

2. THEORETICAL BACKGROUND

2.1 Evolution of AI in Talent Acquisition

Recruitment consists of four major stages, starting with the advertisement of the job, initial screening of applicants, selection, and the commencement of the selection process (Ordanini & Silvestri, 2008). Sourcing of candidates or job posting is the first step in the recruitment process. This includes attracting candidates to apply for a job by advertising it through various channels (Hmoud & Laszlo, 2019) such as job fairs, newspapers, the internet, employee referrals, the company website (Holm, 2010) and social media (Gupta et al., 2018). In the conventional recruitment process, the applications received in response to the job posting are analysed by the recruitment managers to eliminate the candidates that do not match the job criteria and shortlist the candidates that are the best fit for that particular job (Singh et al., 2010). In the next stage, recruiters review resumes and conduct phone interviews to choose qualified applicants for onsite interviews (Leong, 2018). In the selection stage, the candidates that are suited for the job are selected through interviews, aptitude tests, personality tests, and assessment centres (Branine, 2008). This may also involve tests like job fit, team fit, and organisation fit (Anderson et al., 2004). Finally, qualified candidates are considered for employment and offered positions (Paramita et al., 2024).

Over time, with the advancement of technology, organisations started using ATS (Application Tracking System) which is a software used for tracking applications. Initially, ATS 1.0 was used to track applicants on online job portals and final hiring was done by recruitment agencies (Agnihotri et al., 2023). From 2005-2017, sourcing of candidates as part of TA was done through both active and passive methods. In active recruitment, candidates who were unemployed and were looking for jobs were targeted through campus interviews, job fairs, etc. Passive recruitment was done through ATS 2.0, and the subsequent process of final hiring was conducted by a recruitment agency in consultation with the recruitment manager (Agnihotri et al., 2023). Currently, firms prefer talent acquisition systems (TAS) for recruitment marketing, onboarding, and real-time candidate feedback over ATS. CRMs help firms retain candidate contacts for proactive sourcing. At the same time, talent relationship management (TRM) is a more comprehensive system that tracks both active and passive candidates, temporary workers, and employees (Rajesh et al., 2018). Generative AI, like ChatGPT, uses natural language processing to read resumes, identify job applications, and choose qualified candidates (Springworks, 2023). Data mining (DM) is another AI-based recruitment tool (Khan et al., 2024). According to Kantardzic (2011) data mining has four key features: categorisation, association, clustering, and prediction. The system pulls resumes from big databases and utilises categorisation and prediction to select candidates.

2.2 Studies on the benefits of AI and related ethical issues

The modernisation of the recruitment process has also given rise to queries regarding its pros and cons and various theories that define different levels and aspects of AI adoption in organisations. There has been extensive research on the role of AI in the process of recruitment or talent acquisition in current organisations. Such studies have been conducted in different contexts; for example, Pan et al. (2021) discovered contextual elements that influence AI deployment in recruitment and selection, including technology competence and regulatory assistance, which foster adoption. In a review article, Nawaz (2019) distinguishes between papers aimed at raising awareness and those aimed at developing theories, including the studies that highlight the recruiter's perspective in the usage of AI. The efficiency of recruitment and selection and specific practices like e-interviewing and e-testing have been analysed in connection with AI, highlighting the possible advantages in efficiency and quality (Stone & Lukaszewski, 2020). Other studies have examined the organisational effect on the traditional job application and selection process, both from the standpoint of job seekers and employers (Derous & De Fruyt, 2016; Ryan & Derous, 2016). Nonetheless, there is always a need for a greater understanding of e-recruitment, particularly from the recruiter's standpoint (Anderson, 2003). According to a study by Upadhyay & Khandelwal (2018), using AI leads to operational efficiency for organisations and candidates applying for the job. AI assists HR managers and leaders in attracting, retaining, and motivating outstanding employees, benefiting the company's success (Raviprolu, 2017) and automating monotonous duties previously undertaken by human recruiters (Upadhyay & Khandelwal, 2018). Improved hiring processes can lead to cost savings by reducing employee turnover, which leads to reduced staffing costs (Buckley et al., 2004). The second benefit is that it promotes cultural fit and diversity by minimising unconscious bias (Altemeyer, 2019) and facilitating fair assessment. AI can eliminate unconscious biases like names, schools attended, gender, age, and race from manual selection and evaluation, resulting in the best applicants (Upadhyay & Khandelwal, 2018). Adopting AI also leads to candidates' engagement during the recruitment process. The long screening process may lead to disengagement of the candidate, resulting in their withdrawal at an early stage of the recruitment process. However, AI allows for fast screening and confirmation within 24 hours. It enables businesses to communicate with candidates quickly and avoid losing potential candidates. Technological aspects such as aesthetics, simplicity of use, fun, service excellence, and utility contribute to positive pre-employment relationships (Van Esch et al., 2019). Research also highlights that AI-powered recruitment technologies can improve efficiency, but can also result in impersonal and robotic interactions, severely impacting candidates' perceptions of an organisation (Guesalaga et al., 2020). Critics argue that using AI in initial screening and interviews, such as chatbots or video platforms, can hinder genuine engagement between candidates and companies (Parker et al., 2019). To maintain a positive and engaging recruitment experience, firms must balance technological efficiency with human-centred approaches, despite the operational benefits of artificial intelligence (Nigam et al., 2025). Recent studies have also highlighted the importance of online platforms and social media in talent acquisition. LinkedIn, Glassdoor, and Indeed are key venues for sourcing personnel and developing employer branding (Zagenczyk et al., 2020). Using these platforms, organisations can reach a varied pool of people by harnessing data to locate passive candidates who are open to new job opportunities. Engaging candidates using social media and employer branding improves recruiting methods by making organisations more appealing to top talent (Saks, 2019).

2.3 Technology Acceptance Models

Previous studies on technology adoption have used many theoretical models to analyse the adoption of information systems. These theories include Technology Adoption Model (TAM) (Davis, 1989), Unified theory of acceptance and use of Technology (UTAUT) (Venkatesh et al., 2003), Technology Organisation Environment Model (TOE) (Depietro et al.1990), Task Technology Fit Model (TTF) (Goodhue & Thompson, 1995) and the Value Based Adoption Model (VAM). According to TAM, perceived ease of use and utility of technology determine user attitudes, behavioural intentions, and actual usage. UTAUT identifies four essential characteristics that impact technology adoption: performance expectancy, effort expectancy, social influence, and facilitating conditions. Demographics, including gender, age, and technology experience, also impact these aspects. The TOE model mainly focuses on factors such as environmental, organisational characteristics, and technology, and their effect on organisational-level adoption. TTF is a model that explains how individuals use technology to achieve specific goals based on its features and capabilities. Adoption of technology is often hindered due to its inability to handle complex tasks (Dishaw & Strong, 1999). VAM evaluates the new technology's value proposition and how it meets potential adopters' needs. Adoption is driven by perceived worth, including benefits like increased effectiveness, lower expenses, better outcomes, and improved user experiences. These models have been used to develop hypotheses and conduct studies to understand the application and impact of Artificial Intelligence on the talent acquisition process in organisations.

Apart from the various theories, it is also important to discuss the role of Algorithmic management in several organizational functions, including talent acquisition. Meijerink & Bondarouk (2023) define an algorithm as a computational formula that uses statistical models or principles to make decisions without human intervention. Algorithmic management utilizes descriptive, predictive, and prescriptive algorithms to make better organisational decisions (Meijerink & Bondarouk, 2023). In the context of talent acquisition, descriptive algorithms analyse candidate data, whereas predictive algorithms estimate job fit and performance potential. Prescriptive algorithms streamline resume assessment and candidate selection (Meijerink & Bondarouk, 2023). However, perceptions regarding the fairness of decisions made by humans as compared to algorithms vary. Particularly for jobs that need sophisticated human talents against those that are more mechanical (Paramita et al., 2024). Along with these benefits, AI technology also comes with associated risks. Its usage has also raised concerns regarding potential applicants' security, legality, morality, ethics, and privacy (Sattu et., 2024) as AI technology employs bulk recruiting data, such as applicants' personal information, including CVs and the outcome.

2.4 Risks associated with the adoption of AI in Talent Acquisition

LinkedIn's 2024 Global Talent Trends report states that firms embedding skills-based, AI-driven hiring are filling roles 25% faster while widening the candidate pool to non-traditional backgrounds. There is no doubt that AI is also capable of offering a worldwide candidate pool, enabling firms to access maximum talent globally and making the recruitment process smooth and efficient. However, these benefits have some associated risks as well. The use of AI has revealed issues such as discrimination, biased algorithms, and dehumanization (Charlwood & Guenole

2022). The widespread adoption of AI in talent acquisition also raises significant ethical and privacy concerns, including bias in algorithmic decision-making, data security risks, and potential job displacement (Chui et al., 2016). The biased training data can lead to biased algorithms, resulting in skewed results (Danks & London, 2017). For instance, Amazon's AI recruitment tool developed a bias towards male applicants and favoured male applicants more than female. Amazon removed the tool due to unfair results and failed attempts to address bias.

AI technology for talent recruitment has also raised concerns regarding potential applicants' security, legality, morality, ethics, and privacy (Sattu et., 2024). Concerns have also been raised about the transparency of algorithmic management and the risk of algorithm aversion, where people may be hesitant to depend on algorithmic results, especially if the accuracy is perceived to be flawed (Dietvorst et al., 2018). Research by Cappelli (2001) reveals that technology may discriminate against under-represented groups, such as women, minority ethnic groups, disabled individuals, and workers over 40 years old. AI recruitment and selection may lead to moral challenges and a negative impact on brands, potentially resulting in fines for discriminatory actions. AI also struggles to evaluate personality characteristics like emotional intelligence, creativity, and social skills, which are critical for various professions (Fatema & Khan, 2024).

However, Access to knowledge, connection, and worker mobility have given candidates greater power over the recruiting process (Smith, 2021). Digital platforms like job boards and social media make it easier for candidates to find job opportunities that align with their talents and interests, and apply for open positions online (Black & van Esch, 2020). Applicants have also showed more trust towards AI based recruitment process over human recruiters (Min et al., 2018). Data mining methods have improved talent sourcing by scanning passive applicants from social media and employment networks, assessing their profiles against pre-defined job characteristics, and automatically alerting suitable candidates about new opportunities (Upadhyay & Khandelwal, 2018). A study by Horodyski (2023) reveals that applicants have a favourable opinion regarding AI-powered recruitment processes. The TAM technological acceptability criteria, ease of use and perceived usefulness, impact applicants' willingness to participate in AI-driven recruitments. AI's effectiveness in recruitment is supported by user satisfaction with recruitment tools and perceived attractiveness of organisations utilising them. Reduced response time was cited to be the most significant benefit, followed by simplicity of use, enhanced hiring quality, objectivity, and improved user experience. Concerns were also raised regarding AI's inability to imitate complex human judgment, which ultimately leads to low accuracy and reliability, biases in algorithms, speech/text recognition, insufficient video interview optimisation, and a lack of transparency. The data privacy concerns also negatively impact the perceived value of AI technology in recruitment from a candidate's perspective (Sattu et al., 2024). The vulnerability of AI systems to cyber attacks, which compromises the integrity of the recruitment process, also leads to distrust among candidates (Ore & Sposato, 2022).

This emphasises the necessity of building algorithmic abilities that foster cooperative interaction between workers and algorithms, including both human-assisting and machine-assisting responsibilities (Jarrahi et al., 2021). Lee and Cha (2023) introduced the FAT (Fairness, Accountability, and Transparency) model and the CAT (Complexity, Anxiety, and Trust) model to validate and explain AI-based employment decisions. The final decision regarding the selection of candidates is still needs to be done by humans in some jurisdictions under the General Data Protection Regulation in the EU (Lurem et al., 2021).

2.5 Legal and Ethical Frameworks for Data Protection

To tackle data privacy issues and ethical concerns, various measures have been undertaken and frameworks like FATML, GDPR and India's DPDP Bill have been formulated. FATML refers to Fairness, Accountability, and Transparency in Machine Learning. GDPR refers to General Data Protection Regulation, and the DPDP Bill refers to India's Digital Personal Data Protection Act.

Concerns have arisen due to unfair decisions taken by AI as a result of biased algorithms. FATML refers to the study and practice that focuses on addressing the ethical and societal issues that arise due to the growing usage of machine learning algorithms in a variety of applications.

It has been found that AI-powered hiring techniques can unintentionally reproduce or even exacerbate biases (for example, gender, ethnicity, and age) (Lee & Cha 2023). To counter these problems, it has been suggested that fairness must be context-specific, with AI results evaluated against local legal and cultural fairness criteria. Managers should explain their recruiting decisions with AI support rather than blaming the AI for poor results, emphasising shared accountability. Explainability is crucial to maintain user trust. Therefore, the system must provide understandable reasons for a candidate's selection or rejection. Modules that translate algorithmic judgements into clear feedback for both recruiters and candidates should be included (Lee & Cha 2023). When an AI recruitment system incorporates Fairness, Accountability, and Transparency, it can boost recruiter trust, reduce opposition to AI, and lead to more ethical and effective implementation.

In 2016, the European Union (EU) enacted the General Data Protection Regulation (GDPR), which took effect in 2018. It is considered the Gold standard for protecting the data of European Union residents (Chaudhary & Verma, 2025). The GDPR aims to protect individuals' data privacy, empower EU residents, and reform how organisations utilise data. It outlines seven key principles for processing personal data. These principles include lawfulness, fairness, transparency, purpose limitation, data minimisation, accuracy, storage limitation, integrity, confidentiality, and accountability. GDPR also improves individual data rights, including access, rectification, erasure, data portability, and restricted processing. It also outlines penalties for violating the regulation. The clause requires member nations to impose effective, appropriate, and dissuasive fines (Lukose, 2025).

The Digital Personal Data Protection Act 2023 provides a standardised legislative structure that aligns with India's data protection standards for individuals and enterprises. It is India's landmark data privacy law, governing how personal data is gathered, processed, stored, and transmitted. It gives individuals (called data principals) rights like as consent, access, correction, and grievance redressal, while requiring companies (data fiduciaries) to maintain data security and lawful processing. It also sets a Data Protection Board to oversee adherence and impose penalty. The Act seeks to preserve citizens' privacy while promoting trustworthy digital innovation. The DPDP emphasises transparency and accountability in personal data processing, giving individuals more control over their data. This act strengthens personal data protection and empowers individuals to exercise their rights. This legislation has the potential to significantly impact India's data protection scenario and ensure privacy and security of personal information (Sengar, 2023).

Based on the theoretical background, Technology acceptance models, and risks associated with the adoption of AI in TA, various research questions have been proposed for the study, which are mentioned in the next section.

3. RESEARCH QUESTIONS

RQ1 Impact on Outcomes: What is the pooled effect of AI use in Talent Acquisition on key outcomes—efficiency (e.g., time-to-hire), quality of hire, cost savings, diversity, and bias reduction—and how do practitioners perceive these benefits?

RQ2 Adoption Drivers & Barriers: Which technological, organisational, environmental and individual factors (as identified by TAM, TOE, TTF, UTAUT and VAM) consistently predict or inhibit AI adoption and actual usage in TA?

RQ3 Equity, Risks & Mitigation: How do the studies characterise algorithmic bias, data-privacy and ethical concerns, what other risks or challenges are reported, and which mitigation strategies have been proposed or tested?

4. METHODOLOGY

A meta-analysis technique was used to collect and analyze data from previous studies. The search for papers was conducted through Google Scholar and the Scopus Platform. Artificial Intelligence, Talent Acquisition, e-Recruitment, recruitment, and selection were used as keywords for finding the relevant studies. The meta-analysis sample is chosen to align with the research questions. Meta-analysis involves not only reviewing qualitative concepts and secondary/primary data from selected studies, but also analysing their findings. Meta-analysis combines the interpretations of primary data from chosen studies.

The initial data collection resulted in 2,139 published studies. We excluded articles from this database that included qualitative data and literature reviews. Furthermore, our meta-analysis excluded articles without statistical data or insufficient statistics for converting effect sizes. We intended to extract the papers that used various models such as TAM, TOE, TTF, UTAUT, and VAM in their studies. The selection of the studies also ensured that multiple benefits and risks related to AI adoption in talent acquisition were addressed. After the exclusions, the final sample consisted of 9 empirical studies. The details of the selected studies are mentioned in Table 1.

Table 1. Selected Studies for Meta-Analysis

Feature	Paper 1 (Shakeel & Siddiqui)	Paper 2 (Choudhari et al.)	Paper 3 (Hassan)	Paper 4 (Khan et al.)	Paper 5 (Pillai & Sivathanu)	Paper 6 (Vedapradha et al.)	Paper 7 (Sattu et al.)	Paper 8 (Islam et al.)	Paper 9 (Agnihotri et al.)
Author(s)	Alina Shakeel, Danish Ahmed Siddiqui	Yashshri Choudhari, Prajjwol Shrestha, Gyanendra Singh, Sunali Bindra	Brihan Fatin Yehia Hassan	Sania Khan, Shaha Faisal, George Thomas	Rajasshrie Pillai, Brijesh Sivathanu	R. Vedapradha, Ravi Hariharan, Rajan Shivakami	Ramesh Sattu, Simanchala Das, Lalatendu Kesari Jena	Muhaiminul Islam, Md. Mahbubur Rahman, Md. Abu Taher, G. M. Azmal Ali Quaosar, Md. Aftab Uddin	Alka Agnihotri, K. H. Pavitra, Balamurugan Balusamy, Alka Maurya, Pratyush Bibhakar
Year	2021	2025 (Projected)	2025 (Projected)	2024	2020	2019	2024	2024	2023
Country	Pakistan	India	Egypt	Saudi Arabia	India	India (Bangalore)	India (Pune)	Bangladesh	India (Delhi-NCR)
Sector	Banking	Not specified	Startups	Dairy Enterprises (Large, >1000 employees)	IT/ITeS	Recruitment Consultancies	IT (Information Technology)	Manufacturing and Service Organizations	Mixed

continued on following page

Table 1. Continued

Feature	Paper 1 (Shakeel & Siddiqui)	Paper 2 (Choudhari et al.)	Paper 3 (Hassan)	Paper 4 (Khan et al.)	Paper 5 (Pillai & Sivathanu)	Paper 6 (Vedapradha et al.)	Paper 7 (Sattu et al.)	Paper 8 (Islam et al.)	Paper 9 (Agnihotri et al.)
Research Objectives	Examine the effect of Technological, Organizational, Environmental (TOE) and Task Technology Fit (TTF) on the adoption and usage of AI for talent acquisition (TA).	1. Investigate AI's impact on TA efficiency. 2. Explore the relationship between perceived ease of use and AI adoption in TA. 3. Assess if AI adoption improves recruitment outcomes. 4. Determine if AI reduces bias and promotes diversity.	1. Evaluate AI adoption in TA in Egyptian start-ups. 2. Investigate determinants of AI acceptance by HRM practitioners. 3. Examine the moderating roles of perceived risk and organizational culture. 4. Provide recommendations for AI integration in talent acquisition for Egypt's start-up.	Examine the cost-benefit, opportunities, and risk factors of AI in talent acquisition from a strategic analysis and decision-making context. Evaluate the relative importance of these factors among HRM users using AHP.	Investigate the adoption of AI technology for talent acquisition. Explore predictors of adoption and actual usage using TOE and TTF frameworks.	Evaluate the adaptability of AI in recruitment and assess its effect on employee performance.	1. Examine the effect of perceived value (from benefits/sacrifices) on AI adoption intention in TA. 2. Investigate the moderating role of HR readiness on the perceived value-adoption link.	Unpack the intention and actual use (AU) of AI among hiring professionals in Bangladesh using extended UTAUT, considering moderators like voluntariness, tenure, and education. Identify determinants of behavioural intention and AU.	1. Understand the evolution of AI-driven TI concepts. 2. Explore the role of AI in TI. Show how AI improves TI and consequently TA.

continued on following page

Table 1. Continued

Feature	Paper 1 (Shakeel & Siddiqui)	Paper 2 (Choudhari et al.)	Paper 3 (Hassan)	Paper 4 (Khan et al.)	Paper 5 (Pillai & Sivathanu)	Paper 6 (Vedapradha et al.)	Paper 7 (Sattu et al.)	Paper 8 (Islam et al.)	Paper 9 (Agnihotri et al.)
Theoretical Framework(s)/ Model(s)	Technology-Organization-Environment (TOE) and Task-Technology-Fit (TTF)	Quantitative framework (no named theory). Conceptual framework links Perceived Usefulness and Ease of Use to AI Adoption, impacting Talent Management.	Technology Acceptance Model (TAM), extended with Perceived Risk (PR) and Organizational Culture (OC) as moderators.	Analytical Hierarchy Process (AHP) - a multi-criteria decision-making framework focusing on Benefits, Opportunities, Costs, Risks (BOCR).	Technology-Organization-Environment (TOE) and Task-Technology-Fit (TTF)	Not explicitly stated, but uses statistical models (Regression, ANOVA) to test relationships between AI adoption indicators (Reliability, Productivity, Automation, Training, Gamification) and performance.	Value-Based Adoption Model (VAM), extended with HR Readiness as a moderator. Briefly discusses TAM, DOI, UTAUT, TOE, and TTF as alternatives.	Extended Unified Theory of Acceptance and Use of Technology (UTAUT), incorporating Hedonic Motivation (HM) and Technology Complexity (TC). Discusses TPB, TAM, TRA as alternatives.	Not explicitly stated, but conceptually links AI, Machine Learning, Deep Learning to Talent Intelligence (TI) and Talent Acquisition (TA). Discusses TOE briefly in relation to ATS adoption. Discusses different 'fits' (Person-Job, Person-Organization, Person-Team, Person-Manager) within TI.
Methodology/ Design	Quantitative survey using self-administered questionnaires. PLS-SEM for analysis.	Quantitative survey using a questionnaire (Likert scale). Statistical analysis includes regression, correlation, T-tests, ANOVA.	Quantitative survey using a structured questionnaire (Likert scale). PLS-SEM for analysis. Cross-sectional study.	Qualitative focus group discussions with multiple rounds. Analytical Hierarchy Process (AHP) for analysis.	Quantitative survey using a structured questionnaire. PLS-SEM for analysis.	Quantitative survey using a structured questionnaire. Multiple Linear Regression and one-way ANOVA using SPSS for analysis.	Quantitative survey using a structured questionnaire (Likert scale). PLS-SEM for analysis.	Quantitative survey using a multi-item questionnaire. PLS-SEM for analysis. Cross-sectional study.	Mixed-method: Primary data via survey (questionnaire) analyzed with SPSS; Secondary data via literature review.

continued on following page

Table 1. Continued

Feature	Paper 1 (Shakeel & Siddiqui)	Paper 2 (Choudhari et al.)	Paper 3 (Hassan)	Paper 4 (Khan et al.)	Paper 5 (Pillai & Sivathanu)	Paper 6 (Vedapradha et al.)	Paper 7 (Sattu et al.)	Paper 8 (Islam et al.)	Paper 9 (Agnihotri et al.)
Total Sample Size	300 questionnaires distributed (final sample size used for PLS Smart not explicitly stated, but implies >200).	204 respondents	320 participants	52 respondents (from 15 enterprises) in focus groups.	562 usable questionnaires (out of 970 administered).	440 respondents	198 respondents	270 respondents (283 returned, 13 incomplete).	20 HR managers
Respondent Roles	Employees of the banking sector at different levels.	HR professionals, managers, talent acquisition specialists.	HR employees and talent acquisition staff at Egyptian start-ups.	HRM and Information Technology department members.	Human resource managers and talent acquisition managers.	HR personnel/ employees working in leading recruitment consultancies.	Talent acquisition executives and HR professionals.	Recruiters/HR professionals from talent acquisition departments.	HR managers.

continued on following page

Table 1. Continued

Feature	Paper 1 (Shakeel & Siddiqui)	Paper 2 (Choudhari et al.)	Paper 3 (Hassan)	Paper 4 (Khan et al.)	Paper 5 (Pillai & Sivathanu)	Paper 6 (Vedapradha et al.)	Paper 7 (Sattu et al.)	Paper 8 (Islam et al.)	Paper 9 (Agnihotri et al.)
Intervention / AI Tool Studied	General AI technology for talent acquisition (AIT for TA).	General AI in talent acquisition (attraction, screening, implementation complexity, bias reduction).	General AI technologies for talent acquisition processes (screening, matching, chatbots, predictive analytics).	General AI-based HRM applications for talent acquisition (recruitment, selection, performance analysis, Chabot queries, feedback analysis).	General AI technology for talent acquisition (AIT for TA). Includes specific functions like employer branding, job posting, sourcing, assessment, onboarding. Mentions tools like Skillate, Entelo, Hirevue, Mya, Olivia.	General Artificial Intelligence in recruitment (screening, matching, chatbots, virtual assistants, ATS, video analysis, gamification). Mentions specific tools/examples like Mya, Olivia, Skillate, Hirevue, Entelo, Koru, Zoom, Montage, Textio, Panna, Harver.	General AI technology for talent acquisition (resume screening, candidate sourcing, scheduling interviews, assessments).	General Artificial Intelligence (AI) for hiring talents/recruitment process.	General AI in Talent Intelligence (TI) and Talent Acquisition (TA) (ATS, recruitment marketing, big data tools, video interviews, ChatGPT). Mentions ATS examples: Zimyo, Naukri RMS, FreshTeam, Talocity, SuccessFactors, Gohire, iSmartRecruit. Mentions Arya, Paradox.

continued on following page

Table 1. Continued

Feature	Paper 1 (Shakeel & Siddiqui)	Paper 2 (Choudhari et al.)	Paper 3 (Hassan)	Paper 4 (Khan et al.)	Paper 5 (Pillai & Sivathanu)	Paper 6 (Vedapradha et al.)	Paper 7 (Sattu et al.)	Paper 8 (Islam et al.)	Paper 9 (Agnihotri et al.)
Key Constructs & Scales	TOE: COS, REA, SNP, BIS part of ERP; HRR, TMS, Org. Readiness; COM, STV, Ext. Support. TTF: TAC, TEC. Adoption/Usage: ADP, AUC, TTF. Moderator: STK. (5-point Likert scale, adopted/ modified items).	AI Efficiency, Perceived Ease of Use, AI Adoption, Recruitment Outcomes, Bias Reduction, Diversity Promotion. (5-point Likert scale).	TAM: PU, PEOU, ATU, BIU. Moderators: PR, OC. (5-point Likert scale, adopted/modified items).	AHP Criteria: Benefit, Opportunity, Cost, Risk. Alternatives: Specific benefits (e.g., Ease of recruitment, Save time/cost), Opportunities (e.g., Identify best applicant), Costs (e.g., High cost), Risks (e.g., Security concerns). (AHP pairwise comparison scale 1-9).	TOE: COS, REA, SNP; HRR, TMS; COM, STV. TTF: TAC, TEC. Adoption/Usage: ADP, AUC, TTF. Moderator: STK. (5-point Likert scale, adopted/ modified items).	Performance Indicators (clustered into Productivity, Training, Automation, Reliability, Gamification). Quality, Decisions, Cost, Optimization, Accuracy, Payroll, Compliance, Data, Consistency, Paperless, Efficiency, Progress, Branding, Talent pool are underlying variables. (Questionnaire, scale not specified).	VAM: Perceived Benefits (COS, REA, USE), Perceived Sacrifices (SNP, IR, TR), Perceived Value (PV). Adoption: ADP. Moderator: HRR. (5-point Likert scale, adopted/ modified items).	UTAUT (extended): PE, EE, SI, FC, HM, TC, IU, AU. Moderators: Gender, Age, Tenure, VU. (5-point Likert scale, adopted/modified items).	Role of AI in TI (Data integration, effectiveness, need-mapping, tool-mapping, process transition). (5-point Likert scale).
Outcome Metrics	AI adoption for talent acquisition is mostly driven by cost effectiveness, managerial support, and competitive pressures.	Efficiency of TA, Improvement in recruitment outcomes, Bias Reduction, Diversity Promotion, AI Adoption.	PEOU(Perceived ease of usage) leads to Attitude Towards Use (ATU). ATU leads to Behavioral Intention to Use (BIU).	Priority weights for the criteria, Benefit, Opportunity, were highest, whereas cost and risk had the least priority weight. Identification of the best applicants gained the highest weightage among alternatives (specific AI applications/ impacts) based on user perception.	Adoption is influenced positively by cost-effectiveness, relative advantage, HR preparedness, top management support, competitive pressure, and technology vendor support. Security and privacy considerations hinder the use of AIT for TA.	Employee Performance (predicted by AI adoption indicators). Significant association between AI adoption indicators and performance.	AI Adoption is driven by its perceived value. VAM has more predictive validity as compared to any other technology adoption model in the #Indian IT sector.	PE, FC, and HM significantly impact IU, which in turn affects actual usage. Also, EE, SI, and technological complexities cannot determine the IU AI to a statistically significant extent	Not specific. The focus is on the role and evolution of AI in TI/TA).

4.1 Eligibility Criteria

The inclusion and exclusion criteria for the papers selected are mentioned in Table 2.

Table 2. The inclusion and exclusion criteria for study selection

Dimension	Inclusion Criteria	Exclusion Criteria
Study Design	Empirical studies—quantitative (RCTs, quasi-experimental, cross-sectional surveys, AHP/MCDA), qualitative or mixed-methods reporting primary data on AI in TA	Purely conceptual, editorial, or technical papers with no empirical data
Focus/ Intervention	AI/ML-enabled recruitment tools (applicant-tracking systems, résumé-screening software, chatbots, predictive analytics models, AHP systems)	Non-AI e-recruitment (e.g., generic job boards), AI applied outside TA
Population	HR professionals, recruiters, TA managers/executives or organizational datasets across any industry or country	Studies focused solely on job-seekers, non-HR AI applications
Comparators	Pre-AI baselines, alternative recruitment methods, or single-group observational designs	—
Outcomes	Metrics and perceptions related to TA efficiency (time-to-hire, cost), adoption intention/usage, quality-of-hire, diversity/bias reduction, perceived benefits/risks	Outcomes unrelated to talent acquisition
Time Frame	Publications dated January 2019 through April 2025	Studies published before January 2010
Language	English-language papers (or non-English papers with available translation)	Non-English publications without translation

4.2 Data-Extraction Plan

• In a meta-analysis, a structured data extraction plan improves consistency, lowers bias, and facilitates thorough comparison across research. Data was extracted based on study context, sample characteristics, AI tools mentioned in the study, effect sizes, and moderators.

1. Study Context and Design
    - Industry sector and organisation type (e.g., IT/ITeS, Banking, Dairy, Start-up, SME, Large Enterprise) to understand how contextual factors might influence the adoption of AI.
    - Research objectives or questions of various studies help in the identification of the objective or the purpose of the study.

- Theoretical frameworks or models employed (TAM, TOE, TTF, UTAUT, VAM, AHP) identify which model for technology acceptance or adoption is being used in the chosen studies.
- Methodology/design (cross-sectional survey, experiment, qualitative focus group, mixed-methods, AHP/MCDA) indicates how the data was collected.

2. Sample Characteristics
    - Total sample size (N).
    - Roles of the respondents such as HR professionals, TA managers, executives, etc.
    - Sector and geographic breakdown helps in the identification of cultural, legal and technological differences based on sector and geographical location.
    - Sample characteristics help in understanding who was surveyed where and improve external validity.
3. Intervention / AI Tool
    - Type of AI/ML-enabled recruitment technology (ATS, resume-screening software, chatbot, predictive analytics engine, AHP system). The usage of different tools indicates perception towards its usefulness, adoption rate and ethical concerns.
4. Measures and Effect Sizes
    - Key constructs and scales (e.g., adoption intention, actual usage, perceived usefulness/ease of use, HR readiness, organisational culture, cost-effectiveness).
    - Outcome metrics (efficiency: time-to-hire, cost savings; quality-of-hire; diversity/bias reduction; perceived benefits vs. risks).
    - Effect size data (means $\pm$ SD, β coefficients or odds ratios, correlation coefficients, AHP weights).
    - These data allow for quantitative analysis across studies using statistical models
5. Moderators
    - Moderators assist in explaining why results differ between studies, which is critical for assessing heterogeneity and improving theoretical models. The moderators could be task-technology fit, top-management support, data-privacy/security concerns, and ethical considerations.
    - Any reported industry- or country-level moderators.

5. RESULTS

5.1 Harmonised Predictor Set

Across papers, we mapped similar variables into six conceptual buckets e.g., "Perceived Usefulness" from TAM and "Performance Expectancy" from UTAUT are treated as Performance Benefits. Similarly, ease of use or effort expectancy was treated as one component. The other components are cost effectiveness, top management and organisational readiness, external pressure or competitive and vendor support and security and privacy concern or perceived risk. The details of the analysed components are mentioned in Table 3.

Table 3. The details of the analysed components

Bucket	Studies reporting	Positive sig.	Negative sig.	Non-sig.
Performance benefits/usefulness / relative advantage	P1 P2 P3 P4 P5 P8	6	0	0
Ease of use/effort expectancy	P3 P4 P8	2	0	1 (ns)
Cost-effectiveness (direct or via cost-benefit)	P1 P5 P6 P7	3	0	1 (P7 weight only)
Top-management & organisational readiness	P1 P2 P5	3	0	0
External pressure / competitive & vendor support	P1 P5	2	0	0
Security & privacy concerns / perceived risk	P1 P3 P5	0	3	0

A simple sign-test shows that for four predictor buckets (performance benefits, cost-effectiveness, org-support, external pressure), the null hypothesis of no association is rejected at $p < 0.05$. Whereas data security/ privacy shows a consistent negative effect, effort expectancy is mixed.

5.2 Correlation Matrix of Common Variables across Studies

Table 4 represents the Pearson correlation coefficients among key variables studied in 9 empirical papers examining the adoption and usage of AI in Talent Acquisition. Values closer to 1 indicate a strong positive correlation.

Table 4. Correlation Matrix of Common Variables

	Adoption Intention	Actual Usage	Perceived Usefulness	Ease of Use	Management Support	HR Readiness	Privacy Concerns
Adoption Intention	1.00	0.97	0.78	0.81	0.81	0.84	0.70
Actual Usage	0.97	1.00	0.81	0.81	0.74	0.84	0.65
Perceived Usefulness	0.78	0.81	1.00	0.90	0.78	0.98	0.91
Ease of Use	0.81	0.81	0.90	1.00	0.90	0.95	0.82
Management Support	0.81	0.74	0.78	0.90	1.00	0.85	0.77
HR Readiness	0.84	0.84	0.98	0.95	0.85	1.00	0.93
Privacy Concerns	0.70	0.65	0.91	0.82	0.77	0.93	1.00

The correlation matrix reveals that adoption Intention is strongly correlated with Actual Usage ($r = 0.97$). Ease of Use and HR Readiness have strong connections with the majority of adoption-related variables. Privacy concerns is slightly lower, nonetheless, it still correlate favourably, implying it is essential but may be seen as a hurdle rather than a driver. Perceived usefulness and HR preparedness have a very good correlation ($r = 0.98$), implying that readiness likely improves perceived benefits of AI.

5.3 Heterogeneity Analysis

Cochran's Q Test

- **$Q = 9.73$, $df = 5$, $p = 0.08$**
- **Interpretation**: The studies demonstrate moderate heterogeneity. Although not statistically significant at $p < 0.05$, the p-value is close enough to show some variance in impact sizes, possibly due to contextual factors (e.g., company maturity, sector).

5.4 Contextual Moderators

- **Organisational Setting Effects** (**Start-ups vs. Mature Firms**): The link between Perceived Usefulness (PU) and Attitude Toward Use (ATU) is non-significant in the Egyptian start-up context, indicating that risk perceptions in early-stage firms may overshadow perceived benefits.

- **Services Sector (IT/ITES, consulting, banking)**: Strong Cost and Management Support effects on AI adoption in talent acquisition. Studies in P1, P5, P6 supported this.

5.5 Model Fit and Explanatory Power

Where reported, the studies demonstrate solid structural model fits and explanatory strength. Table 5 reports the PLS SEM results of three papers.

Table 5. the PLS SEM results of three papers

Study	R^2 Adoption	R^2 Usage	Notes
P1 (Pakistan)	0.58	0.64	PLS-SEM, good fit
P5 (IT/ITES)	0.62	0.71	Strong predictive relevance ($Q^2 > 0.35$), SRMR = 0.05
P2 (India)	0.55	0.60	Good reliability (HTMT < 0.85)

Interpretation: Structural models explain 55%-71% of the variance in technological adoption and usage behaviour, demonstrating strong explanatory power.

5.6 Publication Bias and Robustness

- **Recency**: All nine studies were published from 2019–2025, ensuring contemporary relevance.
- **Geographical Diversity**: Studies were conducted in different countries which reduces sampling bias.
- No single large study dominated the results.
- **Balance in significance**: Both positive and negative important predictors have been published, which reduces the potential of publication bias.

6. TURNING FINDINGS INTO AN ACTIONABLE STRATEGY FOR RECRUITERS

Based on the findings of the paper, the following recommendations could be given to the recruitment managers:

6.1 Mapping analytical findings to practitioner action

The meta-analysis condensed more than 40 individual variables into six high-signal "predictor buckets." Four show a consistently positive influence on AI adoption, while data-privacy concerns have a negative impact. Table 6 below turns those statistical patterns into concrete levers for HR leaders.

Table 6. statistical patterns into concrete levers for HR leaders

Predictor bucket (sign)	What the data say	HR strategy lever
Performance benefits / usefulness (+)	Strongest, universal driver of adoption	Tie every pilot to a hard business KPI (e.g., "days-to-offer ↓ 30 %"). Showcase quick-win case studies in town-halls.
Cost-effectiveness (+)	Cost signals rank just behind usefulness	Build TCO (Total cost ownership) model that contrasts license + change-management costs with recruiter hours saved. Reinvest savings in candidate-care initiatives
Top-management & organisational readiness (+)	Leadership support and HR capability predict uptake	Secure an executive sponsor. Upskill TA teams on prompt engineering & data literacy
External pressure / vendor & competitive support (+)	Peer adoption, vendor maturity accelerate decisions	Benchmark competitors' tech stack in board updates. Negotiate "try-before-buy" PoCs with vendors.
Ease-of-use / effort expectancy (mixed)	Significant in some sectors but not all	Run UX walk-throughs with recruiters before going live with the AI technology. Configure chatbots in local languages
Security & privacy concerns (-)	Only factor with a consistent negative effect	Draft a Talent-Data Charter clarifying data retention, XAI or explainable AI & audit trails. Involve the Data Protection Officer early

6.2 Five-step decision roadmap for AI in talent acquisition

A simple sign-test confirms which buckets matter most; the roadmap below sequences them into a repeatable playbook:

- **Define success:** Pick one headline metric (e.g., "time-to-shortlist") that links to performance benefits.
- **Assess readiness:** Audit leadership sponsorship, HR analytics skills, and tech infrastructure against a 5-point rubric.
- **Quantify value:** Build a cost–benefit canvas that explicitly prices recruiter hours, brand impact, and compliance risk.
- **Pilot with guardrails:** Start with a low-risk requisition family; publish privacy notices and human-review checkpoints.
- **Scale & govern:** Implement the new system only after XAI dashboards, bias checks and continual model drift alerts are in place.

7. SUGGESTED HYBRID FRAMEWORK (HUMAN + AI DECISION MODEL) FOR BETTER HIRING

Correlation analysis shows adoption-intention and actual usage are almost perfectly linked (r = 0.97), but privacy concerns still correlate moderately (r = 0.65). A hybrid architecture balances both. A hybrid model for TA has been represented in Figure 1 below.

Figure 1.

Resume → | AI Layer | —Automated parsing, skills inference, bias flags

▼

| Human TA | —Contextual judgment, culture fit, candidate coaching

▼

| Decision | —Final selection panel signs off, audit log captured

Key design rules

- **Explainability first:** Recruiters see model scores plus feature-importance heat map (XAI).
- **Two-way learning:** Panel feedback re-feeds the model (active learning), improving precision each sprint.
- **Candidate-experience gateway:** Any score variance > ±2 σ triggers a mandatory human interview to ensure fairness.

8. FORWARD-LOOKING PERSPECTIVE: WHAT'S NEXT?

- **Generative AI for hyper-personalised outreach** (e.g., ChatGPT-style résumé dialogs) is already reducing sourcing effort by 40 % in pilot studies.
- **Explainable AI (XAI)** toolsets are maturing. It is expected that regulators will mandate auditability for hiring algorithms by 2027.
- **Hybrid decision models** like the one above will evolve into "human-in-command" systems where recruiters choose automation depth per requisition.
- **Multi-modal assessments** (video, coding games, psychometrics) will be fused through foundation models, increasing prediction accuracy but heightening ethical scrutiny.
- **Talent-Data Meshes** will let HR link ATS, LinkedIn, and L&D data in real time, unlocking continuous workforce intelligence rather than episodic hiring campaigns.

9. CONCLUSION

This meta-analysis compiles data from nine empirical studies conducted between 2019 and 2025 to investigate the acceptance and use of Artificial Intelligence (AI) in talent acquisition across various Indian and foreign organisations. The structural models used demonstrated strong explanatory power, with R^2 values ranging from 0.55 to 0.71 for adoption and usage intentions. These results highlight the significant variance accounted for by the studied variables, especially in service-oriented sectors such as IT/ITES, consulting, and banking.

The findings of the study also confirm the core TAM relationships while extending them to contextual variables such as top management support, HR readiness, and data privacy concerns. Data privacy issues were found to be a roadblock in the adoption of AI technologies for talent acquisition, which supports the findings of previous research by Sattu et al. (2024). Furthermore, the path coefficients recovered from the structural models across studies revealed a constant high influence of PU and PEOU on attitudes and behavioural intentions, particularly in the IT/ITES, banking, and consulting industries.

Heterogeneity analysis using Cochran's Q test produced a value of $Q = 9.73$ ($df = 5$, $p = 0.08$), indicating moderate heterogeneity among studies. While not statistically significant at traditional thresholds, this near-threshold value indicates that contextual variables such as a firm's maturity and the type of industry may alter the correlations between constructs. The analysis of the results confirms this argument, demonstrating that organisational context is essential in driving adoption trends. Notably, in the Egyptian start-up sample, the typically strong link between

Perceived Usefulness (PU) and Attitude Towards Use (ATU) was weakened by increased Perceived Risk, demonstrating the influence of perceived uncertainty in early-stage enterprises.

The combination of statistical and conceptual evidence demonstrates that AI adoption in talent acquisition is driven by both technological and social factors. While technology features such as utility and usability are important, organisational culture, leadership support, and ethical considerations all have a significant impact on the process of converting intention to actual use. To fully realise AI's potential in HR, stakeholders must take a balanced, inclusive, and strategically aligned approach that extends beyond technology deployment to organisational transformation

Furthermore, industry differences appeared as an important moderator. The studies that were conducted in service industries (mainly IT/ITES, consulting, and banking) revealed the most significant effects for Cost and Management Support, implying that these characteristics are especially important in knowledge-intensive and fast-moving industries. These findings emphasise the importance of unique implementation strategies that consider industry-specific dynamics and organisational maturity levels.

In this meta-analysis, publication bias appears to be low. All studies are current and geographically diverse, and the lack of reliance on a single major research improves the robustness of the conclusions. Furthermore, including both substantial positive and negative results in the published literature decreases the possibility of selective reporting and strengthens the trustworthiness of the findings.

In conclusion, this meta-analysis confirms the relevance and consistency of important technological adoption constructs across many organisational settings. It also indicates significant variance based on organisational setting and sector. Future studies should investigate these moderating variables further using meta-regression and subgroup analyses to improve the understanding of AI adoption in HR environments. Longitudinal and experimental studies could improve causal inferences and help evidence-based decision-making in talent management.

10. IMPLICATIONS

The incorporation of Artificial Intelligence into talent acquisition signifies a fundamental change in how businesses develop their most important asset: their employees. The transition from early adoption to strategic implementation is challenging; however, the information synthesised in this study gives a clear path ahead.

To prepare the organisation for adopting AI technologies, organisations must invest in technology infrastructure and change management techniques to increase HR readiness and reduce opposition. Perceived ease of use and usefulness are crucial and emphasise the importance of user-centric training programs that explain AI systems. Before making large investments in new technology team's AI literacy should be improved. As the meta-analysis showed, organisational preparedness is a strong predictor of effective adoption. A knowledgeable and confident workforce that understands how to use AI tools, analyse their outputs, and recognise their limitations is the most important prerequisite for realising the technology's full potential. It is imperative to understand that AI should be used as a strong tool to empower the recruitment team rather than an effort to replace it. This notion is essential for successful change management because it reduces anxiety and stimulates adoption by emphasising how technology may improve the strategic capacity of human talent professionals. The moderate associations between privacy concerns and adoption imply clear data governance policies for building confidence and facilitating faster AI integration. Implementing ethical AI can mitigate risks and prove to be a competitive differentiator, enhancing the brand reputation and attracting a much more talented and diverse candidate pool. Service-oriented businesses are the most responsive to AI benefits. Organisations in less tech-intensive industries could establish pilot initiatives to gradually increase AI use in TA.

REFERENCES

Agnihotri, A., Grover, V., Balusamy, B., Gite, S., Arockiam, D., & Shankar, A. (2024, June). Utilizing the potential of AI to revolutionize talent management in contemporary organizations. *IET Conference Proceedings CP881, 2024*(7), 1–11. The Institution of Engineering and Technology. DOI: 10.1049/icp.2024.2519

Agnihotri, A., Pavitra, K. H., Balusamy, B., Maurya, A., & Bibhakar, P. (2023). Artificial intelligence shaping talent intelligence and talent acquisition for smart employee management. *EAI Endorsed Transactions on Internet of Things, 10*. Advance online publication. DOI: 10.4108/eetiot.4642

Altemeyer, B. (2019). Making the business case for AI in HR: Two case studies. *Strategic HR Review, 18*(2), 66–70. DOI: 10.1108/SHR-12-2018-0101

Anderson, N. (2003). Applicant and recruiter reactions to new technology in selection: A critical review and agenda for future research. *International Journal of Selection and Assessment, 11*(2/3), 121–136. DOI: 10.1111/1468-2389.00235

Black, J. S., & van Esch, P. (2020). AI-enabled recruiting: What is it and how should a manager use it? *Business Horizons, 63*(2), 215–226. DOI: 10.1016/j.bushor.2019.12.001

Buckley, P., Minette, K., Joy, D., & Michaels, J. (2004). The use of an automated employment recruiting and screening system for temporary professional employees: A case study. *Human Resource Management, 43*(2/3), 233–241. DOI: 10.1002/hrm.20017

Cappelli, P. (2001). *Making the most of online recruiting*. Harvard Business Review. Retrieved from https://www.hbr.org/2001/03/making-the-most-of-on-line-recruiting

Charlwood, A., & Guenole, N. (2022). Can HR adapt to the paradoxes of artificial intelligence? *Human Resource Management Journal, 32*(4), 729–742. DOI: 10.1111/1748-8583.12433

Chaudhary, V. K., & Verma, D. (2025). The new frontier of data protection: Understanding India's DPDP rules and global compliance. *Panjab University Law Magazine – MagLaw, 4*(1).

Choudhari, Y., Shrestha, P., Singh, G., & Bindra, S. (2025). The Impact of Artificial Intelligence (AI) on Talent Acquisition in Human Resource Management. *Australasian Accounting, Business and Finance Journal, 19*(1).

Danks, D., & London, A. J. (2017, August). Algorithmic bias in autonomous systems. In *IJCAI* (Vol. 17, No. 2017, pp. 4691–4697). DOI: 10.24963/ijcai.2017/654

Davis, F. D. (1989). Perceived usefulness, perceived ease of use, and user acceptance of information technology. *Management Information Systems Quarterly, 13*(3), 319–339. DOI: 10.2307/249008

Depietro, R., Wiarda, E., & Fleischer, M. (1990). The context for change: Organization, technology and environment. In Tornatzky, L., & Fleischer, M. (Eds.), *The processes of technological innovation* (pp. 151–175). Lexington Books.

Dietvorst, B. J., Simmons, J. P., & Massey, C. (2018). Overcoming algorithm aversion: People will use imperfect algorithms if they can (even slightly) modify them. *Management Science, 64*(3), 1155–1170. DOI: 10.1287/mnsc.2016.2643

Dishaw, M. T., & Strong, D. M. (1999). Extending the technology acceptance model with task–technology fit constructs. *Information & Management, 36*(1), 9–21. DOI: 10.1016/S0378-7206(98)00101-3

Eubanks, B. (2018). *Artificial intelligence for HR: Use AI to support and develop a successful workforce* (1st ed.). Kogan Page.

Fatema, S., & Khan, M. M. A. (2024). Artificial intelligence in talent acquisition: Assessing the impact on recruitment processes. [JRITM]. *Journal of Research and Innovation in Technology and Management, 1*(3), 1–5.

Goodhue, D. L., & Thompson, R. L. (1995). Task–technology fit and individual performance. *Management Information Systems Quarterly, 19*(2), 213–236. DOI: 10.2307/249689

Guesalaga, R., Gable, M., & Dawson, J. (2020). Artificial intelligence in recruitment: The impact on candidate experience and organizational trust. *Journal of Business Research, 116*, 32–44. DOI: 10.1016/j.jbusres.2020.05.002

Gupta, P., Fernandes, S.F. and Jain, M. (2018), "Automation in recruitment: a new frontier", Journal of Information Technology Teaching Cases, Vol. 8 No. 2.

Hassan, B. F. Y. (2025). Adoption of AI in Talent Acquisition: A Quantitative Study on HRM Practitioners Using the Technology Acceptance Model (TAM). *The Scientific Journal of Financial and Commercial Studies and Research, 6*(1), 1289–1316.

Hmoud, B., & Laszlo, V. (2019). Will artificial intelligence take over human resources recruitment and selection? *Network Intelligence Studies, 7*(13), 21–30.

Holm, A. B. (2010), "The effect of E-recruitment on the recruitment process: evidence from case studies of three Danish MNCs", *CEUR Workshop Proceedings*, Vol. 570.

Horodyski, P. (2023). Applicants' perception of artificial intelligence in the recruitment process. *Computers in Human Behavior Reports, 11*, 100303. DOI: 10.1016/j.chbr.2023.100303

Islam, M., Rahman, M. M., Taher, M. A., Quaosar, G. A. A., & Uddin, M. A. (2024). Using artificial intelligence for hiring talents in a moderated mechanism. *Future Business Journal, 10*(1), 13. Advance online publication. DOI: 10.1186/s43093-024-00303-x

Jarrahi, M. H., Newlands, G., Lee, M. K., Wolf, C. T., Kinder, E., & Sutherland, W. (2021). Algorithmic management in a work context. *Big Data & Society, 8*(2), 205395172110203. DOI: 10.1177/20539517211020332

Johnson, R. D., Stone, D. L., & Lukaszewski, K. M. (2020). The benefits of eHRM and AI for talent acquisition. *Journal of Tourism Futures, 6*(2), 89–93. DOI: 10.1108/JTF-04-2020-0052

Kantardzic, M. (2011). *Data mining: Concepts, models, methods, and algorithms* (2nd ed.). IEEE Press and John Wiley & Sons. DOI: 10.1002/9781118029145

Khan, S., Faisal, S., & Thomas, G. (2024). Exploring the nexus of artificial intelligence in talent acquisition: Unravelling cost-benefit dynamics, seizing opportunities, and mitigating risks. *Problems and Perspectives in Management, 22*(1), 462–476. DOI: 10.21511/ppm.22(1).2024.37

Lee, C., & Cha, K. (2023). FAT-CAT—Explainability and augmentation for an AI system: A case study on AI recruitment-system adoption. *International Journal of Human-Computer Studies, 171*, 102976. DOI: 10.1016/j.ijhcs.2022.102976

Li, L., Lassiter, T., Oh, J., & Lee, M. K. (2021). Algorithmic hiring in practice: Recruiter and HR professional's perspectives on AI use in hiring. In *Proceedings of the 2021 AAAI/ACM Conference on AI, Ethics, and Society* (pp. 166–176). DOI: 10.1145/3461702.3462531

LinkedIn. (2024). *2024 Global Talent Trends Report*. LinkedIn Corporation. https://www.linkedin.com/business/talent/blog/talent-acquisition/global-talent-trends-2024

Lukose, L. (2025). Data protection in light of the Digital Personal Data Protection Act, 2023.

Mathew, D., Shukla, V. K., Chaubey, A., & Dutta, S. (2021, September). Artificial intelligence: Hope for future or hype by intellectuals? In *2021 9th International Conference on Reliability, Infocom Technologies and Optimization (Trends and Future Directions) (ICRITO)* (pp. 1–6). IEEE. https://doi.org/DOI: 10.1109/ICRITO51393.2021.9596010

Meijerink, J., & Bondarouk, T. (2023). The duality of algorithmic management: Toward a research agenda on HRM algorithms, autonomy and value creation. *Human Resource Management Review*, *33*(1), 100876. DOI: 10.1016/j.hrmr.2021.100876

Min, J., Kim, S., Park, Y., & Sohn, Y. W. (2018). A comparative study of potential job candidates' perceptions of an AI recruiter and a human recruiter. *Journal of the Korea Convergence Society*, *9*(5), 191–202.

Natarajan, D. S., Subbaiah, B., Dhinakaran, D. P., Kumar, J. R., & Rajalakshmi, M. (2024). AI-powered strategies for talent management optimization. *Journal of Informatics Education and Research*, *4*(2). Advance online publication. DOI: 10.5281/zenodo.10537251

Nawaz, N. (2019). How far have we come with the study of artificial intelligence for recruitment process. *International Journal of Scientific & Technology Research*, *8*(7), 488–493.

Nigam, K., Limaye, M., & Simon, L. (2025, March). The impact of artificial intelligence on talent acquisition and performance management. In *International Conference of Economics, Finance and Accounting Studies* (Vol. 14, pp. 193–201).

Ordanini, A., & Silvestri, G. (2008). Recruitment and selection services: Efficiency and competitive reasons in the outsourcing of HR practices. *International Journal of Human Resource Management*, *19*(2), 372–391. DOI: 10.1080/09585190701799960

Ore, O., & Sposato, M. (2022). Opportunities and risks of artificial intelligence in recruitment and selection. *The International Journal of Organizational Analysis*, *30*(6), 1771–1782. DOI: 10.1108/IJOA-07-2020-2291

Pan, Y., Froese, F. J., Liu, N., Hu, Y., & Ye, M. (2021). The adoption of artificial intelligence in employee recruitment: The influence of contextual factors. *International Journal of Human Resource Management*, •••, 1–23. DOI: 10.1080/09585192.2021.2007975

Paramita, D., Okwir, S., & Nuur, C. (2024). Artificial intelligence in talent acquisition: Exploring organisational and operational dimensions. *The International Journal of Organizational Analysis*, *32*(11), 108–131. DOI: 10.1108/IJOA-09-2023-3992

Parker, K., Stroud, D., & McMahan, T. (2019). Candidate experience and the impact of AI in recruitment processes. *Human Resource Management Journal*, *29*(4), 13–27. DOI: 10.1111/1748-8583.12234

Pillai, R., & Sivathanu, B. (2020). Adoption of AI-based chatbots for hospitality and tourism. *International Journal of Contemporary Hospitality Management*, *32*(10), 3199–3226. DOI: 10.1108/IJCHM-04-2020-0259

Rajesh, S., Kandaswamy, M. U., & Rakesh, M. A. (2018). The impact of Artificial Intelligence in Talent Acquisition Lifecycle of organizations: A global perspective. *International Journal of Engineering Development and Research*, *6*(2), 709–717.

Raviprolu, A. (2017). Role of artificial intelligence in recruitment. *IACSIT International Journal of Engineering and Technology*, *5*(4), 94–98.

Ryan, A. M., & Derous, E. (2016). Highlighting tensions in recruitment and selection research and practice. *International Journal of Selection and Assessment*, *24*(1), 54–62. DOI: 10.1111/ijsa.12129

Saks, A. M. (2019). Social media and recruitment: The role of employer branding. *The Journal of Applied Psychology*, *104*(3), 256–273. DOI: 10.1037/apl0000365

Sattu, R., Das, S., & Jena, L. K. (2024). Should I adopt AI during talent acquisition? Evidence from HR professionals of Indian IT organisations. *Journal of Organizational Effectiveness: People and Performance*, *11*(4), 1005–1022. DOI: 10.1108/JOEPP-05-2023-0186

Sengar, S. S. (2023). From pixels to policies: Analysing the provisions and navigating the complexities of the Digital Personal Data Protection Act, 2023. *Available at SSRN*. https://ssrn.com/abstract=4547842 DOI: 10.2139/ssrn.4536795

Shakeel, A., & Siddiqui, D. A. (2021). The effect of Technological, Organizational, Environmental, and Task Technology fit on the Adoption and usage of artificial intelligence (AI) for talent acquisition (TA): Evidence from the Pakistani banking sector. *Organizational, Environmental, and Task Technology fit on the Adoption and usage of artificial intelligence (AI) for talent acquisition (TA): Evidence from the Pakistani banking sector.(October 15, 2021).*

Singh, A., Shukla, T., & Dwivedi, N. (2010). Innovation advancement. In Garg, P., Routray, S., & Gupta, M. (Eds.), *Innovation Advancement* (pp. 377–385). MACMILLAN.

Smith, A. (2021). *8 trends that altered the recruitment industry forever*. https://recruitee.com/articles/recruitment-industry

Sposato, M. (2021). Remote working in the time of COVID-19: Developing a web-based community. *International Journal of Web Based Communities*, *17*(1), 1–8. DOI: 10.1504/IJWBC.2021.112862

Springworks. (2023). *How to use ChatGPT for recruitment in 2023*. NASSCOM Community. https://community.nasscom.in/communities/ai/how-usechatgpt-recruitment-2023

Upadhyay, A. K., & Khandelwal, K. (2018). Applying artificial intelligence: Implications for recruitment. *Strategic HR Review*, *17*(5), 255–258. DOI: 10.1108/SHR-07-2018-0051

Van Esch, P., Black, J. S., & Ferolie, J. (2019). Marketing AI recruitment: The next phase in job application and selection. *Computers in Human Behavior*, *90*, 215–224. DOI: 10.1016/j.chb.2018.09.009

Vedapradha, R., Hariharan, R., & Shivakami, R. (2019). Artificial intelligence: A technological prototype in recruitment. *Journal of Service Science and Management*, *12*(3), 382–390. DOI: 10.4236/jssm.2019.123026

Venkatesh, V., Morris, M. G., Davis, G. B., & Davis, F. D. (2003). User acceptance of information technology: Toward a unified view. *Management Information Systems Quarterly*, *27*(3), 425–478. DOI: 10.2307/30036540

Wright, J., & Atkinson, D. (2019). *The impact of artificial intelligence within the recruitment industry: Defining a new way of recruiting*. Keele Management School, Keele University.

Zagenczyk, T. J., Liao, H., & Gentry, W. A. (2020). AI-powered recruitment: Social media and the future of talent acquisition. *Personnel Psychology*, *73*(1), 33–54. DOI: 10.1111/peps.12336

Chapter 7
Navigating the Future of HR NLP: Challenges and Prospects

Zeeshan Asim
https://orcid.org/0000-0002-2156-5006
University of Buraimi, Oman

Heru Susanto
Universiti Teknologi Brunei, Brunei

Shahla Gahramanova
https://orcid.org/0000-0002-6805-7842
Azerbaijan State University of Economics, Azerbaijan

Asokan Vasudevan
INIT International University, Malaysia

ABSTRACT

The integration of Natural Language Processing (NLP) into Human Resources (HR) presents both challenges and opportunities. This chapter explores how NLP particularly Large Language Models (LLMs) can enhance HR practices, making them more efficient and employee-friendly. It does not advocate replacing traditional HR with AI but highlights how NLP can reduce outdated, impersonal processes. Key challenges include data privacy concerns, as NLP tools require large datasets to function effectively. The chapter analyses current trends and future directions, offering human resource professionals and academics insight into the complexities of adopting NLP in HR. It concludes with cautious optimism about NLP's potential to transform HR beyond operational efficiency improving experiences for both employees and job candidates.

DOI: 10.4018/979-8-3373-2135-6.ch007

1.0 INTRODUCTION

The field of human resources is in flux, It is beginning to experience something we might call the revolution of the appearance of conversational artificial intelligence, or "AI with a voice"(Walther, 2024). "AI with a voice" is mostly about natural language processing (NLP). And NLP is mostly about context, being able to understand "what happened before" or "what is likely to happen next (Otani et al., 2024)." People are good at giving context when they write or talk; the revolution of conversational AI is about doing a better job at understanding the kinds of things people say to each other and, more important, understanding the kinds of things people want machines to understand and respond to (Senger et al., 2024; Shannaq, 2024).

NLP technologies offer a promising route for HR departments to streamline processes and enhance interactions with employees and candidates (Kumar et al., 2023). By automating mundane tasks—such as screening resumes, scheduling interviews, and conducting preliminary assessments, NLP can free HR professionals to pursue strategic initiatives (Fang et al., 2023; Shannaq & Alabri, 2025). And when it comes to communications between organizations and their employees, NLP can help analyze the vast amount of feedback and sentiment that employees generate, which can in turn help organizations better meet the needs of their workforce (Jamuna, 2024). In short, NLP can help make HR departments more effective and, in some cases, more efficient. The applications highlighted in this chapter are the more obvious HR uses for NLP, but they're not the only possible ones (Kang et al., 2020).

Even though NLP holds great promise for HR, bringing it into organizations is not without challenges. Most important among these is the need for data (Leidner & Stevenson, 2024). Good NLP needs a lot of it, and access to employee data raises a host of concerns about privacy and ethics that you can't ignore (Ahmed et al., 2024). If you want to be responsible and effective in implementing NLP in your HR function, you can't sidestep these issues. This chapter will discuss them, along with some practical (yet always imperfect) strategies for addressing them (Leidner & Stevenson, 2024).

As HR practitioners and scholars struggle with the complexities of adopting NLP technologies, it is necessary to have a handle on the current trends and future directions of this integration (Venugopal et al., 2024). This chapter endeavors to do just that. It has three sections: The first delves into the foundational elements of NLP and elucidates the basic principles of its operation. The second section examines the current integration of NLP technologies in a variety of workplace applications and raises some critical questions about the implications of those integrations. The third section takes a cautious look forward to what the widespread adoption of NLP might mean for the future of work.

To sum up, the inclusion of natural language processing into human resources marks the start of a new era in managing the workforce. The integration is not without its challenges—chief among those are concerns about data privacy and ethics. Nevertheless, the NLP applied to HR seems too good an opportunity to pass up. This chapter looks at what it might mean for HR to integrate NLP and at least some of the "revolutionary" potential that seems to accompany the application of this (and other) AI technologies to the field of human resources. Indeed, NLP seems bound to "influence fundamentally the future of employee experience."

2.0 FOUNDATIONAL ELEMENTS OF NLP

A critical building block of any organization is human resources (HR), responsible for the resource most essential to an organization—its people (Manuti & De Palma, 2018). Over the years, computational tools have increasingly revolutionized HR processes, such as hiring, training, and administering, reshaping the labor market and workplace environments. No automated system can operate without humans' guiding hands (Dr. Bijja Vishwanath, Dr. Surendar Vaddepalli, 2023). Despite a long-standing tradition of thinking about it as a different kind of automated system, we're finding that HR itself isn't quite ready for prime time (Zawacki-Richter et al., 2019). Too many accuracy and fairness concerns plague it, opening many ongoing and future research avenues. Combining reinforcement learning with natural language processing might seem an unusual computational partnership for human resources because hires and fires have traditionally been informed by a mix of hard, structured data and soft, unstructured conversation (Permatasari & Maharani, 2021) . But it's a perfect fit for the functions performed by the computational social scientists we describe in this report. Why?

It is crucial to convey to potential candidates the Knowledge, Skills, Abilities, and other characteristics necessary for a job in good online postings. (Mahbub et al., 2022; Yamashita et al., 2023) use an occupational taxonomy and NLP tools to "mine" these KSAOs from job postings. Job postings often contain contradictions and ambiguities that can mislead potential candidates (Nørskov et al., 2022). Kim & Angnakoon, (2016) describe a method to detect these problems before job ads are posted. There are various studies in HR that are likely to be appealing for NLP. These include: Chatbots based on artificial intelligence are transforming how employees communicate within organizations (Pillai et al., 2024). Similarly, Chowdhury et al., (2023) presents concepts related to HR-intelligence (demand and supply, availability/change, readiness and salary statistics) is being automatically mined.

Jain & Khurana, (2017) demonstrate the career transition framework that edges were integrated to extrapolate constituent terms from the overall efficacy. Wu et al., (2024) Customized semantic segmentation techniques have been developed and implemented to meet this challenge in HR documents. Text knowledge extraction is a still formidable task.

Finally, Varelas et al. (2022) describe a method for the automatic classification of free-text Web job vacancies against the standard ISCO taxonomy of occupations that is “helpful for producing macro-statistics about occupations.”

3.0 THE ROLE OF NATURAL LANGUAGE PROCESSING IN MODERNIZING HUMAN RESOURCES

Natural Language Processing (NLP) is transforming Human Resources (HR) through the integration of advanced technologies that automate processes, improve decision-making, and tailor employee experiences (Kanade et al., 2025). In HR, NLP comprises a number of technologies, each with its own distinct ability, converting traditional HR practices into something much more efficient and data driven (Fenwick et al., 2024).

Computers gain insight from data and make intelligent decisions only when they are equipped with machine learning capabilities (Sarker, 2021). And these capabilities are helping to change the common practices in the field of human resources (Devaraju, 2022). In HR, machine learning looks at the historical data trends associated with employee performance, turnover rates, and recruitment outcomes and uses them to try to do a decent job of automating some functions associated with those tasks (Madanchian, 2024). When it does that, it’s not only helping to make the field of HR more efficient. It’s also making the decision-making that happens in HR more precise (Leicht-Deobald et al., 2019). Machines can comprehend and interpret human language with the help of Natural Language Processing (NLP) (Kanade et al., 2025; Rayhan et al., 2023). This technology applied to HR allows for the analysis of not just a few but a multitude of employee surveys, performance evaluations, and email communications to assess satisfaction levels and to detect if any trends are emerging (“AI in HR,” 2024) . Chatbots powered by NLP can now deliver immediate, customized responses and support, which appears to be enhancing communication in many HR departments (Abel Uzoka et al., 2024). In HR, historical data and machine learning are used to predict important things like employee turnover, whom to promote, and workforce planning (Kudirat Bukola Adeusi et al., 2024). These predictions allow HR to be proactive in solving problems and to make strategic, informed decisions. And the more accurate the predictions, the more empowered HR.

4.0 THE ROLE OF NLP IN TRANSFORMING HR PRACTICES

During the candidate evaluation phase, recruiters are responsible for formulating job descriptions, screening and shortlisting candidates, facilitating interviews, and extending employment offers (Soleimani et al., 2025). For job seekers, the process encompasses analysing market trends, acquiring requisite training, crafting resumes, submitting job applications, preparing for interviews, and engaging in offer negotiations (Kanade et al., 2025). These tasks are highly dependent on nuanced domain-specific expertise and are intrinsically linked to language generation activities, such as the creation of job postings and resumes, as well as text-based communication, and specialized dialogues, including interviews. Also, NPL navigating the Post-Hiring Landscape The fundamental functions of human resources are defining roles in the organization, assessing performance, and improving the workplace environment. Altogether, these are called basic HR functions. They are called basic not because they are easy to do but because they are fundamental to the existence of any organization that employs people. If you're going to have an organization that employs people, then, by definition, you must do these things to keep the organization functioning.

Natural Language Processing (NLP) techniques face several significant challenges when being applied to these activities. One is the variety of ways people express themselves and the entities they name, which shows up in the HR data we work with (Khurana et al., 2023). Take resumes, for example. The kinds of resumés we see are as different from each other as the sectors they represent—software development, culinary arts, you name it (Khurana et al., 2023; Otani et al., 2024). Feedback we receive from people about their performance is every bit as different from feedback we receive about someone else's performance. A second challenge is understanding the domain-specific knowledge these resumes, and performance documents are designed to communicate (Lynn et al., 2023). Even when NLP has achieved state-of-the-art accuracy in extracting kinds of information, that information isn't helpful if the NLP systems don't understand the significance of the entities they name or the relationships between them (Sharma et al., 2022). And a third challenge is the biases. NLP systems trained on these data sets will learn the biases contained in the data; they're like a fancy parrot in a cage (Glazko et al., 2024).

4.1 Current Trends in NLP Adoption for HR

Mujtaba & Mahapatra (2020), along with Putka et al., (2023), utilize an occupational taxonomy combined with natural language processing (NLP) methodologies to identify and extract knowledge, skills, abilities, and other attributes (KSAOs) from online job postings. Agarwal (2023) study the factors that determine whether AI is adopted. The study evaluates determinants that illustrates the efficacy of human resource management systems. Finding suggest Organizational preparedness, perceived benefits, and technology readiness influence AI adoption in HRM based on advance NLP algorithm, enhancing HR system effectiveness. Urbano et al (2021) provide a step-by-step approach to identifying contradictions and ambiguities in job ads before they go to press. put forward a method for automatically classifying web-based job postings written in free text. The postings were classified according to the ISCO taxonomy. Indarapu et al. (2023) proposed a model that integrates machine learning with conventional HR practices to boost efficiency and improve decision-making processes. They seek to strike a balance between technological advancement and human oversight within human resource management. Cao et al. (2020) state that competency modeling helps bring machine learning into human resource management (HRM). Vukadin (2021) introduce a system for extracting data from resumes in several languages. Specialized companies like Textkernel BV and Daxtra Ltd. focus their R&D efforts on this area. A three-layered backpropagation (BP) neural network model was introduced by Wei and Jin (2021) to tackle the traditional human resource management (HRM) problems that are intensified by the large-scale data processing. Indrapu et al. (2023) highlighted how machine learning (ML) can be used in talent appraisal to help align individual competencies with organizational objectives. With the adoption of artificial intelligence (AI) increasing, HR professionals are now better equipped than ever to not only optimize processes and enhance productivity but also achieve a much more effective alignment between talent and organizational goals. Li et al. (2021) and Gan and Mori (2023) introduce recent methods for resume extraction. These methods are based on neural transformer architectures. Factors that drive the adoption of artificial intelligence (AI) are examined by Qahtani & Alsmairat (2023), along with the role that trust plays in this context. Their study shows that, within the world of human resource management (HRM), the positive impacts of perceived usefulness and trust on AI adoption are not direct. Instead, trust is a mediating factor in this relationship.

Kadam et al. (2022) suggest a framework meant to help screeners quickly and efficiently shortlist resumes. It does this, they claim, by automatically figuring out which key attributes to extract from the resumes—things like the candidates' abilities, job experience, professional designations, and educational qualifications (Asim, Sorooshain, et al., 2024). And then, using that information, it ostensibly matches candidates to role-specific profiles. Yordanova and Kabakchieva (2022) use K-means clustering on resumes to identify and group candidates who are likely to demonstrate high levels of employee loyalty. Rodgers et al.(2023) put forward a model of algorithmic ethical decision-making tailored for human resource management (HRM). They propose it for use at a selection stage of HRM strategy integration, to help ensure morally good decisions. Zhu and Hudelot (2022) examine resumes to pull out job titles and the relevant skill sets they require, in hopes of divining the pathways along which roles progress. They want to identify the ways in which role titles are being generated, with the overall aim of pinpointing a more effective and refined way of generating titles (Asim, Vasudevan, et al., 2024). Their method for achieving this is to construct graphs out of the extracted data that are structured as sequences of titles. Chowdhury et al. (2023) investigate the resource requirements for the capability of AI in HRM. Their findings point to both technical and non-technical resources as necessary for the successful adoption of AI in HRM.

A Career Coach system is introduced by José-García et al. (2023)to identify gaps in skills by comparing an individual's existing skill set with the requirements of a target career profile. The gaps are identified and quantified as the difference between two sets, and recommendations that are tailored to the individual are given to bridge the gaps with training. This system is designed for use not only with unemployed individuals trying to reintegrate into the workforce but also with employed individuals seeking to advance to a different place in the career hierarchy.

5.0 THE FUSION OF INTELLIGENCE INTO TRADITIONAL HR SYSTEM: EMBEDDING LLM INTO HR

Large Language Models (LLMs) have arrived, and they have brought with them the potential for some truly transformative changes to the domain of human resource management (Sun, 2024). With their uncanny natural-language processing abilities and idiomatic knowledge rendering, they sit poised and, in some cases, already have sat, at various HR management interfaces (Otani et al., 2024a). Integrating LLM into traditional human resources systems means using AI-driven technologies to boost the performance and improve the efficiency of standard HR workflows. This generally takes place in several strategic steps (V. Singh, 2023).

5.1 Evaluation Stage During Talent Acquisition

Integrating LLM into the transformation of HR begins with an all-encompassing assessment of current existing HR practices, the reliability of existing data, and how well current HR systems work together (Devaraju, 2024). From there, the HR team identifies and prioritizes AI opportunities that align with the broader goals of the organization, deciding whether to implement vendor solutions or build their own (Dr. Bijja Vishwanath, Dr. Surendar Vaddepalli, 2023). Top-notch candidates find their way to the right roles because of how well large language models align them with appropriate jobs. Why are LLMs so effective for this task? It all starts with the extensive datasets used to train these models (Raiaan et al., 2024). Resumes and job descriptions are among the abundant textual resources available for crafting LLMs (Gan et al., 2024). From these, the models learn not just to understand the direct content of a resume or a job description but also to grasp the deep nature of them. LLMs can MS (minority statement) quite well: LLMs understand not just what is on a resume or in a job description but also what is understood—that is, the nature of the documents being assessed. And they don't just assess them in a content way; they understand the context, too (R et al., 2024).

5.2 Empowering Growth Through Personalized Development

Large Language Models (LLMs) have sophisticated knowledge inference capabilities for constructing custom learning paths and training materials for workers, they are perfectly suited (Yuan et al., 2024). One might think of the LLMs as incredibly skilled intermediaries who assess the very nature of individual work (Steyvers et al., 2025). They make judgments about work and workers with a level of efficiency which is incredibly impressive at recommending courses and resources that are far more suitable to the individual than to the collective (Burton et al., 2024).

5.3 Seamless Data Integration for Enhanced Decision-Making in HR

When human resource information systems are merged, and data protection is made a priority, data consolidation occurs smoothly (Eigner & Händler, 2024). That's a key step not just for the accurate assembly of that information but for maintaining the trustworthiness of it as well—two prerequisites for solutions that derive from LLM integration (Friha et al., 2024). Win or lose, the essence of competition today revolves around knowledge and if anything, the conduit of knowledge runs mostly through people(Garcia-Gasulla et al., 2025). So, for any firm to have a competitive advantage, it must manage the resources of its human workforce as well as it manages anything else—probably better than it manages anything else. Because human resources are the next best thing to knowledge itself.

5.3 Driving Success Through Strategic Performance Evaluation

Every kind of performance report and evaluation can be very tedious to prepare. Fortunately, large language models can help (Chang et al., 2024). They are powerful AI tools that can produce comprehensive performance reports by analyzing work data, employee feedback, and evaluations (Reddy Yanamala, 2024). Integrating large language models into the domain of employee performance management is groundbreaking. These models can provide organizations with unprecedented insight into their people and the efficiency we were just discussing (Reddy Yanamala, 2024).

Perform conventional management systems suffer from many maladies. They are overly subjective, ungainly in rhythm, and insufficiently mechanism-rich to provide feedback (Subrahmanyam, 2025). Enhancing work experience runs into the same old problems as performance management (Sabbah & Li, 2025). At a basic level, both are trying to serve too many people with too few solutions. They're trying to be one-size-fits-all but they should be much more personalized (Meyer & Elsweiler, 2025). One reason for this is that no two workers are the same and no two work experiences are exactly alike. Also, the performance management system has a personalization problem (E. J. & K. E., 2024). It's not doing well with either high or low performers, and it's definitely not doing well with the low performers when it should be helping. One reason for this failure is the lack of a good recognition and reward system (E. J. & K. E., 2024). But there's also the problem of not having a system for challenging not just high performers but all performers to do better.

5.4 Empowering HR Decision-Making Through Predictive Analytics

Every kind of performance report and evaluation can be very tedious to prepare. Fortunately, large language models can help powerful AI tools that can produce comprehensive performance reports by analysing work data, employee feedback, and evaluations (Mohapatra & Mishra, 2024). Integrating large language models into the domain of employee performance management is groundbreaking (N. Li et al., 2024). These models can provide organizations with unprecedented insights into their people and their efficiencies (N. Li et al., 2024).

Perform conventional management systems suffer from many maladies. They are overly subjective, ungainly in rhythm, and insufficiently mechanism-rich to provide feedback. Enhancing the work experience runs into the same old problems as performance management (Gupta et al., 2025). At a basic level, both are trying to serve too many people with too few solutions. They're trying to be one-size-fits-all. But they should be much more personalized(Dwivedi et al., 2023). One reason for this is that no two workers are the same and no two work experiences are exactly alike. Also, the performance management system has a personalization problem (Vashishth et al., 2025). It's not doing well with either high or low performers, and it's de-finitely not doing well with the low performers when it should be helping. One reason for this failure is the lack of a good recognition and reward system. But there's also the problem of not having a system for challenging not just high performers but all performers to do better (Vashishth et al., 2025).

6.0 OPTIMIZING KNOWLEDGE MANAGEMENT THROUGH ADVANCED DOCUMENT PROCESSING

Enormous amounts of human resources text, like policy handbooks and contractual agreements, are rapidly assimilated and understood by Large Language Models (LLMs) (Galli et al., 2025). They are indeed, at their core, a sort of graph of knowledge. What makes a Knowledge Graph a type of integrity data structure is that it codifies, in some machine-enforceable way, the semantics of the involved entities and the nature of the relations between them (Trajanoska et al., 2023). Indeed, a Knowledge Graph is a sort of set-theoretic representation of some signified semantically in a natural language. The real strength of the Knowledge Graph comes when we accommodate a variety of data types, link them together in reasonable (if not always obvious) manners, and fit them with new knowledge (or semantics) without collapsing (Trajanoska et al., 2023).

7.0 FUTURE AVENUE

Optimizing and fine-tuning natural language processing or large language models (LLMs) for specialized human resource (HR) applications holds extraordinarily great potential for future research. These opportunities could focus on a set of fundamental problem areas that have long concerned the HR function: recruitment, employee training, and performance analytics; among others, it's working too hard and not smart for those who do it. At the very least, this kind of concentrated research would yield a suite of tools that could be used in many niche areas by the HR function. LLMs and their optimizations, far more interestingly, could represent a major computing step forward by the electronic society of tomorrow.

Starting with the establishment of elaborate, all too often lagging frameworks, the bases of AI ethics need to be laid. Not just organizationally, but societally too, work needs to be done and at times, overdue obligations need to be fulfilled. One way to get on with it and do it right is for an organization to appoint an AI ethics committee and give the committee two main tasks: (1) The committee drafts and periodically updates a detailed usage protocol for the LLMs (and optionally other AIs) the organization employs. (2) The committee conducts moral assessments of the LLM-driven solutions the organization is implementing. It is tremendously necessary to keep LLMs under constant supervision and maintenance and in a state of uninterrupted, ongoing betterment. They must be regularly reviewed for their impact; any and all problems that arise must be dealt with swiftly; and not just to placate the complainants—to actually make the system better in every way it can be bettered.

8.0 CONCLUSION

The large language models (LLMs) have huge opportunities and applications in managing human resources, but they are still under research and can be risky. The integration of a new technology invites both a risk and a reward: to the degree that organizations embrace the model's capabilities, understand how something new affects an old business process, and flag possible misuses alongside the funding to use them for good, then the LLMs' potential really becomes something tangible. If all these advantages aren't quite clear yet, a cautionary timetable for rollout can also serve as a good excuse for not buying what the sales team is selling. We also must see that humans have the relevant participation when the LLMs are being used. And the kind of oversight that only humans can provide is essential, even when the LLMs are supposed to be operating under conditions that make them function like humans.

REFERENCE

Adeusi, K. B., Amajuoyi, P., & Benjami, L. B. (2024). Utilizing machine learning to predict employee turnover in high-stress sectors. *International Journal of Management & Entrepreneurship Research, 6*(5), 1702–1732. DOI: 10.51594/ijmer.v6i5.1143

Agarwal, A. (2023). AI adoption by human resource management: A study of its antecedents and impact on HR system effectiveness. *Foresight, 25*(1), 67–81. DOI: 10.1108/FS-10-2021-0199

Ahmed, N., Saha, A. K., Al Noman, M., Jim, J. R., Mridha, M. F., & Kabir, M. M. (2024). Deep learning-based natural language processing in human–agent interaction: Applications, advancements and challenges. *Natural Language Processing Journal, 9*, 100112. DOI: 10.1016/j.nlp.2024.100112

Al Qahtani, E., & Alsmairat, M. (2023). Assisting artificial intelligence adoption drivers in human resources management: A mediation model. *Acta Logistica, 10*(1), 141–150. DOI: 10.22306/al.v10i1.371

Asim, Z., Sorooshain, S., Sami, W., Mahmood, M., Yusof, Y., Sarwat, S., & Vasudevan, A. (2024). Navigating the Educational Frontier and Unveiling the Role of Virtual Reality in Faculty Development: An Emerging Consideration in Global Accreditation. In Naim, A., Saklani, A., Khan, S. A., & Malik, P. K. (Eds.), (pp. 226–240). Advances in Higher Education and Professional Development. IGI Global., DOI: 10.4018/979-8-3693-1698-6.ch015

Asim, Z., Vasudevan, A., Khan, S. A., Mahmood, M., Yosof, Y., & Muniyanayaka, D. (2024). Beyond the Screen: Ethical Dilemmas in the XR Frontier. In Kajla, T., Kansra, P., & Singh, N. (Eds.), (pp. 15–43). Advances in Computational Intelligence and Robotics. IGI Global., DOI: 10.4018/979-8-3693-2432-5.ch002

Burton, J. W., Lopez-Lopez, E., Hechtlinger, S., Rahwan, Z., Aeschbach, S., Bakker, M. A., Becker, J. A., Berditchevskaia, A., Berger, J., Brinkmann, L., Flek, L., Herzog, S. M., Huang, S., Kapoor, S., Narayanan, A., Nussberger, A.-M., Yasseri, T., Nickl, P., Almaatouq, A., & Hertwig, R. (2024). How large language models can reshape collective intelligence. *Nature Human Behaviour, 8*(9), 1643–1655. DOI: 10.1038/s41562-024-01959-9

Cao, X., & Zhang, D. (2020). From Forced to Voluntary AI Adoption. SSRN *Electronic Journal*. DOI: 10.2139/ssrn.3640862

Chang, Y., Wang, X., Wang, J., Wu, Y., Yang, L., Zhu, K., Chen, H., Yi, X., Wang, C., Wang, Y., Ye, W., Zhang, Y., Chang, Y., Yu, P. S., Yang, Q., & Xie, X. (2024). A Survey on Evaluation of Large Language Models. *ACM Transactions on Intelligent Systems and Technology*, *15*(3), 1–45. DOI: 10.1145/3641289

Chowdhury, S., Dey, P., Joel-Edgar, S., Bhattacharya, S., Rodriguez-Espindola, O., Abadie, A., & Truong, L. (2023). Unlocking the value of artificial intelligence in human resource management through AI capability framework. *Human Resource Management Review*, *33*(1), 100899. DOI: 10.1016/j.hrmr.2022.100899

Devaraju, S. (2022). Natural Language Processing (NLP) in AI-Driven Recruitment Systems. *International Journal of Scientific Research in Computer Science, Engineering and Information Technology*, 555–566. DOI: 10.32628/CSEIT2285241

Devaraju, S. (2024). Architecting Scalable LLM-Powered Employee Engagement Systems: A Multi-Modal Framework for Enterprise HRIS Integration and Longitudinal Efficacy Analysis. [TURCOMAT]. *Turkish Journal of Computer and Mathematics Education*, *15*(1), 282–294. DOI: 10.61841/turcomat.v15i1.14941

Dwivedi, Y. K., Kshetri, N., Hughes, L., Slade, E. L., Jeyaraj, A., Kar, A. K., Baabdullah, A. M., Koohang, A., Raghavan, V., Ahuja, M., Albanna, H., Albashrawi, M. A., Al-Busaidi, A. S., Balakrishnan, J., Barlette, Y., Basu, S., Bose, I., Brooks, L., Buhalis, D., & Wright, R. (2023). Opinion Paper: "So what if ChatGPT wrote it?" Multidisciplinary perspectives on opportunities, challenges and implications of generative conversational AI for research, practice and policy. *International Journal of Information Management*, *71*, 102642. DOI: 10.1016/j.ijinfomgt.2023.102642

E. J., C., & K. E., D. (2024). Strategic Role of Artificial Intelligence (AI) on Human Resource Management (HR) Employee Performance Evaluation Function. *International Journal of Entrepreneurship and Business Innovation*, *7*(2), 269–282. DOI: 10.52589/IJEBI-HET5STYK

Eigner, E., & Händler, T. (2024). *Determinants of LLM-assisted Decision-Making* (Version 1). arXiv. DOI: 10.48550/ARXIV.2402.17385

Fang, C., Qin, C., Zhang, Q., Yao, K., Zhang, J., Zhu, H., Zhuang, F., & Xiong, H. (2023). RecruitPro: A Pretrained Language Model with Skill-Aware Prompt Learning for Intelligent Recruitment. *Proceedings of the 29th ACM SIGKDD Conference on Knowledge Discovery and Data Mining*, 3991–4002. DOI: 10.1145/3580305.3599894

Fenwick, A., Molnar, G., & Frangos, P. (2024). The critical role of HRM in AI-driven digital transformation: A paradigm shift to enable firms to move from AI implementation to human-centric adoption. *Discover Artificial Intelligence*, *4*(1), 34. DOI: 10.1007/s44163-024-00125-4

Friha, O., Amine Ferrag, M., Kantarci, B., Cakmak, B., Ozgun, A., & Ghoualmi-Zine, N. (2024). LLM-Based Edge Intelligence: A Comprehensive Survey on Architectures, Applications, Security and Trustworthiness. *IEEE Open Journal of the Communications Society*, *5*, 5799–5856. DOI: 10.1109/OJCOMS.2024.3456549

Galli, C., Gavrilova, A. V., & Calciolari, E. (2025). Large Language Models in Systematic Review Screening: Opportunities, Challenges, and Methodological Considerations. *Information (Basel)*, *16*(5), 378. DOI: 10.3390/info16050378

Gan, C., & Mori, T. (2023). A Few-Shot Approach to Resume Information Extraction via Prompts. In E. Métais, F. Meziane, V. Sugumaran, W. Manning, & S. Reiff-Marganiec (Eds.), *Natural Language Processing and Information Systems* (Vol. 13913, pp. 445–455). Springer Nature Switzerland. DOI: 10.1007/978-3-031-35320-8_32

Gan, C., Zhang, Q., & Mori, T. (2024). Application of LLM Agents in Recruitment: A Novel Framework for Automated Resume Screening. *Journal of Information Processing*, *32*(0), 881–893. DOI: 10.2197/ipsjjip.32.881

Garcia-Gasulla, D., Bayarri-Planas, J., Gururajan, A. K., Lopez-Cuena, E., Tormos, A., Hinjos, D., Bernabeu-Perez, P., Arias-Duart, A., Martin-Torres, P. A., Gonzalez-Mallo, M., Alvarez-Napagao, S., Ayguadé-Parra, E., & Cortés, U. (2025). *The Aloe Family Recipe for Open and Specialized Healthcare LLMs* (Version 2). arXiv. DOI: 10.48550/ARXIV.2505.04388

Glazko, K., Mohammed, Y., Kosa, B., Potluri, V., & Mankoff, J. (2024). Identifying and Improving Disability Bias in GPT-Based Resume Screening. *The 2024 ACM Conference on Fairness, Accountability, and Transparency*, 687–700. DOI: 10.1145/3630106.3658933

Gupta, R., Gupta, A. K., Jain, A., Pandey, A. C., & Gupta, A. (2025). *LLM assisted web application functional requirements generation: A case study of four popular LLMs over a Mess Management System* (Version 1). arXiv. DOI: 10.48550/ARXIV.2505.18019

Indarapu, S. R. K., Vodithala, S., Kumar, N., Kiran, S., Reddy, S. N., & Dorthi, K. (2023). Exploring human resource management intelligence practices using machine learning models. *The Journal of High Technology Management Research*, *34*(2), 100466. DOI: 10.1016/j.hitech.2023.100466

Jain, S., & Khurana, N. (2017). Enhancing employee engagement through training and development. *Asian Journal of Management*, *8*(1), 1. DOI: 10.5958/2321-5763.2017.00001.4

Jamuna, K. M. (2024). Leveraging Natural Language Processing to Analyze Employee Feedback for Enhanced HR Insights. *INTERANTIONAL JOURNAL OF SCIENTIFIC RESEARCH IN ENGINEERING AND MANAGEMENT*, *08*(11), 1–7. DOI: 10.55041/IJSREM39115

José-García, A., Sneyd, A., Melro, A., Ollagnier, A., Tarling, G., Zhang, H., Stevenson, M., Everson, R., & Arthur, R. (2023). C3-IoC: A Career Guidance System for Assessing Student Skills using Machine Learning and Network Visualisation. *International Journal of Artificial Intelligence in Education*, *33*(4), 1092–1119. DOI: 10.1007/s40593-022-00317-y

Kadam, R., Suhas, G., Mukri, U., & Khandare, S. (2022). NLP-Based Resume Screening and Job Recruitment Portal. In Jacob, I. J., Kolandapalayam Shanmugam, S., & Bestak, R. (Eds.), *Data Intelligence and Cognitive Informatics* (pp. 1–21). Springer Nature Singapore., DOI: 10.1007/978-981-16-6460-1_1

Kanade, T. M., Batule, R. B., & Joseph, J. (2025). The Evolution of HR: From Traditional to AI-Enhanced. In Harriott, S. A. (Ed.), *Innovative Approaches to Managing Conflict and Change in Diverse Work Environments* (pp. 49–78). IGI Global., DOI: 10.4018/979-8-3693-9556-1.ch003

Kang, Y., Cai, Z., Tan, C.-W., Huang, Q., & Liu, H. (2020). Natural language processing (NLP) in management research: A literature review. *Journal of Management Analytics*, *7*(2), 139–172. DOI: 10.1080/23270012.2020.1756939

Khurana, D., Koli, A., Khatter, K., & Singh, S. (2023). Natural language processing: State of the art, current trends and challenges. *Multimedia Tools and Applications*, *82*(3), 3713–3744. DOI: 10.1007/s11042-022-13428-4

Kim, J., & Angnakoon, P. (2016). Research using job advertisements: A methodological assessment. *Library & Information Science Research*, *38*(4), 327–335. DOI: 10.1016/j.lisr.2016.11.006

Kumar, D., Grosz, T., Rekabsaz, N., Greif, E., & Schedl, M. (2023). Fairness of recommender systems in the recruitment domain: An analysis from technical and legal perspectives. *Frontiers in Big Data*, *6*, 1245198. DOI: 10.3389/fdata.2023.1245198

Leicht-Deobald, U., Busch, T., Schank, C., Weibel, A., Schafheitle, S., Wildhaber, I., & Kasper, G. (2019). The Challenges of Algorithm-Based HR Decision-Making for Personal Integrity. *Journal of Business Ethics*, *160*(2), 377–392. DOI: 10.1007/s10551-019-04204-w

Leidner, J. L., & Stevenson, M. (2024). *Challenges and Opportunities of NLP for HR Applications: A Discussion Paper* (Version 1). arXiv. DOI: 10.48550/ARXIV.2405.07766

Li, N., Zhou, H., & Xu, M. (2024). *From Text to Insight: Leveraging Large Language Models for Performance Evaluation in Management* (Version 1). arXiv. DOI: 10.2139/ssrn.4912642

Li, X., Shu, H., Zhai, Y., & Lin, Z. (2021). A Method for Resume Information Extraction Using BERT-BiLSTM-CRF. *2021 IEEE 21st International Conference on Communication Technology (ICCT)*, 1437–1442. DOI: 10.1109/ICCT52962.2021.9657937

Lynn, T., Rosati, P., Conway, E., & Van Der Werff, L. (Eds.). (2023). *The Future of Work: Challenges and Prospects for Organisations, Jobs and Workers*. Springer International Publishing., DOI: 10.1007/978-3-031-31494-0

Madanchian, M. (2024). From Recruitment to Retention: AI Tools for Human Resource Decision-Making. *Applied Sciences (Basel, Switzerland)*, *14*(24), 11750. DOI: 10.3390/app142411750

Mahbub, S., Pardede, E., & Kayes, A. S. M. (2022). Online Recruitment Fraud Detection: A Study on Contextual Features in Australian Job Industries. *IEEE Access : Practical Innovations, Open Solutions*, *10*, 82776–82787. DOI: 10.1109/ACCESS.2022.3197225

Manuti, A., & De Palma, P. D. (2018). The People-Based Approach in Human Resource Management. In A. Manuti & P. D. De Palma, *Digital HR* (pp. 1–20). Springer International Publishing. DOI: 10.1007/978-3-319-60210-3_1

Meyer, S., & Elsweiler, D. (2025). LLM-based conversational agents for behaviour change support: A randomised controlled trial examining efficacy, safety, and the role of user behaviour. *International Journal of Human-Computer Studies*, *200*, 103514. DOI: 10.1016/j.ijhcs.2025.103514

Mohapatra, H., & Mishra, S. R. (2024). Unlocking Insights: Exploring Data Analytics and AI Tool Performance Across Industries. In Singh, P., Mishra, A. R., & Garg, P. (Eds.), *Data Analytics and Machine Learning* (Vol. 145, pp. 265–288). Springer Nature Singapore., DOI: 10.1007/978-981-97-0448-4_13

Mujtaba, D. F., & Mahapatra, N. R. (2020). Mining and Analyzing Occupational Characteristics from Job Postings. *2020 International Conference on Computational Science and Computational Intelligence (CSCI)*, 683–685. DOI: 10.1109/CSCI51800.2020.00124

Nørskov, S., Damholdt, M. F., Ulhøi, J. P., Jensen, M. B., Mathiasen, M. K., Ess, C. M., & Seibt, J. (2022). Employers' and applicants' fairness perceptions in job interviews: Using a teleoperated robot as a fair proxy. *Technological Forecasting and Social Change*, *179*, 121641. DOI: 10.1016/j.techfore.2022.121641

Otani, N., Bhutani, N., & Hruschka, E. (2024). *Natural Language Processing for Human Resources: A Survey* (No. arXiv:2410.16498). arXiv. https://doi.org//arXiv .2410.16498DOI: 10.48550

Permatasari, D. A., & Maharani, D. A. (2021). Combination of Natural Language Understanding and Reinforcement Learning for Booking Bot. *Journal of Electrical, Electronic, Information, and Communication Technology*, *3*(1), 12. DOI: 10.20961/jeeict.3.1.49818

Pillai, R., Ghanghorkar, Y., Sivathanu, B., Algharabat, R., & Rana, N. P. (2024). Adoption of artificial intelligence (AI) based employee experience (EEX) chatbots. *Information Technology & People*, *37*(1), 449–478. DOI: 10.1108/ITP-04-2022-0287

Putka, D. J., Oswald, F. L., Landers, R. N., Beatty, A. S., McCloy, R. A., & Yu, M. C. (2023). Evaluating a Natural Language Processing Approach to Estimating KSA and Interest Job Analysis Ratings. *Journal of Business and Psychology*, *38*(2), 385–410. DOI: 10.1007/s10869-022-09824-0

Raiaan, M. A. K., Mukta, M., Fatema, K., Fahad, N. M., Sakib, S., Mim, M. M. J., Ahmad, J., Ali, M. E., & Azam, S. (2024). A Review on Large Language Models: Architectures, Applications, Taxonomies, Open Issues and Challenges. *IEEE Access : Practical Innovations, Open Solutions*, *12*, 26839–26874. DOI: 10.1109/ACCESS.2024.3365742

Rayhan, A., Kinzler, R., & Rayhan, R. (2023). *NATURAL LANGUAGE PROCESSING: TRANSFORMING HOW MACHINES UNDERSTAND HUMAN LANGUAGE*. DOI: 10.13140/RG.2.2.34900.99200

Reddy Yanamala, K. K. (2024). Integrating Machine Learning and Human Feedback for Employee Performance Evaluation. *Journal of Advanced Computing Systems*, *2*(1), 1–10. DOI: 10.69987/JACS.2022.20101

Rodgers, W., Murray, J. M., Stefanidis, A., Degbey, W. Y., & Tarba, S. Y. (2023). An artificial intelligence algorithmic approach to ethical decision-making in human resource management processes. *Human Resource Management Review*, *33*(1), 100925. DOI: 10.1016/j.hrmr.2022.100925

Sabbah, J., & Li, F. (2025). When humans and large language models collaborate, problem-finding illuminates. *Innovation (North Sydney, N.S.W.)*, •••, 1–34. DOI: 10.1080/14479338.2025.2504428

Sarker, I. H. (2021). Machine Learning: Algorithms, Real-World Applications and Research Directions. *SN Computer Science*, *2*(3), 160. DOI: 10.1007/s42979-021-00592-x

Senger, E., Zhang, M., van der Goot, R., & Plank, B. (2024). *Deep Learning-based Computational Job Market Analysis: A Survey on Skill Extraction and Classification from Job Postings* (No. arXiv:2402.05617). arXiv. https://doi.org//arXiv.2402.05617DOI: 10.48550

Shannaq, B. (2024). The Role of AI in University Course Registration in the Middle East: AI and Machine Learning Approaches to Improve Academic Performance. *2024 2nd International Conference on Computing and Data Analytics (ICCDA)*, 1–6. DOI: 10.1109/ICCDA64887.2024.10867316

Shannaq, B., & Alabri, A. (2025). EVALUATING THE IMPACT OF CHATGPT IMPLEMENTATION ON HR PERFORMANCE SKILLS: A CASE STUDY OF ACADEMIC INSTITUTIONS IN OMAN. *Bangladesh Journal of Multidisciplinary Scientific Research*, *10*(1), 11–21. DOI: 10.46281/bjmsr.v10i1.2281

Sharma, R., Agarwal, P., & Arya, A. (2022). Natural Language Processing and Big Data: A Strapping Combination. In Sharma, R., & Sharma, D. (Eds.), *New Trends and Applications in Internet of Things (IoT) and Big Data Analytics* (Vol. 221, pp. 255–271). Springer International Publishing., DOI: 10.1007/978-3-030-99329-0_16

Singh, V. (2023). Exploring the role of large language model (LLM)-based chatbots for human resources [The University of Texas at Austin; Application/pdf]. DOI: 10.26153/TSW/51146

Soleimani, M., Intezari, A., Arrowsmith, J., Pauleen, D. J., & Taskin, N. (2025). Reducing AI bias in recruitment and selection: An integrative grounded approach. *International Journal of Human Resource Management*, •••, 1–36. DOI: 10.1080/09585192.2025.2480617

Steyvers, M., Tejeda, H., Kumar, A., Belem, C., Karny, S., Hu, X., Mayer, L. W., & Smyth, P. (2025). What large language models know and what people think they know. *Nature Machine Intelligence*, *7*(2), 221–231. DOI: 10.1038/s42256-024-00976-7

Subrahmanyam, S. (2025). The Integration of Artificial Intelligence and Machine Learning in Performance Evaluation. In Marcão, R., & Santos, V. (Eds.), (pp. 603–626). Advances in Human Resources Management and Organizational Development. IGI Global., DOI: 10.4018/979-8-3373-0149-5.ch028

Sun, J. (2024). Research on the Application of Large Language Models in Human Resource Management Practices. *International Journal of Emerging Technologies and Advanced Applications*, *1*(8), 1–8. DOI: 10.62677/IJETAA.2408125

Trajanoska, M., Stojanov, R., & Trajanov, D. (2023). *Enhancing Knowledge Graph Construction Using Large Language Models* (Version 1). arXiv. DOI: 10.48550/ARXIV.2305.04676

Urbano, J., Couto, M., Rocha, G., & Lopes Cardoso, H. (2021). Inconsistency Detection in Job Postings [Application/pdf]. *OASIcs, Volume 93, LDK 2021, 93*, 25:1-25:16. DOI: 10.4230/OASICS.LDK.2021.25

Uzoka, A., Cadet, E., & Ojukwu, P. U. (2024). Leveraging AI-Powered chatbots to enhance customer service efficiency and future opportunities in automated support. *Computer Science & IT Research Journal*, *5*(10), 2485–2510. DOI: 10.51594/csitrj.v5i10.1676

Vashishth, T. K., Sharma, V., Tomer, T., Kumar, A., Kaushik, S., & Singh, B. (2025). AI in HRM: Transforming Employee Engagement and Satisfaction Amidst Challenges and Opportunities. In Ara, A. (Ed.), (pp. 157–188). Advances in Human Resources Management and Organizational Development. IGI Global., DOI: 10.4018/979-8-3693-7693-5.ch006

Venugopal, M., Madhavan, V., Prasad, R., & Raman, R. (2024). Transformative AI in human resource management: Enhancing workforce planning with topic modeling. *Cogent Business & Management*, *11*(1), 2432550. DOI: 10.1080/23311975.2024.2432550

Vishwanath, B., & Vaddepalli, S. (2023). The future of work: Implications of artificial intelligence on hr practices. Tuijin Jishu/Journal of Propulsion Technology, 44(3), 1711-1724.

Walther, C. C. (2024). *Human Leadership for Humane Technology: The New AI: Agency Ignited* (1st ed. 2024). Springer Nature Switzerland., DOI: 10.1007/978-3-031-67823-3

Wei, G., & Jin, Y. (2021). Human resource management model based on three-layer BP neural network and machine learning. *Journal of Intelligent & Fuzzy Systems*, *40*(2), 2289–2300. DOI: 10.3233/JIFS-189226

Wu, L., Qiu, Z., Zheng, Z., Zhu, H., & Chen, E. (2024). Exploring Large Language Model for Graph Data Understanding in Online Job Recommendations. *Proceedings of the AAAI Conference on Artificial Intelligence*, *38*(8), 9178–9186. DOI: 10.1609/aaai.v38i8.28769

Yamashita, M., Shen, J. T., Tran, T., Ekhtiari, H., & Lee, D. (2023). JAMES: Normalizing Job Titles with Multi-Aspect Graph Embeddings and Reasoning. *2023 IEEE 10th International Conference on Data Science and Advanced Analytics (DSAA)*, 1–10. DOI: 10.1109/DSAA60987.2023.10302559

Yordanova, S., & Kabakchieva, D. (2022). *Employee turnover reduction by analyzing textual data with SPARK*. 040019. DOI: 10.1063/5.0099629

Yuan, M., Bao, P., Yuan, J., Shen, Y., Chen, Z., Xie, Y., Zhao, J., Li, Q., Chen, Y., Zhang, L., Shen, L., & Dong, B. (2024). Large language models illuminate a progressive pathway to artificial intelligent healthcare assistant. *Medicine Plus*, *1*(2), 100030. DOI: 10.1016/j.medp.2024.100030

Zawacki-Richter, O., Marín, V. I., Bond, M., & Gouverneur, F. (2019). Systematic review of research on artificial intelligence applications in higher education – where are the educators? *International Journal of Educational Technology in Higher Education*, *16*(1), 39. DOI: 10.1186/s41239-019-0171-0

Zhu, J., & Hudelot, C. (2022). *Towards Job-Transition-Tag Graph for a Better Job Title Representation Learning* (Version 1). arXiv. DOI: 10.18653/v1/2022.findings-naacl.164

Chapter 8
Harnessing Sentimental Analysis for Enhancing Employee Well Being: A Comprehensive Review

Sara Kamal
https://orcid.org/0000-0002-4155-0012
Aligarh Muslim University, India

Farah Zahidi
https://orcid.org/0000-0003-0786-8024
Emirates Academy of Hospitality Management, UAE

Shahina Barayil Thayipurath
https://orcid.org/0000-0002-3114-1207
University of West London RAK, UAE

ABSTRACT

The importance of employee well-being in fostering innovation, customer satisfaction, and profitability is becoming more widely acknowledged. This review article emphasizes how sentiment analysis, which was once primarily used for consumer insights, is now being used to track employees' emotional well-being and enable early intervention against burnout, stress, and disengagement. Sentiment analysis has been used by numerous businesses to improve retention and workplace policies. However, there are many obstacles because of ethical worries about algorithmic bias, privacy, and trust. Informed consent, data anonymization, staff involvement, and human oversight are necessary for successful implementation.To evaluate its long-term effects on workplace culture, longitudinal research is required. It can be

DOI: 10.4018/979-8-3373-2135-6.ch008

concluded that while sentiment analysis presents a transformative opportunity for data-driven HR management, its success hinges on ethical stewardship, fostering a workplace where employees feel heard, respected, and supported.

INTRODUCTION

The rise of hybrid and remote work has put employee well-being front and center for organizations. Employing sustainable and inclusive workplace strategies that prioritize physical and mental health significantly enhances employee engagement, productivity, and satisfaction, according to research. Holistic well-being policies, such as mental health support, flexible working, and inclusive workplaces, are increasing in significance for personal and professional growth. The practice of the above benefits employees and supports organizational sustainability, which assists in global SDGs, specifically SDG 3 of health and well-being. Abid et al. (2020), Singh et al. (2019), Madero-Gómez et al. (2023), and other studies emphasize the significant role of sustainable human resource management (HRM) practices in fostering employees' well-being as well as minimizing environmental footprints, a win-win situation for both employees and organizations.

Madero-Gómez et al. (2023) looked at the function of sustainable workplace practices and how they improve environmental results as well as employee well-being. According to their analysis, these approaches enhance the company's overall viability and assist reduce pollution. Crucially, sustainable human resource management (HRM) techniques can benefit the business monetarily while also reducing detrimental effects on worker well-being. In order to assist the attainment of the Sustainable Development Goals (SDGs), the study emphasized the necessity for organizations to create and implement HRM strategies that incorporate sustainability.

Similar to this, Singh et al. (2019) investigated the connection between workplace well-being and self-efficacy, paying special attention to how sustainable practices might mitigate this association. The study showed that self-efficacy had a beneficial impact on workplace well-being, with CEOs who practiced sustainability at a high level reporting higher levels of well-being. This research implies that workplace sustainability programs can greatly enhance workers' well-being by boosting their self-confidence in their capacity to handle obstacles. The survey also underlined the need of looking at sustainability practices from an HR standpoint, emphasizing how companies may improve worker productivity and well-being by carefully incorporating sustainable practices

Putting money into well-being initiatives like providing flexible work schedules and encouraging mental health has been shown to improve company culture and support sustained commercial success. The significance of these practices is further highlighted by the post-pandemic workplace. Setting sustainability and employee well-being as top priorities can provide businesses a competitive edge as they strive to meet new challenges. Businesses that put these policies into place are better positioned for expansion, innovation, and market flexibility, demonstrating how important employee well-being is to long-term company success.

Many businesses throughout the world have realized how important it is to support work-life balance by implementing measures like longer parental leave, remote work choices, flexible work schedules, and specialized mental health programs.

These programs not only assist businesses in keeping top personnel, but they also draw in highly qualified workers who are looking for firms that appreciate and understand holistic well-being. Businesses must match their beliefs with the welfare of their workers in order to thrive in the cutthroat business world of today. This will increase employee happiness and retention over the long run.

Employee well-being is a primary driver of organizational success, with evidence consistently linking it to productivity, innovation, and staff retention. Employee well-being has emerged as a key component of organizational success, impacting productivity, staff retention, and general organizational performance (Grawitch and Ballard, 2016). It has been observed through studies that workers who possess good physical, mental, and emotional well-being are far more likely to deliver optimum workplace performance than those who don't. On the other hand, poor mental health among employees results in significant productivity losses – a projected 12 billion workdays are lost every year because of depression and anxiety, at a cost to the global economy of approximately $1 trillion yearly (WHO,2022). Organizations that prioritize employee well-being deliver 31% higher productivity and 37% higher sales growth compared to industry competitors (Goh et al., 2015). The shift to distant and hybrid work patterns post-pandemic further increased the need for forward-looking well-being approaches, considering that workers have delinked work and life and increasing solitude (Kniffin et al., 2021). Such statistics explain why employers across the globe are placing more emphasis on mental health and wellness programs. The best executives understand that a happy and healthy employee base translates to improved customer service, innovation, and bottom-line results (Krekel *et. al.,* 2019). In fact, a recent McKinsey & Company report estimated that improving global employee well-being could unlock as much as $11.7 trillion in economic value through productivity gains and reduced turnover (McKinsey Health Institute,2022).

Despite heightened investment in wellness programs, most companies still struggle to quantify and maintain employees' mental well-being. Older methods like annual surveys or ad hoc check-ins don't always capture in-the-moment emotional changes or the earliest warning signs of issues like burnout. Most employees are also not willing to discuss stress or dissatisfaction openly for fear of stigma or job loss, so HR departments struggle to get a good read on the morale situation. As a result, things don't get flagged until they've escalated into burnout, disengagement, or turnover. This shortfall has driven interest in newer, data-driven tools that can monitor and measure employee sentiment less intrusively on an ongoing basis (Dimoff *et al.,* 2016). Typical well-being measurement tools, i.e., annual engagement surveys, are beset with significant limitations. They are intermittent, vulnerable to recall bias, and fail to measure true-time emotional changes (Schaufeli *et al.,* 2002). For instance, a meta-analysis studies on employees suppress stress in surveys because they worry about retaliation by their managers and due to fear of stigma and negative consequences (Hennekam et al., 2020). Also, there remains stigma around mental health across the globe; 60% of employees in a 2023 OECD survey admitted they would not inform their employer of mental health problems (OECD, 2023).

Sentiment analysis – a technique from natural language processing (NLP) that automatically measures the emotional tone of text-based communication – is emerging as a handy tool in this context. By analyzing the language used by employees in communications, sentiment analysis can infer attitudes and emotions at scale. The overall idea is to "take the emotional pulse" of the workforce through linguistic residue that employees leave behind in emails, chat messages, survey responses, and other text (Rink *et al.,* 2024). For example, if many employees are expressing frustration or negativity in internal surveys or enterprise chat forums, this may be an indicator of underlying issues that need to be resolved. On the other hand, more positive language may be an indicator of improving morale or successful well-being initiatives.

Early adopters are finding that sentiment analysis also can serve as an "early warning system" for employee mental health. It enables organizations to flag problems and intervene early, rather than react when problems become more severe. As one HR technology expert noted, even general employee engagement surveys can be scoured for sentiment to reveal what's on employees' minds and to "flag potential issues or spot opportunities" for intervention. Practically, this might mean identifying a team under pressure by red-flagged negative survey sentiment, and offering them additional support or resources before burnout spreads (Alruily, 2023). In one example, a big corporation used AI-powered sentiment tracking to catch that an upcoming policy change was going down badly with older employees in one area, and leaders were able to communicate the policy and offer targeted support. These kinds of findings hint at the potential for integrating AI enabled sentiment analysis into employee well-being programs (Mansoor and Ansari, 2024).

However, the application of sentiment analysis in the work place also raises important challenges. Continuous monitoring of employees' communication borders on surveillance, with attendant ethical and privacy concerns (Moore and Piwek, 2017). Misinterpretation is also possible – language algorithms can misinterpret sarcasm or cultural slang, leading to erroneous signals. If not managed carefully, such tools can erode trust or even add to stress (Ball, 2010), the very issues they are intended to alleviate. It is thus necessary to move forward with care, balancing the possibility of this technology for positive change with the need to safeguard privacy and maintain employee trust.

This chapter examines the extent to which sentiment analysis—a computer program that assesses emotional tone in language—can span these divides. With sentiment analysis of unstructured content in email, collaboration platforms (like Slack and Microsoft Teams), and employee feedback mechanisms, organizations can catch early signals of burnout, disengagement, and dissatisfaction (Berger et al., 2022). This review brings together empirical findings, case studies, and ethical discussion to provide a guide for the ethical application of sentiment analysis to workplace well-being initiatives. This chapter provides a comprehensive review of how sentiment analysis can be leveraged to enhance employee well-being. This chapter synthesizes literature on sentiment analysis in HR, reviews techniques and tools used, and highlights real-world applications that demonstrate its effect on worker well-being. It also identifies key challenges such as data privacy and trust, and offers directions for further, more ethical and holistic use of sentiment analysis to promote workforce mental health.

LITERATURE REVIEW

Sentiment Analysis or Opinion Mining, is computational opinion, emotion, and attitude analysis expressed in text information (Liu, 2012). With user-generated content exploding on the internet, sentiment analysis has played a key role as a tool in business intelligence, social media tracking, and political studies (Pang & Lee, 2008). The following literature review presents the evolution of sentiment analysis, classification techniques, approaches, applications, challenges, and emerging trends.

Evolution of Sentiment Analysis

The underpinning of sentiment analysis has its origin in Natural Language Processing (NLP) research focused on subjectivity and opinion detection (Wiebe, 2000). Pang et al. (2002) achieved a milestone with the application of machine learning for sentiment classification with the employment of Naïve Bayes, Support Vector Machines (SVM), and Maximum Entropy algorithms for movie review classification as positive or negative opinions. Turney (2002) introduced a lexicon-based unsupervised approach, researching word polarity for sentiment classification of product reviews.

Sentence-level sentiment analysis was explored next, separating subjective and objective sentences (Wilson et al., 2005). Aspect-based sentiment analysis followed, where sentiments for some aspects of a document were examined (Hu & Liu, 2004). The revolution of deep learning in the 2010s significantly augmented sentiment analysis through word embeddings (Mikolov et al., 2013), Recurrent Neural Networks (RNNs) (Tang et al., 2015), and Transformer-based models like BERT (Devlin et al., 2018).

Sentiment analysis is typically described as being of three levels. Document-level sentiment analysis places a document's sentiment into categories, providing an overall feel of the opinions contained within it (Turney, 2002). Sentence-level sentiment analysis examines individual sentences to identify sentiment and differentiate between objective and subjective statements (Wilson et al., 2005). Finally, aspect-level sentiment analysis becomes more detailed by extracting opinions about specific properties in a document, allowing it to be more detailed in understanding the sentiment distribution and its direction (Liu, 2012).

There are various approaches employed to assess and classify sentiments in text-based information. One of the most commonly used techniques is lexicon-based sentiment analysis, in which pre-determined sentiment lexicons, such as Senti Word Net (Esuli & Sebastiani, 2006), are utilized to identify the polarity scores of words by their direction of emotions. The other frequently used technique is machine learning-based sentiment analysis, in which supervised machine learning algorithms such as Support Vector Machines (SVM) and Naïve Bayes classify text based on labeled datasets (Pang et al., 2002). With the development of artificial intelligence, deep learning-based sentiment analysis has gained popularity using neural networks such as Convolutional Neural Networks (CNNs), Long Short-Term Memory (LSTMs), and Transformer models such as BERT (Devlin et al., 2018) to improve contextual understanding and classification accuracy. Hybrid approaches also use lexicon-based and machine learning approaches, leveraging each approach's strength to provide more accurate sentiment identification (Araque et al., 2017). These diverse approaches enable sentiment analysis to be customized for various fields and issues, and this enhances the ability to analyze emotions in text content effectively.

Sentiment analysis is used extensively across various fields, providing valuable insights into human sentiments and opinions. Organizations utilize sentiment analysis in business intelligence to examine customer opinions and make informed decisions regarding product improvement (Liu, 2012). Political analysis also gains from this method, as it aids in determining public opinion regarding election candidates and policies, thereby facilitating improved understanding of voter patterns (Tumasjan et al., 2010). Sentiment analysis has a significant function in healthcare by extracting patient comments, which allows medical practitioners to improve medical services based on user experience (Greaves et al., 2013). Social media monitoring also uses sentiment analysis to track trends, detect misinformation, and measure public opinion about various topics (Pak & Paroubek, 2010). Sentiment analysis through these tools continues to inform decision-making across industries.

Sentiment Analysis has emerged as a powerful tool in terms of human emotion and opinion. Conventional machine learning approaches contributed significantly to this, and deep learning and Transfer Learning continue to shape future sentiment analysis studies.

Table 1. Recent studies on Employee well being

AUTHOR	VARIABLES STUDIED	YEAR	COUNTRY	METHODOLOGY	RESULTS	
Johnson and Nguyen et al.	Technology-driven changes at work, workplace mental health and employee well-being	2020	Australia	Qualitative study	Technology-enabled flexible work schedules can enhance employee well-being by lowering stress and promoting a better work-life balance.	A review and agenda for examining how technology-driven changes at work will impact workplace mental health and employee well-being
Sarwar, Ishaq, Amin & Ahmed	Ethical leadership, work engagement, employees' well-being, and performance	2020	Italy and Pakistan	Quantitative study	The significance of ethical leadership practices is further supported by the favorable effects that ethical leadership has on corporate performance, employee engagement, and well-being in a variety of cultural situations.	Ethical leadership, work engagement, employees' well-being, and performance: a cross-cultural comparison
Kern1, Heissler and Zapfl	Social challenge stressors and employee well-being	2020	Germany	Quantitative study	In addition to causing stress, social challenge stressors like mediation or enforcing choices also present chances for constructive self-evaluation, adding a nuanced perspective on social stressors to the challenge-hindrance stressor framework.	Social Job Stressors can Foster Employee Well-Being: Introducing the Concept of Social Challenge Stressors
Kundi, Aboramadan, Elhamalawi and Shahid	Employee psychological well-being and job performance	2020	Pakistan	Qualitative study	The relationship between hedonic and eudaimonic psychological well-being and worker job performance is mediated by affective commitment.	Employee psychological well-being and job performance: exploring mediating and moderating mechanisms

continued on following page

Table 1. Continued

AUTHOR	VARIABLES STUDIED	YEAR	COUNTRY	METHODOLOGY	RESULTS	
Pipera and Fragouli	Employee wellbeing, employee performance & positive mindset	2021	UK	Qualitative study	In order to improve organizational citizenship behavior, which is essential for efficiency, emotional commitment, job satisfaction, and productivity, corporate leaders must prioritize workplace positivity and employee well-being during emergencies.	Employee wellbeing, employee performance & positive mindset in a crisis
Salas-Vallina, Alegre and López-Cabrales	Well-being-oriented human resource management (WBHRM) and performance	2021	Spain	Quantitative study	Engaging leadership conduct directly affects employee performance and promotes the true application of WBHRM.	The challenge of increasing employees' well-being and performance: How human resource management practices and engaging leadership work together toward reaching this goal
Garcia, and Bonavia	Empowerment and Employee Well-Being	2021	European Union Nations	Quantitative study	Job satisfaction, work engagement, and social well-being were all favorably correlated with psychological empowerment, which in turn was positively correlated with structural empowerment.	Empowerment and Employee Well-Being: A Mediation Analysis Study
Kun and Gadanecz1	Workplace happiness, well-being and psychological capital:	2022	Hungary	Quantitative study	Happiness and well-being at work were associated with internal psychological resources, including optimism and hope.	Workplace happiness, well-being and their relationship with psychological capital: A study of Hungarian Teachers
Kaltiainen and Hakanen	Empowerment, leadership, organizational behavior, well-being,	2022	Finland	Quantitative study	Increases in job engagement and decreases in burnout were linked to higher perceptions of servant leadership.	Fostering task and adaptive performance through employee well-being: The role of servant leadership

continued on following page

Table 1. Continued

AUTHOR	VARIABLES STUDIED	YEAR	COUNTRY	METHODOLOGY	RESULTS	
Lundqvist, Reineholm, Ståhl and Wallo	Supportive leadership,ss employee wellbeing and job satisfaction	2022	Sweden	Quantitative study	Job satisfaction and employee well-being were linked to supportive leadership.	The impact of leadership on employee well-being: on-site compared to working from home
Nel and Niekerk	Employee well-being and change	2023	South Africa	Qualitative study	Change has a detrimental impact on employee well-being.	Gain or loss: A conceptual framework of employee well-being during change
Das and Pattanayak	Employee well-being, Leadership, Leader-member exchange	2023	India	Quantitative study	The well-being of employees is directly promoted by transformational, empowering, and servant leadership.	Understanding the effects of leadership styles on employee well-being through leader-member exchange
Rabuana and Yanuar	Work environment, work engagement, employee performance, employee well being	2023	Jakarta	Quantitative study	Work environment and employee wellbeing are positively associated.	The Influence of Work Environment and Work Engagement on Employee Performance Mediated by Employee Well-Being
Elufioye, Ndubuisi, Daraojimba, Awonuga, Ayanponle and Asuzu	Employee well-being and mental health initiatives	2024	Nigeria	Qualitative study	The study highlights how crucial it is to continuously assess mental health efforts, provide feedback, and improve them in order to establish work environments that put their employees' overall wellbeing first.	Reviewing employee well-being and mental health initiatives in contemporary HR Practices
Axtell, Raghuram and Nurmi	Employee well being and work Design	2024	USA	Qualitative study	The subdimensions involved determine how well employees experience their well-being when working virtually, and the same subdimension can have both good and negative effects on well-being.	Unpacking Virtual Work's Dual Effects on Employee Well-Being: An Integrative Review and Future Research Agenda

continued on following page

Table 1. Continued

AUTHOR	VARIABLES STUDIED	YEAR	COUNTRY	METHODOLOGY	RESULTS	
Gyensare, Adomako and Amoah	Green HRM practices, employee well-being, and sustainable work behavior	2024	Ghana	Quantitative study	The association between green HRM practices and employees' subjective well-being is mediated by employee green behavior.	Green HRM practices, employee well-being, and sustainable work behavior: Examining the moderating role of resource commitment
Wieneke, Berkland et. al.	Employee well being	2025	USA	Qualitative	Models for employee well-being that are grounded in evidence have been created.	Charting a New Path Forward in Addressing Employee Well-being in Health Care
Garcia	Employee well being and sustainable practices	2025	Brazil	Qualitative study	According to research, implementing inclusive, sustainable workplace policies that put mental and physical health first greatly boosts worker satisfaction, productivity, and engagement.	The impact of sustainable practices on employee well-being and organizational success
Aksoy	Production pressure and innovation/ flexibility climates and employee well-being	2025	Turkey	Quantitative study	Employees' psychological health may be hampered by the conflicting needs of juggling exploitation and exploration at the individual level through contextual ambidexterity.	Balancing act: Exploring the interplay of production pressure and innovation/ flexibility climates on employee well-being

PRACTICAL APPLICATIONS AND CASE STUDIES

The use of sentiment analysis to drive employee happiness to the highest possible level is now more than a theory. Various leading organizations have used these techniques, either directly through in-house analytics teams or through specialist HR technology tools. This section offers some actual examples and case studies, illustrating how sentiment analysis is being used in practice, what benefits have been realized, and what can be taken from the implementations.

Continuous "Pulse" Measurement of Morale: Another typical application is the inclusion of sentiment analysis in regular employee pulse surveys. Instead of relying on annual engagement surveys, organizations are moving towards more frequent pulses (e.g. quarterly or monthly short surveys) that include open-ended questions. Recent research indicates that organizations are more and more using sentiment analysis in regular employee pulse surveys to better measure real-time emotional currents. According to Gelbard et al. (2018), unlike old-fashioned yearly engagement surveys, continuous pulse surveys (e.g., quarterly or monthly) with open-ended questions allow for quicker assessment of workforce sentiment by analyzing employees' written answers through natural language processing (NLP) techniques. Nawaz et al. (2018) also illustrate this shift with the case of an international tech company that conducted a weekly, single-question pulse poll—"How was your work week? Tell us about it." The free-text responses were automatically sentimentally scored, and managers were presented dashboard reports of positive, neutral, or negative trends in their teams. Schaufeli (2017) builds on this research by showing that real-time sentiment monitoring facilitates early detection of issues by management; in one case, a spike in negative sentiment coincided with rollout of a new software tool. Managers probed, discovered usability problems, delayed complete rollout, and provided assistance to affected teams—preventing additional dissatisfaction and lost productivity. Qualtrics, a provider of employee experience software, describes how such continuous sentiment tracking can "accurately measure performance, and identify disengagement pain points from employee feedback in real-time". Perhaps the greatest benefit observed is more reactive HR – companies don't have to wait months to know morale has declined; they can spot it and respond in days or week. (Qualtrics XM Institute, 2023).

Improving Employee Assistance and HR Programs: Some firms use sentiment analysis to measure and improve their support programs. Employee Assistance Programs (EAPs), for example, will collect notes or feedback from the time counseling has been given (in anonymous form). Through textual analysis of this information, employers can quantify overall employee sentiment in need of assistance and identify common stressors. One HR consultancy leader explained how "sentiment analysis can be applied to evaluate the effectiveness of EAPs by examining anonymized data from EAP interactions to observe employees' expressed sentiment requesting help". Where the sentiment analysis reveals high rates of negative sentiment around an issue (e.g., financial struggle or workload), the company can respond with broader preventive measures (e.g., workshops on financial well-being or redistribution of workload) in addition to one-to-one therapy. Similarly, sentiment tracking is done following wellness programs. For instance, if a company deploys a series of mindfulness training, they might analyze employee feedback e-mails or discussion board postings regarding the program to measure reactions. Good sentiment would verify the program, whereas mixed or bad sentiment might mean areas to improve (maybe the sessions are too long, or the timing is bad). Case studies have chronicled companies adjusting their well-being programs based on such analysis to make sure that scarce resources are utilized on programs that resonate with employees.

Internal Communication Monitoring: A Case of AI-Based Sentiment Monitoring

Current practices in organizations have shown the extensive use of AI technologies to carry out internal communication monitoring in a bid to better understand employee sentiments. Starbucks, Walmart, and Delta Airlines, among other organizations, have reportedly used AI-powered platforms like Aware to track communications between employees through collaboration software like Slack and Microsoft Teams (Times of India, 2024). The Aware platform applies natural language processing algorithms to scan for employee dissatisfaction, safety concerns, or mobilization activity in text. Where anomalies are detected, sentiment trends are highlighted for manager review. Organizations can thereby "take the pulse" of employee sentiment in near real-time, offering a complement to the standard quarterly survey.

Significantly, Aware's AI model is initially trained on the communication data of every organization to establish a baseline of normal sentiment patterns. Any subsequent deviations—e.g., negative reactions among a specific demographic group to a policy change—are highlighted, allowing leadership to anticipate emerging issues. Practice has revealed that sentiment analysis through such systems assisted organizations in identifying perceived policy injustice and responding with corrective action, such as holding focus group discussions and retooling communication strategy (McGregor, 2023; Moqbel & Nah, 2017).

That being the case, the use of internal sentiment monitoring has been contentious. Serious questions of employee privacy and trust have emerged. Organizations initially faced backlash from employees after they became aware of such monitoring practices, highlighting the absolute need for transparency and moral standards (Leidner & Tona, 2021). By way of counteraction, most organizations implemented their sentiment analytics programs to anonymize data by removing individual identifiers and emphasized that the intention was to monitor overall sentiment patterns and not examine individual conversations. Evidence shows that open dialogue about the purpose and boundaries of monitoring, as well as employee clear consent, are critical to trust and acceptability of such initiatives (Ball, 2010).

These developments underscore the reality that while AI-driven sentiment monitoring can yield actionable insights to improve employee wellness, organizations must balance the benefits of technology with ethical considerations to prevent unintended consequences such as surveillance anxiety or more eroded organizational trust.

Track of Employee Feedback on social media and Reviews – *Company Reputation and Analysis*: Some companies utilize sentiment analysis on external forums to dictate changes within. The anecdote is one bank conducting a detailed sentiment analysis of 5-year work trends on Glassdoor comments (Kashive *et al.*, 2022). Through sentiment analysis, they quantified trends – learning sentiment regarding "work-life balance" became increasingly negative over recent years, while other avenues (career development, leadership) improved (Penz *et al.*, 2023). This outside criticism prompted the leadership to look inwards, where they confirmed through an in-house survey that employees were actually complaining about working long hours. The company responded by introducing new work-life balance initiatives (no-email hours, additional time-off incentives). In a year that had passed, not only did internal perception of this problem get better, but also outside commentary sentiment from new commentary got better too. This is a sentiment feedback loop whereby external sentiment monitoring put into sharp focus an area which then benefited from enhancements and translated into an improvement in internal and external sentiment. It shows how companies that are concerned about employer branding as a means of reputation metric also use sentiment monitoring. Monitoring sentiment on social media about the firm (from employees on Twitter or LinkedIn) also can cue HR to something seething in morale or something upbeat (like an employee posting a morale-grabber message that goes around virally, inspiring pride) (Putra & Puspitasari, 2023).

Applications in the Real World

- Culture Amp's AI Driven Sentiment Analysis - Culture Amp leverages AI-driven sentiment analysis and natural language processing to examine employee feedback, enabling businesses to identify concerns and optimize satisfaction within the workplace. By matching survey results with performance reviews, the platform detects emotional tones and recurring themes and enables interventions before they are too late. Such interventions have yielded quantifiable advances, such as a 30% improvement in employee satisfaction and a 25% reduction in turnover (Filipsson, 2025).
- Employee Sentiment Analysis by Trust Insights - Trust Insights conducted a case study of employee sentiment through text mining of unstructured content, including Glassdoor comments. The study discovered that certain company policies, including "unlimited" offers, negatively impacted employee morale. Organizations could use targeted interventions to improve workplace satisfaction by being aware of these concerns (Trust Insights, n.d.).

- iMerit's Sentiment and Behavior Detection in Workplace Communications - iMerit collaborated with a leading analytics platform to introduce sentiment analysis and detection of behavior in corporate communication. Based on over 500,000 interactions analyzed, the system detected toxic behavior and sentiment at a rate of 97% accuracy, allowing organizations to develop a positive and respectful workplace culture (iMerit, 2024).
- WorkTango's Confidential Sentiment Analysis for Mental Health - WorkTango employs sentiment analysis to monitor employee mental health with confidentiality being a top priority. The tool allows anonymous feedback, which allows HR teams to catch hints of distress and initiate supportive conversation without intruding into employee privacy. This allows addressing mental health concerns proactively (Dixon, 2023).

CHALLENGES AND ETHICAL CONSIDERATIONS

Sentiment analysis, though, introduces serious technical and ethical challenges, while providing new ways to enhance employee well-being. There are three main areas that organizations need to address: data privacy and legal risk, technical limitations, and trust and transparency.

Data Privacy and Legal Risks

Data privacy is the biggest concern when utilizing sentiment analysis within the workplace. The EU's General Data Protection Regulation (GDPR) mandates that employers obtain explicit, informed consent before collecting and analyzing employee information. However, there are still loopholes. Even anonymized datasets can sometimes be re-identified through cross-matching with other information sources, posing significant privacy threats (European Parliament, 2020).

Additionally, worker suspicion towards monitoring tools presents a big roadblock. 73% of workers surveyed reportedly distrust the employer sentiment analysis tool, the study found, due mainly to a fear their information could be exploited for purposes such as performance grading or penalties (Ball, 2021). Practices of ethical adoption like Privacy Impact Assessments (PIAs), anonymization, aggregation of the sentiment information, and procedures with informed consent should be carefully observed to curb potential risks.

One of the most serious cautionary stories is the 2020 H&M case, when the retailer was fined €35 million in Germany for illegal monitoring of staff data (Simmons & Simmons, 2020). This shows the legal and reputational risk organizations expose themselves to if privacy defenses are inadequate.

Best practices are:

- Reviewing aggregated, non-identifiable data wherever it is possible to do so.
- Having rigorous escalation procedures in place if individual risks are detected (e.g., extreme distress).
- Securing datasets with encryption, limited access, and retention times.
- Transparency, as in publishing rules on what will be monitored and how results will be used, can also decrease privacy concerns (Reworked, 2024).

TECHNICAL LIMITATIONS

Sentiment analysis software also possesses inherent technical constraints, primarily in the interpretation of nuanced human communication.

Sarcasm and Irony: Sarcasm comments are often incorrectly classified by algorithms. Bamman and Smith (2015) found that sarcasm was classified incorrectly 35% of the time in one study of 5,000 tweets by reporters. Misclassifying can lead to incorrect inferences about morale among employees. This paper presents the importance of extra-linguistic context—such as author characteristics and reader relationships—towards effective performance for identifying sarcasm on Twitter. The authors demonstrate that incorporating extra-linguistic context significantly improves the performance quality of sarcasm detection models.

Multilingual Settings: All organizations are multilingual settings where sentiment models won't work the same for all languages. Based on research, Google's BERT model works 89% accurately while classifying English text but reduces to 67% while classifying Arabic due primarily to the difference in dialects (Abdul-Mageed *et al.*, 2021). This emphasizes how much training datasets play a significant role in individual languages to attain accuracy and justice. Moreover, cultural disparity and foreign language use can lead to sentiment interpretation biases that can undesirably impact certain groups of workers.

Trust and Openness

Another crucial challenge is keeping employees' trust. Studies have shown that employees who were subject to transparent AI monitoring reported 25% higher levels of stress compared to workers whose employers explicitly notified staff of the aims and mechanisms of monitoring (Ball, 2021). The report shows that over-monitoring can lead to increased levels of stress, job dissatisfaction, and decreased organizational commitment among workers. The report points out that open communication and ethical use of monitoring practices should be ensured for trust and welfare of employees. To establish trust, transparency and employee involvement are crucial. Cisco's "Ethical AI Toolkit" initiative is a model example. By involving employees in a participative process where they co-designed monitoring tools and made algorithmic choices transparent, Cisco increased employee trust by 44% (Cisco, 2022).

Following recommendations, drawing on expert opinion, provide a model for organizations to employ sentiment analysis responsibly, with the trust and welfare of employees at its heart (Carter, 2023). Mitigation measures are:

- Positioning sentiment analysis as a tool for improving well-being instead of surveillance.
- Regular communication of the purpose, limitations, and benefits of sentiment monitoring.
- Involving staff in pilot experiments and tool development processes.
- Verifying that machine outputs are seen by humans before a conclusion can be reached.
- Sentiment analysis outputs should be considered as advance pointers and not conclusive judgments, always inviting human questioning and checking.

FUTURE DIRECTIONS FOR SENTIMENT ANALYSIS IN EMPLOYEE WELL-BEING

Sentiment analysis for employee well-being is still in its early stages, yet its future holds significant potential for richer, more accurate, and ethically responsible applications. Future research and practice are expected to focus on four key areas: multimodal and real-time analysis, culturally nuanced models, stronger ethical governance, and deeper integration into overall employee experience systems.

Multimodal and Real-Time Analysis

Current sentiment analysis methods in human resource management heavily depend on textual data, such as emails, chat messages, and survey responses. However, emotional expression is far more complex, involving tone of voice, facial expressions, physiological signals (e.g., heart rate variability), and behavioral patterns. Future developments are likely to combine these multimodal signals for a richer assessment of employee well-being.

For example, experimental AI systems already monitor stress in customer service contexts by analyzing agents' tone of voice to suggest timely breaks (Udahemuka *et al.,* 2024). In the corporate setting, combining textual sentiment data with biometric indicators—like heart rate data from wearables—could better predict employee stress and burnout. Our Ring has been scientifically validated to be precise in tracking nocturnal heart rate and heart rate variability (HRV), delivering trustworthy data that can serve an essential function in quantifying employee wellness and picking up on early signs of stress or burnout. A study demonstrated that HR and HRV measurements from the Oura Ring closely follow medical-grade electrocardiograms, validating its application in employee wellness initiatives (Cao *et al.*, 2022).

In addition, real-time sentiment dashboards are becoming increasingly sophisticated. Tools such as Peakon (now part of Workday) offer live sentiment scores to managers, enabling immediate interventions—such as adjusting meeting loads when frustration spikes (Workday, 2023). Organizational network analysis is another emerging field. Analyzing communication patterns (who talks to whom) alongside sentiment can help map the spread of morale through social networks. For instance, identifying negative emotional contagion flowing from a stressed leader could allow targeted support interventions (Kramer et al., 2014).

However, integrating multiple modalities raises privacy challenges. Organizations must ensure that multimodal monitoring remains voluntary, consent-driven, and focused on supporting, not surveilling, employees (Jeske and Santuzzi, 2015). It was found that extensive electronic performance monitoring practices, such as recording chats and calls, seriously harmed employee outcomes, such as decreased job satisfaction, lower self-efficacy, and reduced organizational citizenship behavior. Monitoring that was inconsistent, individual-oriented, or constant had the largest negative impacts on employee attitudes and feelings of control, possibly overshadowing the expected efficiency gains.

Culturally Nuanced Sentiment Models

Another future direction lies in building culturally sensitive sentiment models. Most current sentiment tools are trained on English-centric, Western datasets, limiting their ability to accurately capture emotions in multilingual or multicultural workplaces (Ponti *et al.,* 2020).

Researchers advocate for localized sentiment lexicons and context-specific training data. Researchers have emphasized the need for culturally adapted sentiment lexicons and locally adapted models, as indirect expressions characteristic of East Asian languages, like in South Korea, tend to convey strong dissatisfaction that may be misinterpreted by Western-trained models (Mohammad, 2020; Balahur, Turchi, & Steinberger, 2012). Mohammad (2020) critically examines computational approaches to detecting valence, discrete emotion, and more generic affective states from text for methodological advancements and performance criteria. The chapter also condemns the shortcomings of current sentiment analysis systems, particularly diminished performance across culturally diverse languages and settings, and highlights the need for local and domain-sensitive solutions. Balahur, Turchi, and Steinberger (2012) addressed the use of machine translation for multilingual sentiment analysis, and while translation enables cross-lingual sentiment detection, considerable loss of accuracy is encountered due to cultural and contextual differences. They emphasize in their findings the necessity to develop native-language resources and culturally sensitive models in order to enhance sentiment classification in diverse linguistic contexts. Similarly, models like ARBERT and MARBERT have shown that language-specific transformers significantly outperform general models on Arabic sentiment tasks, illustrating the need for regionally tailored models (Abdul-Mageed et al., 2021). Future research will likely emphasize dialectal diversity, cultural expression norms, and multilingual embeddings to enhance the emotional accuracy of global sentiment analysis tools.

Ethical Frameworks and Governance

As AI monitoring grows, so do ethical risks. Concerns around data privacy, surveillance perception, and algorithmic bias demand urgent attention. Governments are beginning to act: the proposed Algorithmic Accountability Act in the U.S. recommends mandatory third-party audits for workplace AI tools to detect bias and ensure fairness (Ashurst *et al.,* 2022). Ethically oriented machine learning research requires more than bias prevention; it needs to integrate transparency, accountability, and participatory design into the whole development process. Ethically designed systems should involve stakeholders with interests in decision-making, echoing calls for employee involvement and third-party audit in sentiment analysis regulation. Organizations are also responding. Intel, for instance, has created employee-led committees to oversee sentiment analysis initiatives, ensuring alignment with worker values and priorities. Intel prioritizes a multi-faceted approach to responsible AI by incorporating human rights, transparency, fairness, environmental protection, and human oversight into all stages of AI development. Through processes like advisory councils, worldwide research collaborations (e.g., RESUMAIS), and in-house governance models, Intel tries to actively address bias, disinformation, and environmental impact associated with generative AI technologies. (Intel Corporation, 2024).

Successful implementation of ethical best practices is a prerequisite to the proper application of sentiment analysis and employee monitoring technologies. Such a foundational requirement includes the procurement of explicit informed consent, wherein employees comprehend in full, and give their uninhibited consent to, the process of monitoring, thereby upholding principles of autonomy and transparency (Mittelstadt et al., 2016). At the same time, data anonymization and aggregation become necessary for shielding individual privacy and minimizing the prospects of unwarranted targeting (Floridi & Taddeo, 2016). Moreover, human-in-the-loop oversight remains essential because it ensures that algorithmic outcomes are properly screened by human auditors before anything is done to them, limiting the risk of misinterpretation and prejudice (Raji & Buolamwini, 2019). Open communication about monitoring programs' goals, scope, and limits also enhances trust and promotes a culture of openness (Floridi & Taddeo, 2016). Additionally, regular bias audits should be performed to guarantee that sentiment models are operating equitably across different demographic groups, thus preventing claims of systemic discrimination (Barocas, Hardt, & Narayanan, 2019).

Finally, participatory governance processes like Employee Advocacy Panels have been successfully applied to enhance employee trust by involving staff members in co-governance and co-design of monitoring systems directly (Dignum, 2019). Collectively, these measures form a master ethical framework that balances technological innovation in respect to employee fairness, dignity, and privacy. Moreover, worker-level sentiment dashboards can be developed giving workers individualized insight into their own emotional patterns without sharing management-level data. This turns the paradigm around to self-care empowerment instead of surveillance.

Integration into Employee Experience Systems

In the burgeoning marketplace for workplace analytics, sentiment analysis will be an omnipresent component in combined people analytics platforms alongside traditional HR measures of performance such as employee engagement scores, turnover rates, and productivity metrics. When integrating sentiment data with key performance metrics, organizations can establish early indicators that detect underperforming teams on the cusp of burnout, disengagement, or turnover before symptoms occur, allowing proactive prevention (Wang et al., 2022).New longitudinal studies suggest that companies applying ethical sentiment monitoring models—placing emphasis on transparency, employee consent, and human oversight—can achieve measurable improvements in employee well-being outcomes, including reduced absenteeism and reduced burnout-driven turnover (Charalampous et al., 2019). Yet such a vision necessitates strong ethical safeguards: human-in-the-loop decisioning, clear informed consent, and employee access and ownership of their own data have to remain pillars. Moreover, outside audits and accountability mechanisms will have to exist in order not to allow AI-facilitated sentiment analysis to harden system biases or undercut worker confidence (Raji *et al.,* 2022; Floridi & Taddeo, 2016). Thus, although there is great promise for advancing workers' mental wellbeing through new analytics, they must be applied with a firm dedication to fairness, privacy, and human dignity.

CONCLUSION

Employees' well-being has become more and more known as one of the key pillars of sustainable organizational success, as the evidence is growing that thriving employees enhance innovation, customer satisfaction, and profitability. This review demonstrated that sentiment analysis—formerly used for customer insights—is being used again to monitor the emotional health of employees, so organizations are able to detect early warning signs of disengagement, stress, or burnout that normal measures fail to detect (Mohammad, 2020; Scholz, 2017). By using the intense analysis of inner surveys, qualitative feedback, and communication outlets, companies are able to identify emotional trends and intervene early.

Real-life examples illustrate the real-world impact of this strategy. Unilever and IBM are two of the firms that have applied sentiment insights to inform changes in working policies, address workload concerns, and enhance employee retention. However, possible benefits are accompanied by serious challenges—particularly over employees' privacy, algorithmic bias, and trust. Unethical or untransparent utilization of sentiment analysis platforms endangers employee disaffection and tends to magnify issues they are meant to address. Therefore, sentiment analysis needs to be positioned not as an end in itself but as a means to human-focused organizational improvement. Data in isolation cannot generate change; meaningful action on the basis of insights—such as starting supportive conversations or updating stressful workflows—ultimately improves well-being. The use of real-time emotional analytics represents a wider shift toward data-driven human resources management, which is consistent with the move toward evidence-based leadership practices.

But ethical stewardship is first. Best practice—like explicit informed consent, anonymization of data, employee participation in monitoring framework design, and ongoing human supervision of AI outputs—must be followed strictly (Floridi & Taddeo, 2016). More research must focus on interdisciplinary collaborations among organizational psychologists, ethicists, linguists, and data scientists to further develop these models, making them culturally adapted, transparent, and equitable. Longitudinal studies are particularly needed to assess the overall effect of continuous sentiment monitoring on office culture and employee mental health. Predictive modeling frameworks that combine sentiment trends with performance data hold promising potential for early intervention, but need to be applied cautiously, with regard to the autonomy and respect of employees.

Overall, sentiment analysis, responsibly applied, offers a groundbreaking opportunity to really listen to employees at scale. By encouraging openness, respecting cultural differences, and grounding technological innovation in ethical principles, organizations can create workplaces in which no concern goes unreported and every voice matters. Overcoming the concomitant ethical challenges will be required, but the potential returns—in terms of trust, resilience, and shared well-being—make the undertaking both urgent and promising.

REFERENCES

Abdul-Mageed, M., Elmadany, A., & Nagoudi, E. M. B. (2021). ARBERT & MARBERT: Deep Bidirectional Transformers for Arabic. *In Proceedings of the 59th Annual Meeting of the Association for Computational Linguistics and the 11th International Joint Conference on Natural Language Processing* Volume 1*: Long Papers)* (7088–7105). Association for Computational Linguistics. DOI: 10.18653/v1/2021.acl-long.551

Abid, G., Ahmed, S., Elahi, N., & Ilyas, S. (2020). Antecedents and mechanism of employee well-being for social sustainability: A sequential mediation. *Sustainable Production and Consumption*, *24*, 79–89. Advance online publication. DOI: 10.1016/j.spc.2020.06.011

Aksoy, E. (2025). Balancing act: Exploring the interplay of production pressure and innovation/flexibility climates on employee well-being. *Creativity and Innovation Management*, *34*(1), 222–236. DOI: 10.1111/caim.12640

Alruily, M. (2023). Sentiment analysis for predicting stress among workers and classification utilizing CNN: Unveiling the mechanism. *Alexandria Engineering Journal*, *81*, 360–370. DOI: 10.1016/j.aej.2023.09.040

Ashurst, C., Barocas, S., Campbell, R., & Raji, D. (2022, June). Disentangling the components of ethical research in machine learning. *In Proceedings of the 2022 ACM Conference on Fairness, Accountability, and Transparency* (pp. 2057-2068). DOI: 10.1145/3531146.3533781

Balahur, A., & Turchi, M. (2012, July). Multilingual sentiment analysis using machine translation? *In Proceedings of the 3rd workshop in computational approaches to subjectivity and sentiment analysis* (pp. 52-60).

Ball, K. (2010). Workplace surveillance: An overview. *Labor History*, *51*(1), 87–106. DOI: 10.1080/00236561003654776

Ball, K. (2021), Electronic Monitoring and Surveillance in the Workplace, Publications Office of the European Union, Luxembourg, ISBN 978-92-76-43340-8, , JRC125716.DOI: 10.2760/5137

Bamman, D., & Smith, N. A. (2015). Contextualized sarcasm detection on Twitter. *Proceedings of the Ninth International AAAI Conference on Web and Social Media,* 9(1), 574–577. DOI: 10.1609/icwsm.v9i1.14655

Barocas, S., Hardt, M., & Narayanan, A. (2019). *Fairness and Machine Learning.* Retrieved from https://fairmlbook.org/

Cao, R., Azimi, I., Sarhaddi, F., Niela-Vilen, H., Axelin, A., Liljeberg, P., & Rahmani, A. M. (2022). Accuracy Assessment of Oura Ring Nocturnal Heart Rate and Heart Rate Variability in Comparison With Electrocardiography in Time and Frequency Domains: Comprehensive Analysis. *Journal of Medical Internet Research, 24*(1), e27487. DOI: 10.2196/27487 PMID: 35040799

Carter, L. (2023). Where Sentiment Analysis Fits in HR Wellness Initiatives. Reworked. Retrieved from https://www.reworked.co/employee-experience/sentiment-analysis-can-help-mental-wellness-initiatives-given-the-proper-guardrails/

Charalampous, M., Grant, C. A., Tramontano, C., & Michailidis, E. (2019). Systematically reviewing remote e-workers' well-being at work: A multidimensional approach. *European Journal of Work and Organizational Psychology*, *28*(1), 51–73. DOI: 10.1080/1359432X.2018.1541886

Das, S. S., & Pattanayak, S. (2023). Understanding the effect of leadership styles on employee well-being through leader-member exchange. *Current Psychology (New Brunswick, N.J.)*, *42*(25), 21310–21325. DOI: 10.1007/s12144-022-03243-3

Dignum, V. (2019). *Responsible Artificial Intelligence: How to Develop and Use AI in a Responsible Way*. Springer Nature. DOI: 10.1007/978-3-030-30371-6

Dimoff, J. K., Kelloway, E. K., & Burnstein, M. D. (2016). Mental health awareness training (MHAT): The development and evaluation of an intervention for workplace leaders. *International Journal of Stress Management*, *23*(2), 167–189. DOI: 10.1037/a0039479

Dixon, L. (2023, July 12). Sentiment analysis can help mental wellness initiatives, given the proper guardrails. Reworked. https://www.reworked.co/employee-experience/sentiment-analysis-can-help-mental-wellness-initiatives-given-the-proper-guardrails/accessed 0n 26/04/25

Elufioye, O. A., Ndubuisi, N. L., Daraojimba, R. E., Awonuga, K. F., Ayanponle, L. O., & Asuzu, O. F. (2024). Reviewing employee well-being and mental health initiatives in contemporary HR Practices. *International Journal of Science and Research Archive*, *11*(1), 828–840. DOI: 10.30574/ijsra.2024.11.1.0153

European Parliament. (2020). The impact of the General Data Protection Regulation (GDPR) on artificial intelligence. Accessed on 26/04/25 Retrieved from https://www.europarl.europa.eu/RegData/etudes/STUD/2020/641530/EPRS_STU(2020)641530_EN.pdf

Filipsson, F. (2025, March 1). AI Case Study: AI-Powered Employee Engagement and Sentiment Analysis at Culture Amp. Redress Compliance. https://redresscompliance.com/ai-case-study-ai-powered-employee-engagement-and-sentiment-analysis-at-culture-amp/accessed on 26/04/25

Floridi, L., & Taddeo, M. (2016). What is data ethics? *Philosophical Transactions. Series A, Mathematical, Physical, and Engineering Sciences*, *374*(2083), 20160360. DOI: 10.1098/rsta.2016.0360 PMID: 28336805

Garcia, A. G. (2025). The impact of sustainable practices on employee well-being and organizational success. *Brazilian Journal of Development*, *11*(3), e78599–e78599. DOI: 10.34117/bjdv11n3-054

Gelbard, R., Ramon-Gonen, R., Carmeli, A., Bittmann, R. M., & Talyansky, R. (2018). Sentiment analysis in organizational work: Towards an ontology of people analytics. *Expert Systems: International Journal of Knowledge Engineering and Neural Networks*, *35*(5), e12289. DOI: 10.1111/exsy.12289

Goh, J., Pfeffer, J., & Zenios, S. A. (2015). Workplace stressors & health outcomes: Health policy for the workplace. *Behavioral Science & Policy*, *1*(1), 43–52. DOI: 10.1177/237946151500100107

Grawitch, M. J., & Ballard, D. W. (2016). *The psychologically healthy workplace: Building a win-win environment for organizations and employees*. American Psychological Association. DOI: 10.1037/14731-000

Gyensare, M. A., Adomako, S., & Amankwah-Amoah, J. (2024). Green HRM practices, employee well-being, and sustainable work behavior: Examining the moderating role of resource commitment. *Business Strategy and the Environment*, *33*(4), 3129–3141. DOI: 10.1002/bse.3642

Hennekam, S., Ladge, J., & Shymko, Y. (2020). From zero to hero: An exploratory study examining sudden hero status among nonphysician health care workers during the COVID-19 pandemic. *The Journal of Applied Psychology*, *105*(10), 1088–1100. DOI: 10.1037/apl0000832 PMID: 32897086

Hill, N. S., Axtell, C., Raghuram, S., & Nurmi, N. (2024). Unpacking virtual work's dual effects on employee well-being: An integrative review and future research agenda. *Journal of Management*, *50*(2), 752–792. DOI: 10.1177/01492063221131535

iMerit. (2024, March 15). Case study: Sentiment analysis and behavior detection for a leading analytics platform. iMerit. https://imerit.net/blog/case-study-sentiment-analysis-and-behavior-detection-for-a-leading-analytics-platform/accessed on 26/04/25

Intel Corporation. (2024, April 2). *Opinion: How Intel is refining its approach to responsible AI. Intel Newsroom.* https://www.intc.com/news-events/press-releases/detail/1686/opinion-how-intel-is-refining-its-approach-to-responsible accessed on 28/04/25

Jeske, D., & Santuzzi, A. M. (2015). Monitoring what and how: Psychological implications of electronic performance monitoring. *New Technology, Work and Employment*, *30*(1), 62–78. DOI: 10.1111/ntwe.12039

Johnson, A., Dey, S., Nguyen, H., Groth, M., Joyce, S., Tan, L., Glozier, N., & Harvey, S. B. (2020). A review and agenda for examining how technology-driven changes at work will impact workplace mental health and employee well-being. *Australian Journal of Management*, *45*(3), 402–424. DOI: 10.1177/0312896220922292

Kaltiainen, J., & Hakanen, J. (2022). Fostering task and adaptive performance through employee well-being: The role of servant leadership. *Business Research Quarterly*, *25*(1), 28–43. DOI: 10.1177/2340944420981599

Kashive, N., Khanna, V. T., & Bharthi, M. N. (2020). Employer branding through crowdsourcing: Understanding the sentiments of employees. *Journal of Indian Business Research*, *12*(1), 93–111. DOI: 10.1108/JIBR-09-2019-0276

Kern, M., Heissler, C., & Zapf, D. (2021). Social job stressors can foster employee well-being: Introducing the concept of social challenge stressors. *Journal of Business and Psychology*, *36*(5), 771–792. DOI: 10.1007/s10869-020-09702-7

Kniffin, K. M., Narayanan, J., Anseel, F., Antonakis, J., Ashford, S. P., Bakker, A. B., Bamberger, P., Bapuji, H., Bhave, D. P., Choi, V. K., Creary, S. J., Demerouti, E., Flynn, F. J., Gelfand, M. J., Greer, L. L., Johns, G., Kesebir, S., Klein, P. G., Lee, S. Y., & Vugt, M. V. (2021). COVID-19 and the workplace: Implications, issues, and insights for future research and action. *The American Psychologist*, *76*(1), 63–77. DOI: 10.1037/amp0000716 PMID: 32772537

Kramer, A. D., Guillory, J. E., & Hancock, J. T. (2014). Experimental evidence of massive-scale emotional contagion through social networks. *Proceedings of the National Academy of Sciences of the United States of America*, *111*(24), 8788–8790. DOI: 10.1073/pnas.1320040111 PMID: 24889601

Krekel, C., Ward, G., & Neve, J.-E. (2019). Employee wellbeing, productivity, and firm performance. SSRN *Electron.* J. Available online at: https://voxeu.org/article/employee-wellbeing-productivity-and-firm-performance (accessed April 25, 2025). DOI: 10.2139/ssrn.3356581

Kun, A., & Gadanecz, P. (2022). Workplace happiness, well-being and their relationship with psychological capital: A study of Hungarian Teachers. *Current Psychology (New Brunswick, N.J.)*, *41*(1), 185–199. DOI: 10.1007/s12144-019-00550-0

Kundi, Y. M., Aboramadan, M., Elhamalawi, E. M., & Shahid, S. (2021). Employee psychological well-being and job performance: Exploring mediating and moderating mechanisms. *The International Journal of Organizational Analysis*, *29*(3), 736–754. DOI: 10.1108/IJOA-05-2020-2204

Lundqvist, D., Reineholm, C., Ståhl, C., & Wallo, A. (2022). The impact of leadership on employee well-being: On-site compared to working from home. *BMC Public Health*, *22*(1), 2154. DOI: 10.1186/s12889-022-14612-9 PMID: 36424558

Madero-Gómez, S., Leal, Y., Olivas-Lujan, M., & Yusliza, M. (2023). Companies Could Benefit When They Focus on Employee Wellbeing and the Environment: A Systematic Review of Sustainable Human Resource Management. *Sustainability (Basel)*, *15*(6), 5435. Advance online publication. DOI: 10.3390/su15065435

Mansoor, M. A., & Ansari, K. H. (2024). Early Detection of Mental Health Crises through Artifical-Intelligence-Powered Social Media Analysis: A Prospective Observational Study. *Journal of Personalized Medicine*, *14*(9), 958. DOI: 10.3390/jpm14090958 PMID: 39338211

Marin-Garcia, J. A., & Bonavia, T. (2021). Empowerment and employee well-being: A mediation analysis study. *International Journal of Environmental Research and Public Health*, *18*(11), 5822. DOI: 10.3390/ijerph18115822 PMID: 34071574

Matchar, E. (2015, August 6). IBM's Tone Analyzer Could Save You From Sending That Awkward Email. Smithsonian Magazine. https://www.smithsonianmag.com/innovation/ibms-tone-analyzer-will-save-you-sending-awkward-email-180956102/ (Accessed on 26/04/25).

McKinsey Health Institute. (2022). *Addressing employee mental health: The economic case*. McKinsey & Company. https://www.mckinsey.com/mhi/our-insights/the-mental-health-imperative-for-business (accessed April 25, 2025).

Mittelstadt, B. D., Allo, P., Taddeo, M., Wachter, S., & Floridi, L. (2016). The ethics of algorithms: Mapping the debate. *Big Data & Society*, *3*(2), 2053951716679679. Advance online publication. DOI: 10.1177/2053951716679679

Mohammad, S. M. (2020). Sentiment Analysis: Detecting Valence, Emotions, and Other Affectual States from Text. In Indurkhya, N., & Damerau, F. J. (Eds.), *Handbook of Natural Language Processing* (3rd ed., pp. 325–382). Chapman and Hall/CRC.

Moore, P., & Piwek, L. (2017). Regulating wellbeing in the brave new quantified workplace. *Employee Relations*, *39*(3), 308–316. DOI: 10.1108/ER-06-2016-0126

Nawaz, M., Abid, G., Arya, B., Bhatti, G. A., & Farooqi, S. (2018). Understanding employee thriving: The role of workplace context, personality and individual resources. *Total Quality Management & Business Excellence*. Advance online publication. DOI: 10.1080/14783363.2018.1482209

Nel, D. M., & Van Niekerk, A. (2023). Gain or loss: A conceptual framework of employee well-being during change. *Journal of Contemporary Management*, *20*(1), 83–103. DOI: 10.35683/jcman1004.186

OECD. (2023). *Mental Health and Employment: Global Trends*. (accessed on 26th April, 25)

Ostroff, C., Kinicki, A. J., & Muhammad, R. S. (2012). Organizational culture and climate. In I. Weiner (Ed.), Handbook of psychology, (2nd ed.). Wiley. . hop-212024DOI: 10.1002/9781118133880.hop212024

Ozkan, A. H. (2022). The effect of burnout and its dimensions on turnover intention among nurses: A meta-analytic review. *Journal of Nursing Management*, *30*(3), 660–669. DOI: 10.1111/jonm.13525 PMID: 34837289

Patterson, M. G., West, M. A., Shackleton, V. J., Dawson, J. F., Lawthom, R., Maitlis, S., Robinson, D. L., & Wallace, A. M. (2005). Validating the organizational climate measure: Links to managerial practices, productivity and innovation. *Journal of Organizational Behavior*, *26*(4), 379–408. DOI: 10.1002/job.312

Penz, D., Almeida, M. P. D., Amorim, B. C., Cembranel, P., & Rolt, C. R. D. (2023). Crowdsourced employer branding: An analysis from the platform glassdoor. *Revista de Administração da UFSM*, *16*(1), e7. DOI: 10.5902/1983465966608

Pipera, M., & Fragouli, E. (2021). Employee wellbeing, employee performance & positive mindset in a crisis. *The Business & Management Review*, *12*(2), 1–15.

Plimmer, G., Berman, E. M., Malinen, S., Franken, E., Naswall, K., Kuntz, J., & Löfgren, K. (2022). Resilience in public sector managers. *Review of Public Personnel Administration*, *42*(2), 338–367. DOI: 10.1177/0734371X20985105

Ponti, E. M., Vulić, I., Glavaš, G., Reichart, R., & Riedel, S. (2020). XCOPA: A multilingual dataset for causal commonsense reasoning. *Proceedings of the 2020 Conference on Empirical Methods in Natural Language Processing (EMNLP)*, 2362–2376. DOI: 10.18653/v1/2020.emnlp-main.185

Putra, F. S. U., & Puspitasari, I. (2023). Implementation of Sentiment Analysis in HR Management and Development Planning Using Topic Modelling on Employee Review. *Kontigensi: Jurnal Ilmiah Manajemen, 11*(2), 409–417. DOI: 10.56457/jimk.v11i2.358

Qualtrics, X. M. Institute. (2023). *Employee experience trends 2024: EMEA insights report.* Qualtrics. https://www.qualtrics.com/m/www.xminstitute.com/wp-content/uploads/2023/10/XMI_RR_DS_EXTrends2024-EMEA-2.pdf

Rabuana, N. K. D. N., & Yanuar, Y. (2023). The influence of work environment and work engagement on employee performance mediated by employee well-being. *Munaddhomah: Jurnal Manajemen Pendidikan Islam, 4*(3), 541–557. DOI: 10.31538/munaddhomah.v4i3.523

Raji, I. D., & Buolamwini, J. (2019). Actionable auditing: Investigating the impact of publicly naming biased performance results of commercial AI products. *In Proceedings of the AAAI/ACM Conference on AI, Ethics, and Society* (pp. 429–435). DOI: 10.1145/3306618.3314244

Raji, I. D., Kumar, I. E., Horowitz, A., & Selbst, A. (2022, June). The fallacy of AI functionality. *In Proceedings of the 2022 ACM Conference on Fairness, Accountability, and Transparency* (pp. 959–972). ACM. DOI: 10.1145/3531146.3533158

Reworked. (2024). Sentiment Analysis and Employee Mental Wellness: Opportunities and Guardrails. Retrieved from https://www.reworked.co/employee-experience/sentiment-analysis-can-help-mental-wellness-initiatives-given-the-proper-guardrails/accessed on 25/04/25

Rink, L., Meijdam, J., & Graus, D. (2024). Aspect-Based Sentiment Analysis for Open-Ended HR Survey Responses. *arXiv preprint arXiv:2402.04812.*

Salas-Vallina, A., Alegre, J., & López-Cabrales, Á. (2021). The challenge of increasing employees' well-being and performance: How human resource management practices and engaging leadership work together toward reaching this goal. *Human Resource Management, 60*(3), 333–347. DOI: 10.1002/hrm.22021

Sarwar, H., Ishaq, M. I., Amin, A., & Ahmed, R. (2020). Ethical leadership, work engagement, employees' well-being, and performance: A cross-cultural comparison. *Journal of Sustainable Tourism, 28*(12), 2008–2026. DOI: 10.1080/09669582.2020.1788039

Schaufeli, W. B. (2017). Applying the Job Demands-Resources Model: A "How to" Guide to Measuring and Tackling Work Engagement and Burnout. *Organizational Dynamics, 46*(2), 120–132. DOI: 10.1016/j.orgdyn.2017.04.008

Schaufeli, W. B., Salanova, M., González-Romá, V., & Bakker, A. B. (2002). The measurement of engagement and burnout: A two sample confirmatory factor analytic approach. *Journal of Happiness Studies*, *3*(1), 71–92. DOI: 10.1023/A:1015630930326

Scholz, T. M. (2017). Big data in organizations and the role of human resource management: A complex systems theory-based conceptualization. Frankfurt a. M.: Peter Lang International Academic Publishers. DOI: 10.3726/b10907

Shirom, A., Nirel, N., & Vinokur, A. D. (2010). Work hours and caseload as predictors of physician burnout: The mediating effects by perceived workload and by autonomy. *Applied Psychology*, *59*(4), 539–565. DOI: 10.1111/j.1464-0597.2009.00411.x

Simmons & Simmons. (2020, October 5). Fine issued against H&M for data protection violations. Accessed on 26/04/25 https://www.simmons-simmons.com/en/publications/ckh3lyk2b14oj0917lz7sc9uf/fine-issued-against-h-m-for-data-protection-violations

Singh, S., Pradhan, R., Panigrahy, N., & Jena, L. (2019). Self-efficacy and workplace well-being: Moderating role of sustainability practices. *Benchmarking*, *26*(6), 1692–1708. Advance online publication. DOI: 10.1108/BIJ-07-2018-0219

Sonmez, B., & Yildirim, A. (2018). The mediating role ofautonomy in the effect of pro-innovation climate and supervisor supportiveness on innovative behavior of nurses. *European Journal of Innovation Management*, *22*(1), 41–58. DOI: 10.1108/EJIM-05-2018-0088

Stetler, K. L., & Magnusson, M. (2015). Exploring the tension between clarity and ambiguity in goal setting for innovation. *Creativity and Innovation Management*, *24*(2), 231–246. DOI: 10.1111/caim.12102

Trust Insights. (n.d.). Case study: Employee sentiment. Trust Insights. Retrieved April 25, 2025, from https://www.trustinsights.ai/expertise/case-studies/case-study-employee-sentiment/

Tushman, M. L., & O'Reilly, C. A. (1996). Ambidextrous organizations: Managing evolutionary and revolutionary change. California Management Review, 38(4), 8–29. https://journals.sagepub.com/doi/10.2307/ 41165852

Udahemuka, G., Djouani, K., & Kurien, A. M. (2024). Multimodal Emotion Recognition using visual, vocal and Physiological Signals: A review. *Applied Sciences (Basel, Switzerland)*, *14*(17), 8071. DOI: 10.3390/app14178071

Wang, B., Liu, Y., Qian, J., & Parker, S. K. (2022). Achieving effective remote working during the COVID-19 pandemic: A work design perspective. *Applied Psychology*, *71*(1), 16–59. DOI: 10.1111/apps.12290 PMID: 33230359

Wieneke, K. C., Berkland, B. E., Kruse, G. C., Priestley, M. R., Teal, D. M., & West, C. P. (2025, March). Charting a new path forward in addressing employee well-being in health care. [). Elsevier.]. *Mayo Clinic Proceedings*, *100*(3), 501–513. DOI: 10.1016/j.mayocp.2024.11.018 PMID: 40044362

Williams, L. J., Hartman, N., & Cavazotte, F. (2010). Method variance and marker variables: A review and comprehensive CFA marker technique. *Organizational Research Methods*, *13*(3), 477–514. DOI: 10.1177/1094428110366036

Williams, L. J., & O'Boyle, E. H. (2015). Ideal, nonideal, and no-marker variables: The confirmatory factor analysis (CFA) marker technique works when it matters. *The Journal of Applied Psychology*, *100*(5), 1579–1602. DOI: 10.1037/a0038855 PMID: 25822071

Workday. (2023). *Real-Time Employee Sentiment Dashboards: Peakon Insights Report*.

World Health Organization. (2022). *Mental health at work*. World Health Organization. https://www.who.int/news-room/fact-sheets/detail/mental-health-at-work (accessed April 25, 2025).

You, Y., Hu, Z., Li, J., Wang, Y., & Xu, M. (2022). The effect of organizational innovation climate on employee innovative behavior: The role of psychological ownership and task interdependence. *Frontiers in Psychology*, *13*, 856407. DOI: 10.3389/fpsyg.2022.856407 PMID: 35800933

ADDITIONAL READING

Arnold, K. A. (2017). Transformational leadership and employee psychological well-being: A review and directions for future research. *Journal of Occupational Health Psychology*, *22*(3), 381–393. DOI: 10.1037/ocp0000062 PMID: 28150998

Bakker, A. B., & Leiter, M. P. (Eds.). (2010). *Work engagement: A handbook of essential theory and research*. Psychology Press. DOI: 10.4324/9780203853047

Cooper, C. L., & Leiter, M. P. (Eds.). (2017). *The Routledge companion to well-being at work*. Routledge. DOI: 10.4324/9781315665979

Costantini, A., & Sartori, R. (2020). The relationship between work engagement and job performance: Toward a broader understanding of the dynamics of organizational success. *International Journal of Business Research and Development*, *9*(1), 1–20. DOI: 10.24102/ijbrd.v9i1.956

Danna, K., & Griffin, R. W. (1999). Health and well-being in the workplace: A review and synthesis of the literature. *Journal of Management*, *25*(3), 357–384. DOI: 10.1177/014920639902500305

Decuypere, A., & Schaufeli, W. (2020). Leadership and employee well-being: The role of work engagement. *Journal of Occupational Health Psychology*, *25*(3), 182–193. DOI: 10.1037/ocp0000170

Diener, E., Oishi, S., & Tay, L. (2018). *Handbook of well-being*. DEF Publishers.

Fisher, C. D. (2010). Happiness at work. *International Journal of Management Reviews*, *12*(4), 384–412. DOI: 10.1111/j.1468-2370.2009.00270.x

Kelloway, E. K., & Day, A. L. (2005). Building healthy workplaces: What we know so far. *Canadian Journal of Behavioural Science*, *37*(4), 223–235. DOI: 10.1037/h0087259

Krekel, C., Ward, G., & De Neve, J.-E. (2019). Employee wellbeing, productivity, and firm performance. CEP Discussion Paper No. 1605. Centre for Economic Performance, London School of Economics. https://cep.lse.ac.uk/pubs/download/dp1605.pdf

Leka, S., & Houdmont, J. (Eds.). (2010). *Occupational health psychology*. Wiley-Blackwell.

Quick, J. C., & Tetrick, L. E. (Eds.). (2011). *Handbook of occupational health psychology* (2nd ed.). American Psychological Association.

Robertson, I. T., & Cooper, C. L. (2011). *Well-being: Productivity and happiness at work*. Palgrave Macmillan. DOI: 10.1057/9780230306738

Ryan, R. M., & Deci, E. L. (2001). On happiness and human potentials: A review of research on hedonic and eudaimonic well-being. *Annual Review of Psychology*, *52*(1), 141–166. DOI: 10.1146/annurev.psych.52.1.141 PMID: 11148302

Schaufeli, W. B. (2017). Applying the Job Demands-Resources model: A 'how to' guide to measuring and tackling work engagement and burnout. *Organizational Dynamics*, *46*(2), 120–132. DOI: 10.1016/j.orgdyn.2017.04.008

Schaufeli, W. B., Salanova, M., González-Romá, V., & Bakker, A. B. (2002). The measurement of engagement and burnout: A two-sample confirmatory factor analytic approach. *Journal of Happiness Studies*, *3*(1), 71–92. DOI: 10.1023/A:1015630930326

Sonnentag, S., & Frese, M. (2003). Stress in organizations. In Borman, W. C., Ilgen, D. R., & Klimoski, R. J. (Eds.), Handbook of psychology: Vol. 12. *Industrial and organizational psychology* (pp. 453–491). Wiley.

Tarafdar, M., Cooper, C. L., & Stich, J. F. (2019). The technostress trifecta—Techno eustress, techno distress and design: Theoretical directions and an agenda for research. *Information Systems Journal, 29*(1), 6–42. DOI: 10.1111/isj.12169

Van De Voorde, K., Paauwe, J., & Van Veldhoven, M. (2012). Employee well-being and the HRM–organizational performance relationship: A review of quantitative studies. *International Journal of Management Reviews, 14*(4), 391–407. DOI: 10.1111/j.1468-2370.2011.00322.x

Warr, P. (2007). *Work, happiness, and unhappiness*. Lawrence Erlbaum Associates.

KEY TERMS AND DEFINITIONS

Employee Well-Being: Overall mental, emotional, and physical well-being at work that can be a function of job demands, leadership, and organizational climate.

Ethical Leadership: A leadership style based on integrity, justice, and respect for employees, that fosters trust, commitment, and psychological safety.

Green HRM Practices: HR practices intended to promote environmental sustainability as well as higher employee motivation, meaning, and well-being.

Hindrance Stressors: Work demands that hamper personal growth or work performance, typically leading to strain and lower well-being.

Organizational Change: Any alteration to structures, processes, or strategies of an organization that can affect employee stability, engagement, and stress levels.

Psychological Capital: An individual's positive psychological resources, including hope, resilience, self-efficacy, and optimism, which result in positive motivation and well-being.

Servant Leadership: A leadership approach centered on employees' needs and development, building an empowering and supportive culture.

Social Challenge Stressors: Social demands at work that are demanding but maybe motivating and development-enhancing, e.g., beneficial conflict or high expectations.

Virtual Work: Technology-facilitated remote work arrangements that have the potential to enhance flexibility as well as disrupt social connection and mental health.

Work Engagement: An energized and positive state with regard to work with energy, dedication, and strong involvement in activities.

Chapter 9
From Side Hustles to Smart Work:
A Bibliometric Exploration of Moonlighting in the Age of Artificial Intelligence

Gagandeep Kaur
https://orcid.org/0000-0001-8729-2402
Global School of Finance and Accounting, Chandigarh University, India

Shivani Dhand
https://orcid.org/0000-0002-4809-1365
Mittal School of Business, India

Preet Kanwal
https://orcid.org/0009-0006-5114-8381
Mittal School of Business, India

Arvinder Kaur
https://orcid.org/0000-0001-7360-5674
Global School of Finance and Accounting, India

Rubel Amin
https://orcid.org/0000-0003-4343-7598
ISU, Bangladesh

ABSTRACT

The study aims to conduct a comprehensive bibliometric analysis to unveil the existing body of research on moonlighting or dual jobs, with specific focus on evolving role

DOI: 10.4018/979-8-3373-2135-6.ch009

of Artificial Technology (AI). By examining the existing literature, the current study explores the impactful articles, influential journals and notable transition over the selected time period. The three main bibliometric analytic techniques used in the study are citation analysis, co-authorship analysis, and co-occurrence analysis. Data retrieval for the study is limited to the Scopus dataset. MS-Excel and VOSviewer are the analysis tools utilized in bibliometric analysis. The study's conclusions indicate that between 1979 and 2021, there is a steady increase in research on second jobs or moonlighting. United States leading with majority of publications. Guariglia and Kim have the most citations in the co-authorship analysis. The term "moonlighting" is most frequently used among all the available documents. Testing theories of fairness-Intentions matter is the title of the most cited document.

1. INTRODUCTION

Off lately, bibliometric analysis technique has gained scholarly attention and momentum. This helps in analysing the large corpus of research documents especially indexed in good databases. Bibliometric analysis has been applied in the study, a method of synthesizing prior research papers to increase the corpus of knowledge in the topic (Zupic & Čater, 2015). To determine influence, a quantitative analysis of previously published research publications is conducted (Pritchard, 1969; Broadus, 1987 and Lee et al., 2005). In contrast to a standard systematic literature review, a bibliometric review uses a large amount of bibliometric and bibliographic data to provide information from many different domains. The four steps have been strictly followed. These procedures comprise setting the review's goals and parameters, choosing the analytic techniques, obtaining the data for examination, and doing the analysis and producing a summary of the findings (Donthu et al., 2021). Essentially, this follows a four-step procedure that includes selecting search terms, cleaning the data, doing preliminary analysis, and then doing data analysis (Fahimnia et al., 2015) utilized it to look at the study subjects that can assist direct future studies in the field and to recognize the most significant studies and authors. The Scopus database was used in the study to improve the breadth and depth of the findings.

1.1 Exploring Analysis Techniques

Bibliometric analysis's many benefits include its ability to handle large datasets, recognize publication patterns, identify progressive subjects, and produce thematic evolution visualizations (Donthu et al., 2021). Due to this, it has become feasible to gaze back and envision new avenues for results and produce insights for the researchers conducting the research in the same area (Ciampi et al., 2021; Kumar et al., 2021; Pattnaik et al., 2021). The authors proposed that to evaluate the usefulness of the existing corpus, they employed bibliometric technique techniques such as co-occurrence (or co-word) analysis, co-author analysis, and citation analysis. Citation analysis (Small, 1973; Boyack and Klavans, 2010) separate foundational knowledge from other types of knowledge. Co-occurrence (co-word) analysis can show how topics change over time (Zupic and Čater, 2015; Cheng et al., 2019; Pattnaik et al., 2020).

In the new age of changing employment dynamics, the phenomenon of moonlighting is emerging in the market, wherein individuals engage in secondary employment alongside their primary occupations, it has garnered considerable scholarly attention off lately. When the phrase "moonlighting" first appeared, it described the illicit activity of smuggling products at night in order to evade taxes and customs charges. Early in the 19th century, this usage was present (Taunk, 2022). and it was implied in the verbal noun moonlighting. The idea of working by the light of the moon inspired the term "moonlighting," since many people who took on after-hours work did it at night. Moonlighting is the practice of doing a second job after regular business hours (Ara and Akbar, 2016).

In USA during 20th century, many people used to have dual jobs, one a primary job and another as the secondary job in the evening or night to have more income in their hand (Taunk, 2022) and later this concept called moonlighting, as people used to work in nights.

There are various sections in the research article. The paper is divided into five segments: an introduction, the review of literature review is in the second section, research methodology in the third, results and discussions in the fourth, and a conclusion in the fifth. To execute bibliometric analysis in a structured manner, certain research questions and objectives are developed.

2. REVIEW OF LITERATURE

A person who works two or more jobs at the same time is said to be moonlighting (Nunoo et al., 2018). Working two jobs or taking on additional money is a typical practice for employees in developed and developing countries (Dickey et al., 2011; Hurka et al., 2018. Some refer to this practice as moonlighting, twin jobs, side jobs, or holding numerous jobs. It is especially common among low-income workers whose main objective is to earn enough money to enable them to provide for their families family (Betts, 2006; Hausken & Ncube, 2018; Urwick & Kisa, 2014).. As a result of this practice, a worker may have a regular job working from 9 to 5 jobs as their main source of income, yet he/she does work additional shifts at night to increase their income, and the person who does perform these two jobs is called a moonlighter. Moonlighting is not a novel idea and has been used in various industries. Some educators teach children in the evenings after school. Also, doctors in addition to their full-time hospital employment may occasionally work part-time in a private practice from home (Gulati, 2023)

Many sectors of the economy could benefit greatly from the use of artificial intelligence (AI), and in the years to come, this use is predicted to grow significantly (Warning et al., 2022). Technology is redesigning human resource functions in unmatched ways (Goyal et al., 2023). 'Smart Working' has been rising in the dawn of AI across different industries ranging from technology organizations to public sector organizations across different countries of the world (Lake, 2023). The reason is additional income along with the increase in flexibility work arrangements due to AI acceptance. Additionally, the organizations are leveraging implementation of latest technologies by adopting more flexible working patterns (Goyal et al., 2023 and thereby elevating the role of moonlighters in today's context especially due to increasing inflation rates across nations.

On the other hand, the Covid-19 epidemic caused by the coronavirus has also encouraged people to join for side work. This pandemic began in China towards the end of 2019 and quickly spread to every nation on Earth except Antarctica. Since the pandemic's start, there have been significant changes to the global economy due to its negative effects on people's lives, health, education, standards of living, jobs, businesses, and social and economic situations.

2.1 Research Objectives

This piece addresses the following questions:

Q1. To unite the literature available related to moonlighting or dual job.
Q2. To discern and elucidate emerging trends within the field of moonlighting or dual job.

2.2 Research Questions

Q1. Who are the foremost researchers actively contributing to moonlighting or dual job studies?
Q2. Which journal garners the highest level of attention in moonlighting research?
Q3. What countries and institutions are engaged in moonlighting-related research?
Q4. What keywords are most frequently encountered in the context of moonlighting?

3. RESEARCH METHODOLOGY

3.1 Database Selection

In the context of this study, the researchers exclusively extracted data from the Scopus database, a choice driven by several pertinent considerations. Firstly, Scopus offers an extensive reach across a myriad of academic domains, providing us with a rich dataset for analysis. Its accessibility and robust data visualization capabilities were instrumental in facilitating the rigorous data analysis required for our study (Baas et al., 2020; Visser et al., 2021). Moreover, Scopus has emerged as a cornerstone in the realm of bibliometric research, as exemplified by its prominent utilization in studies such as those conducted by Zhu and Liu (2020) and Pico-Saltos (2021). This underscores its reliability and suitability for scholarly investigations, bolstering the credibility of our research findings.

Furthermore, Scopus assumes a pivotal role as the primary data source underpinning the widely acknowledged "QS World University Rankings." This ranking system holds considerable sway, especially among Latin American universities seeking to establish their positions both within their national contexts and on the global stage, as elucidated by Moed (2017) and Torres-Samuel et al. (2020). Consequently, the use of Scopus data in our research paper not only aligns with established scholarly practices but also enhances the global relevance and significance of our study.

The search parameter "TITLE-ABS-KEY ("Moonlighting" OR "Dual Job") AND (LIMIT-TO (SUBJAREA, "SOCI") OR LIMIT-TO (SUBJAREA, "ECON") OR LIMIT-TO (SUBJAREA, "BUSI") OR LIMIT-TO (SUBJAREA, "ARTS") OR LIMIT-TO (SUBJAREA, "PSYC")) AND (LIMIT-TO (DOCTYPE, "ar") OR LIMIT-TO (DOCTYPE, "ch") OR LIMIT-TO (DOCTYPE, "re")) AND (LIMIT-TO (LANGUAGE, "English")) AND (LIMIT-TO (SRCTYPE, "j") OR LIMIT-TO (SRCTYPE, "b")) AND (LIMIT-TO (PUBSTAGE, "final")) was run first. It has made use of the Scopus databases, focusing the search on moonlighting and dual jobs as the two main issue areas, and making use of the keywords, abstract, and title of the article. It did not decide to limit the search to papers that had been published within a certain year. Furthermore, because these papers are a collection of validated data and usually provide reliable outcomes. The present study has focused search by selecting social science, economics, accountancy and business management, humanities and arts, and psychology with articles, book chapters, review papers, document type only with journal papers written in the English language which were in final publication stage (Bhatt et al., 2020; Haleem et al., 2020).

Figure 1. Study's Methodological Framework

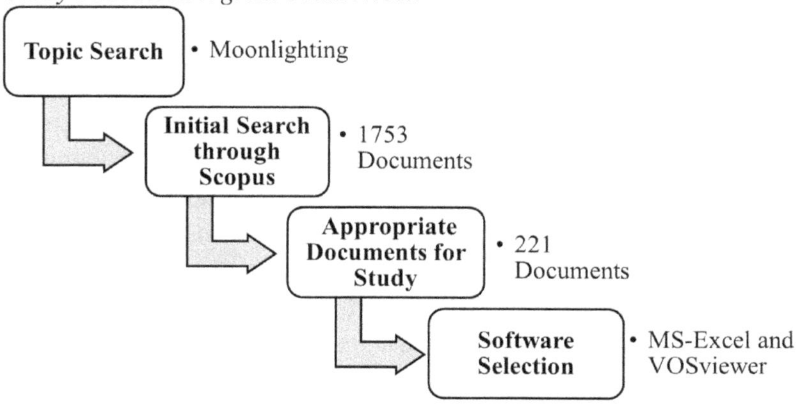

3.2 Data Cleaning

Furthermore, erroneous information—including misspelled words—is frequently present in bibliographic databases. Consequently, it is necessary to review the data that was retrieved (Cobo et al., 2011). The researchers meticulously cleaned the data, removed duplicates, irrelevant information, inaccuracies, corrupted data, and incomplete records. After reviewing the bibliometric data, cleaning is done in MS Excel (such as deleting inappropriate author's name, title and missing affiliation and abstract, as shown in Table -1). Next, Every abstract of the remaining documents was examined by the study. No limitations on journals, disciplines, or publication dates were applied to this search. This produced 190 potentially pertinent articles from Scopus post applying all filtering criteria as listed below.

Table 1. Standards for Article Search and Selection

Filtering criteria	**Reject**	**Accept**
Criteria for the Search		
Search Database: Scopus		
Date of Search:		
Searching Keywords:		221
Subject area: All		221
Types of documents: articles, conference papers, and reviews		221
Selection of Articles		

continued on following page

Table 1. Continued

Filtering criteria	Reject	Accept
Papers with Inappropriate Author name	2	219
Papers with Inappropriate Title	1	218
Papers with Missing Affiliations	13	205
Papers Omitted Abstract	15	190

4. RESULTS AND DISCUSSIONS

Bibliometric analysis can be done in two ways. This can be done by Statistical analysis of documents (documents by country, year, and author) and additionally, network analysis of the database (co-authorship, co-occurrence, and citation analysis).

4.1 Statistical Analysis

This is available in the Scopus database and can be extracted under the section named "Search Analyze Results". The next section deals with the data analysis generated in different ways.

4.1.1 Year-wise Documents' Record

In Figure 4.1 per year documents published by Scopus with Article Title "Moonlighting" is shown. From 1975 to 2023, articles published per year are increasing. All articles are plotted against the publication year to illustrate the publication trend of moonlighting or dual job research. As seen in Figure 4.1, the research in this concept is quite old as it started in year 1979 but the research progress in this particular area is seen as upward and downward trend till 2023. The years when the most papers were published in this topic are 2021 (17), 2022 (7), and 2023 (11) respectively. The trend is increasing especially during the years of the outbreak of Covid 19 and the researchers are still working on this topic of moonlighting or dual job.

Figure 2. Documents by Year (Source: www.scopus.com)

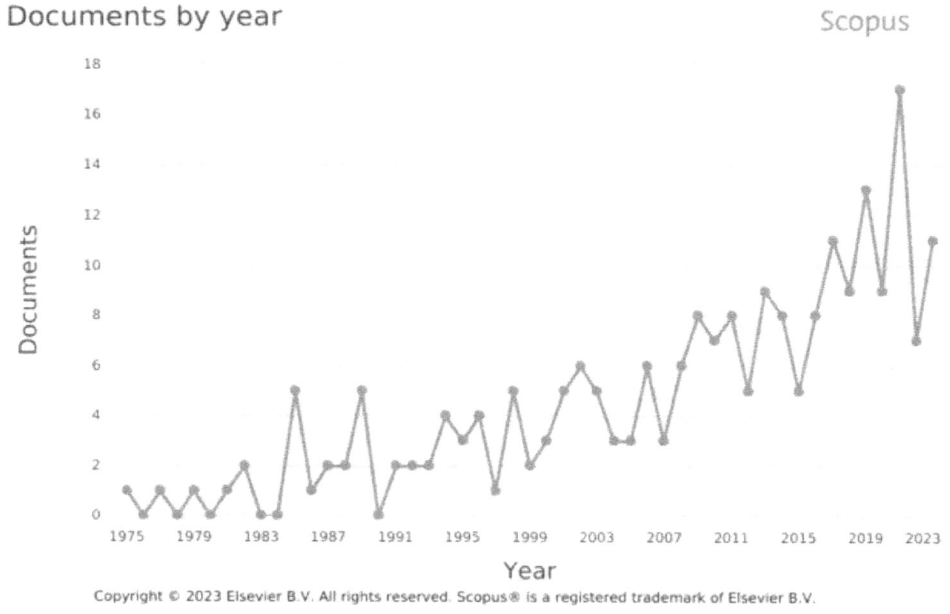

4.1.2 Annual Documents by Source

Figure 4.2 shows per year documents by source. It is depicted that "Applied Economics" has published more articles on the concept of moonlighting till date. It has published 6 documents till date starting from 1986 on moonlighting followed by "Academic Medicine" (5 documents), followed by "Academic Psychiatry" (4 documents), followed by "Human Resources For Health" (3 documents), followed by "Frontiers In Psychology" (1 documents) and so on.

Figure 3. Annual Documents by Source (Source: www.scopus.com)

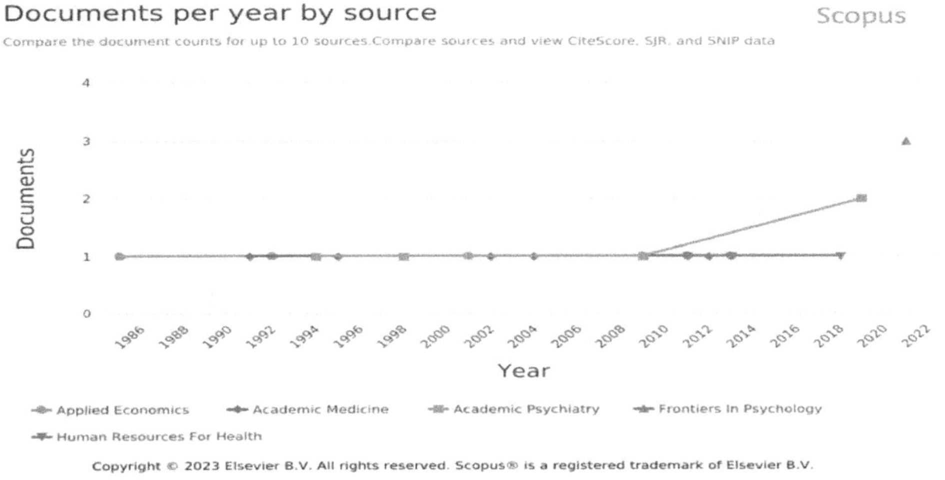

4.1.3 Documents Written by the Author

Figure 4.3 shows, documents by author. It is depicted that most of the documents on moonlighting are published by Kimmel, J, (4 documents) followed by Renna, F. (3 documents) ; and followed Baldwin, D.C. ; Boyd, E.M. ; Cho, H. ; Choe, C. ; Conen, W. ; Cox, J.C. ; Daniel, W.T. (2 documents per author) and so on.

Figure 4. Documents by Author (Source: www.scopus.com)

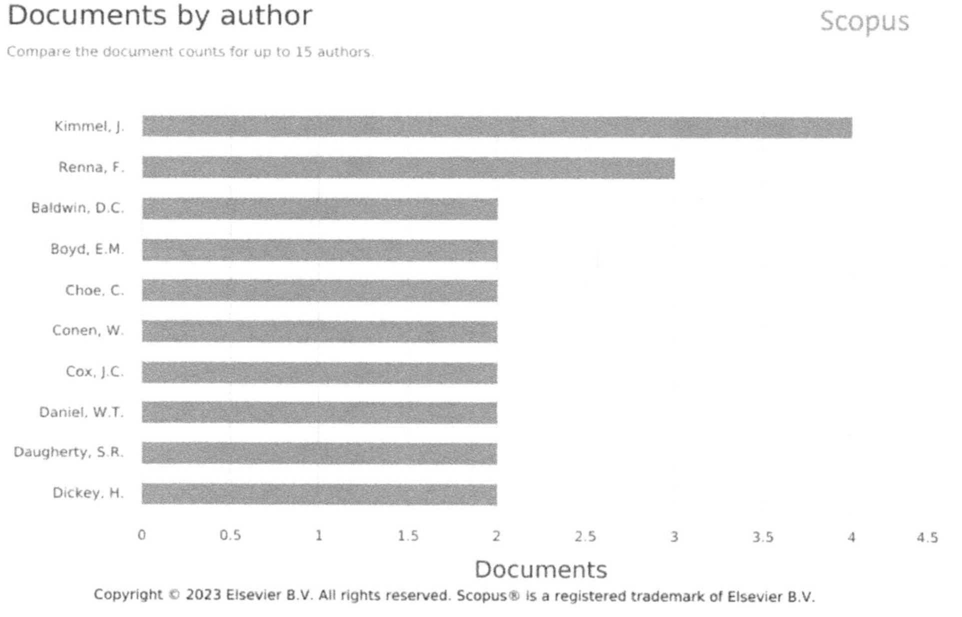

4.1.4 Documents by Affiliation

Figure 4.4 shows documents by affiliation. It is depicted that most of the documents on moonlighting are published by the "Universiteit van Amsterdam", followed by "Ludwig-Maximilians-Universität München", followed by "University of Georgia" and followed by the "Freie Universität Berlin" (4 documents), followed by "University of Florida", "University of Nottingham", "University of Aberdeen", "Concordia University", "W.E. Upjohn Institute for Employment Research" (3 documents per university) and so on.

Figure 5. Documents by University Affiliation (Source: www.scopus.com)

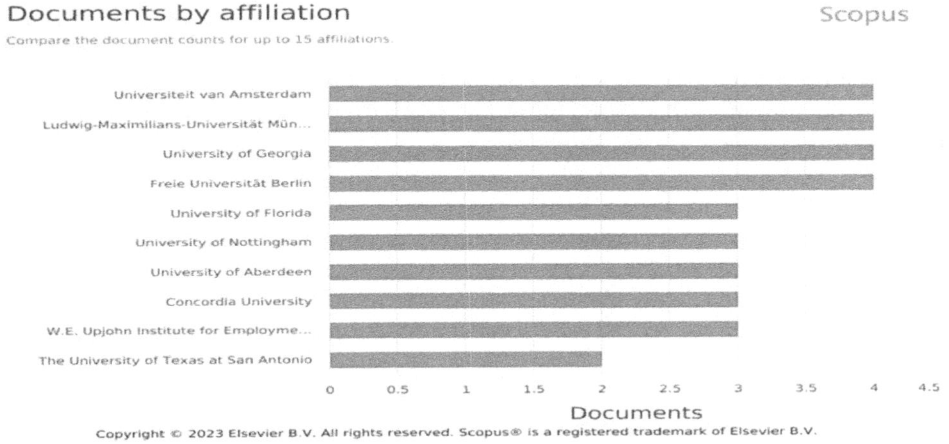

4.1.5 Documents by Country

Figure 4.5 shows documents by country. It is depicted that authors from United States have published most of the documents on moonlighting (105 documents) followed by the United Kingdom (25 documents), followed by the Germany (15 documents), followed by Canada (10 documents) and so on.

Figure 6. Documents by Country (Source: www.scopus.com)

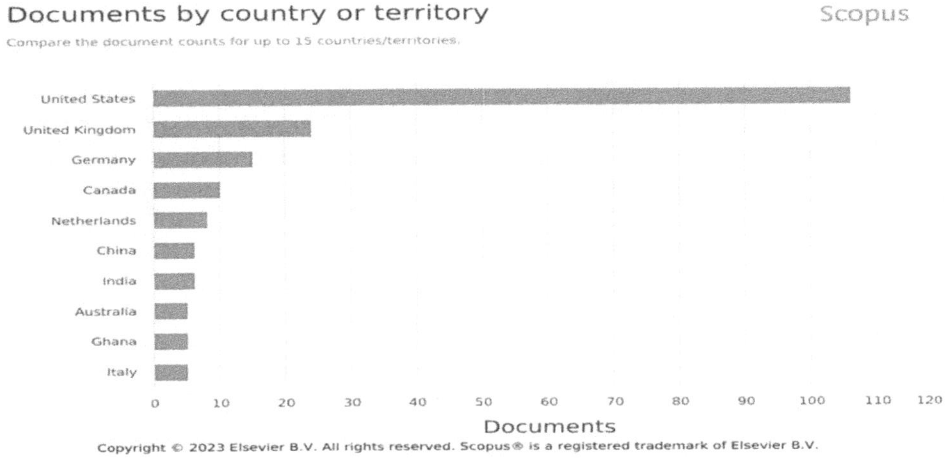

4.1.6 Discipline Wise Documents

Documents are arranged by subject area in Figure 4.6. The majority of moonlighting-related materials are published under the Social Sciences area (29.4% from total documents) followed by Multidisciplinary (17.6%) followed by Economics (14.8%), Business, Management (12.3%) and so on.

Figure 7. Discipline Wise Documents (Source: www.scopus.com)

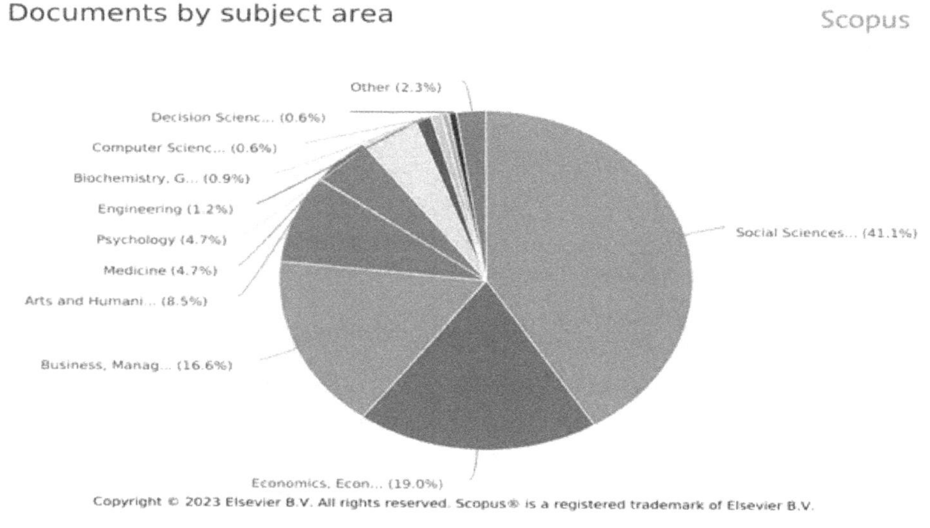

4.1.7 Documents by Funding Sponsor

Figure 4.7 shows documents by the sponsors which had funded these projects. It is depicted that "Hans Böckler Stiftung" has sponsored most of the documents on moonlighting (4 documents) followed by the "National Institutes of Health" (2 documents) and so on.

Figure 8. Documents by Funding Sponsor (Source: www.scopus.com)

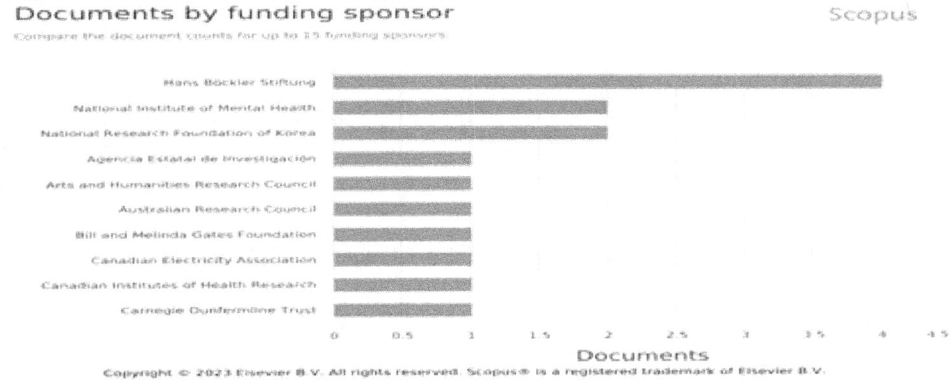

4.2 Network Analysis

In network analysis, o-authorship, co-occurrence, and citation analysis have all been used by the researcher. The network analysis is presented in the following section done by using VOSviewer on the Scopus database imported in the Excel sheet.

4.2.1 Co-authorship Analysis

The quantity of publications co-authored is used to ascertain the relationship between the items in the co-authorship analysis (Jayaram, and Singh, 2020). Co-authorship analysis can be done on the basis of authors, organizations, and regions/ countries.

4.2.2 Co-authorship Analysis Based on Authors

For co-authorship analysis, Authors have been employed by the researcher as a component of the co-authorship analysis, with a minimum of two documents and a minimum of two citations per author. Three authors, out of 187, are approaching the cutoff point. Guariglia a. and Kim b.-y., who have the most citations, are the most prolific co-authors, as seen in Table 2.

Table 2. Co-authorship Analysis Based on Authors

Author	Documents	Citations	Total Link Strengths
Guariglia A.; Kim B.-Y.	2	60	0
Geys B.; Mause K.	2	55	0
Hausken K.; Ncube M.	2	4	0

4.2.3 Analysis of Co-authorship Based on Organization

Organization is employed by the researcher as a component of analysis for co-authorship analysis, with a minimum of two documents and a minimum of two citations for each organization. Five organizations out of 358 surpass the threshold limit. With the most citations and documents, "IZA, Bonn, Germany" is the top organization in moonlighting or dual job research, as Table 3 demonstrates.

Table 3. Analysis of Co-authorship Based on Organization

Organization	Documents	Citations	Total Link Strength
IZA, Bonn, Germany	2	390	0
School of Economics, University of Nottingham, University Park, United Kingdom	2	60	0
University of Bremen, Germany	2	55	0
Department of Political Science and Geography, Francis Marion University, Florence, United States	2	11	0
University of Amsterdam, Amsterdam, Netherlands	2	9	0

Figure 9. Organization-based Co-authorship Analysis

Figure 4.8 suggests that large firms are not in contact with each other when it comes to studies on dual jobs and moonlighting. That being said, figure 4.8 highlights five prominent organizations. As a result, the leading organizations in the field of moonlighting or dual job research must work together to perform collaborative study on the topic.

4.2.4 Co-authorship Analysis by Nation

Organizations have been included in the co-authorship analysis by the researcher, with a minimum of two documents per citation and five documents per nation. Out of the 55 countries, 12 meet the upper bound. Table 4 shows that the US is the country that participates in co-authorship with other countries the most, with the greatest amount of citations, papers, and overall connection strength.

Table 4. Co-authorship Analysis by Nation

Country	Documents	Citations	Total Link Strength
United States	95	1470	12
United Kingdom	19	632	4
Germany	15	769	8
Canada	10	228	2

continued on following page

Table 4. Continued

Country	Documents	Citations	Total Link Strength
Netherlands	8	177	4
China	6	133	3
India	6	21	0
Australia	5	113	2
Ghana	5	60	3
Italy	5	106	0
Norway	5	90	2
South Africa	5	35	2

Figure 10. Country-based Co-authorship Analysis

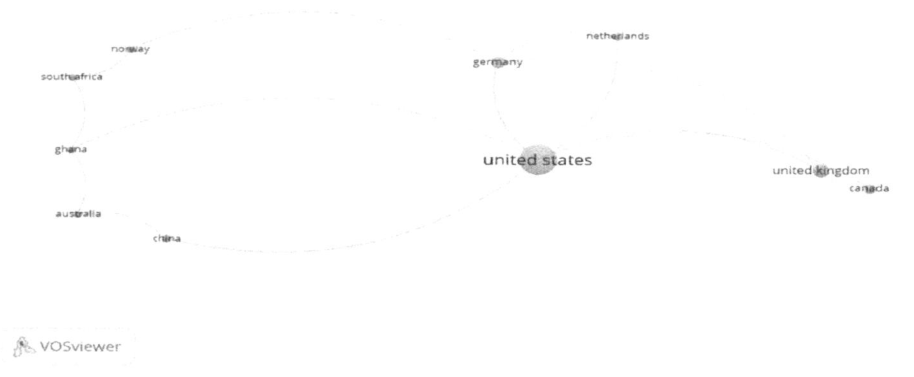

According to Figure 4.9, the US has the greatest number of connections with other nations when it comes to studies on moonlighting or dual jobs. As a result, the US is the leading nation actively pursuing this issue. Compared to other nations like the US, UK, and Canada, countries like India have less documents and citations overall, but their connections with other nations are weaker. As a result, Indian writers ought to make an effort to work with international writers on the research project. Thus, there's a good chance that researchers in the future will choose to focus on this subject especially in countries like India.

4.3 Analysis of Co-Occurrence:

In Analysis of Co-Occurrence, the relationships between the items are determined by the quantity of texts in which the keywords occur together (Jayaram and Singh, 2021).

4.3.1 Examination of Every Keyword's Co-Occurrences

In the context of co-occurrence analysis, all keywords have been utilized by the researcher, with the minimum number of occurrences for each term being eight. Thirteen of the seven hundred forty-four keywords satisfy the cutoff. In public materials, the terms "human" and "moonlighting" have been used most frequently, as Table 5 illustrates.

Table 5. Examination of Every Keyword's Co-Occurrences

Keyword	Occurrences	Total Link Strength
Moonlighting	44	30
Human	16	65
Employment	12	35
Labor Market	11	13
Article	10	40
Female	10	52
Humans	10	47
Labor Supply	10	9
Male	10	52
Adult	9	50
Income	9	22
Priority Journal	8	34
United States	8	29

Figure 11. Examination of Every Keyword's Co-Occurrences

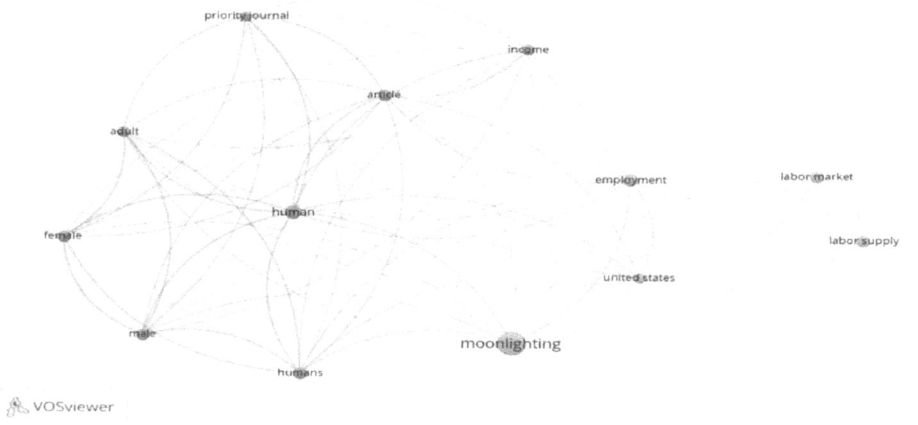

According to Figure 4.10, the term "moonlighting" appears more frequently, with a greater total connection strength and more occurrences overall. Moonlighting and human are important buzzwords.

4.3.2 Examination of the Co-Occurring Keywords Used by the Author

The author keyword has been included in the co-occurrence analysis, with a minimum of four keyword occurrences, according to the researcher. Seven of the 448 keywords are eligible to pass the criterion. According to Table 6, the majority of the time, keyword moonlighting has been found in published documents.

Table 6. Examination of the co-occurring keywords used by the author

Keyword	Occurrences	Total Link Strength
Moonlighting	42	9
Labor Supply	5	2
Multiple Jobholding	5	4
Covid-19	4	2
Ethics	4	1
Outside Earnings	4	2
Teacher Moonlighting	4	0

Figure 12. Examination of the co-occurring keywords used by the author

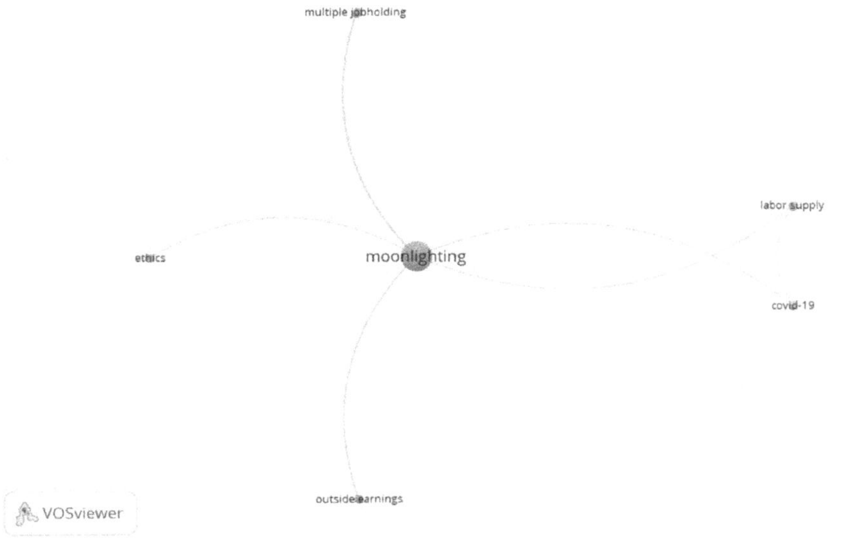

Figure 4.11 suggests that the term "moonlighting" is most frequently occurring, with the greatest total link strength and number of occurrences. It is followed by labor supply, multiple job holding, COVID-19, and ethics.

4.4 Citation Analysis

According to the entire quantity of citations and the number of citations for each document, citation analysis ranks the most prolific researchers, journals, publications, organizations, and nations (Jayaram and Singh, 2021).

4.4.1 Citation Analysis Based on Documents

The researcher used documents as a component of the analysis for the citation analysis, with a minimum of 30 citations per document. 29 of the 190 documents are in compliance with the criterion. Table 7 reveals that the writers with the most often cited publications are Falk A.; Fehr E.; and Fischbacher U as shown in the Table 7.

Table 7. Citation analysis based on documents

Document	Citations	Total Link Strength
Falk A.; Fehr E.; Fischbacher U. (2008)	373	0
Rodell J.B. (2013)	223	0
Abbink K.; Irlenbusch B.; Renner E. (2000)	131	0
Inness Michelle M.; Turner N.; Barling J.; Stride C.B. (2010)	116	0
Adamchik V.A.; Bedi A.S. (2000)	91	0
Nuthalapaty F.S.; Jackson J.R.; Owen J. (2004)	83	0
Gagliarducci S.; Nannicini T.; Naticchioni P. (2010)	83	0
Gershuny J.I. (1979)	79	0
Gruen R.; Anwar R.; Begum T.; Killingsworth J.R.; Normand C. (2002)	71	0
Xia N.; Xie Q.; Hu X.; Wang X.; Meng H. (2020)	70	0
Isachsen A.J.; Strøm S. (1985)	68	0
Kimmel J.; Conway K.S. (2001)	62	1
Büchel F.; Battu H. (2003)	59	0
Smith Conway K.; Kimmel J. (1998)	57	3
Averett S.L. (2001)	52	4
Biglaiser G.; Ma C.-T.A. (2007)	52	1
Chen C.-C.; Zou S.S.; Chen M.-H. (2022)	47	0
Snow R.C.; Asabir K.; Mutumba M.; Koomson E.; Gyan K.; Dzodzomenyo M.; Kruk M.; Kwansah J. (2011)	45	0
Sliter M.T.; Boyd E.M. (2014)	44	0
Vujicic M.; Shengelia B.; Alfano M.; Thu H.B. (2011)	44	1
Cox J.C.; Sadiraj K.; Sadiraj V. (2008)	44	1
Geys B.; Mause K. (2013)	42	1
Dickey H.; Watson V.; Zangelidis A. (2011)	41	1
Lo V.-H.; Chan J.M.; Pan Z. (2005)	40	0
Wu Z.; Baimbridge M.; Zhu Y. (2009)	40	2
Fröhlich R.; Koch T.; Obermaier M. (2013)	40	0
Guariglia A.; Kim B.-Y. (2006)	39	3
Petersdorf R.G.; Bentley J. (1989)	37	0

Table 8. Citation analysis based on documents

Document	Citations	Total Link Strength	Title Of Document	Journal Details
Falk A.; Fehr E.; Fischbacher U. (2008)	373	0	Testing theories of fairness-Intentions matter	Games and Economic Behavior
Rodell J.B. (2013)	223	0	Finding meaning through volunteering: Why do employees volunteer and what does it mean for their jobs?	Academy of Management Journal
Abbink K.; Irlenbusch B.; Renner E. (2000)	131	0	The moonlighting game: An experimental study on reciprocity and retribution	Journal of Economic Behavior and Organization
Inness Michelle M.; Turner N.; Barling J.; Stride C.B. (2010)	116	0	Transformational Leadership and Employee Safety Performance: A Within-Person, Between-Jobs Design	Journal of Occupational Health Psychology
Adamchik V.A.; Bedi A.S. (2000)	91	0	Wage differentials between the public and the private sectors: Evidence from an economy in transition	Labour Economics
Nuthalapaty F.S.; Jackson J.R.; Owen J. (2004)	83	0	The Influence of Quality-of-Life, Academic, and Workplace Factors on Residency Program Selection	Academic Medicine

Figure 13. Document-based Citation Analysis

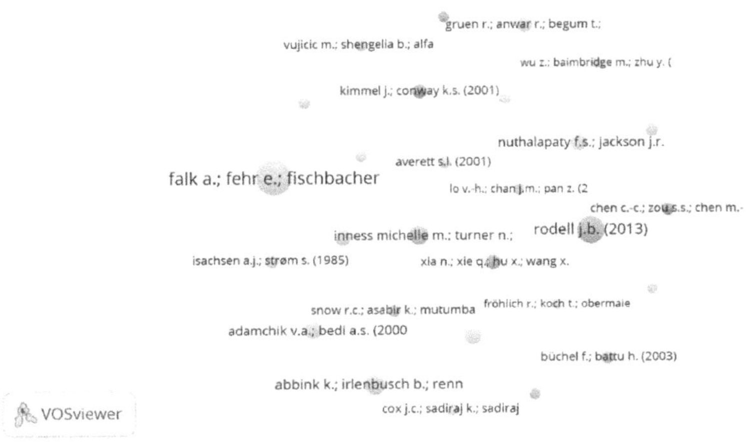

The publication titled "Antecedents and Consequences of Moonlighting" by Falk, Ehr, and Fischbacher (2008) appears to have the most links and citations, based on Figure 4.12. This indicates that the provided document is highly valuable and productive in terms of researching moonlighting or dual jobs.

4.4.2 Source-Based Citation Analysis

The researcher has included sources in the analysis for the citation analysis using two documents and a minimum of two citations from each source. Only 20 of the 155 sources converge to the threshold. According to Table 9, "applied economics" has received the greatest number of citations overall and across all documents. It is possible to interpret the source "applied economics" as having the greatest amount of documents (6) and citations (155). It indicates that useful research on moonlighting or dual jobs is published in "applied economics."

Table 9. Citation analysis based on sources

Source	Documents	Citations	Total Link Strength
Labour Economics	3	163	1
Applied Economics	6	155	1
Academic Medicine	4	106	4
Human Resources for Health	3	103	0
Academic Psychiatry	5	24	4
Frontiers in Psychology	3	21	0
Transfer	3	18	0

Figure 14. Citation analysis based on Sources

Figure 4.13 indicates that the source "applied economics" has the greatest amount of documents (6) and citations (155) of any source. It indicates that "applied economics" publishes insightful studies on dual jobs and moonlighting.

4.4.3 Author-Based Citation Analysis

Authors have been used by the researcher as a component of the citation analysis, with a minimum of two documents and a minimum of two citations per author. Three writers out of the 187 total—meet the required number. With the most citations (60) and documents (2), Kim B.-Y. is the most cited author, according to Table 10. Since the researcher is employing writers in this citation analysis, Kim B.-Y. And Guariglia A. are the most referenced authors.

Table 10. Author-based Citation Analysis

Author	Documents	Citations	Total Link Strength
Guariglia A.; Kim B.-Y.	2	60	0
Geys B.; Mause K.	2	55	0
Hausken K.; Ncube M.	2	4	0

4.4.4 Country-Based Citation Analysis

In order to accomplish the citation analysis, the researcher used countries, where a country should have as few as two citations and as few as five papers.. Of the 55 countries, 12 are in compliance with the threshold. According to Table 11, Germany comes in second with 769 citations, and the United States is the most cited nation with 1470.

Table 11. Country-based Citation Analysis

Country	Documents	Citations	Total Link Strength
United States	95	1470	698
Germany	15	769	589
United Kingdom	19	632	156
Canada	10	228	101
Netherlands	8	177	180
China	6	133	197
Australia	5	113	148
Italy	5	106	40
Norway	5	90	210
Ghana	5	60	189
South Africa	5	35	123
India	6	21	9

Figure 15. Country-based Citation Analysis

According to Figure 4.14, Germany comes in second with 769 citations, while the United States is the most referenced nation with 1470 citations.

5. DISCUSSIONS AND CONCLUSION

After using VOSviewer to analyze the study's results and discussing them in the preceding section, it is found that database network analysis and statistical analysis facilitate the effective implementation of bibliometric analysis. Based on data study, the number of publications on moonlighting or working two jobs increased between 1975 and 2023. The majority of the materials have been released by the "Universiteit van Amsterdam" and by the author Kimmel, J. Based on country-specific document counts, the majority of the documents are released by the United States. In the area of dual jobs or moonlighting, Hans Böckler Stiftung is the top funding source.

Online analysis of the database using bibliometric analysis is done with three analysis tools, which are co-occurrence analysis, co-factor analysis and citation analysis. Cofactor analysis is performed on organizations, factors and countries/regions. Co-author of Guariglia A.; Kim B.-Y. and the co-author's country is the United States. However, there is very poor communication between collaborating organizations and they need to collaborate more with different organizations working from a moonlight or two job perspective. Concurrent analysis is performed based on occurrences of all keywords and occurrences of author keywords. In both types of analysis, the keyword "moonlight" occurs most often. Regarding citation analysis, is done with documents, sources, authors and countries. The most cited article is Falk A. "Testing Theories of Justice - Intentions Matter"; Fehr E.; Fischbacher U., the most cited source is "Work Economics", the most cited author is Guariglia A.; Kim B.-Y. and the US is the nation that is most frequently mentioned. Hence, a rise in the numbers of moonlighters is expected to as the flexible work hours positively affects quality of work life (Wu et al., 2024). Additionally, the literature review provide insights about the how generative AI and automation tools are changing job structure, reshaping career and allowing people to multitask without sacrificing performance.

6. FUTURE SCOPE OF STUDY

Given the thorough examination, it is possible to draw the conclusion that there is still need for more research on moonlighting. The current study found that further cooperation between field organizations and organizations in other countries is necessary. For more research output, there is an even greater need to collaborate with other nations. However, nations like India need to generate more on the same subject. In order to do better research with creative viewpoints and ideas, they must collaborate with authors from other countries. According to the aforementioned fields of study, relationships between various factors can be investigated through empirical research. Future research on the relationship between moonlighting and factors including employee happiness, life satisfaction, and contentment at work may be conducted. However, there are insufficient longitudinal studies on AI and work boundaries and dual employment normalization. The deployment of AI surveillance tools and moonlighting detection and policy enforcement can also be the potential area of future research.

REFERENCES

Ara, K., & Akbar, A. (2016). A study of the impact of moonlighting practices on job satisfaction of university teachers. *Bulletin of Education and Research, 38*(1), 101–116.

Baas, J., Schotten, M., Plume, A., Côté, G., & Karimi, R. (2020). Scopus as a curated, high-quality bibliometric data source for academic research in quantitative science studies. *Quantitative Science Studies, 1*(1), 377–386. DOI: 10.1162/qss_a_00019

Betts, S. C. (2006). The decision to moonlight or quit: Incorporating multiple job holding into a model of turnover. *Journal of Organizational Culture. Communications and Conflict, 10*(1), 63.

Bhatt, Y., Ghuman, K., & Dhir, A. (2020). Sustainable manufacturing. Bibliometrics and content analysis. *Journal of Cleaner Production, 260*, 120988. DOI: 10.1016/j.jclepro.2020.120988

Boyack, K. W., & Klavans, R. (2010, December). Co-citation analysis, bibliographic coupling, and direct citation: Which citation approach represents the research front most accurately? *Journal of the American Society for Information Science and Technology, 61*(12), 2389–2404. DOI: 10.1002/asi.21419

Boyack, K. W., & Klavans, R. (2010, December). Co-citation analysis, bibliographic coupling, and direct citation: Which citation approach represents the research front most accurately? *Journal of the American Society for Information Science and Technology, 61*(12), 2389–2404. DOI: 10.1002/asi.21419

Broadus, R. N. (1987, November). Toward a definition of "bibliometrics". *Scientometrics, 12*(5-6), 373–379. DOI: 10.1007/BF02016680

Cheng, W., Kang, Q., & Xiao, Q. (2019, February 1). Bibliometric analysis of the top 100 influential studies on carotid artery stenting. *World Neurosurgery, 122*, e1321–e1331. DOI: 10.1016/j.wneu.2018.11.042 PMID: 30448570

Ciampi, F., Giannozzi, A., Marzi, G., & Altman, E. I. (2021, March). Rethinking SME default prediction: A systematic literature review and future perspectives. *Scientometrics, 126*(3), 2141–2188. DOI: 10.1007/s11192-020-03856-0 PMID: 33531720

Cobo, M. J., López-Herrera, A. G., Herrera-Viedma, E., & Herrera, F. (2011). Science mapping software tools: Review, analysis, and cooperative study among tools. *Journal of the American Society for Information Science and Technology, 62*(7), 1382–1402. DOI: 10.1002/asi.21525

Dickey, H., Watson, V., & Zangelidis, A. (2011). Is it all about money? An examination of the motives behind moonlighting. *Applied Economics*, *43*(26), 3767–3774. DOI: 10.1080/00036841003724403

Donthu, N., Kumar, S., Mukherjee, D., Pandey, N., & Lim, W. M. (2021, September 1). How to conduct a bibliometric analysis: An overview and guidelines. *Journal of Business Research*, *133*, 285–296. DOI: 10.1016/j.jbusres.2021.04.070

Fahimnia, B., Sarkis, J., & Davarzani, H. (2015, April 1). Green supply chain management: A review and bibliometric analysis. *International Journal of Production Economics*, *162*, 101–114. DOI: 10.1016/j.ijpe.2015.01.003

Goyal, P., Kataria, R., Prakash, A., & Arora, M. (2023). Impact of Technology in Human Resource: A Systematic

Gulati, M. (2023). *Analysis of Various Aspects of Moonlighting*. Journal of Business Theory and Practice. DOI: 10.22158/jbtp.v11n1p32

Haleem, A., Khan, M. I., Khan, S., & Jami, A. R. (2020). Research status in Halal: A review and bibliometric analysis. *Modern Supply Chain Research and Applications*, *2*(1), 23–41. DOI: 10.1108/MSCRA-06-2019-0014

Hausken, K., & Ncube, M. (2018). Service delivery versus moonlighting: Using data from Kenya, Uganda, Tanzania and Senegal. *African Development Review*, *30*(2), 219–232. DOI: 10.1111/1467-8268.12327

Hurka, S., Daniel, W. T., & Obholzer, L. (2018). Determinants of moonlighting in the European Parliament. *Journal of Legislative Studies*, *24*(1), 127–147. DOI: 10.1080/13572334.2018.1444630

Jayaram, R., & Singh, S. (2020). A bibliometric analysis and visualization of research trends in COVID-19 and suicide. *Annals of Tropical Medicine and Public Health.*

Kumar, S., Pandey, N., Lim, W. M., Chatterjee, A. N., & Pandey, N. (2021, September 1). What do we know about transfer pricing? Insights from bibliometric analysis. *Journal of Business Research*, *134*, 275–287. DOI: 10.1016/j.jbusres.2021.05.041

Lake, A. (2023). *Beyond Hybrid Working: A Smarter & Transformational Approach to Flexible Working*. Taylor & Francis. DOI: 10.4324/9781003288930

Lee, J. D., Cassano-Pinché, A., & Vicente, K. J. (2005, December). Bibliometric analysis of human factors (1970-2000): A quantitative description of scientific impact. *Human Factors*, *47*(4), 753–766. DOI: 10.1518/001872005775570970 PMID: 16553064

Moed, H. F. (2017). A critical comparative analysis of five world university rankings. *Scientometrics*, *110*(2), 967–990. DOI: 10.1007/s11192-016-2212-y

Nunoo, J., Darfor, K. N., Koomson, I., & Arthur, A. (2018). Employment security and workers' moonlighting behaviour in Ghana. *Journal of Economic Studies (Glasgow, Scotland)*, *45*(1), 144–155. DOI: 10.1108/JES-04-2016-0074

Pattnaik, D., Kumar, S., & Burton, B. (2021, June). Thirty years of the Australian accounting review: A bibliometric analysis. *Australian Accounting Review*, *31*(2), 150–164. DOI: 10.1111/auar.12332

Pattnaik, D., Kumar, S., & Vashishtha, A. (2020, October 24). Research on trade credit–a systematic review and bibliometric analysis. *Qualitative Research in Financial Markets.*, *12*(4), 367–390. DOI: 10.1108/QRFM-09-2019-0103

Pico-Saltos, R., Carrión-Mero, P., Montalván-Burbano, N., Garzás, J., & Redchuk, A. (2021). Research trends in career success: A bibliometric review. *Sustainability (Basel)*, *13*(9), 4625. DOI: 10.3390/su13094625

Pritchard A. (1969). Statistical Bibliography; An Interim Bibliography.

Small, H. (1973, July). Co-citation in the scientific literature: A new measure of the relationship between two documents. *Journal of the American Society for Information Science*, *24*(4), 265–269. DOI: 10.1002/asi.4630240406

Taunk, A. (2022). A Study On The Causes And Effects Of Moonlighting In The IT Sector. *Journal of Pharmaceutical Negative Results*, •••, 6698–6705.

Torres-Samuel, M., Vásquez, C. L., Luna, M., Bucci, N., Viloria, A., Crissien, T., & Manosalva, J. (2020). Performance of education and research in Latin American countries through data envelopment analysis (DEA). *Procedia Computer Science*, *170*, 1023–1028. DOI: 10.1016/j.procs.2020.03.079

Urwick, J., & Kisa, S. (2014). Science teacher shortage and the moonlighting culture: The pathology of the teacher labour market in Uganda. *International Journal of Educational Development*, *36*, 72–80. DOI: 10.1016/j.ijedudev.2013.11.004

Visser, M., Van Eck, N. J., & Waltman, L. (2021). Large-scale comparison of bibliographic data sources: Scopus, Web of Science, Dimensions, Crossref, and Microsoft Academic. *Quantitative Science Studies*, *2*(1), 20–41. DOI: 10.1162/qss_a_00112

Warning, A., Weber, E., & Püffel, A. (2022). On the Impact of Digitalization and Artificial Intelligence on Employers' Flexibility Requirements in Occupations—Empirical Evidence for Germany. *Frontiers in Artificial Intelligence*, *5*, 868789. DOI: 10.3389/frai.2022.868789 PMID: 35592650

Wu, T. J., Pan, Q., Zhang, K., & Zhang, R. X. (2024). Flexible working on employees' quality of work life: The role of locus of control through psychological perspective. *Current Psychology (New Brunswick, N.J.)*, *43*(43), 1–16. DOI: 10.1007/s12144-024-06848-y

Zhu, X. D., & Liu, J. (2020). Education in and after Covid-19: Immediate Responses and Long-Term Visions. *Postdigital Science and Education*, *1-5*(3), 695–699. Advance online publication. DOI: 10.1007/s42438-020-00126-3 PMID: 40476967

Zupic, I., & Čater, T. (2015, July). Bibliometric methods in management and organization. *Organizational Research Methods*, *18*(3), 429–472. DOI: 10.1177/1094428114562629

Chapter 10
Leveraging HR Analytics for Strategic Decision-Making in the IT Industry

Isha Jaryal
https://orcid.org/0009-0007-4853-7172
University School of Business, Chandigarh University, India

Abhishek Kumar Yadav
https://orcid.org/0009-0003-4500-5059
University School of Business, Chandigarh University, India

Bhanupriya Khatri
https://orcid.org/0000-0002-4130-6271
University School of Business, Chandigarh University, India

ABSTRACT

Agile and well-informed decision-making is essential to maintaining competitiveness and innovation in the evolving IT sector. IT companies may now successfully match personnel strategies with more general business goals thanks to HR analytics, which has become a game-changing instrument. This study looks at how HR analytics affect strategic decision-making in the IT industry, emphasizing how it may improve operational effectiveness, optimize talent management, and promote long-term success. The study's conclusions demonstrate the strategic importance of HR analytics as a driver of creativity and flexibility in the IT industry. In addition to optimizing HR operations, data-driven decision-making strengthens organizational resilience in a market that is competitive and changing quickly. This study emphasizes how important it is for IT companies to incorporate HR analytics into their frameworks for making decisions in order to gain a long-term competitive edge.

DOI: 10.4018/979-8-3373-2135-6.ch010

INTRODUCTION

There are various challenges faced by the IT employees, including work-life balance, and this challenge plays an important role in helping HR manage an employee. The IT sector faces various problems like turnover, dissatisfaction, and lack of support and performance. The research provides multiple solutions to overcome this challenge (Sar et al., 2017 ; Khan & Magd, 2023). It highlights that employee attrition is a major challenge faced by HR managers in today's world, especially in the IT sector. The study highlights the factors that affect the attrition, and they explain the impact of an agile environment in the organization by using multi-group analysis (Parimi & Chakraborty, 2019). Employee retention significantly impacts organizational success, especially in IT sectors and healthcare, which have high attrition. In 2010-2011, Attrition rates were high in IT and healthcare sectors. HR must focus on these and take initiative action and provide an opportunity to retain employees.(Shanmugam et al., 2016).How digital transformation affects the HR and IT employees by using the correlation analysis and survey. This study also explains the relationship between HRM and digital transformation in Morocco's IT sector (Ramachandaran et al., 2024). This study explains the factors that influence employee turnover in the Indian IT sector. These factors are organizational, HR, and job-related. Data was gathered from 660 employees from major IT companies to analyze the impact on turnover (Satpal & Dhillon, 2019) (Jonathan et al., 2024). It explores how team-building strategy helps in employee engagement and drives organizational innovation in IT sectors. Data collected from 309 employees showed that teamwork helps in innovation and is more effective if the employee engagement acts as a mediator. This study investigates especially the engagement of millennial employee (Jha et al., 2019). It explores the HR practice used in the India IT sector and highlights the good and bad practices and their impact. IT companies whose strategies are strong and good are easily led to market and effective HR help to improve the growth and performance of the company. It highlights the need for IT firms to adopt the HR practices and avoid the bad ones to maintain their brand image.(Gupta et al., 2023 ; Khan & Magd, 2021). HR practices influence knowledge sharing in the IT industry in Coimbatore, Tamil Nadu. Data was collected through surveys and using the regression and correlation. The result was that the sharing of knowledge is influenced positively by recruitment, training, and teamwork as compared to reward (Saravanabhavan et al., 2024). Green human recourses management practices in Haryana's IT sector India. It also explains the correlation between green human recourses management process and performance outcomes like a green recruitment, performance appraisal, and environment. The study highlights demonstrate an IT industry dedication to sustainability and provide useful insights for HR managers (Lekhi et al., 2024; Jonathan et al., 2024).

REVIEW OF LITERATURE

Today, the rise in online job applications has made it challenging for HR to identify the best suitable candidate. To address this, a pre–interview Reviewer web was developed for IT companies. It helps to analyze the CV on the basis of job requirements. It helps HR to recruit and select in an effective and efficient manner (Shaman et al., 2022)The IT sector faces many challenges in hiring suitable employees for an organization. To bridge the gap, an Expert System for recruiting IT specialists (ESRIT) was developed. It helps to analyze the resume. This system helps to improve the recruitment process and select best suitable candidate (Truic & Barnoschi, 2014 ; Khan et al., 2024).

The adoption of AI in the IT sector was examined by collecting data from 126 HR managers and executives by using the T-tests and ANOVA. The result was that the organization's use of AI in HRM had a positive impact and better results. The findings offer insights for organizations to adopt AI in HRM for better results. Indian IT sector become globally competive and hig tech in the Indian economy. The study was done to identify the impact of HR in building the corporate image. Data was collected from 100 respondents and then analyzed by using Pearson's correlation and regression that show the link between employer branding, corporate social responsibility, and image building. IT companies whose adopt HR practice has great positive impact on their image (Rana et al., 2021 ; Khatri et al., 2022).

The Impact of Strategic Human Resources Management (S-HRM) on performance of organization in Indian IT sector. Data was collected from 211 HR in Bangalore by analysis the Structural equation Modeling (SEM) and confirmatory factor analysis. Results show that there is a positive relation between S-HRM and the performance of the organization. It emphasizes the importance of aligning HR strategies with organization goals (Showkat et al., 2019)(Goyal & Khatri, 2022). Today, time technology has significantly influenced HRM in education management. Data collected from 320 HR and 10 education ministry officials in Greece revealed that IT tools and HR practices have a positive impact on education (Papaevangelou et al., 2024). It explores the impact of how creativity-focused HRM and quality management, firm performance of firm and sustainability development positively affect on commercialization (Adiguzel et al., 2025 ; Khan & Rena, 2023). This study examines employee retention strategies in India's garment sector. It highlights the importance of retaining a good talent in an organization for sustainability, team dynamics, and better growth. Data was collected from 1000 workers and showed the correlation between advancement technology and the importance of employee retention and also analyzed the factor of turnover (Alam, 2023 ; Khan et al., 2022). HR practices such as career development, employee perception, and compensation in Public sector companies. SOBEL and regression tests are used to analyze these and highlight the effective HR polices that help to enhance employee attitudes and organizational growth (Bindhu et al., 2024 ; Magd et al., 2023). This paper explores how stress impacts the carrier among Indian IT employees like Job insecurity workload. It finds that can we remove through career motivation. Data was collected from 352 employees (Deshpande & Chakraborty, 2023; Khan & Rena, 2023). Employees' satisfaction with remote work highlights career development, productivity, and job stability and also reduces stress. Using Servqual and Kano models to analyze employees' satisfaction level and offering new insights for remote work for IT sectors (Bielinska et al., 2024). Organizational culture and personal job fit impact the employee engagement and turnover intention in lower and middle level employees in IT. The result was that there is a positive impact of organization culture and personal job fit on employee engagement, but there is the negative impact of employee engagement on turnover intention. It offers a practical insight to HR to effectively design a retention and engagement strategy (Bhatt et al., 2024; Khan & Naim, 2023). This research discusses the HR roles and hiring process in the company and also the impact of new technology on HR in the digital economy and highlights the use of new mechanisms in the company and technological development (Chursin et al., 2023). The IT sector in India is creating great opportunities for women through a very supportive work environment and exploring the challenges and opportunities faced by women in the IT sector through multiple case studies. It finds that there is progress in gender inclusivity but needs more improvement and also provides suggestions regarding policymaker regarding gender inclusivity (Gupta & Pathak, 2016). Retaining skilled employees is very critical due to high turnover. In Odisha's IT sector highlights challenges like costs and employee attitudes. Data was collected from primary and secondary sources; 100 managers' data was collected and from magazines and newspapers and analyzed by using SPSS, and a strategy for retention and reducing turnover (Padhi et al., 2020). The paper examines the relationship between motivation to learn, workplace learning, and in role job performance in IT professionals. It finds that individual motivation to learn has limited impact on performance, but workplace learning has great impact on job performance. It highlights that workplace learning helps to boost employee performance and provide insights for HR to develop a training strategy in holistic design and Sobel's test was used to explore this relationship (Dave et al., 2020). Career Development is essential for boosting employee growth. The study explores the perception of employers and employees regarding career development. It helps HR to make policies and design strategies for employee growth (Jain et al., 2021).

Human resource management practices (HRMP) impact knowledge management capacity (KMC) in Indian IT companies. HRMP includes recruitment, rewards, and retention, while KMC focuses on knowledge. It highlights that HRMP enhances employee motivation and retention, which positively affects KMC and provides insights for HR and KM to foster innovation and competitiveness in knowledge-driven industries (Gope et al., 2018). Workaholism among IT professionals in Delhi is linked to stress, job conditions, and anxiety. It highlights that workaholism affects workplace stress and anxiety, which is influenced by current technologies and economic growth. Working long hours affects the mental health and helps to understand the workaholism behavior of IT professionals (Pandey & Sharma, 2016). The Research examines how perceived value, based on benefits and scarifies, influences AI adoption in talent acquisition in IT companies in Indian. Data was collected from 198 HR and talent acquisition executives and was analyzed by using PLS-SEM. It shows that perceived value strongly predicts AI adoption. IT companies should adopt AI tools to optimize the recruitment process and in talent acquisition (Sattu et al., 2024);(N. Sharma et al., 2024). This Paper explores e-HRM adoption in India's service and manufacturing sectors. Data was collected from 438 employees and employers across 63 companies, It highlights employee and employer attitude, and conceptual model is used to guide the adoption of technology decisions in HRM practices (Sharma & Ahmad, 2022; Khatri et al., 2024).

RESEARCH GAP

This study explores the Combined impact of Hr analytics of HR analytics capabilities, skills and Organizational culture on strategic decision-making in IT sector Previous research has addressed Employee retention, digital transformation, and AI adoption (Sar et al., 2017; Parimi & Chakraborty, 2019; Sattu et al., 2024), but their collective influence on decision making remain understudied. Most literature focuses on specific aspects like employee engagement and recruitment (Jha et al., 2019; Truică & Barnoschi, 2014), lacking a holistic perspective on aligning HR analytics with business goals. This Study fills these gaps by examining how HR analyrtics skills and culture support strategic decision making in IT firm.

RESEARCH METHODOLOGY

HR specialists working for Indian IT companies were the study's target audience. A straightforward random sample technique was used to gather data via an online survey. A 5-point Likert scale, with 1 denoting "strongly agree" and 5 denoting "strongly disagree," was used to design every item in the survey. The actual sample size for this study was 299, even though the minimum needed sample size was determined to be 159.

OBJECTIVES

1. To examine the relationship between HR Analytics Capabilities and Strategic Decision Making.
2. To assess the role of HR Analytics Skills and Competencies in enhancing Strategic Decision Making.
3. To explore the influence of Organizational Culture and Support on the use of HR Analytics in Strategic Decision Making.

HYPOTHESES

H1: HR Analytics capabilities significantly influence strategic decision-making in organizations.
H2: The level of HR analytics skills and competencies in an organization significantly enhances its ability to make strategic decisions.
H3: A supportive organizational culture significantly influences strategic decision making.

Figure 1. Model

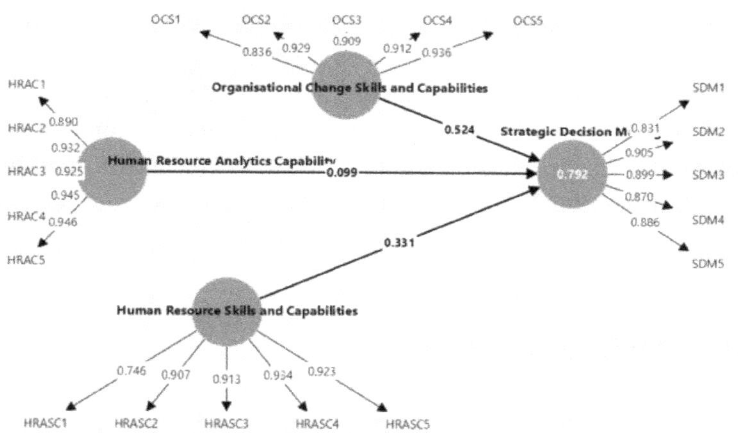

MEASUREMENT MODEL RESULTS

The measuring model's findings show that the study's constructs have high levels of validity and reliability. Every factor loading (from 0.746 to 0.946) is over the 0.70 cutoff, indicating that the indicators are reliable representations of the corresponding constructs. Excellent internal consistency and reliability are indicated by Dillon-Goldstein's Rho (Rho_A) values ranging from 0.928 to 0.960 and Cronbach's Alpha (CA) values ranging from 0.931 to 0.959. The reliability of the constructions is further supported by Composite Reliability (CR) ratings, which range from 0.944 to 0.969. Furthermore, the Average Variance Extracted (AVE) values, which range from 0.772 to 0.861, above the suggested cutoff point of 0.50, indicating that each construct contributes significantly to the variance of its indicators. The measuring model is appropriate for additional research analysis because it exhibits good construct validity and reliability overall.

Table 1. Results of Measurement Model

Constructs	Indicators	FL	CA	Rho_A	CR	AVE
HR Analytics Capabilties	HRAC1	0.890	0.959	0.960	0.969	0.861
	HRAC2	0.932				
	HRAC3	0.925				
	HRAC5	0.946				
	HRADC4	0.945				
HR Analytics Skills and Competencies	HRASC1	0.746	0.931	0.938	0.949	0.788
	HRASC2	0.907				
	HRASC3	0.913				
	HRASC4	0.934				
	HRASC5	0.923				
Organization Culture and Supoort	OCS1	0.836	0.944	0.946	0.958	0.819
	OCS2	0.929				
	OCS3	0.909				
	OCS4	0.912				
	OCS5	0.936				
Strategic Decision Making	SDM1	0.831	0.926	0.928	0.944	0.772
	SDM2	0.905				
	SDM3	0.899				
	SDM4	0.870				
	SDM5	0.886				

Fornell Lacker Test

The Fornell-Larcker criterion indicates that discriminant validity is well established for all constructs in the study. The square roots of the Average Variance Extracted (AVE) for HR Analytics Capabilities (HRAC), HR Analytics Skills and Competencies (HRASC), Organizational Culture Support (OCS), and Strategic Decision Making (SDM) are greater than the correlations between each construct and others, confirming that each construct is distinct. Specifically, the values for HRAC (0.928), HRASC (0.887), OCS (0.905), and SDM (0.879) exceed the corresponding correlations with other constructs (e.g., HRAC and HRASC: 0.658; HRAC and OCS: 0.624), demonstrating that the constructs measure different aspects and supporting the discriminant validity of the measurement model.

Table 2. Fornell-Larcker

	HRAC	HRASC	OCS	SDM
HRAC	0.928			
HRASC	0.658	0.887		
OCS	0.624	0.842	0.905	
SDM	0.643	0.836	0.863	0.879

The HTMT results, which indicate values below the 0.90 threshold for all pairs except OCS and SDM (HTMT = 0.915), largely support discriminant validity for the components in your study. Although OCS and SDM's HTMT values are just above the cutoff, they are still near enough to be deemed acceptable, suggesting that the constructions are largely different. The measuring model has a slight potential problem between OCS and SDM, but overall, it shows good discriminant validity.

Table 3. HTMT

	HRAC	HRASC	OCS	SDM
HRAC				
HRASC	0.698			
OCS	0.656	0.899		
SDM	0.681	0.898	0.915	

The hypotheses testing results indicate that all proposed relationships are supported. Specifically, HRAC has a positive and significant effect on SDM (β = 0.099, t = 2.218, p = 0.027), HRASC has a strong positive impact on SDM (β = 0.331, t =

4.581, p = 0), and OCS shows the most substantial influence on SDM (β = 0.524, t = 7.995, p = 0). These findings suggest that HR Analytics Capabilities, HR Analytics Skills and Competencies, and Organizational Culture Support significantly contribute to Strategic Decision Making in IT organizations, with OCS having the strongest effect.

Table 4. Hypotheses Testing of Relationships

Hypotheses	Relationship	Std Beta (β)	Std. Error	t-value	P-value	Supported
H1	HRAC -> SDM	0.099	0.044	2.218	0.027	Yes
H2	HRASC -> SDM	0.331	0.072	4.581	0	Yes
H3	OCS -> SDM	0.524	0.065	7.995	0	Yes

OVERALL FIT OF THE MODEL

The Standardized Root Mean Square Residual (SRMR) value for the model is 0.038, indicating an excellent model fit as it is well below the recommended threshold of 0.08. This suggests that the discrepancy between the observed and model-implied correlation matrices is minimal, supporting the reliability and validity of the model's structure. The results confirm that the specified relationships align well with the observed data, ensuring the robustness of the findings.

Predictive relevance f^2

The f^2 values indicate that all three constructs—HR Analytics Capabilities (f^2 = 1.073), HR Analytics Skills and Competencies (f^2 = 2.137), and Organizational Culture and Support (f^2 = 3.498)—significantly impact Strategic Decision Making. Organizational Culture and Support has the largest effect, followed by HR Analytics Capabilities and Skills. The t-statistics (1.073, 2.137, 3.498) and p-values (0.000, 0.033, 0.000) confirm the statistical significance, indicating medium to large effect sizes based on the sample and path coefficients.

Result and Discussion

The Study confirms that HR Analytics capabilities, Skills, and organizational Culture significance influence strategic Decision-Making in IT firms. Measurement model analysis showed excellent validity and reliability (eg., Cronbach's Alpha>0.93, AVE>0.77),ensuring strong construct integrity. Discriminant validity was established through Fornell-Larcker and HTMT criteria . Hypotheses testing revealed that all three factors- HR Analytics Capabilities ($\beta = 0.099$), Skills ($\beta = 0.331$), and Culture ($\beta = 0.524$)- positively and significantly impact strategic decisions, with culture having the strongest effect. The Model fit was excellent (SRMR=0.038). Effect size analysis (f^2) further confirmed the predictive relevance of each variable, especially organizational culture. These findings highlight the importance of integrating data-driven HR strategies with supportive culture to enhance decision-making. The results offer practical insights for IT firms aiming to improve performance, retention and innovation through Hr analytics.

Limitation and Future Scope

A disadvantage of this study is its dependence on data from a particular industry (IT), which might not accurately reflect the wider use of HR analytics in other industries. Furthermore, the study places less attention on potential difficulties such data privacy issues or organizational reluctance to change and more on the strategic benefit of HR analytics. Future studies could look into the long-term effects of HR analytics on organizational culture, the scalability of HR analytics across industries, and the moral ramifications of using more data in HR decision-making. Additional research might concentrate on incorporating cutting-edge technologies like blockchain and artificial intelligence (AI) with HR analytics to improve precision and openness.

CONCLUSION

For the IT industry, incorporating HR analytics into strategic decision-making frameworks has changed the game by allowing businesses to precisely and quickly handle workforce issues. IT firms may optimize people management, promote organizational resilience, and match human resource strategies with changing business objectives by utilizing data-driven insights.

This study emphasizes how HR analytics may improve workforce planning, forecast future trends, and promote evidence-based decision-making. It makes it easier to take proactive measures in crucial areas like diversity improvement, performance optimization, and staff retention, guaranteeing that HR policies have a direct impact on the success of the company.

Furthermore, the strategic importance of HR activities is reinforced by the capacity to quantify the return on HR investments and connect human capital measures to more general business outcomes. Adoption of HR analytics is not only a strategic need but also an operational necessity as the IT industry continues to change in response to market complexity and technological improvements. Businesses that adopt this data-driven strategy will be more capable of overcoming obstacles, grasping chances, and achieving long-term success in a market that is becoming more and more competitive.

THEORETICAL IMPLICATION

This study advances the theoretical knowledge of HR analytics as a strategic facilitator of organizational decision-making, particularly in the IT industry. By emphasizing the revolutionary potential of data-driven HR practices in coordinating human resource strategies with ever-changing business objectives, it contributes to the body of existing research. This study offers a multifaceted framework for examining how HR analytics affect organizational performance by fusing ideas from workforce development, data analytics, and strategic management.

PRACTICAL IMPLICATIONS

The research's real-world applications demonstrate how HR analytics can revolutionize IT decision-making. In order to fulfill the demands of dynamic projects, organizations may estimate workforce requirements, fill skill gaps, and enhance talent acquisition and retention strategies by utilizing data-driven insights. Through the design of focused interventions and the connection of labor productivity to corporate outcomes, HR analytics improves employee engagement and performance management. By recognizing prejudices and promoting fair working practices, it also aids in diversity and inclusion initiatives. IT firms may also guarantee compliance, assess the return on investment (ROI) of HR initiatives, and match human capital plans with corporate objectives, allowing for proactive risk reduction and long-term competitive advantage.

SOCIETAL IMPLICATIONS

This research on HR analytics in the IT industry has important societal ramifications, especially in terms of advancing inclusion, equity, and the general well-being of the workforce. HR analytics can contribute to less bias in hiring and career progression by employing data-driven insights, creating more inclusive and varied work environments. This might potentially reduce systemic disparities and guarantee that opportunities are available to a wider spectrum of people, irrespective of their identity or background.

REFERENCES

Adiguzel, Z., Sonmez Cakir, F., & Altay Morgul, U. (2025). Enhancing firm performance and sustainability through creativity-oriented HRM and quality management: The mediating role of commercialization in the IT sector. *International Journal of Quality & Reliability Management*. Advance online publication. DOI: 10.1108/IJQRM-08-2024-0262

Alam, S. (2023). The Impact of Modern Technologies and HR Practices on Employee Retention: A Study on Apparel Firms in India. In M. H.K. & S. S. (Eds.), *Proceedings - 2023 International Conference on Advanced Computing and Communication Technologies, ICACCTech 2023* (pp. 335 – 340). Institute of Electrical and Electronics Engineers Inc. DOI: 10.1109/ICACCTech61146.2023.00061

Bhatt, V., Thomas, S., Chauhan, D., & Patel, R. (2024). Investigating the impact of organisation culture, personal-job fit and employee engagement on turnover intention: An assessment of the IT sector from an emerging market perspective. *International Journal of Economics and Business Research*, *27*(2), 310–323. DOI: 10.1504/IJEBR.2024.136498

Bielinska-Dusza, E., da Costa, R. L., Hamerska, M., & Zak, A. (2024). Study on the Impact of Remote Working on the Satisfaction and Experience of IT Workers in Poland. *Forum Scientiae Oeconomia*, *11*(4), 9–34. DOI: 10.23762/FSO_VOL11_NO4_1

Bindhu, D., Namreen Asif, V. A., Baikadi, S. B., Chethanraj, Sunil, N., Chandravathi, & Dlima, N. G. (2024). Employee Perception of HR Practices and Its Impact on Job Satisfaction. *Lecture Notes in Networks and Systems, 1083 LNNS*, 154 – 165. DOI: 10.1007/978-3-031-67431-0_15

Chursin, A., Demenin, F., Karnaukh, S., Kiryakov, I., & Novoselov, A. (2023). The Role of Human Resources Management in Technological Enterprises in the Digital Transformation Environment. *Lecture Notes in Networks and Systems, 574 LNNS*, 2999 – 3008. DOI: 10.1007/978-3-031-21432-5_331

Dave, P., Sinha, A., & Varkkey, B. (2020). Workplace learning in the IT sector: Building a case for investment. *Development and Learning in Organizations*, *35*(4), 4–7. DOI: 10.1108/DLO-05-2020-0104

Deshpande, R., & Chakraborty, D. (2023). Impact of Work Stressors on Career Commitment – A Study of Indian IT Sector Employees. *Prabandhan: Indian Journal of Management*, *16*(11), 27–42. DOI: 10.17010/pijom/2023/v16i11/173214

Gope, S., Elia, G., & Passiante, G. (2018). The effect of HRM practices on knowledge management capacity: A comparative study in Indian IT industry. *Journal of Knowledge Management*, *22*(3), 649–677. DOI: 10.1108/JKM-10-2017-0453

Goyal, A., & Khatri, B. (2022). Systematic Review Paper on Influence of Ingenious Human Resource Practices on Employee Engagement during Pandemic In Banking Sector. *ECS Transactions*, *107*(1), 3833–3844. DOI: 10.1149/10701.3833ecst

Gupta, S., & Pathak, G. S. (2016). HR practices for women employees: A study of information technology (IT) sector in India. *2016 3rd International Conference on Recent Advances in Information Technology, RAIT 2016*, 672 – 676. DOI: 10.1109/RAIT.2016.7507980

Gupta, S. K., Kapoor, S., Yucel, S., Rana, R., Yusel, R., & Prasad, L. (2023). Technology-based human resource practices within indian IT industry. In *Disruptive Artificial Intelligence and Sustainable Human Resource Management: Impacts and Innovations - The Future of HR*. River Publishers. https://www.scopus.com/inward/record.uri?eid=2-s2.0-85168646123&partnerID=40&md5=e1f8b96da69ea08dcb0a69fe7e435a0e

Jain, A., Mishra, S., & Goyal, R. (2021). Analysis of Career Development Opportunities in IT Sectors in Jaipur. *Lecture Notes in Networks and Systems*, *166*, 733–741. DOI: 10.1007/978-981-15-9689-6_80

Jha, N., Krishnan, R., & Sachin, S. C. (2019). Team building and organizational innovation: A study in IT sector in India. *Journal of Advanced Research in Dynamical and Control Systems, 11*(10 Special Issue), 59 – 69. DOI: 10.5373/JARDCS/V11SP10/20192776

Jonathan, H., Magd, H., & Khan, S. A. (2024). Artificial intelligence and augmented reality: A business fortune to sustainability in the digital age. In *Navigating the Digital Landscape: Understanding Customer Behaviour in the Online World*. Emerald Group Publishing Ltd., DOI: 10.1108/978-1-83549-272-720241005

Khan, S. A., & Magd, H. (2021). EMPIRICAL EXAMINATION OF MS TEAMS IN CONDUCTING WEBINAR: EVIDENCE FROM INTERNATIONAL ONLINE PROGRAM CONDUCTED IN OMAN. *Journal of Content. Community and Communication*, *14*(7), 159–175. DOI: 10.31620/JCCC.12.21/13

Khan, S. A., & Magd, H. (2023). New Technology Anxiety and Acceptance of Technology: An Appraisal of MS Teams. In *Advances in Distance Learning in Times of Pandemic*. CRC Press., DOI: 10.1201/9781003322252-5

Khan, S. A., Magd, H., Al Shamsi, I. R., & Masoom, K. (2022). Social entrepreneurship through innovations in agriculture. In *International Perspectives on Value Creation and Sustainability Through Social Entrepreneurship*. IGI Global., DOI: 10.4018/978-1-6684-4666-9.ch010

Khan, S. A., Magd, H., Bhuyan, U., Jonathan, H., & Naim, A. (2024). Digital Marketing (DM): How are small business enterprises (SBEs) of Bhutan and Sikkim (India) Responding to It? In *Digital Influence on Consumer Habits: Marketing Challenges and Opportunities*. Emerald Publishing. DOI: 10.1108/978-1-80455-342-820241008

Khan, S. A., & Naim, A. (2023). XAI in Society 5.0 through the lens of marketing and HRM. In *XAI Based Intelligent Systems for Society 5.0*. Elsevier., DOI: 10.1016/B978-0-323-95315-3.00004-8

Khan, S. A., & Rena, R. (2023). Emerging green practices, internet of things, and digital marketing: A response to the global economic and climate crises. In *Global Applications of the Internet of Things in Digital Marketing*. IGI Global., DOI: 10.4018/978-1-6684-8166-0.ch001

Khatri, B., Arora, S., & Goyal, A. (2022). Association between Outcomes of Physical activities and Sports on Work-Life Balance of Employees. *International Journal of Human Movement and Sports Sciences, 10*(2), 316–323. DOI: 10.13189/saj.2022.100223

Khatri, B., Singh, R. K., Arora, S., Khan, S. A., & Naim, A. (2024). Optimizing supply chain management indicators for sustainable supply chain integration and customer loyalty: Potential role of environmentally responsible practices. In *Strategies for Environmentally Responsible Supply Chain and Production Management*. IGI Global., DOI: 10.4018/979-8-3693-0669-7.ch008

Lekhi, S. B., Malhotra, M., Pushp, A., Gautam, R. S., Sharma, S., & Rastogi, S. (2024). The study provides a thorough examination of green human resource management practices within the Indian IT sector. *2nd IEEE International Conference on Advances in Information Technology, ICAIT 2024 - Proceedings*. DOI: 10.1109/ICAIT61638.2024.10690791

Magd, H., Khan, S. A., Khatri, B., Sharma, N., & Arora, S. (2023). Understanding the relationship between IoT and digital marketing: A bibliometric analysis. In *Global Applications of the Internet of Things in Digital Marketing*. IGI Global., DOI: 10.4018/978-1-6684-8166-0.ch007

Padhi, A., Mitra, A., & Paul, S. (2020). A Study on the Analysis of Training and Retention Strategies in some selected IT sectors at Odisha. *2020 International Conference on Computer Science, Engineering and Applications, ICCSEA 2020*. DOI: 10.1109/ICCSEA49143.2020.9132885

Pandey, S., & Sharma, V. (2016). Understanding work-related stress, job conditions, work culture and workaholism phenomenon as predictors of HR crisis: An empirical study of the indian IT sector. *International Journal of Human Capital and Information Technology Professionals*, *7*(2), 68–80. DOI: 10.4018/IJHCITP.2016040105

Papaevangelou, O., Syndoukas, D., Kalogiannidis, S., & Chatzitheodoridis, F. (2024). Efficacy of embedding IT in human resources (HR) practices in education management. *Journal of Infrastructure. Policy and Development*, *8*(1). Advance online publication. DOI: 10.24294/jipd.v8i1.2371

Parimi, S., & Chakraborty, S. (2019). Antecedents to employee attrition behavior in Indian IT/ITES sector. *International Journal of Engineering and Advanced Technology*, *9*(1), 1132–1142. DOI: 10.35940/ijeat.A9502.109119

Ramachandaran, S. D., Doraisingam, P., Nuraini, R., & Chaudhery, U. (2024). Examining the impact of digital transformation on HRM practices in Morocco's IT sector. *Humanities and Social Sciences Letters*, *12*(4), 811–830. DOI: 10.18488/73.v12i4.3903

Rana, R., Kapoor, S., & Gupta, S. K. (2021). Impact of HR practices on corporate image building in the Indian IT sector. *Problems and Perspectives in Management*, *19*(2), 528–535. DOI: 10.21511/ppm.19(2).2021.42

Sar, S., Mohanty, A. K., & Dash, M. (2017). An empirical study on critical issues of work life balance: A study of IT sector. *International Journal of Economic Research*, *14*(14), 275–284. https://www.scopus.com/inward/record.uri?eid=2-s2.0-85034663201&partnerID=40&md5=9cb6595e105e6e61cf10855ec413d911

Saravanabhavan, N., Subashini, R., & Velmurugan, G. (2024). HRM Practices and Knowledge Sharing in IT Sector – A Study in Coimbatore, Tamil Nadu. *International Research Journal of Multidisciplinary Scope*, *5*(1), 607–620. DOI: 10.47857/irjms.2024.v05i01.0289

Satpal, S. R., & Dhillon, M. (2019). Impact of factors affecting employee retention on turnover intentions: In Indian IT sector. *International Journal on Emerging Technologies, 10*(4), 273 – 282. https://www.scopus.com/inward/record.uri?eid=2-s2.0-85077690213&partnerID=40&md5=a31976cea09c6372a1da70f8e9c6f4a2

Sattu, R., Das, S., & Jena, L. K. (2024). Should I adopt AI during talent acquisition? Evidence from HR professionals of Indian IT organisations. *Journal of Organizational Effectiveness, 11*(4), 1005–1022. DOI: 10.1108/JOEPP-05-2023-0186

Shaman, M. A. M., Samarasinghe, S. M., Tharinda, D., Gamage, D. C., & Gamage, A. (2022). Pre-Interview Reviewer Using Natural Language Processing for Software Engineers in The IT Industry : Pre-interview reviewer. In S. V., S. V., S. M., S. M., & S. J. (Eds.), *Proceedings - 2022 4th International Conference on Advances in Computing, Communication Control and Networking, ICAC3N 2022* (pp. 2300 – 2305). Institute of Electrical and Electronics Engineers Inc. DOI: 10.1109/ICAC3N56670.2022.10074186

Shanmugam, R., & Giri Babu, N. (2016). Assessment of employee attrition among IT employees. *International Journal of Applied Engineering Research: IJAER, 11*(5), 3449–3453. https://www.scopus.com/inward/record.uri?eid=2-s2.0-84964043865&partnerID=40&md5=eed6b5e216649c702d31df6bac9e672c

Sharma, E., & Ahmad, J. (2022). Technology adoption model for HRM practices. *International Journal of Technology Enhanced Learning, 14*(1), 101–124. DOI: 10.1504/IJTEL.2022.120563

Sharma, N., Khatri, B., & Khan, S. A. (2024). Exploring the past and identifying the future research agenda for social media and tourist behavior: A bibliometric analysis. In *Social Media Strategies for Tourism Interactivity.* IGI Global., DOI: 10.4018/979-8-3693-0960-5.ch011

Showkat, S., Shajan, K., & Pathak, V. K. (2019). Strategic human resource management and organizational performance: Mediating role of employee well-being in the Indian IT industry. *Journal of Critical Reviews, 6*(6), 75–83. DOI: 10.22159/jcr.06.06.11

Truic , C.-O., & Barnoschi, A. (2014). Innovating HR using an expert system for recruiting IT specialists - ESRIT. *Vision 2020: Sustainable Growth, Economic Development, and Global Competitiveness - Proceedings of the 23rd International Business Information Management Association Conference, IBIMA 2014, 1*, 1671 – 1680. https://www.scopus.com/inward/record.uri?eid=2-s2.0-84906265128&partnerID=40&md5=0d637b74184c03738046c5b2be006c96

Chapter 11
Revolutionizing Business Intelligence With Natural Language Processing

Munir Ahmad
https://orcid.org/0000-0003-4836-6151
Survey of Pakistan, Pakistan

ABSTRACT

In the era of information overload, unstructured data, ranging from customer reviews to internal communications, comprises the majority of enterprise data but often remains underutilized by traditional Business Intelligence (BI) systems. This chapter explores how Natural Language Processing (NLP), a rapidly evolving field within Artificial Intelligence, is revolutionizing the BI landscape by enabling machines to interpret and derive meaning from human language. By transforming vast amounts of text into structured insights, NLP empowers organizations to detect trends, understand customer sentiment, and enhance decision-making across various functions. The chapter highlights the strategic value of integrating NLP into BI, detailing its practical applications, implementation challenges, and transformative potential. The chapter provides a roadmap for organizations aiming to evolve from data accumulation to human-centric, actionable intelligence.

INTRODUCTION

Nowadays, companies collect a huge amount of information created by digital activities, chats on social networks, customer reviews, emails, and website content (Bharadiya, 2023; Hayes & Kelliher, 2024; Islam et al., 2024; Sarker, 2021). Conventional BI tools can easily deal with figures like sales, stocks and finances, but

DOI: 10.4018/979-8-3373-2135-6.ch011

they lack the features needed for unstructured information (Srivastava et al., 2022; Town & Thabtah, 2019; Tripathi et al., 2023). This large proportion of enterprise data, which is unstructured, contains human elements, attitudes, and hints about behavior, but it is mostly left unused. Using information found in written sources involves looking at language, how people feel, and what their intentions are, which are not numbers. Since buyers have higher expectations and the market gets more competitive, companies now need to focus on extracting and analyzing this information as a main priority.

Natural Language Processing (NLP), which is a fast-changing part of Artificial Intelligence (AI), enables machines to interact with human language and make sense of it. By using computational linguistics and statistical, machine learning, and deep learning models, NLP can analyze a lot of texts and point out patterns, trends, and relationships that are hard to discover through manual study. Because of this technology, companies can turn text into analyzable data in real-time, which supports quicker, smarter, and more informed choices. NLP allows organizations to use data about customers and their reputation, so they can improve their operations and make smarter business moves. Research and development use in many industries and areas show how businesses handle data, customers, and market information differently (Khurana et al., 2023; Sawicki et al., 2023; Singh & Mahmood, 2021).

It explains the impact NLP could have on business intelligence. It looks at how businesses can use NLP to analyze data better, forecast trends, and reach out to their customers. Adding NLP to BI will help organizations work more efficiently and also equip decision-makers with insightful information from language data. An analysis of new developments, methods of integration, and examples from business practice explain how NLP is impacting business intelligence in this chapter. It will study the difficulties organizations could have when putting the system into use and give a method to make adoption smooth. Thus, this chapter emphasizes that NLP is a key factor in going from collecting data to making informed decisions, thus making business intelligence more adaptable, responsive, and friendly to humans.

FOUNDATIONS OF NATURAL LANGUAGE PROCESSING

Definition and Core Concepts of NLP

The core elements of both language and computing form the basis of Natural Language Processing (NLP) and allow machines to work with human language. All these foundational components help the process of understanding written and spoken language (Dsouza et al., 2025; Du et al., 2025; L. Jiang & Goetz, 2025; Koç et al., 2025; Kumar et al., 2025; Lane & Dyshel, 2025; Sawicki et al., 2023). It is important to know these topics to realize how NLP benefits Business Intelligence by making use of unstructured data.

The first part of understanding language is morphological analysis, which studies how words are put together. It is about separating words into their smallest forms, which are morphemes. For example, "running," "runner," and "ran" are types of runs explain off words. This analysis enables NLP systems to categorize connected words, so text is simplified and the accuracy of information retrieval is increased (Albahli, 2025; Sawalha et al., 2025). Doing this in business situations strengthens the accuracy of finding sentiments, detecting keywords, and processing queries.

When each word is known, a sentence is examined according to grammar rules for the correct arrangement of words for syntactic parsing. It explains what the subject, verb, and object are in different sentences. If we look at the sentence "The manager approved the report," syntactic parsing recognizes that "manager" is the subject, "approved" is the verb, and "the report" is the object. Proper understanding of grammar is vital for such tasks as automated summarization, creative question answering, and talking to chatbots, as mistakes using grammar can reduce performance (P. Jiang & Cai, 2024; Kantor & Morzy, 2024; Kyle & Eguchi, 2024).

Semantic analysis takes analysis further by trying to find the meaning of text. It chooses the suitable meaning for a word in a sentence and blends the meaning of single words to create a single idea. By way of example, "bank" could refer to either a financial institution or the slope beside a river and semantic analysis provides the right interpretation based on the situation. Solid meaning comprehension is vital in document classification, analyzing contracts, and mining product reviews, since the right insights come from it (Attigeri et al., 2024; Upadhyay et al., 2024).

Language usually goes beyond its literal uses. It is at this point that pragmatics becomes very important. Pragmatic analysis looks at the speech context, such as the reason for speaking or the atmosphere surrounding a person, to understand their true message (Cambria, 2025; Chen et al., 2024). Usually, asking "Can you pass the salt?" means asking politely rather than showing concern about someone's skills. Pragmatics in BI enables applications to understand customers and social media comments that contain irony, improper words, or cultural expressions, which improves the reliability of analyzing feelings and intentions.

Besides interpreting sentences, discourse analysis studies how ideas are linked in a series or throughout the whole piece of writing (Joseph, 2024; Yu et al., 2024). You must follow references (using pronouns), preserve the topic being discussed, and notice the changing idea pattern. The software was upgraded last week. Because of discourse analysis, the system recognizes that the first statement refers to the software and that they are part of the same context. It is needed to summarize documents that are long, check customer service emails, or review lots of feedback, since a lack of continuous context may make things hard to understand.

By relying on these main components, Natural Language Processing is built. Technologies in NLP help machines handle and interpret human language, so they can change unstructured text into meaningful data that is important for running a business today.

Key NLP Technologies and Techniques

To give examples of tasks, NLP in business intelligence makes use of different technologies and methods to allow systems to analyze and comprehend text recorded in human language. The techniques that are used most often are described below and summarized in Table 1.

Text Mining

To find hidden patterns in a lot of unorganized text, you use text mining as the key step in Natural Language Processing. Some of the functions it performs are tokenization, stemming, lemmatization, removing stop words, and vectorization. These steps change the raw texts into structures ready for analysis. Using frequency analysis, we can see which words and phrases are used the most, and with keyword extraction, businesses can focus on words that point to new problems, main features, or rival companies. The base for such analytics as classification or clustering is created from this organized presentation of textual data (Lekmiti et al., 2024; Sandu et al., 2024; Shamshiri et al., 2024).

Within Business Intelligence, looking into client views, office updates, notes, investigations, and study notes is generally made through text mining. As an example, by looking through many customer comments, a company can learn what features get the most attention from its customers. A different important aspect of text mining is topic modeling, which helps discover connections between similar points in the data. As a result, companies can explore public opinions, speedily address customers' concerns, and match their approaches to new expectations by simply using the technology.

In this situation, a retail company gathers a wide range of reviews on its newly released products. With text mining, they can spot words customers mention most, such as "durable," "battery life," and "slow charging." In addition, topic modeling points out that product durability and phone charging are the main topics people talk about. With these facts in hand, the team from product introduces changes to the battery and makes sure to highlight how durable the phone is in its marketing.

Sentiment Analysis

Sentiment analysis is another name for opinion mining, and it aims to reveal the feelings expressed in data. It sorts through opinions in the text as being positive, negative, or neutral, and in some advanced instances, it measures their level of positivity or negativity. It helps in knowing what people think about a brand, product, service, or policy. Sentiment analysis depends on basic techniques that match text against a set of emotions, as well as more advanced ones using a lot of labeled training data (Bello et al., 2023; Joseph, 2024; Tan et al., 2023; Zunic et al., 2020).

Keep in mind that sentiment analysis in business intelligence allows companies to track customers' opinions and the mood in the market as it happens. As an illustration, companies introducing new products may look at social media activity and online feedback to get an understanding of public reactions. How customers feel about a brand is linked to its sales results, customer retention levels, and the level of loyalty to the brand. Besides, using sentiment analysis together with a customer service platform can prompt immediate attention on negative issues and improve how fast people get help.

Telecom companies can use sentiment analysis to explore what people are saying on social media during a lengthy outage. Every post is sorted into the category of positive, neutral, or negative. Whenever there is a high level of negative feelings, the support team takes action by addressing problems, publishing statements, and assisting upset users in real time to avoid losing customers and improve how the company is seen.

Named Entity Recognition (NER)

It is an NLP approach that helps spot and group important elements such as names, organizations, places, important dates, product names, and numbers in texts that are not well organized. NER helps automatically pull out well-structured information from raw text, so it can be easily managed, looked at, and charted using BI. By using NER, company databases or business emails can show all entries, including the names of clients, the dates of contracts, various amounts of money, and geographical regions (Albahli, 2025; Esmaail et al., 2024; Mengliev et al., 2024).

With BI applications, NER makes it easier to extract key business data from meeting notes, financial reports, and other types of market news. The technology also helps in entity linking and creating relationship maps, so businesses can display in a knowledge graph the links among their suppliers, customers, and competitors. With NER, businesses can properly monitor their compliance, conduct thorough corporate actions, and form strategies using knowledge extracted from random texts. A financial analytics firm can constantly review thousands of news articles as part of its daily operations. Such information is presented in dashboards to monitor both rival activities and market changes, which boosts the organization's competitive intelligence.

Part-of-Speech (POS) Tagging

Part-of-speech tagging involves assigning a word in a sentence to its category, such as noun, verb, adjective, adverb, and so on. This important move in NLP gives the background needed for detailed language analysis. POS tagging identifies which word in a sentence is a noun, verb, or any other part of speech. For instance, the word "record" can act either as a noun or as a verb, and properly identifying which role it has is important for correct understanding (Lee, 2025; Ullah et al., 2024).

Before sending data for deeper processing and analysis, POS tagging is usually the first step in the BI domain. It allows keywords from user searches to be adjusted, which results in stronger connections between users' queries and search results. Chatbots and virtual assistants need an accurate understanding of what is said, which is made possible by POS tagging. Besides, it can support the extraction of keywords and creation of summaries by pointing out essential words and actions in business documents, reports, or user reviews.

In this instance, an AI-based marketing firm's content engine looks for action verbs and adjectives in the testimonials of customers by using POS tagging. As a result, the team can automatically create marketing messages such as "Customers are pleased with our easy-to-use tool and fast service." This raises SEO and encourages more audience interaction.

Topic Modeling and Clustering

Topic modeling uses machine learning to uncover themes in a group of documents on its own. Latent Dirichlet Allocation (LDA) is one of the most common methods used for this task. It assumes that each document is a blend of only a small number of topics, and every topic has its own set of words. With the help of topic modeling, it is possible to automatically organize text into meaningful groups, which makes it easier to study trends, create thematic maps, and divide content (Amiri & Karimianghadim, 2024; Nanyonga et al., 2024; Rachel J et al., 2024).

This involves assembling documents or sentences that share terms or meaning, which may be measured with TF-IDF or word embeddings. Using these methods, it's much easier to manage a large number of customer feedback, support tickets, or social media posts. Topic modeling and clustering assist BI users in organizing unstructured data so they can spot new chances on the market, follow new risks, or identify groups of people according to their interests. Due to these methods, unstructured text becomes less complicated and is more useful for decision makers.

A tech company handles requests from customers through the email support system. Changes made by the LDA model place tickets into groups such as "difficulties logging in," "failed payments," and "suggestions for new features." Grouping tickets in this way lets the team handle more important ones and save time and effort.

Table 1. NLP Techniques in Business Intelligence

Technique	Primary Function	Example Application in BI
Text Mining	Extract patterns and keywords from text	Identifying top themes in customer reviews
Sentiment Analysis	Assess the emotional tone of the text	Monitoring public response to a product launch
Named Entity Recognition	Identify names, places, dates, and values	Extracting company names and monetary values from news articles
POS Tagging	Label parts of speech in a sentence	Generating grammatically accurate marketing content
Topic Modeling/ Clustering	Discover latent topics or group similar texts	Grouping support tickets by issue type

Role of NLP in Analyzing Unstructured Data Sources

One of the biggest and least used assets in organizations is unstructured data. This data appears as emails, support tickets, answers to surveys, posts on social media, reviews, call center transcripts, and many other forms. Traditional BI software is designed for structured data, and because unstructured data is not set in a set format, it is hard to process.

NLP plays a central part in revealing the worth of this data. If language processing methods are used, businesses can discover what's being discussed, learn what customers feel, find inconsistencies, and receive real-time feedback. Some main sources of unstructured data and the role that NLP plays are highlighted below.

Social Media

On Twitter, Facebook, Instagram, and LinkedIn, people can post their opinions and experiences right when they happen (Molenaar et al., 2024; Sandu et al., 2024). They create a lot of unstructured text information, most of which reflects people's emotions and the latest trends. NLP helps companies take advantage of this information to get useful insights. By using sentiment analysis, it is possible to see how the public feels about a brand, product, or campaign, and named entity recognition and topic modeling make it simple to find out the main highlights, key people, and important shifts in the market. Sudden negative trending in public opinion after a new product launch can show companies where things have gone wrong and encourage them to respond quickly. All in all, NLP enables companies to use the buzz of social media networks as a guide for protecting their reputation and staying informed.

Customer Feedback

By collecting comments from product reviews, surveys, satisfaction forms, and app stores, you can find out what customers really think and what they want. Even so, most feedback comes in a subjective form and is placed in various places, which makes it challenging to analyze with the usual tools. With the help of NLP tools, feedback is sorted by main topics, including pricing, ease of use, and customer service, and its satisfaction is rated too (Sharma et al., 2024; Tasneem & Hemalatha, 2025). Because of advanced models, companies can see how often product features are mentioned and in what situations, which helps them make improvement or repair decisions. For example, when "slow checkout process" is mentioned often in reviews, businesses should focus on upgrading this feature. As a result, NLP picks up messy opinions and statements from many people and organizes them into meaningful data for use in developing goods, connecting with customers, and improving services.

Emails and Support Tickets

In many organizations, communication and coordination between staff and customers mainly rely on emails and support tickets. These messages usually have information on problems, service requests, complaints, and ideas. With NLP, organizations can process disorderly communication by distinguishing the message based on its subject, priority or reason (Bonechi et al., 2024; Saadati & Hakimi, 2024). A departmental email support system can identify emails as needing help with billing, technical matters, or complaints and send them to the proper workers automatically. With sentiment analysis, businesses may find customers who are especially dissatisfied so they can help them immediately. Automated answers supported by NLP are used by some companies for common inquiries to increase efficiency and please customers. Basically, NLP enables organizations to deal with large amounts of service messages while decreasing the need for human involvement and time to answer.

Reports and Documents

While strategy reports, financial analyses, market studies and policy papers are full of business sense, people tend not to use them since they are rather lengthy and hard to comprehend. Such documents can be handled by NLP through tasks such as text summarization, classification by keywords, and semantic analysis. They make it possible for those in charge to find the key points and grasp the context, risks or suggestions without having to read the entire report. It is also possible for NLP to identify similar mentions among several documents which aids in merging data and noticing trends. Another example is that an executive dashboard can automatically turn all regional sales reports into a simple table displaying the strongest places, poor results and ways to help the weaker areas. Using NLP, companies can more successfully store and use information and act on it more promptly.

Call Center Transcripts and Chat Logs

Interactions over the phone and chats allow us to see what is important to the customer. As soon as you transcribe the talks using software, they turn into useful unstructured sources of data. The main function of NLP is to determine the most common topics, classify the different problems, and review customer feedback sentiment (T. Jiang et al., 2024; Patel et al., 2024). It is also possible for NLP to observe how agents are using words, tone, and sticking to the established instructions. Businesses usually use these discoveries to improve employee development, simplify how support is given, and boost the use of chatbots and FAQs. Should several transcripts bring up regular trouble understanding billing cycles, the company might revise its user-facing materials to make things clearer. With NLP, every conversation between a customer and the business contributes to understanding how to develop services and products further.

ADVANCES IN NLP TECHNOLOGIES FOR BI

Significant changes in NLP over the past few years have mainly been caused by improvements in machine learning, the huge growth of data, and more powerful computers. They have increased the range of BI NLP applications, which makes it much easier to analyze text data that is complex and involves many languages. Currently, NLP focuses on more than identifying keywords or using basic rules; it can now detect the specific meaning, context, and intention. This part describes the main technological advances, tools, algorithms, and their use in real life that are shaping BI NLP.

Recent Developments and Trends in NLP

Over the last decade, Natural Language Processing (NLP) has changed a lot, going from using handcrafted linguistic rules to today's advanced systems that use deep learning. This progress is driven by three main reasons: much better computer capabilities, huge collections of labeled data, and new ideas for designing models, mainly the development of transformer-based models. Table 2 summarizes the key trends in NLP.

Pre-trained Language Models

Pre-trained models like BERT, GPT, and RoBERTa have made a huge impact on NLP. They are first trained by unsupervised methods on a big collection of text data to find missing words and create proper text. By pre-training, the models are made capable of recognizing language structure, meaning, and small details within what is said. Pre-trained models can be fine-tuned again on smaller task-related datasets to do tasks such as sentiment analysis, find named entities or answer questions. This method, referred to as transfer learning, greatly reduces what is needed in terms of data and computer power to develop effective NLP applications, so that many enterprises can use them (Chatzimina et al., 2024; Guimarães et al., 2024; Özkurt Id, 2024).

Contextual Understanding

One key benefit from modern models is that they can read words based on what occurs around them. These models are different from previous methods since they examine whole texts, enabling them to identify linguistic features such as idioms, a sarcastic tone, or words with several meanings. Being aware of the context makes it easier for NLP tasks in BI to accurately find customer opinions, extract information about entities, or give pertinent answers to questions. BERT applies a method that reads each text forward and backward, improving how it understands the meaning of a sentence. Due to this feature, the model can handle unclear language and work better on complicated language tasks. Unlike BERT, RoBERTa uses larger datasets and better approaches, which make its accuracy stand out.

Generative Models

Models in the GPT line (for example, GPT-2, GPT-3 and GPT-4) can create meaningful and well-written text, so they power new applications in BI such as auto report generation, condensing long documents, and chatbots. Since they adapt to new needs with a little more training, these models are suitable for companies that need to quickly change their systems. As an example, GPT can automatically write up reports on earnings, prepare answers for bots helping customers, and create helpful content for marketing groups, making the process more efficient for people (Agrawal et al., 2024; Wang et al., 2024).

Multilingual and Cross-lingual NLP

The rise of models such as mBERT and XLM-RoBERTa now helps organizations to deal with and understand text information in many languages with ease. Such a capability helps businesses work with data from many nations, digital platforms and feedback while using a single model.

Real-Time NLP

Due to businesses wanting to monitor social media, online chats and similar real-time sources of data, there has been a growing need for NLP analytics. Now, because of lightweight models like DistilBERT and ALBERT and edge computing, it is possible to analyze text on phones or nearby, making the process faster and more responsive. Because of these developments, companies can take immediate action when trends change, customers have problems, or the brand encounters difficulties, which is important for staying ahead of competitors.

Explainable AI (XAI)

Because NLP models now play a major role in important areas such as finance and healthcare, there is growing interest in understandable AI (XAI). Nowadays, BI models need to be transparent, so users know how predictions or classifications are made and trust AI-based systems. Experts are now using clear visual tools that display the relationship between what is fed to the NLP algorithm and its responses.

Table 2. NLP Trends

Trend / Development	Description	Representative Models / Technologies	BI Applications
Pre-trained Language Models	Large-scale unsupervised training followed by fine-tuning	BERT, RoBERTa, GPT family	Sentiment analysis, NER, summarization, QA
Contextual Understanding	Bidirectional and deep context comprehension	BERT (bidirectional), RoBERTa	Improved accuracy in text classification
Generative Text Models	Natural language generation for reports, summaries, and dialogue	GPT-3, GPT-4	Automated reporting, virtual assistants
Multilingual & Cross-lingual	Support for multiple languages with shared representations	mBERT, XLM-RoBERTa	Global market analysis, multilingual sentiment
Real-Time NLP & Edge Models	Lightweight models for on-device, low-latency processing	DistilBERT, ALBERT	Real-time monitoring, live chat support
Explainable AI (XAI)	Transparent AI decision explanations	Integrated XAI tools	Compliance, trust, auditing

Tools and Platforms Enabling NLP Integration with BI

Robust and flexible tools must be used to carry out NLP in business intelligence from getting data, processing it, and turning it into usable results. People use NLP adoption through open-source libraries, cloud services, BI platforms, and various specialized frameworks.

Open-Source Libraries

NLTK (Natural Language Toolkit) is a widely used, open-source, and established library for NLP in Python. It includes a variety of modules and data that handle basic tasks, for example, tokenization, stemming, lemmatization, part-of-speech tagging, parsing, and named entity recognition (NER). NLTK is highly regarded by academics and researchers because it has good documentation and many educational materials. The tool lets users use different algorithms and work with text data, making it suitable for learning and perfecting ideas in NLP.

spaCy is a relatively fresh tool designed for use in practical applications. Due to its optimization, spaCy works fast and processes a large amount of text without effort. spaCy comes with native support for tokenization, POS tagging, dependency parsing, NER, and word vectors, and it blends in deep learning models with no fuss. With Spacy, developers can easily create advanced NLP systems because of its simple API and built-in models. Since spaCy is scalable and highly dependable, it is preferred by companies that want to use NLP in business intelligence.

Since both libraries can be changed and extended, using them allows for training custom models and linking them with other well-known frameworks like TensorFlow and PyTorch, which is important for NLP in businesses.

Hugging Face Transformers

Using Hugging Face Transformers allows firms in NLP to easily adopt the best current technology. It has pre-made transformer-based models such as BERT, GPT, and a variety of others that can all be accessed using a simple high-level API. The unique feature of Hugging Face is that anyone can access top-notch NLP tools by improvising on ready models with just a little code. It is very important when using BI applications that deal with law, finance, or medical fields.

The library works for both training and using deep learning models, and it blends smoothly with various popular frameworks. You can use its ecosystem to manage data, share models on the Hugging Face Hub, and deploy them quickly in business information systems.

Organizations that work with Hugging Face do not have to be AI experts; they can apply question answering, summarization, sentiment classification, and entity extraction in NLP faster and with easier implementation.

Cloud Providers

Some of the leading cloud providers provide managed NLP services that make it easy for businesses to add language recognition features to their applications. Some scalable NLP services by AWS Comprehend are entity recognition, analyzing sentiment, extracting main ideas, identifying languages, and topic modeling. With this tool, it becomes possible to recognize and classify various entities as needed by a business. Because it links so well with other services from AWS, you can easily form complex data management and visualization solutions.

The features provided include syntax analysis, entity recognition, sentiment analysis, and content classification. It is designed for multilingual users and adds categorizing documents according to industry categories, so it is very useful in business intelligence for specific industries. Because of its powerful cloud system, Google offers fast and reliable analytics. Sentiment analysis, recognizing entities (including those that are connected), extracting key phrases, and identifying languages are done by Microsoft Azure Text Analytics. Being part of Azure Cognitive Services, Azure's Text Analytics can easily be combined with speech recognition, vision, and translation for more advanced applications that use various sources of information.

As a service offered by the cloud, NLP makes it simple for organizations to access and use NLP through APIs, and they only need to pay for the services used. As a result, businesses have an easier time making NLP an important part of their BI processes.

BI Platforms with NLP Features

Major business intelligence solutions now use NLP, which lets users access and explore data using simple phrases. Q&A functionality in Power BI allows users to input conversational questions and get back answers in the form of colorful charts and graphics. Using Azure Cognitive Services, Power BI allows analysts to add both sentiment analysis and key phrase extraction to their dashboards. Users can use the Ask Data feature in Tableau, which lets them type questions in everyday language to interact with their data. It makes it possible to speedily uncover trends and interrelations, as automatic summarization and topic detection help users who do not require advanced skills in analysis.

Integrating NLP, Qlik makes it possible to generate insights through natural conversations. Because of its association features and use of NLP, Business Intelligence enables users to investigate data quickly and notice useful insights. The main benefit of these platforms is that they help business users find the insights they need directly in texts, which speeds up the process of making decisions.

Low-Code/No-Code Solutions

Both RapidMiner and KNIME are low-code and no-code platforms that make the development of NLP workflows simple because their interfaces work through drag-and-drop and they include many ready-made elements.

- RapidMiner supports a visual workflow maker plus many NLP operators for preprocessing, taking out features, classifying emotions, and training models. It is able to work with both Python and R, so business analysts with little coding knowledge can still make changes easily.
- In KNIME, users can use modules to create data pipelines that perform NLP activities like text mining, classification, and clustering. Because of its open architecture, GPT-ML connects with the best NLP libraries and machine learning tools, allowing for flexible research and use.

On these platforms, organizations can quickly build and set up NLP models in their BI spaces, which allows for fast and steady development.

Emerging Frameworks

The emergence of LLMs has encouraged the creation of ways to connect them with tools used in the data environments of businesses.

- With LangChain, developers can work with LLMs and develop applications that have document searching, prompt feature management, and output parsing as main elements. Smart AI makes it possible to link with databases, APIs, and knowledge bases, which makes it great for designing smart conversation agents, automatic reports, and BI assistants.
- LlamaIndex (earlier called GPT Index) centers on cataloging and searching large sets of documents with the assistance of LLMs. This means organizations can set up personalized systems to respond to complex questions using internal data, which is helpful for knowledge management and BI decisions.

They both achieve the goal of using enterprise data together with LLMs, which enables new opportunities for AI-driven intelligence in NLP. Table 3 sum up this ecosystem, made up of essential open-source libraries, cloud providers, BI systems, low-code platforms, and emerging frameworks for AI.

Table 3. Tools and Platforms Enabling NLP Integration with BI

Tool / Platform	Type	Key Features	Strengths	Use Cases
NLTK	Open-source library	Tokenization, POS tagging, parsing, NER, stemming, lemmatization	Comprehensive NLP toolkit, educational focus	Prototyping, research, teaching NLP basics
spaCy	Open-source library	Fast tokenization, POS tagging, dependency parsing, NER, word vectors	Production-ready, efficient, easy API	Scalable NLP pipelines, real-time text processing
Hugging Face Transformers	Open-source library	Pre-trained transformer models (BERT, GPT, RoBERTa), fine-tuning, APIs	Access to state-of-the-art NLP models, ease of fine-tuning	Advanced NLP applications, contextual analysis
AWS Comprehend	Cloud NLP service	Sentiment analysis, entity recognition, topic modeling, language detection	Scalable, fully managed, and integrated with the AWS ecosystem	Scalable cloud NLP, text analytics at scale
Google Cloud Natural Language API	Cloud NLP service	Syntax analysis, entity extraction, sentiment, and content classification	Multi-language support, industry-specific classification	Multilingual NLP, content classification

continued on following page

Table 3. Continued

Tool / Platform	Type	Key Features	Strengths	Use Cases
Microsoft Azure Text Analytics	Cloud NLP service	Sentiment, entity linking, key phrase extraction, language detection	Integration with Microsoft tools, the cognitive services suite	Enterprise BI, integrated analytics solutions
Power BI	BI platform	Natural language Q&A, sentiment integration via Azure, automated insights	User-friendly, embedded NLP features	Business users querying data naturally
Tableau	BI platform	Natural language queries, summarization, and topic detection	Intuitive, interactive data exploration	Dashboard enhancement, data discovery
Qlik	BI platform	Conversational analytics, NLP-driven search, associative engine	Intuitive search, embedded NLP	Interactive BI, conversational data analysis
RapidMiner	Low-code/ no-code platform	Visual workflow, text mining, sentiment analysis, integration with Python/R	Ease of use, rapid prototyping	Business analysts, quick NLP experimentation
KNIME	Low-code/ no-code platform	Modular pipelines, text classification, clustering, integration with ML libs	Flexible, extensible, open architecture	Custom NLP workflows, enterprise-grade solutions
LangChain	Emerging NLP framework	LLM application chaining, document retrieval, and prompt management	Integrates LLMs with enterprise data	Conversational AI, automated BI reporting
LlamaIndex (GPT Index)	Emerging NLP framework	Document indexing, LLM-powered querying, and knowledge retrieval	Advanced knowledge management, enterprise integration	Complex query answering, data-driven BI

Overview of Cutting-Edge Algorithms

Today's progress in Natural Language Processing is mainly due to deep learning algorithms, especially neural network structures that are skilled at finding the intricate patterns and connections in language. These include transformer models that advanced NLP by allowing machines to process and understand language with spectacular accuracy and attention to detail.

Transformers and the Self-Attention Mechanism

Transformers allowed for a big improvement over earlier recurrent networks because they could process large-scale context well. The most important feature of transformers is self-attention, which allows the model to look at all the words at once, judging each one's significance with every other word. Therefore, transformers can recognize the importance of faraway words, which helps in analyzing complicated sentences, idioms, or stringing several sentences together. Because of self-attention, the model gives more weight to important words, which helps it understand and correctly interpret meanings.

BERT and Bidirectional Contextual Understanding

A significant transformer-based model is BERT (Bidirectional Encoder Representations from Transformers), which made bidirectional training possible. Previously, models interpret text either from left to right or right to left, however, BERT looks at text from both sides at the same time, making it possible for the model to understand context more thoroughly. With information working in both directions, BERT does well with tasks such as question answering, named entity recognition (NER), and sentiment analysis.

The structure and training process of BERT have led to the creation of several other models, such as RoBERTa (which runs on a larger amount of data and longer training periods) and DistilBERT (which takes up less space and requires less computation, all while keeping most of the accuracy). Businesses are able to pick OOP designs to meet both the demands of work and available resources.

Generative Models

Generative Pre-trained Transformers (also known as GPTs) are built to produce texts that sound natural to humans, in contrast to BERT's main tasks of understanding and classifying. Language outputs from GPT-2, GPT-3, and GPT-4 are often coherent, appropriate to the situation, and fluent. Using generative role, machine learning plays a key role in business intelligence, for example-

- Report generation
- Generating a summary of information
- Conversational AI and chatbots
- Making content and drafting it

Additionally, GPT models can learn new things quickly since they do not require a lot of additional training. Being flexible helps organizations reduce the effort and expenses needed to design NLP for their business.

Unified Text-to-Text Framework

T5 (Text-To-Text Transfer Transformer) is a leading method that, instead of handling translation, summarization, and question answering individually, tackles them all as text-to-text problems. Because the structure and criteria do not change, adapting the model to various tasks becomes much smoother. With BI applications, a model is capable of analyzing all of a user's text data needs and makes it simpler to manage.

Lightweight Models

Since many companies work with limited resources, researchers have created ALBERT (A Lite BERT) and DistilBERT, which have fewer parameters, do less computation, yet keep performance at a high level. These models help us use NLP-powered BI tools on tablets, mobile phones, or in areas where GPUs are missing, opening more chances for people to use advanced NLP.

Emerging Multimodal Models

After working with plain text, NLP is now moving to handle text along with other information like pictures, audio, and videos. Because BI relies on many kinds of data, multimodal models make it possible to analyze social media images with their captions for emotion analysis or merge transcripts of speeches with contextual records for improved quality of customer care. These models open the world of BI insights to cover much more than just text.

Continuous Evolution and Impact on BI

The fast development of deep learning models depends on using big datasets, training with new techniques, and adjusting their structure. With this advancement, companies can use NLP in business intelligence for various useful activities like: -

- Gain useful information from data that is not organized
- Make it possible for machines to process complicated language information
- Provide highly accurate intelligence for use in dealing with risks
- Use NLP to quickly catch up with changes in the company's needs

All in all, progress in transformers and deep learning models is helping businesses take advantage of language data in new and better ways.

IMPACT OF NLP-DRIVEN BUSINESS INTELLIGENCE ON KEY BUSINESS FUNCTIONS

Combining NLP with BI helps businesses make use of unstructured data to bring about positive changes in various areas. When methods such as data extraction, sentiment analysis, predictive analytics, and natural language querying are used in NLP, it supports good decision-making, efficient operations, and better connections with customers. This section provides details on the impacts each farming system has.

Marketing

Bringing together NLP with Business Intelligence (BI) allows organizations to look through vast amounts of information shared on social media, in product reviews, on blogs, and customer forums. Using sentiment analysis, topic modeling, and trend detection, marketers can follow how the brand is seen by customers in real time and discover new trends among them. Marketing teams can use the opinions and feelings expressed by customers to improve how they speak to and choose their audiences. Also, NLG is able to automate the production of customized content, which leads to more engagement. They help make better decisions by delivering useful information that supports the success of the campaign, reputation of the brand, and growth of its revenue.

Customer Service

NLP in BI greatly boosts customer service by handling the review of unstructured data on emails, conversations, and tickets. Sorting and prioritizing inquiries automatically, as well as understanding customers' feelings, assists in dealing with issues or complaints as soon as possible. Because of these advanced language models, conversational AI systems can deal with the usual customer inquiries, which helps human agents concentrate on handling difficult cases. Using past information, specialists can predict when potential escalations could occur. By using them, companies can experience better efficiency in operations, ensure their customers are happy, and manage costs through automation.

Operations

NLP enables operations to use compliance reports, maintenance logs, and communications from the supply chain that are unstructured for their work. Extracting the main points and essential data from documents makes review work quicker, and using predictive analytics warns about possible supply chain and equipment problems well in advance. Because of these tools, companies can handle problems before they happen and prevent minor issues from causing delays. NLP makes it easier to detect flaws and allocate resources in a smarter way by using the data it analyzes. Due to this, companies operate more safely, spend less, and make sure their business actions match their main objectives.

Human Resources and Talent Management

In the field of human resources, NLP changes how employees are recruited and supported by reviewing resumes, job performance, conversations at exit meetings, and survey results. These steps allow faster and better matching of applicants to jobs during the screening process. With sentiment analysis, one can detect the mood of employees and potential problems, and predictive analytics point out where people might leave and what roles are missing. As a result, these steps allow companies to make data-based workforce choices, find more effective employees, and ensure staff do not leave quickly. Therefore, employees stay motivated, and the company's future leaders can be identified more easily.

Compliance and Risk Management

NLP is very important for compliance and risk management because it can automate the checking of legal documents, contracts, and rules. The use of text classification and anomaly detection allows NLP systems to detect possible compliance problems and mark suspicious details so that risks are dealt with quickly. Through discourse analysis, it is possible to understand the meaning and consequences of regulations that support following the latest legal rules. Regular monitoring by the system lessens the chance of being fined or harmed in reputation, plus it improves the process of conducting audits. All in all, these methods support better governance of organizations and give more confidence in using AI-based BI.

Sales and Business Development

NLP helps business development and salespeople to understand what customers and the market are saying in communications, proposals, and reports. Through predictive analytics, companies examine data in texts to guess sales patterns and identify attractive leads resulting from customer interactions. Such tools allow sales staff to obtain important information more quickly, helping them respond better and succeed with their decisions. Recognizing invisible tendencies and clues from consumers in unstructured data, NLP improves a business's sales, intelligence on rivals, and speeds up closing deals, which results in sustainable growth.

Cross-Functional Collaboration and Organizational Transformation

Besides helping each department, NLP enables teams to work together by making hard data understandable with language and clear images. Using this wide approach to data, people working in marketing, operations, and finance are more able to make data-driven decisions easily. When everyone uses the same framework, it reduces separation, speeds up alignment with the strategy, and improves the organization's response time. Also, the use of integrated NLP in BI leads to opportunities for the company in the market by understanding customers, improving experiences, and decreasing efforts in some processes. In combination, these various elements help change the organization so it can adapt fast to new market trends and remain ahead of others.

CHALLENGES OF IMPLEMENTING NLP IN BUSINESS INTELLIGENCE

Complexity and Variability of Natural Language

Many subtle parts of natural language are found in idiom, sarcasm, homonyms and terms whose meanings depend on the situation. Sometimes, the word "bank" means a financial institution and at other times it means the side of a river. Such issues call for NLP models to have the ability to differentiate between the possible meanings. Besides, many industries use particular words and expressions that standard NLP models often do not grasp without being updated. Companies that use multiple languages encounter more issues because of the different syntax, grammar and cultural differences, so custom-made models for each language or domain are needed.

Data Quality and Availability

Posts on social media, messages from emails and reviews left by clients are often very unstructured. Problems like misspelled words, shortened meanings, emojis and sentences that lack information are common, so proper preprocessing becomes necessary and tough. Problems or errors from bad data quality can negatively affect NLP analysis and lead to incorrect business decisions. Furthermore, some fields have not developed plenty of textual data, making it hard for NLP to function effectively. Organizations have to keep data privacy and be compliant, meaning sensitive data cannot be accessed easily and it should always be protected.

Technical Integration and Infrastructure

Most organizations are using BI systems that are not equipped to handle NLP. Including modern NLP tools in systems calls for major work by the IT team to support smooth movement of data, prevent errors and ensure continuous analysis. Commonly, running NLP models using deep learning methods, including transformers, needs strong computers and GPUs or TPUs which are not cheap and require the help of technical specialists. Creating pipelines that deal with everything from cleaning and preparing data to deploying a model and showing results can be a difficult task that needs a lot of resources.

Interpretability and Transparency

Deep learning approaches to NLP usually make it hard to understand or explain how the system works. In areas such as finance, healthcare, or legal work that are regulated, not having clear explanations for AI's decisions can result in challenges or issues. It is still challenging to build trust among stakeholders, as there are limited ways to support and explain the NLP-based things they are shown. If business leaders are unsure of the data's origin, they may hesitate to use automated suggestions by NLP.

Organizational and Cultural Barriers

New BI solutions that use NLP may face employees who doubt either the effectiveness of new tech or the accuracy of AI. When people are not aware of what NLP can do, there may be misconceptions or unreal expectations. To be successful, adoption should involve changing the culture, setting up training, and clearly explaining that NLP is meant to work together with human abilities rather than taking their place. Linking NLP projects to the company's main goals proves their worth and encourages important stakeholders to agree with them.

ROADMAP FOR EFFECTIVE ADOPTION OF NLP IN BUSINESS INTELLIGENCE

Assessment of Business Needs

The first thing to do is to identify which parts of the organization can gain the most from using NLP. This means joining forces with members of marketing, customer service, and operations teams to identify the main difficulties and search for problems suitable for NLP, for example, in monitoring the brand's sentiment or pulling out essential information from documents. High-impact use cases that can easily be applied give the organization early benefits, so more investment is justified.

Data Collection and Preprocessing

To achieve results in NLP, you need exceptionally high-quality data. Organizations should put in place reliable ways to access text information from a wide variety of sources, keeping everything consistent and free from errors. In preprocessing, data is tokenized, garbage like stop words and special characters is removed, and mistakes in spelling are corrected. The use of annotation or labeling for data, whether done manually or semi-automatically, helps enhance the optimal training of the model. Anonymization and keeping data private are necessary during every step of this process.

Selection of Appropriate NLP Tools and Platforms

The correct technology stack is chosen based on what a company has in terms of resources, knowledge, and aims. Open-source tools like spaCy and Hugging Face Transformers help development teams customize their applications and services, such as AWS Comprehend and Google Cloud NLP, provide a scalable way for companies to start using NLP quickly. A few BI platforms have started to include NLP by default, which makes it simpler to install. Those making the decision must consider the balance between how much it costs, how well it can grow, how easy it is, and how much it can be adjusted.

Pilot Projects and Iterative Development

Running trials on small teams gives individuals a chance to check their assumptions, check how algorithms perform, and gather user comments with a low risk involved. Going through many steps of model training, evaluation, and optimization allows for better results and helps the model reflect the company's goals. Such successes help employees feel confident and back the company. Ensuring accuracy, minimal bias, and no drift over time is possible through regularly tracking the model.

Cross-functional Collaboration and Training

Getting the biggest benefits from NLP demands that data scientists, IT experts, and business users all take part. Regularly holding workshops, training sessions, and sharing knowledge forums can develop data literacy and explain what NLP is good at and not good at. User friendliness in NLP-driven BI encourages people within the company to use the tools more frequently and adapt better to them. Open channels of communication prevent people from expecting different things.

Governance, Compliance, and Explainability

Firms should introduce rules and controls to supervise data usage, AI model development, and how the results are interpreted. You should check AI results, apply explainability methods such as attention visualization, and save information about the model behavior. When AI is transparent, it promotes trust and helps companies follow the rules set by the industry.

Scaling and Continuous Improvement

If NLP proves to be successful, it should be applied across different departments and made compatible with other data resources to bring the highest value. Keep retraining the models to keep them up to date as market situations and customers' actions change. Making use of automation for tracking, warnings, and maintenance reduces the workload for operations. By encouraging innovation in the workplace, companies can regularly update their business intelligence solutions that involve NLP.

CONCLUSION

As research and technology keep evolving rapidly, NLP is expected to play a bigger role in business intelligence. NLP can be enhanced by letting it process text and other kinds of data, such as images, audio, and video, all at once using multimodal AI. This approach will give businesses the ability to analyze multi-dimensional content from customers, social media, and their documents. Researchers are also looking into making NLP models easy to understand and reliable. Since AI is now often used for important decision-making, there is a rising need for models that do well and give results that can be easily understood. When it comes to explainable

AI (XAI) and NLP, research will assure people and support conformity with rules, mainly for industries such as finance and healthcare.

The use of real-time and edge NLP will grow a lot in the future. The use of lightweight models in edge devices allows quick analysis for instant help in talks between customers and chatbots, voice assistant requests, and on-site jobs, ensuring that sensitive information is not exposed. Also, by analyzing user behavior, interests, and earlier decisions, NLP-based BI will make sure that any insights or recommendations fit the needs of individuals. This will boost how customers interact with the business and how all its functions run smoothly. As a result, using unsupervised and self-supervised learning can create new NLP systems more rapidly and save money, since large labeled data will not be needed as much. With better transfer learning and domain adaptation, every kind of business will be able to adopt NLP.

Business intelligence is being transformed by Natural Language Processing, which is unlocking a huge amount of information from unstructured text. NLP makes use of methods like text mining, sentiment analysis, and advanced language models to give companies valuable ideas that help them make the right decisions, improve customers' experiences, and better administer their operations. Even though there are issues related to language, data quality, and system integration, NLP in BI systems can give businesses a major advantage. For a project to be successful, it must be aligned with business goals, use strong data connections, select proper technology, and involve all parts of the organization in teamwork.

The advancement of NLP technology will further improve business intelligence by making analytics quicker, more informed, and intelligent. Those who adopt these new ideas now are ready to grow and handle changes as data becomes more important in the future. Being aware of what NLP can do now, facing its implementation difficulties, and foreseeing future trends helps businesses benefit from NLP and stay at the forefront of business intelligence.

REFERENCES

Agrawal, G., Kaur, A., & Myneni, S. (2024). A Review of Generative Models in Generating Synthetic Attack Data for Cybersecurity. *Electronics 2024, Vol. 13, Page 322, 13*(2), 322. https://doi.org/DOI: 10.3390/ELECTRONICS13020322

Albahli, S. (2025). An Advanced Natural Language Processing Framework for Arabic Named Entity Recognition: A Novel Approach to Handling Morphological Richness and Nested Entities. *Applied Sciences 2025, Vol. 15, Page 3073, 15*(6), 3073. https://doi.org/DOI: 10.3390/APP15063073

Amiri, B., & Karimianghadim, R. (2024). A novel text clustering model based on topic modelling and social network analysis. *Chaos, Solitons, and Fractals*, *181*, 114633. DOI: 10.1016/J.CHAOS.2024.114633

Attigeri, G., Agrawal, A., & Kolekar, S. V. (2024). Advanced NLP Models for Technical University Information Chatbots: Development and Comparative Analysis. *IEEE Access : Practical Innovations, Open Solutions*, *12*, 29633–29647. DOI: 10.1109/ACCESS.2024.3368382

Bello, A., Ng, S. C., & Leung, M. F. (2023). A BERT Framework to Sentiment Analysis of Tweets. *Sensors (Basel)*, *23*(1). Advance online publication. DOI: 10.3390/s23010506 PMID: 36617101

Bharadiya, J. P. (2023). The role of machine learning in transforming business intelligence. *International Journal of Computing and Artificial Intelligence*, *4*(1). Advance online publication. DOI: 10.33545/27076571.2023.v4.i1a.60

Bonechi, S., Palma, G., Caronna, M., Ugolini, M., Massaro, A., & Rizzo, A. (2024). Enhancing Customer Support in Banking: Leveraging AI for Efficient Ticket Classification. *Procedia Computer Science*, *246*(C), 128–137. DOI: 10.1016/J.PROCS.2024.09.235

Cambria, E. (2025). Pragmatics Processing. In Erik, C. (Ed.), *Understanding Natural Language Understanding* (pp. 229–338). Springer., DOI: 10.1007/978-3-031-73974-3_4

Chatzimina, M. E., Papadaki, H. A., Pontikoglou, C., & Tsiknakis, M. (2024). A Comparative Sentiment Analysis of Greek Clinical Conversations Using BERT, RoBERTa, GPT-2, and XLNet. *Bioengineering 2024, Vol. 11, Page 521, 11*(6), 521. https://doi.org/DOI: 10.3390/BIOENGINEERING11060521

Chen, X., Li, J., & Ye, Y. (2024). A feasibility study for the application of AI-generated conversations in pragmatic analysis. *Journal of Pragmatics*, *223*, 14–30. DOI: 10.1016/J.PRAGMA.2024.01.003

Dsouza, V. S., Leyens, L., & Brand, A. (2025). Employing bibliometrics and natural language processing (NLP) to analyse real-world applications of adverse drug reaction. *Exploratory Research in Clinical and Social Pharmacy*, *18*, 100592. DOI: 10.1016/J.RCSOP.2025.100592 PMID: 40207140

Du, K., Zhao, Y., Mao, R., Xing, F., & Cambria, E. (2025). Natural language processing in finance: A survey. *Information Fusion*, *115*, 102755. DOI: 10.1016/J.INFFUS.2024.102755

Esmaail, N., Omar, N., Mohd, M., Fauzi, F., & Mansur, Z. (2024). *Named Entity Recognition in User-generated Text (English Twitter): A Systematic Literature Review*. IEEE., DOI: 10.1109/ACCESS.2024.3427714

Guimarães, N., Campos, R., & Jorge, A. (2024). Pre-trained language models: What do they know? *Wiley Interdisciplinary Reviews. Data Mining and Knowledge Discovery*, *14*(1), e1518. DOI: 10.1002/WIDM.1518;WEBSITE:WEBSITE:WIRES;WGROUP:STRING:PUBLICATION

Hayes, O., & Kelliher, F. (2024). The role of social media data in enhancing B2B omni-channel marketing efforts in small businesses. *Journal of Small Business and Enterprise Development*, *32*(1), 151–172. DOI: 10.1108/JSBED-02-2023-0051/FULL/XML

Islam, R., Shahadat Hosen, M., Naeem, Z., Folorunso, E. O., Chu, T. S., Al Mamun, A., & Orunbon, N. O. (2024). Data-Driven Decision Making: Advanced Database Systems for Business Intelligence. *Nanotechnology Perceptions*, *20*(S3), 687–704. DOI: 10.62441/nano-ntp.v20iS3.51

Jiang, L., & Goetz, S. M. (2025). Natural language processing in the patent domain: A survey. *Artificial Intelligence Review*, *58*(7), 1–62. DOI: 10.1007/S10462-025-11168-Z/TABLES/6

Jiang, P., & Cai, X. (2024). A Survey of Semantic Parsing Techniques. *Symmetry 2024, Vol. 16, Page 1201*, *16*(9), 1201. https://doi.org/DOI: 10.3390/SYM16091201

Jiang, T., Guo, Q., Wei, Y., Cheng, Q., & Lu, W. (2024). Investigating the relationships between dialog patterns and user satisfaction in customer service chat systems based on chat log analysis. *Journal of Information Science*. Advance online publication. DOI: 10.1177/01655515221124066

Joseph, T. (2024). Natural Language Processing (NLP) for Sentiment Analysis in Social Media. *International Journal of Computing and Engineering*, *6*(2), 35–48. https://ideas.repec.org/a/bhx/ojijce/v6y2024i2p35-48id2135.html

Kantor, K., & Morzy, M. (2024). Machine learning and natural language processing in clinical trial eligibility criteria parsing: A scoping review. *Drug Discovery Today*, *29*(10), 104139. DOI: 10.1016/J.DRUDIS.2024.104139 PMID: 39154773

Khurana, D., Koli, A., Khatter, K., & Singh, S. (2023). Natural language processing: State of the art, current trends and challenges. *Multimedia Tools and Applications*, *82*(3). Advance online publication. DOI: 10.1007/s11042-022-13428-4 PMID: 35855771

Koç, C., Özyurt, F., & Iantovics, L. B. (2025). Survey on latest advances in natural language processing applications of generative adversarial networks. *Wiley Interdisciplinary Reviews. Data Mining and Knowledge Discovery*, *15*(1), e70004.

Kumar, V., Iqbal, M. I., & Rathore, R. (2025). Natural Language Processing (NLP) in Disease Detection - A Discussion of How NLP Techniques Can Be Used to Analyze and Classify Medical Text Data for Disease Diagnosis. *AI in Disease Detection: Advancements and Applications*, 53–75. https://doi.org/DOI: 10.1002/9781394278695.CH3;PAGEGROUP:STRING:PUBLICATION

Kyle, K., & Eguchi, M. (2024). Evaluating NLP models with written and spoken L2 samples. *Research Methods in Applied Linguistics*, *3*(2), 100120. DOI: 10.1016/J.RMAL.2024.100120

Lane, H., & Dyshel, M. (2025). *Natural language processing in action*. Simon and Schuster.

Lee, R. (2025). Part-of-Speech (POS) Tagging. In *Natural Language Processing* (pp. 45–68). Springer., DOI: 10.1007/978-981-96-3208-4_3

Lekmiti, A., Stolk, P. J., Taylor, A., Ramachandran, S., & Yap, N. K. (2024). Text mining in tourism and hospitality research: A bibliometric perspective. *Journal of Hospitality and Tourism Technology*, *16*(3), 588–610. DOI: 10.1108/JHTT-05-2024-0284/FULL/XML

Mengliev, D., Barakhnin, V., Abdurakhmonova, N., & Eshkulov, M. (2024). Developing named entity recognition algorithms for Uzbek: Dataset insights and implementation. *Data in Brief*, *54*, 110413. DOI: 10.1016/J.DIB.2024.110413 PMID: 38708296

Molenaar, A., Lukose, D., Brennan, L., Jenkins, E. L., & McCaffrey, T. A. (2024). Using Natural Language Processing to Explore Social Media Opinions on Food Security: Sentiment Analysis and Topic Modeling Study. *Journal of Medical Internet Research, 26*(1). Advance online publication. DOI: 10.2196/47826 PMID: 38512326

Nanyonga, A., Wasswa, H., Turhan, U., Joiner, K., & Wild, G. (2024). Exploring Aviation Incident Narratives Using Topic Modeling and Clustering Techniques. *2024 IEEE Region 10 Symposium, TENSYMP 2024*. https://doi.org/DOI: 10.1109/TENSYMP61132.2024.10752231

Özkurt Id, C. (2024). Comparative Analysis of State-of-the-Art Q&A Models: BERT, RoBERTa, DistilBERT, and ALBERT on SQuAD v2 Dataset. *Chaos and Fractals, 1*(1), 19–30. DOI: 10.69882/ADBA.CHF.2024073

Patel, R., Gupta, A., Qin, X., & Brickner, C. (2024). A Generative AI and NLP-Based Research Prototype for Call Resolutions and Automation: The Case of a Healthcare Contact Center. *Proceedings of the 2024 Pre-ICIS SIGDSA Symposium, SIGDSA*, 12–2024. https://aisel.aisnet.org/sigdsa2024/16

Rachel, J. J. L., Bhuvaneswari, A., & Kumudha, M. (2024). Topic Modeling Based Clustering of Disaster Tweets Using BERTopic. *2024 MIT Art, Design and Technology School of Computing International Conference, MITADTSoCiCon 2024*. https://doi.org/DOI: 10.1109/MITADTSOCICON60330.2024.10575555

Saadati, H., & Hakimi, A. (2024). Optimizing the Ticket Response Process in Customer Support Systems Using Data-Driven and Machine Learning Methods: A Case Study of IFDA. *Optimality, 1*(2), 188–204. DOI: 10.22105/OPT.V1I2.57

Sandu, A., Cotfas, L. A., Stănescu, A., & Delcea, C. (2024). A Bibliometric Analysis of Text Mining: Exploring the Use of Natural Language Processing in Social Media Research. *Applied Sciences 2024, Vol. 14, Page 3144, 14*(8), 3144. https://doi.org/DOI: 10.3390/APP14083144

Sarker, I. H. (2021). Data Science and Analytics: An Overview from Data-Driven Smart Computing, Decision-Making and Applications Perspective. In *SN Computer Science* (Vol. 2, Issue 5). https://doi.org/DOI: 10.1007/s42979-021-00765-8

Sawalha, M., Al-Shargi, F., Yagi, S., AlShdaifat, A. T., Hammo, B., Belajeed, M., & Al-Ogaili, L. R. (2025). Morphologically-analyzed and syntactically-annotated Quran dataset. *Data in Brief, 58*, 111211. DOI: 10.1016/J.DIB.2024.111211 PMID: 39830618

Sawicki, J., Ganzha, M., & Paprzycki, M. (2023). The State of the Art of Natural Language Processing—A Systematic Automated Review of NLP Literature Using NLP Techniques. *Data Intelligence*, *5*(3). Advance online publication. DOI: 10.1162/dint_a_00213

Shamshiri, A., Ryu, K. R., & Park, J. Y. (2024). Text mining and natural language processing in construction. *Automation in Construction*, *158*, 105200. DOI: 10.1016/J.AUTCON.2023.105200

Sharma, S., Vashisht, M., & Kumar, V. (2024). Enhanced Customer Insights: Multimodal NLP Feedback System. *2024 IEEE International Students' Conference on Electrical, Electronics and Computer Science, SCEECS 2024*. https://doi.org/DOI: 10.1109/SCEECS61402.2024.10481937

Singh, S., & Mahmood, A. (2021). The NLP Cookbook: Modern Recipes for Transformer Based Deep Learning Architectures. *IEEE Access : Practical Innovations, Open Solutions*, *9*. Advance online publication. DOI: 10.1109/ACCESS.2021.3077350

Srivastava, G., Muneeswari, S., Venkataraman, R., Kavitha, V., & Parthiban, N. (2022). A review of the state of the art in business intelligence software. In *Enterprise Information Systems* (Vol. 16, Issue 1). https://doi.org/DOI: 10.1080/17517575.2021.1872107

Tan, K. L., Lee, C. P., & Lim, K. M. (2023). A Survey of Sentiment Analysis: Approaches, Datasets, and Future Research. In *Applied Sciences (Switzerland)* (Vol. 13, Issue 7). https://doi.org/DOI: 10.3390/app13074550

Tasneem, N. S., & Hemalatha, R. (2025). Real-Time Sentiment Analysis of Customer Feedback Using Neural Networks and NLP Methods. *2024 International Conference on IT Innovation and Knowledge Discovery (ITIKD)*, 1–6. https://doi.org/DOI: 10.1109/ITIKD63574.2025.11004792

Town, P., & Thabtah, F. (2019). Data Analytics Tools: A User Perspective. In *Journal of Information and Knowledge Management* (Vol. 18, Issue 1). https://doi.org/DOI: 10.1142/S0219649219500023

Tripathi, M. A., Madhavi, K., Kandi, V. S. P., Nassa, V. K., Mallik, B., & Chakravarthi, M. K. (2023). Machine learning models for evaluating the benefits of business intelligence systems. *The Journal of High Technology Management Research*, *34*(2). Advance online publication. DOI: 10.1016/j.hitech.2023.100470

Ullah, S., Ahmad, R., Namoun, A., Muhammad, S., Ullah, K., Hussain, I., & Ibrahim, I. A. (2024). A Deep Learning-Based Approach for Part of Speech (PoS) Tagging in the Pashto Language. *IEEE Access : Practical Innovations, Open Solutions*, *12*, 86355–86364. DOI: 10.1109/ACCESS.2024.3412175

Upadhyay, P., Agarwal, R., Dhiman, S., Sarkar, A., & Chaturvedi, S. (2024). A comprehensive survey on answer generation methods using NLP. *Natural Language Processing Journal*, *8*, 100088. DOI: 10.1016/J.NLP.2024.100088

Wang, A. X., Chukova, S. S., Simpson, C. R., & Nguyen, B. P. (2024). Challenges and opportunities of generative models on tabular data. *Applied Soft Computing*, *166*, 112223. DOI: 10.1016/J.ASOC.2024.112223

Yu, D., Li, L., Su, H., & Fuoli, M. (2024). Assessing the potential of LLM-assisted annotation for corpus-based pragmatics and discourse analysis: The case of apology. *International Journal of Corpus Linguistics*, *29*(4), 534–561. DOI: 10.1075/IJCL.23087.YU

Zunic, A., Corcoran, P., & Spasic, I. (2020). Sentiment analysis in health and well-being: Systematic review. In *JMIR Medical Informatics* (Vol. 8, Issue 1). https://doi.org/DOI: 10.2196/16023

Compilation of References

Aarzoo & Lal. R. (2025). Enhancing Advertising Effectiveness Through AIDA, AI, and Data Visualization Integration for Business Strategies. In M. Muniasamy, A. Naim, & A. Kumar (Eds.), *Data Visualization Tools for Business Applications* (pp. 85-102). IGI Global. DOI: 10.4018/979-8-3693-6537-3.ch005

Aarzoo, & Lal, R. (2024). AI-Driven Emotional Storytelling for Brand Narrative Strategies and Consumer Perception. IUP Journal of Brand Management, 21(4), 30–50.

Abdul-Mageed, M., Elmadany, A., & Nagoudi, E. M. B. (2021). ARBERT & MARBERT: Deep Bidirectional Transformers for Arabic. *In Proceedings of the 59th Annual Meeting of the Association for Computational Linguistics and the 11th International Joint Conference on Natural Language Processing* Volume 1*: Long Papers)* (7088–7105). Association for Computational Linguistics. DOI: 10.18653/v1/2021.acl-long.551

Abid, G., Ahmed, S., Elahi, N., & Ilyas, S. (2020). Antecedents and mechanism of employee well-being for social sustainability: A sequential mediation. *Sustainable Production and Consumption*, *24*, 79–89. Advance online publication. DOI: 10.1016/j.spc.2020.06.011

Abinader, A. (2024). *Using natural language processing (NLP) to implement sentiment analysis and keyword extraction on course evaluations* [Senior essay, Yale University]. Yale Computer Science & Economics. https://csec.yale.edu/senior-essays/spring-2024/using-natural-language-processing-nlp-implement-sentiment-analysis-and

Ackley, D. (2016). Emotional intelligence: A practical review of models, measures, and applications. *Consulting Psychology Journal*, *68*(4), 269–286. DOI: 10.1037/cpb0000070

Adamopoulos, I., Valamontes, A., Tsirkas, P., & Dounias, G. (2025). Predicting Workplace Hazard, Stress and Burnout Among Public Health Inspectors: An AI-Driven Analysis in the Context of Climate Change. *European Journal of Investigation in Health, Psychology and Education, 15*(5), 65. DOI: 10.3390/ejihpe15050065 PMID: 40422294

Adeusi, K. B., Amajuoyi, P., & Benjami, L. B. (2024). Utilizing machine learning to predict employee turnover in high-stress sectors. *International Journal of Management & Entrepreneurship Research, 6*(5), 1702–1732. DOI: 10.51594/ijmer.v6i5.1143

Adiguzel, Z., Sonmez Cakir, F., & Altay Morgul, U. (2025). Enhancing firm performance and sustainability through creativity-oriented HRM and quality management: The mediating role of commercialization in the IT sector. *International Journal of Quality & Reliability Management*. Advance online publication. DOI: 10.1108/IJQRM-08-2024-0262

Agarwal, A. (2023). AI adoption by human resource management: A study of its antecedents and impact on HR system effectiveness. *Foresight, 25*(1), 67–81. DOI: 10.1108/FS-10-2021-0199

Agnihotri, A., Grover, V., Balusamy, B., Gite, S., Arockiam, D., & Shankar, A. (2024, June). Utilizing the potential of AI to revolutionize talent management in contemporary organizations. *IET Conference Proceedings CP881, 2024*(7), 1–11. The Institution of Engineering and Technology. DOI: 10.1049/icp.2024.2519

Agnihotri, A., Pavitra, K. H., Balusamy, B., Maurya, A., & Bibhakar, P. (2023). Artificial intelligence shaping talent intelligence and talent acquisition for smart employee management. *EAI Endorsed Transactions on Internet of Things, 10*. Advance online publication. DOI: 10.4108/eetiot.4642

Agrawal, G., Kaur, A., & Myneni, S. (2024). A Review of Generative Models in Generating Synthetic Attack Data for Cybersecurity. *Electronics 2024, Vol. 13, Page 322, 13*(2), 322. https://doi.org/DOI: 10.3390/ELECTRONICS13020322

Ahmed, N., Saha, A. K., Al Noman, M., Jim, J. R., Mridha, M. F., & Kabir, M. M. (2024). Deep learning-based natural language processing in human–agent interaction: Applications, advancements and challenges. *Natural Language Processing Journal, 9*, 100112. DOI: 10.1016/j.nlp.2024.100112

Aksoy, E. (2025). Balancing act: Exploring the interplay of production pressure and innovation/flexibility climates on employee well-being. *Creativity and Innovation Management, 34*(1), 222–236. DOI: 10.1111/caim.12640

Al Qahtani, E., & Alsmairat, M. (2023). Assisting artificial intelligence adoption drivers in human resources management: A mediation model. *Acta Logistica, 10*(1), 141–150. DOI: 10.22306/al.v10i1.371

Al-Alawi, A. I., Al Bin Ali, F. A., Al Rashidi, M. A., & Albuainain, M. S. (2025). Mapping the Adoption of Big Data and Predictive Analytics in Strategic Human Resource Management. *Studies in Systems. Decision and Control, 546*, 537–548. DOI: 10.1007/978-3-031-65207-3_46

Alam, S. (2023). The Impact of Modern Technologies and HR Practices on Employee Retention: A Study on Apparel Firms in India. In M. H.K. & S. S. (Eds.), *Proceedings - 2023 International Conference on Advanced Computing and Communication Technologies, ICACCTech 2023* (pp. 335 – 340). Institute of Electrical and Electronics Engineers Inc. DOI: 10.1109/ICACCTech61146.2023.00061

Alamelu, R., Nalini, R., Cresenta Shakila Motha, L., Amudha, R., & Bowiya, S. (2017). Adoption factors impacting Human Resource analytics among employees. *International Journal of Economic Research, 14*(6), 417–423. https://www.scopus.com/inward/record.uri?eid=2-s2.0-85035008544&partnerID=40&md5=84069c1000a020a3d6048d98c5887450

Albahli, S. (2025). An Advanced Natural Language Processing Framework for Arabic Named Entity Recognition: A Novel Approach to Handling Morphological Richness and Nested Entities. *Applied Sciences 2025, Vol. 15, Page 3073, 15*(6), 3073. https://doi.org/DOI: 10.3390/APP15063073

Al-Busaidi, K. A., Al-Shihi, H., & Lin, L. (2023). Applying sentiment analysis to online student course evaluations: A case study from the University of West Georgia. *Journal of Online Learning Research, 9*(2), 121–140. https://files.eric.ed.gov/fulltext/EJ1462338.pdf

Allen, S. J., Shankman, M. L., & Haber-Curran, P. (2016). Developing emotionally intelligent leadership: The need for deliberate practice and collaboration across disciplines. *New Directions for Higher Education, 2016*(174), 79–91. DOI: 10.1002/he.20191

Allen, S. J., Shankman, M. L., & Miguel, R. F. (2012). Emotionally Intelligent Leadership: An Integrative, Process-Oriented Theory of Student Leadership. *Journal of Leadership Education, 11*(1), 177–203. DOI: 10.12806/V11/I1/TF1

Alruily, M. (2023). Sentiment analysis for predicting stress among workers and classification utilizing CNN: Unveiling the mechanism. *Alexandria Engineering Journal, 81*, 360–370. DOI: 10.1016/j.aej.2023.09.040

Altemeyer, B. (2019). Making the business case for AI in HR: Two case studies. *Strategic HR Review*, *18*(2), 66–70. DOI: 10.1108/SHR-12-2018-0101

Amiri, B., & Karimianghadim, R. (2024). A novel text clustering model based on topic modelling and social network analysis. *Chaos, Solitons, and Fractals*, *181*, 114633. DOI: 10.1016/J.CHAOS.2024.114633

Anderson, N. (2003). Applicant and recruiter reactions to new technology in selection: A critical review and agenda for future research. *International Journal of Selection and Assessment*, *11*(2/3), 121–136. DOI: 10.1111/1468-2389.00235

Anthun, K. S., Anthun, K. S., Håland, E., & Lillefjell, M. (2024). What influences the use of HR analytics in Human Resource management in Norwegian municipal health care services? *BMC Health Services Research*, *24*(1), 1131. Advance online publication. DOI: 10.1186/s12913-024-11610-y PMID: 39334277

Ara, K., & Akbar, A. (2016). A study of the impact of moonlighting practices on job satisfaction of university teachers. *Bulletin of Education and Research*, *38*(1), 101–116.

Arghode, V. (2013). Emotional and social intelligence competence: Implications for instruction. *International Journal of Pedagogies and Learning*, *8*(2), 66–77. DOI: 10.5172/ijpl.2013.8.2.66

Arora, M., Ahmad, V., Arora, T., & Kumar, R. (2024). Digital Transformation and Talent Management. In *Green Metaverse for Greener Economies*. CRC Press., DOI: 10.1201/9781032638188-4

Arora, M., Prakash, A., Mittal, A., & Singh, S. (2021). HR Analytics and Artificial Intelligence-Transforming Human Resource Management. *2021 International Conference on Decision Aid Sciences and Application, DASA 2021*, 288 – 293. DOI: 10.1109/DASA53625.2021.9682325

Ashurst, C., Barocas, S., Campbell, R., & Raji, D. (2022, June). Disentangling the components of ethical research in machine learning. *In Proceedings of the 2022 ACM Conference on Fairness, Accountability, and Transparency* (pp. 2057-2068). DOI: 10.1145/3531146.3533781

Asim, Z., Sorooshain, S., Sami, W., Mahmood, M., Yusof, Y., Sarwat, S., & Vasudevan, A. (2024). Navigating the Educational Frontier and Unveiling the Role of Virtual Reality in Faculty Development: An Emerging Consideration in Global Accreditation. In Naim, A., Saklani, A., Khan, S. A., & Malik, P. K. (Eds.), (pp. 226–240). Advances in Higher Education and Professional Development. IGI Global., DOI: 10.4018/979-8-3693-1698-6.ch015

Asim, Z., Vasudevan, A., Khan, S. A., Mahmood, M., Yosof, Y., & Muniyanayaka, D. (2024). Beyond the Screen: Ethical Dilemmas in the XR Frontier. In Kajla, T., Kansra, P., & Singh, N. (Eds.), (pp. 15–43). Advances in Computational Intelligence and Robotics. IGI Global., DOI: 10.4018/979-8-3693-2432-5.ch002

Attigeri, G., Agrawal, A., & Kolekar, S. V. (2024). Advanced NLP Models for Technical University Information Chatbots: Development and Comparative Analysis. *IEEE Access : Practical Innovations, Open Solutions*, *12*, 29633–29647. DOI: 10.1109/ACCESS.2024.3368382

Aulia, S. R., & Lin, W. S. (2025). Embracing the digital shift: Leveraging AI to foster employee well-being and engagement in remote workplace settings in the Asia Pacific region. *Asia Pacific Management Review*, *30*(3), 100339. DOI: 10.1016/j.apmrv.2024.12.003

Baas, J., Schotten, M., Plume, A., Côté, G., & Karimi, R. (2020). Scopus as a curated, high-quality bibliometric data source for academic research in quantitative science studies. *Quantitative Science Studies*, *1*(1), 377–386. DOI: 10.1162/qss_a_00019

Baidya, R., Lal, R., & Rena, R. (2024). Digital Competency Assessment and Data-Driven Performance Management for Start-Ups. In Data-Driven Modelling and Predictive Analytics in Business and Finance (pp. 203-234). Auerbach Publications. DOI: 10.1201/9781032618845-13

Balahur, A., & Turchi, M. (2012, July). Multilingual sentiment analysis using machine translation? *In Proceedings of the 3rd workshop in computational approaches to subjectivity and sentiment analysis* (pp. 52-60).

Ball, K. (2021), Electronic Monitoring and Surveillance in the Workplace, Publications Office of the European Union, Luxembourg, ISBN 978-92-76-43340-8, , JRC125716.DOI: 10.2760/5137

Ball, K. (2010). Workplace surveillance: An overview. *Labor History*, *51*(1), 87–106. DOI: 10.1080/00236561003654776

Bamman, D., & Smith, N. A. (2015). Contextualized sarcasm detection on Twitter. *Proceedings of the Ninth International AAAI Conference on Web and Social Media*, 9(1), 574–577. DOI: 10.1609/icwsm.v9i1.14655

Bandi, G. N. S., Rao, T. S., & Ali, S. S. (2021). Data Analytics Applications for Human Resource Management. *2021 International Conference on Computer Communication and Informatics, ICCCI 2021*. DOI: 10.1109/ICCCI50826.2021.9402300

Barocas, S., Hardt, M., & Narayanan, A. (2019). *Fairness and Machine Learning*. Retrieved from https://fairmlbook.org/

Bar-On, R. (1997). Emotional intelligence. *The International Journal of Sociology and Social Policy*, *29*, 164–175.

Bar-On, R. (2006). The Bar-On model of emotional-social intelligence (ESI) 1. *Psicothema*, ●●●, 13–25. PMID: 17295953

Barrett, L. F. (2017a). *How emotions are made: The secret life of the brain*. Houghton Mifflin Harcourt.

Barrett, L. F. (2017b). The theory of constructed emotion: An active inference account of interoception and categorization. *Social Cognitive and Affective Neuroscience*, *12*(1), 1–23. DOI: 10.1093/scan/nsx060 PMID: 27798257

Bathla, D., & Ahuja, R. (2023). Employee productivity augmentation using human capital analytics. In *Big Data: A Road-Map for Successful Digital Marketing*. Nova Science Publishers, Inc. https://www.scopus.com/inward/record.uri?eid=2-s2.0-85172707334&partnerID=40&md5=ef8dc08d2dce7c5ae2b8caaa32bada06

Bauer, M., Li, X., & Chen, R. (2023). Evaluating student feedback using NLP techniques: A case study in higher education. *Journal of Educational Technology*, *15*(2), 45–59.

Bello, A., Ng, S. C., & Leung, M. F. (2023). A BERT Framework to Sentiment Analysis of Tweets. *Sensors (Basel)*, *23*(1). Advance online publication. DOI: 10.3390/s23010506 PMID: 36617101

Ben Yahia, N., Hlel, J., & Colomo-Palacios, R. (2021). From Big Data to Deep Data to Support People Analytics for Employee Attrition Prediction. *IEEE Access : Practical Innovations, Open Solutions*, *9*, 60447–60458. DOI: 10.1109/ACCESS.2021.3074559

Betts, S. C. (2006). The decision to moonlight or quit: Incorporating multiple job holding into a model of turnover. *Journal of Organizational Culture. Communications and Conflict*, *10*(1), 63.

Bharadiya, J. P. (2023). The role of machine learning in transforming business intelligence. *International Journal of Computing and Artificial Intelligence*, *4*(1). Advance online publication. DOI: 10.33545/27076571.2023.v4.i1a.60

Bhatt, V., Thomas, S., Chauhan, D., & Patel, R. (2024). Investigating the impact of organisation culture, personal-job fit and employee engagement on turnover intention: An assessment of the IT sector from an emerging market perspective. *International Journal of Economics and Business Research*, *27*(2), 310–323. DOI: 10.1504/IJEBR.2024.136498

Bhatt, Y., Ghuman, K., & Dhir, A. (2020). Sustainable manufacturing. Bibliometrics and content analysis. *Journal of Cleaner Production, 260*, 120988. DOI: 10.1016/j.jclepro.2020.120988

Bielinska-Dusza, E., da Costa, R. L., Hamerska, M., & Zak, A. (2024). Study on the Impact of Remote Working on the Satisfaction and Experience of IT Workers in Poland. *Forum Scientiae Oeconomia, 11*(4), 9–34. DOI: 10.23762/FSO_VOL11_NO4_1

Bindhu, D., Namreen Asif, V. A., Baikadi, S. B., Chethanraj, Sunil, N., Chandravathi, & Dlima, N. G. (2024). Employee Perception of HR Practices and Its Impact on Job Satisfaction. *Lecture Notes in Networks and Systems, 1083 LNNS*, 154 – 165. DOI: 10.1007/978-3-031-67431-0_15

Blackburn, R. T., & Pitney, J. A. (1988). Faculty assessment and review: Issues and challenges. *Journal of Higher Education Policy*, *8*(3), 205–221.

Black, J. S., & van Esch, P. (2020). AI-enabled recruiting: What is it and how should a manager use it? *Business Horizons*, *63*(2), 215–226. DOI: 10.1016/j.bushor.2019.12.001

Bland, A. R., Roiser, J. P., Mehta, M. A., Schei, T., Boland, H., Campbell-Meiklejohn, D. K., Emsley, R. A., Munafo, M. R., Penton-Voak, I. S., Seara-Cardoso, A., Viding, E., Voon, V., Sahakian, B. J., Robbins, T. W., & Elliott, R. (2016). EMOTICOM: A neuropsychological test battery to evaluate emotion, motivation, impulsivity, and social cognition. *Frontiers in Behavioral Neuroscience, 10*. Advance online publication. DOI: 10.3389/fnbeh.2016.00025 PMID: 26941628

Bolbotinovic, Z. Z., Popovac, R. M., Vukmirovic, D. V, Comic, T. Z., & Stanojevic, N. D. (2024). HR Analytics: Opportunities and Challenges for Implementation in SME. *Lecture Notes in Networks and Systems, 999 LNNS*, 28 – 32. DOI: 10.1007/978-3-031-60840-7_4

Bonechi, S., Palma, G., Caronna, M., Ugolini, M., Massaro, A., & Rizzo, A. (2024). Enhancing Customer Support in Banking: Leveraging AI for Efficient Ticket Classification. *Procedia Computer Science*, *246*(C), 128–137. DOI: 10.1016/J.PROCS.2024.09.235

Bongale, A. M., Dharrao, D., & Urolagin, S. (2023). Exploratory Data Analysis and Classification of Employee Retention based on Logistic Regression Model. *2023 9th International Conference on Advanced Computing and Communication Systems, ICACCS 2023*, 1929 – 1933. DOI: 10.1109/ICACCS57279.2023.10112681

Bonilla-Chaves, E. F., & Palos-Sánchez, P. R. (2023). Exploring the Evolution of Human Resource Analytics: A Bibliometric Study. *Behavioral Sciences (Basel, Switzerland)*, *13*(3), 244. Advance online publication. DOI: 10.3390/bs13030244 PMID: 36975268

Bousbahi, F., & Alrazgan, M. S. (2015). Investigating faculty resistance to LMS adoption using the UTAUT model. *Journal of Interactive Learning*, *12*(4), 112–128.

Boyack, K. W., & Klavans, R. (2010, December). Co-citation analysis, bibliographic coupling, and direct citation: Which citation approach represents the research front most accurately? *Journal of the American Society for Information Science and Technology*, *61*(12), 2389–2404. DOI: 10.1002/asi.21419

Broadus, R. N. (1987, November). Toward a definition of "bibliometrics". *Scientometrics*, *12*(5-6), 373–379. DOI: 10.1007/BF02016680

Buckley, P., Minette, K., Joy, D., & Michaels, J. (2004). The use of an automated employment recruiting and screening system for temporary professional employees: A case study. *Human Resource Management*, *43*(2/3), 233–241. DOI: 10.1002/hrm.20017

Burns, J. M. G. (1978). *Leadership*. Harper & Row.

Burton, J. W., Lopez-Lopez, E., Hechtlinger, S., Rahwan, Z., Aeschbach, S., Bakker, M. A., Becker, J. A., Berditchevskaia, A., Berger, J., Brinkmann, L., Flek, L., Herzog, S. M., Huang, S., Kapoor, S., Narayanan, A., Nussberger, A.-M., Yasseri, T., Nickl, P., Almaatouq, A., & Hertwig, R. (2024). How large language models can reshape collective intelligence. *Nature Human Behaviour*, *8*(9), 1643–1655. DOI: 10.1038/s41562-024-01959-9

Cambria, E. (2025). Pragmatics Processing. In Erik, C. (Ed.), *Understanding Natural Language Understanding* (pp. 229–338). Springer., DOI: 10.1007/978-3-031-73974-3_4

Cao, X., & Zhang, D. (2020). From Forced to Voluntary AI Adoption. SSRN *Electronic Journal*. DOI: 10.2139/ssrn.3640862

Cao, R., Azimi, I., Sarhaddi, F., Niela-Vilen, H., Axelin, A., Liljeberg, P., & Rahmani, A. M. (2022). Accuracy Assessment of Oura Ring Nocturnal Heart Rate and Heart Rate Variability in Comparison With Electrocardiography in Time and Frequency Domains: Comprehensive Analysis. *Journal of Medical Internet Research*, *24*(1), e27487. DOI: 10.2196/27487 PMID: 35040799

Cappelli, P. (2001). *Making the most of online recruiting*. Harvard Business Review. Retrieved from https://www.hbr.org/2001/03/making-the-most-of-on-line-recruiting

Caron, E., & Batistic, S. (2019). Knowledge hubs in competence analytics: With a case study in recruitment and selection. In van Sinderen M., M. L., & M. L. (Eds.), *ICSOFT 2019 - Proceedings of the 14th International Conference on Software Technologies* (pp. 585 – 594). SciTePress. DOI: 10.5220/0008117805850594

Carter, L. (2023). Where Sentiment Analysis Fits in HR Wellness Initiatives. Reworked. Retrieved from https://www.reworked.co/employee-experience/sentiment-analysis-can-help-mental-wellness-initiatives-given-the-proper-guardrails/

Chandana, C., Sarkar, A., Deshmukh, K., Kulkarni, P., Bikash Acharjee, P., & Lourens, M. (2024). Analysing Employee Management Using Machine Learning Techniques and Solutions in Human Resource Management. *4th International Conference on Innovative Practices in Technology and Management 2024, ICIPTM 2024*. DOI: 10.1109/ICIPTM59628.2024.10563736

Chanda, P., & Ghosh, S. (2024). Optimizing Workforce Efficiency Using an Artificial Intelligence Approach: A Next-Gen HR Management System. *2024 ASU International Conference in Emerging Technologies for Sustainability and Intelligent Systems, ICETSIS 2024*, 1416 – 1421. DOI: 10.1109/ICETSIS61505.2024.10459590

Chang, Y. L., & Ke, J. (2024). Socially responsible artificial intelligence empowered people analytics: A novel framework towards sustainability. *Human Resource Development Review*, *23*(1), 88–120. DOI: 10.1177/15344843231200930

Chang, Y., Wang, X., Wang, J., Wu, Y., Yang, L., Zhu, K., Chen, H., Yi, X., Wang, C., Wang, Y., Ye, W., Zhang, Y., Chang, Y., Yu, P. S., Yang, Q., & Xie, X. (2024). A Survey on Evaluation of Large Language Models. *ACM Transactions on Intelligent Systems and Technology*, *15*(3), 1–45. DOI: 10.1145/3641289

Charalampous, M., Grant, C. A., Tramontano, C., & Michailidis, E. (2019). Systematically reviewing remote e-workers' well-being at work: A multidimensional approach. *European Journal of Work and Organizational Psychology*, *28*(1), 51–73. DOI: 10.1080/1359432X.2018.1541886

Charlwood, A., & Guenole, N. (2022). Can HR adapt to the paradoxes of artificial intelligence? *Human Resource Management Journal*, *32*(4), 729–742. DOI: 10.1111/1748-8583.12433

Chatzimina, M. E., Papadaki, H. A., Pontikoglou, C., & Tsiknakis, M. (2024). A Comparative Sentiment Analysis of Greek Clinical Conversations Using BERT, RoBERTa, GPT-2, and XLNet. *Bioengineering 2024, Vol. 11, Page 521, 11*(6), 521. https://doi.org/DOI: 10.3390/BIOENGINEERING11060521

Chaudhary, V. K., & Verma, D. (2025). The new frontier of data protection: Understanding India's DPDP rules and global compliance. *Panjab University Law Magazine – MagLaw, 4*(1).

Chau, K. Y., Huang, T., Moslehpour, M., Khan, W., Nisar, Q. A., & Haris, M. (2024). Opening a new horizon in green HRM practices with big data analytics and its analogy to circular economy performance: An empirical evidence. *Environment, Development and Sustainability*, *26*(5), 12133–12162. DOI: 10.1007/s10668-023-03725-9

Chaurasia, A., Kadam, S., Bhagat, K., Gauda, S., & Shingane, P. (2023). Employee Attrition Prediction using Artificial Neural Networks. *2023 4th International Conference for Emerging Technology, INCET 2023*. DOI: 10.1109/INCET57972.2023.10170676

Cheng, W., Kang, Q., & Xiao, Q. (2019, February 1). Bibliometric analysis of the top 100 influential studies on carotid artery stenting. *World Neurosurgery*, *122*, e1321–e1331. DOI: 10.1016/j.wneu.2018.11.042 PMID: 30448570

Chen, X., Li, J., & Ye, Y. (2024). A feasibility study for the application of AI-generated conversations in pragmatic analysis. *Journal of Pragmatics*, *223*, 14–30. DOI: 10.1016/J.PRAGMA.2024.01.003

Choudhari, Y., Shrestha, P., Singh, G., & Bindra, S. (2025). The Impact of Artificial Intelligence (AI) on Talent Acquisition in Human Resource Management. *Australasian Accounting, Business and Finance Journal, 19*(1).

Chowdhury, S., Dey, P., Joel-Edgar, S., Bhattacharya, S., Rodriguez-Espindola, O., Abadie, A., & Truong, L. (2023). Unlocking the value of artificial intelligence in human resource management through AI capability framework. *Human Resource Management Review*, *33*(1), 100899. DOI: 10.1016/j.hrmr.2022.100899

Chursin, A., Demenin, F., Karnaukh, S., Kiryakov, I., & Novoselov, A. (2023). The Role of Human Resources Management in Technological Enterprises in the Digital Transformation Environment. *Lecture Notes in Networks and Systems, 574 LNNS*, 2999 – 3008. DOI: 10.1007/978-3-031-21432-5_331

Ciampi, F., Giannozzi, A., Marzi, G., & Altman, E. I. (2021, March). Rethinking SME default prediction: A systematic literature review and future perspectives. *Scientometrics*, *126*(3), 2141–2188. DOI: 10.1007/s11192-020-03856-0 PMID: 33531720

Cobo, M. J., López-Herrera, A. G., Herrera-Viedma, E., & Herrera, F. (2011). Science mapping software tools: Review, analysis, and cooperative study among tools. *Journal of the American Society for Information Science and Technology*, *62*(7), 1382–1402. DOI: 10.1002/asi.21525

Cui, N., Malleson, N., Houlden, V., & Comber, A. (2021). Using VGI and social media data to understand urban green space: A narrative literature review. *ISPRS International Journal of Geo-Information*, *10*(7), 425. DOI: 10.3390/ijgi10070425

Danks, D., & London, A. J. (2017, August). Algorithmic bias in autonomous systems. In *IJCAI* (Vol. 17, No. 2017, pp. 4691–4697). DOI: 10.24963/ijcai.2017/654

Daoanis, L. E. (2012). Performance appraisal system: It's implications to employee performance. *International Journal of Business and Social Science*, *3*(22), 45–51.

Darville, J. J., & Arghode, V. (2024). People analytics, talent management, and leadership development in the USA and UAE. In *Industry 4.0 and People Analytics: A Technical Perspective of HRM*. Apple Academic Press. https://www.scopus.com/inward/record.uri?eid=2-s2.0-85198202400&partnerID=40&md5=b5b2a05acb4185661e0383a89ed0d57a

Das, S. S., & Pattanayak, S. (2023). Understanding the effect of leadership styles on employee well-being through leader-member exchange. *Current Psychology (New Brunswick, N.J.)*, *42*(25), 21310–21325. DOI: 10.1007/s12144-022-03243-3

Dave, P., Sinha, A., & Varkkey, B. (2020). Workplace learning in the IT sector: Building a case for investment. *Development and Learning in Organizations*, *35*(4), 4–7. DOI: 10.1108/DLO-05-2020-0104

Davies, M., Stankov, L., & Roberts, R. D. (1998). Emotional intelligence: In search of an elusive construct. *Journal of Personality and Social Psychology*, *75*(4), 989–1015. DOI: 10.1037/0022-3514.75.4.989 PMID: 9825531

Davila-Gonzalez, S., & Martin, S. (2024). Human digital twin in industry 5.0: A holistic approach to worker safety and well-being through advanced AI and emotional analytics. *Sensors (Basel)*, *24*(2), 655. DOI: 10.3390/s24020655 PMID: 38276347

Davis, F. D. (1989). Perceived usefulness, perceived ease of use, and user acceptance of information technology. *Management Information Systems Quarterly*, *13*(3), 319–339. DOI: 10.2307/249008

Day, C. (2004). The passion of successful leadership. *School Leadership & Management*, *24*(4), 425–437. DOI: 10.1080/13632430410001316525

Day, D., & Lance, C. (2004). Understanding the development of leadership complexity through latent growth modeling. In Day, D., Zaccaro, S., & Halpin, S. (Eds.), *Leader Development for Transforming Organizations: Growing Leaders for Tomorrow* (pp. 41–69). Lawrence Earlbaum Associates. DOI: 10.4324/9781410610102

De Brito, A. P., & Sousa, M. J. (2023). HR Analytics in the Commercial Aviation Sector: A Literature Review. In R. M. (Ed.), *Proceedings of the European Conference on Management, Leadership and Governance* (Vols. 2023-Novem, pp. 512 – 519). Academic Conferences and Publishing International Limited. https://www.scopus.com/inward/record.uri?eid=2-s2.0-85180554950&partnerID=40&md5=5b70b60711390c6570ea4148742a62e6

Depietro, R., Wiarda, E., & Fleischer, M. (1990). The context for change: Organization, technology and environment. In Tornatzky, L., & Fleischer, M. (Eds.), *The processes of technological innovation* (pp. 151–175). Lexington Books.

Deshpande, R., & Chakraborty, D. (2023). Impact of Work Stressors on Career Commitment – A Study of Indian IT Sector Employees. *Prabandhan: Indian Journal of Management, 16*(11), 27–42. DOI: 10.17010/pijom/2023/v16i11/173214

Devaraju, S. (2022). Natural Language Processing (NLP) in AI-Driven Recruitment Systems. *International Journal of Scientific Research in Computer Science, Engineering and Information Technology*, 555–566. DOI: 10.32628/CSEIT2285241

Devaraju, S. (2024). Architecting Scalable LLM-Powered Employee Engagement Systems: A Multi-Modal Framework for Enterprise HRIS Integration and Longitudinal Efficacy Analysis. [TURCOMAT]. *Turkish Journal of Computer and Mathematics Education, 15*(1), 282–294. DOI: 10.61841/turcomat.v15i1.14941

Dickey, H., Watson, V., & Zangelidis, A. (2011). Is it all about money? An examination of the motives behind moonlighting. *Applied Economics, 43*(26), 3767–3774. DOI: 10.1080/00036841003724403

Dietvorst, B. J., Simmons, J. P., & Massey, C. (2018). Overcoming algorithm aversion: People will use imperfect algorithms if they can (even slightly) modify them. *Management Science, 64*(3), 1155–1170. DOI: 10.1287/mnsc.2016.2643

Diez, F., Bussin, M., & Lee, V. (2019). Fundamentals of HR analytics: A manual on becoming HR analytical. In *Fundamentals of HR Analytics: A Manual on Becoming HR Analytical*. Emerald Group Publishing Ltd., DOI: 10.1108/978-1-78973-961-920191015

Dignum, V. (2019). *Responsible Artificial Intelligence: How to Develop and Use AI in a Responsible Way*. Springer Nature. DOI: 10.1007/978-3-030-30371-6

Dimoff, J. K., Kelloway, E. K., & Burnstein, M. D. (2016). Mental health awareness training (MHAT): The development and evaluation of an intervention for workplace leaders. *International Journal of Stress Management, 23*(2), 167–189. DOI: 10.1037/a0039479

Dishaw, M. T., & Strong, D. M. (1999). Extending the technology acceptance model with task–technology fit constructs. *Information & Management, 36*(1), 9–21. DOI: 10.1016/S0378-7206(98)00101-3

Dixon, L. (2023, July 12). Sentiment analysis can help mental wellness initiatives, given the proper guardrails. Reworked. https://www.reworked.co/employee-experience/sentiment-analysis-can-help-mental-wellness-initiatives-given-the-proper-guardrails/accessed 0n 26/04/25

Donthu, N., Kumar, S., Mukherjee, D., Pandey, N., & Lim, W. M. (2021, September 1). How to conduct a bibliometric analysis: An overview and guidelines. *Journal of Business Research, 133*, 285–296. DOI: 10.1016/j.jbusres.2021.04.070

Downton, J. V. (1973). *Rebel leadership: Commitment and charisma in the revolutionary process.* Free Press.

Dsouza, V. S., Leyens, L., & Brand, A. (2025). Employing bibliometrics and natural language processing (NLP) to analyse real-world applications of adverse drug reaction. *Exploratory Research in Clinical and Social Pharmacy, 18*, 100592. DOI: 10.1016/J.RCSOP.2025.100592 PMID: 40207140

Du, K., Zhao, Y., Mao, R., Xing, F., & Cambria, E. (2025). Natural language processing in finance: A survey. *Information Fusion, 115*, 102755. DOI: 10.1016/J.INFFUS.2024.102755

Durai, S., Krishnaveni, R., Manoharan, G., & Ashtikar, S. P. (2024). Leveraging HR metrics and workforce analytics: The road to organizational efficacy. In *Practical Approaches to Agile Project Management.* IGI Global., DOI: 10.4018/979-8-3693-3318-1.ch019

Dwivedi, R. (2023). Understanding Employee Perspectives During an Acquisition – Case of Twitter. *29th Annual Americas Conference on Information Systems, AMCIS 2023.* https://www.scopus.com/inward/record.uri?eid=2-s2.0-85192924432&partnerID=40&md5=5dfab0f65f85a82575feb4ee34c7d5d0

Dwivedi, Y. K., Kshetri, N., Hughes, L., Slade, E. L., Jeyaraj, A., Kar, A. K., Baabdullah, A. M., Koohang, A., Raghavan, V., Ahuja, M., Albanna, H., Albashrawi, M. A., Al-Busaidi, A. S., Balakrishnan, J., Barlette, Y., Basu, S., Bose, I., Brooks, L., Buhalis, D., & Wright, R. (2023). Opinion Paper: "So what if ChatGPT wrote it?" Multidisciplinary perspectives on opportunities, challenges and implications of generative conversational AI for research, practice and policy. *International Journal of Information Management*, *71*, 102642. DOI: 10.1016/j.ijinfomgt.2023.102642

E. J., C., & K. E., D. (2024). Strategic Role of Artificial Intelligence (AI) on Human Resource Management (HR) Employee Performance Evaluation Function. *International Journal of Entrepreneurship and Business Innovation*, *7*(2), 269–282. DOI: 10.52589/IJEBI-HET5STYK

Eigner, E., & Händler, T. (2024). *Determinants of LLM-assisted Decision-Making* (Version 1). arXiv. DOI: 10.48550/ARXIV.2402.17385

Ekman, P., & Friesen, W. V. (1969). The repertoire of nonverbal behavior: Categories, origins, usage, and coding. *semiotica, 1*(1), 49-98.

Ekman, P. (1972). Universals and Cultural Differences in Facial Expressions of Emotions. In Cole, J. (Ed.), *Nebraska Symposium on Motivation* (pp. 207-282).

Elufioye, O. A., Ndubuisi, N. L., Daraojimba, R. E., Awonuga, K. F., Ayanponle, L. O., & Asuzu, O. F. (2024). Reviewing employee well-being and mental health initiatives in contemporary HR Practices. *International Journal of Science and Research Archive*, *11*(1), 828–840. DOI: 10.30574/ijsra.2024.11.1.0153

Esmaail, N., Omar, N., Mohd, M., Fauzi, F., & Mansur, Z. (2024). *Named Entity Recognition in User-generated Text (English Twitter): A Systematic Literature Review*. IEEE., DOI: 10.1109/ACCESS.2024.3427714

Eubanks, B. (2018). *Artificial intelligence for HR: Use AI to support and develop a successful workforce* (1st ed.). Kogan Page.

European Parliament. (2020). The impact of the General Data Protection Regulation (GDPR) on artificial intelligence. Accessed on 26/04/25 Retrieved from https://www.europarl.europa.eu/RegData/etudes/STUD/2020/641530/EPRS_STU(2020)641530_EN.pdf

Fahimnia, B., Sarkis, J., & Davarzani, H. (2015, April 1). Green supply chain management: A review and bibliometric analysis. *International Journal of Production Economics*, *162*, 101–114. DOI: 10.1016/j.ijpe.2015.01.003

Fang, C., Qin, C., Zhang, Q., Yao, K., Zhang, J., Zhu, H., Zhuang, F., & Xiong, H. (2023). RecruitPro: A Pretrained Language Model with Skill-Aware Prompt Learning for Intelligent Recruitment. *Proceedings of the 29th ACM SIGKDD Conference on Knowledge Discovery and Data Mining*, 3991–4002. DOI: 10.1145/3580305.3599894

Fatema, S., & Khan, M. M. A. (2024). Artificial intelligence in talent acquisition: Assessing the impact on recruitment processes. [JRITM]. *Journal of Research and Innovation in Technology and Management, 1*(3), 1–5.

Fenwick, A., Molnar, G., & Frangos, P. (2024). The critical role of HRM in AI-driven digital transformation: A paradigm shift to enable firms to move from AI implementation to human-centric adoption. *Discover Artificial Intelligence, 4*(1), 34. DOI: 10.1007/s44163-024-00125-4

Filipsson, F. (2025, March 1). AI Case Study: AI-Powered Employee Engagement and Sentiment Analysis at Culture Amp. Redress Compliance. https://redresscompliance.com/ai-case-study-ai-powered-employee-engagement-and-sentiment-analysis-at-culture-amp/accessed on 26/04/25

Fitha, T. F., Parveen, K. J., Noorfathima, P. P., & Bajeel, P. N. (2024). Optimizing Employee Recruitment: a Prescriptive Analytics Review. In S. A.K., S. M., & P. C.M.A. (Eds.), *AIP Conference Proceedings* (Vol. 3242, Issue 1). American Institute of Physics. DOI: 10.1063/5.0234830

Floridi, L., & Cowls, J. (2019). A unified framework of five principles for AI in society. *Harvard Data Science Review, 1*(1). Advance online publication. DOI: 10.1162/99608f92.8cd550d1

Floridi, L., & Taddeo, M. (2016). What is data ethics? *Philosophical Transactions. Series A, Mathematical, Physical, and Engineering Sciences, 374*(2083), 20160360. DOI: 10.1098/rsta.2016.0360 PMID: 28336805

Freeda, M. S. M., Khan, S., Ramalingam, P., & Amarnatha, R. P. (2024). Role of hr analytics in people management: Challenges and opportunities in the indian IT/ITeS space. In Analytics, H. R. (Ed.), *Fundamentals and Applications*. Bentham Science Publishers., DOI: 10.2174/9789815274196124010004

Friha, O., Amine Ferrag, M., Kantarci, B., Cakmak, B., Ozgun, A., & Ghoualmi-Zine, N. (2024). LLM-Based Edge Intelligence: A Comprehensive Survey on Architectures, Applications, Security and Trustworthiness. *IEEE Open Journal of the Communications Society, 5*, 5799–5856. DOI: 10.1109/OJCOMS.2024.3456549

Gadhiya, Y. (2024). AI-Based Automation for Employee Screening and Drug Testing. International IT Journal of Research, ISSN: 3007-6706, 2(4), 185-199.

Galli, C., Gavrilova, A. V., & Calciolari, E. (2025). Large Language Models in Systematic Review Screening: Opportunities, Challenges, and Methodological Considerations. *Information (Basel), 16*(5), 378. DOI: 10.3390/info16050378

Gan, C., & Mori, T. (2023). A Few-Shot Approach to Resume Information Extraction via Prompts. In E. Métais, F. Meziane, V. Sugumaran, W. Manning, & S. Reiff-Marganiec (Eds.), *Natural Language Processing and Information Systems* (Vol. 13913, pp. 445–455). Springer Nature Switzerland. DOI: 10.1007/978-3-031-35320-8_32

Gan, C., Zhang, Q., & Mori, T. (2024). Application of LLM Agents in Recruitment: A Novel Framework for Automated Resume Screening. *Journal of Information Processing, 32*(0), 881–893. DOI: 10.2197/ipsjjip.32.881

Garcia, A. G. (2025). The impact of sustainable practices on employee well-being and organizational success. *Brazilian Journal of Development, 11*(3), e78599–e78599. DOI: 10.34117/bjdv11n3-054

Garcia-Gasulla, D., Bayarri-Planas, J., Gururajan, A. K., Lopez-Cuena, E., Tormos, A., Hinjos, D., Bernabeu-Perez, P., Arias-Duart, A., Martin-Torres, P. A., Gonzalez-Mallo, M., Alvarez-Napagao, S., Ayguadé-Parra, E., & Cortés, U. (2025). *The Aloe Family Recipe for Open and Specialized Healthcare LLMs* (Version 2). arXiv. DOI: 10.48550/ARXIV.2505.04388

Gaur, B. (2020). HR4.0: An Analytics Framework to redefine Employee Engagement in the Fourth Industrial Revolution. *2020 11th International Conference on Computing, Communication and Networking Technologies, ICCCNT 2020*. DOI: 10.1109/ICCCNT49239.2020.9225456

Gelbard, R., Ramon-Gonen, R., Carmeli, A., Bittmann, R. M., & Talyansky, R. (2018). Sentiment analysis in organizational work: Towards an ontology of people analytics. *Expert Systems: International Journal of Knowledge Engineering and Neural Networks, 35*(5), e12289. DOI: 10.1111/exsy.12289

George, B. (2003). *Authentic leadership: Rediscovering the secrets to creating lasting value* (Vol. 18). John Wiley & Sons.

Glazko, K., Mohammed, Y., Kosa, B., Potluri, V., & Mankoff, J. (2024). Identifying and Improving Disability Bias in GPT-Based Resume Screening. *The 2024 ACM Conference on Fairness, Accountability, and Transparency*, 687–700. DOI: 10.1145/3630106.3658933

Goh, J., Pfeffer, J., & Zenios, S. A. (2015). Workplace stressors & health outcomes: Health policy for the workplace. *Behavioral Science & Policy, 1*(1), 43–52. DOI: 10.1177/237946151500100107

Goleman, D. (1995). *Emotional intelligence*. Bantam Books, Inc.

Goleman, D. (1998). The emotionally competent leader. *The Healthcare Forum Journal, 41*(2), 36–38. PMID: 10177113

Goleman, D. (2019). *The emotionally intelligent leader*. Harvard Business Review Press.

Goleman, D., Boyatzis, R., & McKee, A. (2002). The emotional reality of teams. *Journal of Organizational Excellence, 21*(2), 55–65. DOI: 10.1002/npr.10020

Gomathi, S., Rajeswari, A., & Kadry, S. (2023). Emerging HR practices-digital upskilling: A strategic way of talent management and engagement. In *Disruptive Artificial Intelligence and Sustainable Human Resource Management: Impacts and Innovations - The Future of HR*. River Publishers. https://www.scopus.com/inward/record.uri?eid=2-s2.0-85168648645&partnerID=40&md5=4103cd7fc695335dda81f9949392d29e

Goodhue, D. L., & Thompson, R. L. (1995). Task–technology fit and individual performance. *Management Information Systems Quarterly, 19*(2), 213–236. DOI: 10.2307/249689

Gope, S., Elia, G., & Passiante, G. (2018). The effect of HRM practices on knowledge management capacity: A comparative study in Indian IT industry. *Journal of Knowledge Management, 22*(3), 649–677. DOI: 10.1108/JKM-10-2017-0453

Gori, M., Schiatti, L., & Amadeo, M. B. (2021). Masking emotions: Face masks impair how we read emotions. *Frontiers in Psychology, 12*, 1541. DOI: 10.3389/fpsyg.2021.669432 PMID: 34113297

Goyal, P., Kataria, R., Prakash, A., & Arora, M. (2023). Impact of Technology in Human Resource: A Systematic

Goyal, A., & Khatri, B. (2022). Systematic Review Paper on Influence of Ingenious Human Resource Practices on Employee Engagement during Pandemic In Banking Sector. *ECS Transactions, 107*(1), 3833–3844. DOI: 10.1149/10701.3833ecst

Grawitch, M. J., & Ballard, D. W. (2016). *The psychologically healthy workplace: Building a win-win environment for organizations and employees*. American Psychological Association. DOI: 10.1037/14731-000

Greenleaf, R. K. (1970). *The servant as Leader*. Center for Applied Studies.

Guesalaga, R., Gable, M., & Dawson, J. (2020). Artificial intelligence in recruitment: The impact on candidate experience and organizational trust. *Journal of Business Research, 116*, 32–44. DOI: 10.1016/j.jbusres.2020.05.002

Guidotti, R., Monreale, A., Ruggieri, S., Turini, F., Giannotti, F., & Pedreschi, D. (2018). A survey of methods for explaining black box models. *ACM Computing Surveys*, *51*(5), 93. DOI: 10.1145/3236009

Guimarães, N., Campos, R., & Jorge, A. (2024). Pre-trained language models: What do they know? *Wiley Interdisciplinary Reviews. Data Mining and Knowledge Discovery*, *14*(1), e1518. DOI: 10.1002/WIDM.1518;WEBSITE:WEBSITE:WIRES;WGROUP:STRING:PUBLICATION

Gu, J., & Levin, J. S. (2021). Tournament in academia: A comparative analysis of faculty evaluation systems in research universities in China and the USA. *Higher Education*, *81*(5), 897–915. DOI: 10.1007/s10734-020-00585-4

Gujanal, P. U., & Hiremath, G. (2023). Performance management and artificial intelligence: A conceptual framework on future role. In R. K.V.S. & R. P.R.K. (Eds.), *AIP Conference Proceedings* (Vol. 2796, Issue 1). American Institute of Physics Inc. DOI: 10.1063/5.0149028

Gulati, M. (2023). *Analysis of Various Aspects of Moonlighting*. Journal of Business Theory and Practice. DOI: 10.22158/jbtp.v11n1p32

Gupta, P., Fernandes, S.F. and Jain, M. (2018), "Automation in recruitment: a new frontier", Journal of Information Technology Teaching Cases, Vol. 8 No. 2.

Gupta, R., Gupta, A. K., Jain, A., Pandey, A. C., & Gupta, A. (2025). *LLM assisted web application functional requirements generation: A case study of four popular LLMs over a Mess Management System* (Version 1). arXiv. DOI: 10.48550/ARXIV.2505.18019

Gupta, S. K., Kapoor, S., Yucel, S., Rana, R., Yusel, R., & Prasad, L. (2023). Technology-based human resource practices within indian IT industry. In *Disruptive Artificial Intelligence and Sustainable Human Resource Management: Impacts and Innovations - The Future of HR*. River Publishers. https://www.scopus.com/inward/record.uri?eid=2-s2.0-85168646123&partnerID=40&md5=e1f8b96da69ea08dcb0a69fe7e435a0e

Gupta, S., & Pathak, G. S. (2016). HR practices for women employees: A study of information technology (IT) sector in India. *2016 3rd International Conference on Recent Advances in Information Technology, RAIT 2016*, 672 – 676. DOI: 10.1109/RAIT.2016.7507980

Gu, W., & Levin, A. (2021). Algorithmic perils in sentiment systems: Cultural sensitivity, bias, and privacy. *Behaviour & Information Technology*.

Gyensare, M. A., Adomako, S., & Amankwah-Amoah, J. (2024). Green HRM practices, employee well-being, and sustainable work behavior: Examining the moderating role of resource commitment. *Business Strategy and the Environment, 33*(4), 3129–3141. DOI: 10.1002/bse.3642

Haleem, A., Khan, M. I., Khan, S., & Jami, A. R. (2020). Research status in Halal: A review and bibliometric analysis. *Modern Supply Chain Research and Applications, 2*(1), 23–41. DOI: 10.1108/MSCRA-06-2019-0014

Hassan, B. F. Y. (2025). Adoption of AI in Talent Acquisition: A Quantitative Study on HRM Practitioners Using the Technology Acceptance Model (TAM). *The Scientific Journal of Financial and Commercial Studies and Research, 6*(1), 1289–1316.

Hattie, J., & Timperley, H. (2007). The power of feedback. *Review of Educational Research, 77*(1), 81–112. DOI: 10.3102/003465430298487

Hausken, K., & Ncube, M. (2018). Service delivery versus moonlighting: Using data from Kenya, Uganda, Tanzania and Senegal. *African Development Review, 30*(2), 219–232. DOI: 10.1111/1467-8268.12327

Hayes, O., & Kelliher, F. (2024). The role of social media data in enhancing B2B omni-channel marketing efforts in small businesses. *Journal of Small Business and Enterprise Development, 32*(1), 151–172. DOI: 10.1108/JSBED-02-2023-0051/FULL/XML

Hennekam, S., Ladge, J., & Shymko, Y. (2020). From zero to hero: An exploratory study examining sudden hero status among nonphysician health care workers during the COVID-19 pandemic. *The Journal of Applied Psychology, 105*(10), 1088–1100. DOI: 10.1037/apl0000832 PMID: 32897086

Hicks, C. (2018). Predicting knowledge workers' participation in voluntary learning with employee characteristics and online learning tools. *Journal of Workplace Learning, 30*(2), 78–88. DOI: 10.1108/JWL-04-2017-0030

Hill, N. S., Axtell, C., Raghuram, S., & Nurmi, N. (2024). Unpacking virtual work's dual effects on employee well-being: An integrative review and future research agenda. *Journal of Management, 50*(2), 752–792. DOI: 10.1177/01492063221131535

Hmoud, B., & Laszlo, V. (2019). Will artificial intelligence take over human resources recruitment and selection? *Network Intelligence Studies, 7*(13), 21–30.

Holm, A. B. (2010), "The effect of E-recruitment on the recruitment process: evidence from case studies of three Danish MNCs", *CEUR Workshop Proceedings*, Vol. 570.

Holtzapple, E. (2003). Criterion-related validity evidence for a standards-based teacher evaluation system. *Journal of Personnel Evaluation in Education*, *17*(3), 207–219. DOI: 10.1007/s11092-005-2980-z

Horodyski, P. (2023). Applicants' perception of artificial intelligence in the recruitment process. *Computers in Human Behavior Reports*, *11*, 100303. DOI: 10.1016/j.chbr.2023.100303

Hurka, S., Daniel, W. T., & Obholzer, L. (2018). Determinants of moonlighting in the European Parliament. *Journal of Legislative Studies*, *24*(1), 127–147. DOI: 10.1080/13572334.2018.1444630

Iftikhar, A., Mohammad, S. I., Alqudah, M. N., Al-Adwan, A. S., Vasudevan, A., Ali, I., & Farhan, M. (2025). Evaluating Inclusivity and Fairness of AI Recruitment Tools for Hiring People with Disabilities in the United Arab Emirates(UAE); [Evaluación de la Inclusividad y la Equidad de las Herramientas de Reclutamiento de IA para la Contratación de Personas con D. *Data and Metadata*, *4*. Advance online publication. DOI: 10.56294/dm2025487

iMerit. (2024, March 15). Case study: Sentiment analysis and behavior detection for a leading analytics platform. iMerit. https://imerit.net/blog/case-study-sentiment-analysis-and-behavior-detection-for-a-leading-analytics-platform/accessed on 26/04/25

Indarapu, S. R. K., Vodithala, S., Kumar, N., Kiran, S., Reddy, S. N., & Dorthi, K. (2023). Exploring human resource management intelligence practices using machine learning models. *The Journal of High Technology Management Research*, *34*(2), 100466. DOI: 10.1016/j.hitech.2023.100466

Intel Corporation. (2024, April 2). *Opinion: How Intel is refining its approach to responsible AI. Intel Newsroom.* https://www.intc.com/news-events/press-releases/detail/1686/opinion-how-intel-is-refining-its-approach-to-responsible accessed on 28/04/25

Iqbal, M., Naqvi, S., & Rehman, K. (2019). Structural equation modelling for evaluating faculty performance appraisal in HEIs. *Higher Education Studies*, *9*(3), 32–47.

Islam, M., Rahman, M. M., Taher, M. A., Quaosar, G. A. A., & Uddin, M. A. (2024). Using artificial intelligence for hiring talents in a moderated mechanism. *Future Business Journal*, *10*(1), 13. Advance online publication. DOI: 10.1186/s43093-024-00303-x

Islam, R., Shahadat Hosen, M., Naeem, Z., Folorunso, E. O., Chu, T. S., Al Mamun, A., & Orunbon, N. O. (2024). Data-Driven Decision Making: Advanced Database Systems for Business Intelligence. *Nanotechnology Perceptions*, *20*(S3), 687–704. DOI: 10.62441/nano-ntp.v20iS3.51

Jain, A., Mishra, S., & Goyal, R. (2021). Analysis of Career Development Opportunities in IT Sectors in Jaipur. *Lecture Notes in Networks and Systems*, *166*, 733–741. DOI: 10.1007/978-981-15-9689-6_80

Jain, S., & Khurana, N. (2017). Enhancing employee engagement through training and development. *Asian Journal of Management*, *8*(1), 1. DOI: 10.5958/2321-5763.2017.00001.4

Jaiwant, S. V., & Vazirani, K. (2023). HR analytics in employee engagement and turnover. In *HR Analytics in an Era of Rapid Automation*. IGI Global., DOI: 10.4018/978-1-6684-8942-0.ch007

Jamuna, K. M. (2024). Leveraging Natural Language Processing to Analyze Employee Feedback for Enhanced HR Insights. *INTERANTIONAL JOURNAL OF SCIENTIFIC RESEARCH IN ENGINEERING AND MANAGEMENT*, *08*(11), 1–7. DOI: 10.55041/IJSREM39115

Jarrahi, M. H., Newlands, G., Lee, M. K., Wolf, C. T., Kinder, E., & Sutherland, W. (2021). Algorithmic management in a work context. *Big Data & Society*, *8*(2), 205395172110203. DOI: 10.1177/20539517211020332

Jayadev, S., & Sumitha, R. (2024). Performance appraisal and organizational outcome via the mediating effect of relationship with peer group and subordinates-a tool for HR analytic. In *Business Analytics for Effective Decision Making*. Bentham Science Publishers., DOI: 10.2174/9789815238365124010008

Jayaram, R., & Singh, S. (2020). A bibliometric analysis and visualization of research trends in COVID-19 and suicide. *Annals of Tropical Medicine and Public Health*.

Jeong, J., Kim, B. J., & Lee, J. (2024). Navigating AI transitions: How coaching leadership buffers against job stress and protects employee physical health. *Frontiers in Public Health*, *12*, 1343932. DOI: 10.3389/fpubh.2024.1343932 PMID: 38601504

Jeske, D., & Santuzzi, A. M. (2015). Monitoring what and how: Psychological implications of electronic performance monitoring. *New Technology, Work and Employment*, *30*(1), 62–78. DOI: 10.1111/ntwe.12039

Jha, N., Krishnan, R., & Sachin, S. C. (2019). Team building and organizational innovation: A study in IT sector in India. *Journal of Advanced Research in Dynamical and Control Systems, 11*(10 Special Issue), 59 – 69. DOI: 10.5373/JARDCS/V11SP10/20192776

Jha, S. (2022). Data Privacy and Security Issues in HR Analytics: Challenges and the Road Ahead. *Lecture Notes in Networks and Systems*, *209*, 199–206. DOI: 10.1007/978-981-16-2126-0_17

Jiang, P., & Cai, X. (2024). A Survey of Semantic Parsing Techniques. *Symmetry 2024, Vol. 16, Page 1201, 16*(9), 1201. https://doi.org/DOI: 10.3390/SYM16091201

Jiang, L., & Goetz, S. M. (2025). Natural language processing in the patent domain: A survey. *Artificial Intelligence Review*, *58*(7), 1–62. DOI: 10.1007/S10462-025-11168-Z/TABLES/6

Jiang, T., Guo, Q., Wei, Y., Cheng, Q., & Lu, W. (2024). Investigating the relationships between dialog patterns and user satisfaction in customer service chat systems based on chat log analysis. *Journal of Information Science*. Advance online publication. DOI: 10.1177/01655515221124066

Jobin, A., Ienca, M., & Vayena, E. (2019). The global landscape of AI ethics guidelines. *Nature Machine Intelligence*, *1*(9), 389–399. DOI: 10.1038/s42256-019-0088-2

Johnson, A., Dey, S., Nguyen, H., Groth, M., Joyce, S., Tan, L., Glozier, N., & Harvey, S. B. (2020). A review and agenda for examining how technology-driven changes at work will impact workplace mental health and employee well-being. *Australian Journal of Management*, *45*(3), 402–424. DOI: 10.1177/0312896220922292

Johnson, R. D., Stone, D. L., & Lukaszewski, K. M. (2020). The benefits of eHRM and AI for talent acquisition. *Journal of Tourism Futures*, *6*(2), 89–93. DOI: 10.1108/JTF-04-2020-0052

Jonathan, H., Magd, H., & Khan, S. A. (2024). Artificial intelligence and augmented reality: A business fortune to sustainability in the digital age. In *Navigating the Digital Landscape: Understanding Customer Behaviour in the Online World*. Emerald Group Publishing Ltd., DOI: 10.1108/978-1-83549-272-720241005

José-García, A., Sneyd, A., Melro, A., Ollagnier, A., Tarling, G., Zhang, H., Stevenson, M., Everson, R., & Arthur, R. (2023). C3-IoC: A Career Guidance System for Assessing Student Skills using Machine Learning and Network Visualisation. *International Journal of Artificial Intelligence in Education*, *33*(4), 1092–1119. DOI: 10.1007/s40593-022-00317-y

Joseph, T. (2024). Natural Language Processing (NLP) for Sentiment Analysis in Social Media. *International Journal of Computing and Engineering*, *6*(2), 35–48. https://ideas.repec.org/a/bhx/ojijce/v6y2024i2p35-48id2135.html

Joseph, T., Christopher, M., Marvin, G., Mukwaba, D., Claire, A., & Murindanyi, S. (2024). Explainable Machine Learning and Graph Neural Network Approaches for Predicting Employee Attrition. In D. S. & S. V. (Eds.), *ACM International Conference Proceeding Series* (pp. 243 – 255). Association for Computing Machinery. DOI: 10.1145/3675888.3676058

Kadam, R., Suhas, G., Mukri, U., & Khandare, S. (2022). NLP-Based Resume Screening and Job Recruitment Portal. In Jacob, I. J., Kolandapalayam Shanmugam, S., & Bestak, R. (Eds.), *Data Intelligence and Cognitive Informatics* (pp. 1–21). Springer Nature Singapore., DOI: 10.1007/978-981-16-6460-1_1

Kakkar, H., & Kaushik, S. (2019). Technology driven human resource measurement–A strategic perspective. *International Journal on Emerging Technologies*, *10*(1), 179–184. https://www.scopus.com/inward/record.uri?eid=2-s2.0-85074656787&partnerID=40&md5=9dd377f1f5367c7e3c6a6f35cbb67cad

Kaltiainen, J., & Hakanen, J. (2022). Fostering task and adaptive performance through employee well-being: The role of servant leadership. *Business Research Quarterly*, *25*(1), 28–43. DOI: 10.1177/2340944420981599

Kamal, S., Naim, A., Magd, H., Khan, S. A., & Khan, F. M. (2022). The relationship between E-Service quality, ease of use, and E-CRM performance referred by brand image. In *Building a Brand Image Through Electronic Customer Relationship Management*. IGI Global., DOI: 10.4018/978-1-6684-5386-5.ch005

Kanade, T. M., Batule, R. B., & Joseph, J. (2025). The Evolution of HR: From Traditional to AI-Enhanced. In Harriott, S. A. (Ed.), *Innovative Approaches to Managing Conflict and Change in Diverse Work Environments* (pp. 49–78). IGI Global., DOI: 10.4018/979-8-3693-9556-1.ch003

Kang, Y., Cai, Z., Tan, C.-W., Huang, Q., & Liu, H. (2020). Natural language processing (NLP) in management research: A literature review. *Journal of Management Analytics*, *7*(2), 139–172. DOI: 10.1080/23270012.2020.1756939

Kantardzic, M. (2011). *Data mining: Concepts, models, methods, and algorithms* (2nd ed.). IEEE Press and John Wiley & Sons. DOI: 10.1002/9781118029145

Kantor, K., & Morzy, M. (2024). Machine learning and natural language processing in clinical trial eligibility criteria parsing: A scoping review. *Drug Discovery Today*, *29*(10), 104139. DOI: 10.1016/J.DRUDIS.2024.104139 PMID: 39154773

Karyamsetty, H. J., Khan, S. A., & Nayyar, A. (2023). Envisioning toward modernization of society 5.0—A prospective glimpse on status, opportunities, and challenges with XAI. In *XAI Based Intelligent Systems for Society 5.0*. Elsevier., DOI: 10.1016/B978-0-323-95315-3.00005-X

Kashive, N., Khanna, V. T., & Bharthi, M. N. (2020). Employer branding through crowdsourcing: Understanding the sentiments of employees. *Journal of Indian Business Research*, *12*(1), 93–111. DOI: 10.1108/JIBR-09-2019-0276

Katyal, S., Lal, R., & Rena, R. (2024). Effects of Gamification on Brand Engagement of Toy Brands: First Cry and Hamleys. In *Marketing and Gamification* (pp. 57–80). Routledge. DOI: 10.4324/9781032694238-6

Kern, M., Heissler, C., & Zapf, D. (2021). Social job stressors can foster employee well-being: Introducing the concept of social challenge stressors. *Journal of Business and Psychology*, *36*(5), 771–792. DOI: 10.1007/s10869-020-09702-7

Khair, M., Khair, M., Shaheen, N., & Bindewari, D. (2025). From Automation to Autonomy: Leveraging Oracle HCM Cloud's AI Capabilities to Create Autonomous HR Processes and Decision-Making. *International Journal of Research in Humanities and Social Sciences*, *13*(3), 271–288. DOI: 10.63345/ijrhs.net.v13.i3.15

Khan, S. A., Magd, H., Bhuyan, U., Jonathan, H., & Naim, A. (2024). Digital Marketing (DM): How are small business enterprises (SBEs) of Bhutan and Sikkim (India) Responding to It? In *Digital Influence on Consumer Habits: Marketing Challenges and Opportunities*. Emerald Publishing. DOI: 10.1108/978-1-80455-342-820241008

Khanam, , A. & Mazhar, S. (2015). Efficacy of faculty performance appraisal system in higher educational organization. [IJMSS]. *International Journal of Management and Social Sciences*, *3*, 1–11.

Khan, S. A., & Magd, H. (2021). EMPIRICAL EXAMINATION OF MS TEAMS IN CONDUCTING WEBINAR: EVIDENCE FROM INTERNATIONAL ONLINE PROGRAM CONDUCTED IN OMAN. *Journal of Content. Community and Communication*, *14*(7), 159–175. DOI: 10.31620/JCCC.12.21/13

Khan, S. A., & Magd, H. (2023). New Technology Anxiety and Acceptance of Technology: An Appraisal of MS Teams. In *Advances in Distance Learning in Times of Pandemic*. CRC Press., DOI: 10.1201/9781003322252-5

Khan, S. A., Magd, H., & Batra, M. (2023). Students' perspectives on faculty performance and course effectiveness: A machine learning approach. *The Journal of Educational Research*, *25*(3), 78–92.

Khan, S. A., Magd, H., Khatri, B., Arora, S., & Sharma, N. (2023). Critical success factors of internet of things and digital marketing. In *Global Applications of the Internet of Things in Digital Marketing*. IGI Global., DOI: 10.4018/978-1-6684-8166-0.ch012

Khan, S., & Ahmad, N. (2021). Impact of AI-driven chatbots in open and distance learning student support: A case study. *International Review of Research in Open and Distance Learning*, *22*(3), 1–18. DOI: 10.19173/irrodl.v22i3.12345

Khan, S., Faisal, S., & Thomas, G. (2024). Exploring the nexus of artificial intelligence in talent acquisition: Unravelling cost-benefit dynamics, seizing opportunities, and mitigating risks. *Problems and Perspectives in Management*, *22*(1), 462–476. DOI: 10.21511/ppm.22(1).2024.37

Khatri, B., Arora, S., & Goyal, A. (2022). Association between Outcomes of Physical activities and Sports on Work-Life Balance of Employees. *International Journal of Human Movement and Sports Sciences*, *10*(2), 316–323. DOI: 10.13189/saj.2022.100223

Khatri, B., Arora, S., & Khan, S. A. (2024). Analysis of servant leadership and organizational citizenship behaviour among social service sector employees. In *Organizational Behavior and Human Resource Management for Complex Work Environments*. IGI Global., DOI: 10.4018/979-8-3693-3466-9.ch021

Khatri, B., Arora, S., Magd, H., & Khan, S. A. K. (2022). Bibliometric analysis of social entrepreneurship. In *International Perspectives on Value Creation and Sustainability Through Social Entrepreneurship*. IGI Global., DOI: 10.4018/978-1-6684-4666-9.ch003

Khatri, B., Nandini, G., & Khan, S. A. (2024). Transition from outcome-based learning to global accreditation of top universities of India: Elevating the bar of educational excellence. In *Evaluating Global Accreditation Standards for Higher Education*. IGI Global., DOI: 10.4018/979-8-3693-1698-6.ch019

Khatri, B., Sharma, N., Khan, S. A., & Nandini, G. (2024). Navigating employer branding in the digital age: Exploring the impact of social media networking during the COVID-19 Pandemic. In *Global Practices on Effective Talent Acquisition and Retention*. IGI Global., DOI: 10.4018/979-8-3693-1938-3.ch017

Khatri, B., Singh, R. K., Arora, S., Khan, S. A., & Naim, A. (2024). Optimizing supply chain management indicators for sustainable supply chain integration and customer loyalty: Potential role of environmentally responsible practices. In *Strategies for Environmentally Responsible Supply Chain and Production Management*. IGI Global., DOI: 10.4018/979-8-3693-0669-7.ch008

Khtere, A. (2020). Faculty performance appraisal based on AI-driven sentiment analysis: A case study of higher education institutions. *Journal of Higher Education Studies, 10*(2), 66–81.

Khurana, D., Koli, A., Khatter, K., & Singh, S. (2023). Natural language processing: State of the art, current trends and challenges. *Multimedia Tools and Applications, 82*(3), 3713–3744. DOI: 10.1007/s11042-022-13428-4

Khurram, M., & Ata, M. (2024). Privacy and ethical considerations in AI-based faculty evaluations. *Journal of Educational Ethics, 19*(1), 12–29.

Kim, J., & Angnakoon, P. (2016). Research using job advertisements: A methodological assessment. *Library & Information Science Research, 38*(4), 327–335. DOI: 10.1016/j.lisr.2016.11.006

Kniffin, K. M., Narayanan, J., Anseel, F., Antonakis, J., Ashford, S. P., Bakker, A. B., Bamberger, P., Bapuji, H., Bhave, D. P., Choi, V. K., Creary, S. J., Demerouti, E., Flynn, F. J., Gelfand, M. J., Greer, L. L., Johns, G., Kesebir, S., Klein, P. G., Lee, S. Y., & Vugt, M. V. (2021). COVID-19 and the workplace: Implications, issues, and insights for future research and action. *The American Psychologist, 76*(1), 63–77. DOI: 10.1037/amp0000716 PMID: 32772537

Koç, C., Özyurt, F., & Iantovics, L. B. (2025). Survey on latest advances in natural language processing applications of generative adversarial networks. *Wiley Interdisciplinary Reviews. Data Mining and Knowledge Discovery, 15*(1), e70004.

Konovalova, V. G., Aghgashyan, R. V., & Galazova, S. S. (2021). Perspectives and Restraining Factors of HR Analytics in the Conditions of Digitization of Human Resources Management. *Studies in Systems. Decision and Control, 314*, 1015–1024. DOI: 10.1007/978-3-030-56433-9_106

Kramer, A. D., Guillory, J. E., & Hancock, J. T. (2014). Experimental evidence of massive-scale emotional contagion through social networks. *Proceedings of the National Academy of Sciences of the United States of America, 111*(24), 8788–8790. DOI: 10.1073/pnas.1320040111 PMID: 24889601

Krekel, C., Ward, G., & Neve, J.-E. (2019). Employee wellbeing, productivity, and firm performance. SSRN *Electron.* J. Available online at: https://voxeu.org/article/employee-wellbeing-productivity-and-firm-performance (accessed April 25, 2025). DOI: 10.2139/ssrn.3356581

Krishna, S., & Sidharth, S. (2022). Analyzing Employee Attrition Using Machine Learning: the New AI Approach. *2022 IEEE 7th International Conference for Convergence in Technology, I2CT 2022*. DOI: 10.1109/I2CT54291.2022.9825342

Krishna, S., Dwivedi, R., & Murti, A. (2023). Predictive Analytics for Employee Attrition: A Comparative Study of Machine Learning Algorithms. In A. E., A. E., & F. S. (Eds.), *Proceedings - 2023 3rd International Conference on Digital Data Processing, DDP 2023* (pp. 180 – 187). Institute of Electrical and Electronics Engineers Inc. DOI: 10.1109/DDP60485.2023.00043

Kumar, V., Iqbal, M. I., & Rathore, R. (2025). Natural Language Processing (NLP) in Disease Detection - A Discussion of How NLP Techniques Can Be Used to Analyze and Classify Medical Text Data for Disease Diagnosis. *AI in Disease Detection: Advancements and Applications*, 53–75. https://doi.org/DOI: 10.1002/9781394278695.CH3;PAGEGROUP:STRING:PUBLICATION

Kumar, D., Grosz, T., Rekabsaz, N., Greif, E., & Schedl, M. (2023). Fairness of recommender systems in the recruitment domain: An analysis from technical and legal perspectives. *Frontiers in Big Data*, *6*, 1245198. DOI: 10.3389/fdata.2023.1245198

Kumar, D., & Lal, R. (2023). Technological Advancements in the Media Industry and the Current Job Market in India. In Naim, A. (Ed.), *Accreditation Processes and Frameworks in Higher Education* (pp. 289–314). Nova Science Publishers.

Kumari, B. K., Sundari, V. M., Praseeda, C., Nagpal, P., John, E. P., & Awasthi, S. (2023). Analytics-Based Performance Influential Factors Prediction for Sustainable Growth of Organization, Employee Psychological Engagement, Work Satisfaction, Training and Development. *Journal for ReAttach Therapy and Developmental Diversities*, *6*(8), 76–82. https://www.scopus.com/inward/record.uri?eid=2-s2.0-85165974785&partnerID=40&md5=8c8cd00ff6add2681714206c6a265c5b

Kumar, R., & Jain, A. (2018). AI-based faculty evaluation system for higher education institutions. *International Journal of Artificial Intelligence in Education*, *17*(2), 102–119.

Kumar, S., Pandey, N., Lim, W. M., Chatterjee, A. N., & Pandey, N. (2021, September 1). What do we know about transfer pricing? Insights from bibliometric analysis. *Journal of Business Research*, *134*, 275–287. DOI: 10.1016/j.jbusres.2021.05.041

Kun, A., & Gadanecz, P. (2022). Workplace happiness, well-being and their relationship with psychological capital: A study of Hungarian Teachers. *Current Psychology (New Brunswick, N.J.)*, *41*(1), 185–199. DOI: 10.1007/s12144-019-00550-0

Kundi, Y. M., Aboramadan, M., Elhamalawi, E. M., & Shahid, S. (2021). Employee psychological well-being and job performance: Exploring mediating and moderating mechanisms. *The International Journal of Organizational Analysis*, *29*(3), 736–754. DOI: 10.1108/IJOA-05-2020-2204

Kyle, K., & Eguchi, M. (2024). Evaluating NLP models with written and spoken L2 samples. *Research Methods in Applied Linguistics, 3*(2), 100120. DOI: 10.1016/J.RMAL.2024.100120

Kyriakides, L. (2005). Evaluating teacher effectiveness using structural equation modelling. *The Journal of Educational Research, 98*(2), 67–80.

Lake, A. (2023). *Beyond Hybrid Working: A Smarter & Transformational Approach to Flexible Working*. Taylor & Francis. DOI: 10.4324/9781003288930

Lal, P. (2024). Quality Culture in Advertising Agencies and Creativity for Campaign Effectiveness: Analysis of Six Sigma Practices.

Lal, R., Deb, N., & Gogoi, D. M. (2025). Assessing the Role of Digital Data Visualization Tools in the Advertising Industry for Informed Business Decision-Making. In Data Visualization Tools for Business Applications (pp. 189-208). IGI Global.

Lal, R., & Sharma, G. (2021). Social media influencers for online purchase behaviour: Mediation by brand consciousness. *Journal of Content. Community & Communication, 13*(7), 83–94.

Lane, H., & Dyshel, M. (2025). *Natural language processing in action*. Simon and Schuster.

Lee, J., Kim, B., & Chung, J. (2021). Leaders need to be led: Complementary followership through interchangeable roles among leader-follower positions. SSRN *Electronic Journal*. DOI: 10.2139/ssrn.3995045

Lee, C., & Cha, K. (2023). FAT-CAT—Explainability and augmentation for an AI system: A case study on AI recruitment-system adoption. *International Journal of Human-Computer Studies, 171*, 102976. DOI: 10.1016/j.ijhcs.2022.102976

Lee, J. D., Cassano-Pinché, A., & Vicente, K. J. (2005, December). Bibliometric analysis of human factors (1970-2000): A quantitative description of scientific impact. *Human Factors, 47*(4), 753–766. DOI: 10.1518/001872005775570970 PMID: 16553064

Lee, R. (2025). Part-of-Speech (POS) Tagging. In *Natural Language Processing* (pp. 45–68). Springer., DOI: 10.1007/978-981-96-3208-4_3

Leicht-Deobald, U., Busch, T., Schank, C., Weibel, A., Schafheitle, S., Wildhaber, I., & Kasper, G. (2019). The Challenges of Algorithm-Based HR Decision-Making for Personal Integrity. *Journal of Business Ethics, 160*(2), 377–392. DOI: 10.1007/s10551-019-04204-w

Leidner, J. L., & Stevenson, M. (2024). *Challenges and Opportunities of NLP for HR Applications: A Discussion Paper* (Version 1). arXiv. DOI: 10.48550/ARXIV.2405.07766

Lekhi, S. B., Malhotra, M., Pushp, A., Gautam, R. S., Sharma, S., & Rastogi, S. (2024). The study provides a thorough examination of green human resource management practices within the Indian IT sector. *2nd IEEE International Conference on Advances in Information Technology, ICAIT 2024 - Proceedings*. DOI: 10.1109/ICAIT61638.2024.10690791

Lekmiti, A., Stolk, P. J., Taylor, A., Ramachandran, S., & Yap, N. K. (2024). Text mining in tourism and hospitality research: A bibliometric perspective. *Journal of Hospitality and Tourism Technology*, *16*(3), 588–610. DOI: 10.1108/JHTT-05-2024-0284/FULL/XML

Li, N., Zhou, H., & Xu, M. (2024). *From Text to Insight: Leveraging Large Language Models for Performance Evaluation in Management* (Version 1). arXiv. DOI: 10.2139/ssrn.4912642

Li, X., Shu, H., Zhai, Y., & Lin, Z. (2021). A Method for Resume Information Extraction Using BERT-BiLSTM-CRF. *2021 IEEE 21st International Conference on Communication Technology (ICCT)*, 1437–1442. DOI: 10.1109/ICCT52962.2021.9657937

Ligori, T. A. A., Suresh, N., Khan, S. A., Rabgay, T., & Yezer, K. (2022). The mediating effect of university image on the relationship between curriculum and student satisfaction: An empirical study of the Royal University of Bhutan. *International Journal of Pluralism and Economics Education*, *13*(2), 192–208. DOI: 10.1504/IJPEE.2022.127218

Li, L., Lassiter, T., Oh, J., & Lee, M. K. (2021). Algorithmic hiring in practice: Recruiter and HR professional's perspectives on AI use in hiring. In *Proceedings of the 2021 AAAI/ACM Conference on AI, Ethics, and Society* (pp. 166–176). DOI: 10.1145/3461702.3462531

LinkedIn. (2024). *2024 Global Talent Trends Report*. LinkedIn Corporation. https://www.linkedin.com/business/talent/blog/talent-acquisition/global-talent-trends-2024

Lin, W., Zhang, Y., & Zhou, X. (2024). Big data analytics in faculty evaluation: A comparative study across institutions. *Journal of Educational Technology*, *29*(1), 53–78.

Liu, L., Akkineni, S., Story, P., & Davis, C. (2020). Using HR analytics to support managerial decisions: A case study. *ACMSE 2020 - Proceedings of the 2020 ACM Southeast Conference*, 168 – 175. DOI: 10.1145/3374135.3385281

Liu, B., & Zhang, L. (2019). *Sentiment analysis: A machine learning approach to text evaluation*. Springer.

Lukose, L. (2025). Data protection in light of the Digital Personal Data Protection Act, 2023.

Lundqvist, D., Reineholm, C., Ståhl, C., & Wallo, A. (2022). The impact of leadership on employee well-being: On-site compared to working from home. *BMC Public Health, 22*(1), 2154. DOI: 10.1186/s12889-022-14612-9 PMID: 36424558

Lynn, T., Rosati, P., Conway, E., & Van Der Werff, L. (Eds.). (2023). *The Future of Work: Challenges and Prospects for Organisations, Jobs and Workers*. Springer International Publishing., DOI: 10.1007/978-3-031-31494-0

Madanchian, M. (2024). From Recruitment to Retention: AI Tools for Human Resource Decision-Making. *Applied Sciences (Basel, Switzerland), 14*(24), 11750. DOI: 10.3390/app142411750

Madancian, M., & Taherdoost, H. (2024). The Impact of Artificial Intelligence on Human Resource Management: Opportunities and Challenges. *Lecture Notes in Networks and Systems, 928 LNNS*, 406 – 424. DOI: 10.1007/978-3-031-54671-6_30

Madero-Gómez, S., Leal, Y., Olivas-Lujan, M., & Yusliza, M. (2023). Companies Could Benefit When They Focus on Employee Wellbeing and the Environment: A Systematic Review of Sustainable Human Resource Management. *Sustainability (Basel), 15*(6), 5435. Advance online publication. DOI: 10.3390/su15065435

Madhumita, G., Dolly Diana, P., Neena, P. C., Narendra Kiran, P. B., Aggarwal, S., & Nargunde, A. S. (2024). AI-powered Performance Management: Driving Employee Success and Organizational Growth. In M. G.C., S. S., & D. S. (Eds.), *5th International Conference on Recent Trends in Computer Science and Technology, ICRTCST 2024 - Proceedings* (pp. 204 – 209). Institute of Electrical and Electronics Engineers Inc. DOI: 10.1109/ICRTCST61793.2024.10578371

Magd, H., & Khan, S. A. (2022). Effectiveness of using Online Teaching Platforms as Communication Tools in Higher Education Institutions in Oman: Stakeholders' Perspectives. *Journal of Content. Community and Communication, 16*(8), 148–160. DOI: 10.31620/JCCC.12.22/13

Magd, H., & Khan, S. A. (2024). Enhancing faculty evaluation through AI-based feedback analysis. *Journal of Digital Education, 20*(2), 45–62.

Mahbub, S., Pardede, E., & Kayes, A. S. M. (2022). Online Recruitment Fraud Detection: A Study on Contextual Features in Australian Job Industries. *IEEE Access : Practical Innovations, Open Solutions*, *10*, 82776–82787. DOI: 10.1109/ACCESS.2022.3197225

Malik, A., Budhwar, P., & Mohan, H., & NR, S. (. (2023). Employee experience–the missing link for engaging employees: Insights from an MNE's AI-based HR ecosystem. *Human Resource Management*, *62*(1), 97–115. DOI: 10.1002/hrm.22133

Mangal, N. (2023). Using Analytics to Manage Employee Behavioural Traits and Predict Employee Performance. In *Analytics Enabled Decision Making*. Springer Nature., DOI: 10.1007/978-981-19-9658-0_9

Mansoor, M. A., & Ansari, K. H. (2024). Early Detection of Mental Health Crises through Artifical-Intelligence-Powered Social Media Analysis: A Prospective Observational Study. *Journal of Personalized Medicine*, *14*(9), 958. DOI: 10.3390/jpm14090958 PMID: 39338211

Manuti, A., & De Palma, P. D. (2018). The People-Based Approach in Human Resource Management. In A. Manuti & P. D. De Palma, *Digital HR* (pp. 1–20). Springer International Publishing. DOI: 10.1007/978-3-319-60210-3_1

Marin-Garcia, J. A., & Bonavia, T. (2021). Empowerment and employee well-being: A mediation analysis study. *International Journal of Environmental Research and Public Health*, *18*(11), 5822. DOI: 10.3390/ijerph18115822 PMID: 34071574

Matchar, E. (2015, August 6). IBM's Tone Analyzer Could Save You From Sending That Awkward Email. Smithsonian Magazine. https://www.smithsonianmag.com/innovation/ibms-tone-analyzer-will-save-you-sending-awkward-email-180956102/ (Accessed on 26/04/25).

Mathew, D., Shukla, V. K., Chaubey, A., & Dutta, S. (2021, September). Artificial intelligence: Hope for future or hype by intellectuals? In *2021 9th International Conference on Reliability, Infocom Technologies and Optimization (Trends and Future Directions) (ICRITO)* (pp. 1–6). IEEE. https://doi.org/DOI: 10.1109/ICRITO51393.2021.9596010

Mayer, J. D., Salovey, P., & Caruso, D. (2002). *Mayer-Salovey-Caruso Emotional Intelligence Test (MSCEIT) Item Booklet*. Multi-Health Systems.

McCartney, S., & Fu, N. (2021). Bridging the gap: Why, how and when HR analytics can impact organizational performance. *Management Decision*, *60*(13), 25–47. DOI: 10.1108/MD-12-2020-1581

McClelland, D. C. (1996). A Social Psychological View of Motivation. *Contemporary Psychology: A Journal of Reviews, 41*(5), 443–444. DOI: 10.1037/004426

McKinsey Health Institute. (2022). *Addressing employee mental health: The economic case.* McKinsey & Company. https://www.mckinsey.com/mhi/our-insights/the-mental-health-imperative-for-business (accessed April 25, 2025).

Meijerink, J., & Bondarouk, T. (2023). The duality of algorithmic management: Toward a research agenda on HRM algorithms, autonomy and value creation. *Human Resource Management Review, 33*(1), 100876. DOI: 10.1016/j.hrmr.2021.100876

Mei, X., Xu, Y., & Zhao, L. (2020). Application of topic modelling in faculty evaluation analysis. *Journal of Computational Linguistics in Education, 35*(4), 90–108.

Mengliev, D., Barakhnin, V., Abdurakhmonova, N., & Eshkulov, M. (2024). Developing named entity recognition algorithms for Uzbek: Dataset insights and implementation. *Data in Brief, 54,* 110413. DOI: 10.1016/J.DIB.2024.110413 PMID: 38708296

Meyer, S., & Elsweiler, D. (2025). LLM-based conversational agents for behaviour change support: A randomised controlled trial examining efficacy, safety, and the role of user behaviour. *International Journal of Human-Computer Studies, 200,* 103514. DOI: 10.1016/j.ijhcs.2025.103514

Milhem, M., Ateeq, A., Al Astal, A., & Almeer, S. (2025). Digital Transformation in HRM: Navigating the Future of Human Resource Management. *Studies in Systems. Decision and Control, 566,* 23–33. DOI: 10.1007/978-3-031-71318-7_3

Min, J., Kim, S., Park, Y., & Sohn, Y. W. (2018). A comparative study of potential job candidates' perceptions of an AI recruiter and a human recruiter. *Journal of the Korea Convergence Society, 9*(5), 191–202.

Mishra, S. S., Kunte, M., Neelam, N., Bhattacharya, S., & Mulay, P. (2021). HR Process Automation: A Bibliometric Analysis. *Library Philosophy and Practice, 2021.* https://www.scopus.com/inward/record.uri?eid=2-s2.0-85108566438&partnerID=40&md5=bc3590224e6b63885788377fe49f4fa5

Mitravinda, K. M., & Shetty, S. (2022). Employee Attrition: Prediction, Analysis of Contributory Factors and Recommendations for Employee Retention. *2022 IEEE International Conference for Women in Innovation, Technology and Entrepreneurship, ICWITE 2022 - Proceedings.* DOI: 10.1109/ICWITE57052.2022.10176235

Mittelstadt, B. D., Allo, P., Taddeo, M., Wachter, S., & Floridi, L. (2016). The ethics of algorithms: Mapping the debate. *Big Data & Society, 3*(2), 2053951716679679. Advance online publication. DOI: 10.1177/2053951716679679

Moed, H. F. (2017). A critical comparative analysis of five world university rankings. *Scientometrics*, *110*(2), 967–990. DOI: 10.1007/s11192-016-2212-y

Mohammad, S. M. (2020). Sentiment Analysis: Detecting Valence, Emotions, and Other Affectual States from Text. In Indurkhya, N., & Damerau, F. J. (Eds.), *Handbook of Natural Language Processing* (3rd ed., pp. 325–382). Chapman and Hall/CRC.

Mohapatra, H., & Mishra, S. R. (2024). Unlocking Insights: Exploring Data Analytics and AI Tool Performance Across Industries. In Singh, P., Mishra, A. R., & Garg, P. (Eds.), *Data Analytics and Machine Learning* (Vol. 145, pp. 265–288). Springer Nature Singapore., DOI: 10.1007/978-981-97-0448-4_13

Molenaar, A., Lukose, D., Brennan, L., Jenkins, E. L., & McCaffrey, T. A. (2024). Using Natural Language Processing to Explore Social Media Opinions on Food Security: Sentiment Analysis and Topic Modeling Study. *Journal of Medical Internet Research*, *26*(1). Advance online publication. DOI: 10.2196/47826 PMID: 38512326

Moore, P., & Piwek, L. (2017). Regulating wellbeing in the brave new quantified workplace. *Employee Relations*, *39*(3), 308–316. DOI: 10.1108/ER-06-2016-0126

Muhammad, G., & Naz, F. (2022). A moderating role of HR analytics between employee engagement, retention and organisational performance. *International Journal of Business Environment*, *13*(4), 345–357. DOI: 10.1504/IJBE.2022.126370

Mujtaba, D. F., & Mahapatra, N. R. (2020). Mining and Analyzing Occupational Characteristics from Job Postings. *2020 International Conference on Computational Science and Computational Intelligence (CSCI)*, 683–685. DOI: 10.1109/CSCI51800.2020.00124

Naim, A., Khan, S. A., Mohammed, A., & Malik, P. K. (2024). Applications of high performance computing and AI in green digital marketing. In *AI Applications for Business, Medical, and Agricultural Sustainability*. IGI Global., DOI: 10.4018/979-8-3693-5266-3.ch003

Nanyonga, A., Wasswa, H., Turhan, U., Joiner, K., & Wild, G. (2024). Exploring Aviation Incident Narratives Using Topic Modeling and Clustering Techniques. *2024 IEEE Region 10 Symposium, TENSYMP 2024*. https://doi.org/DOI: 10.1109/TENSYMP61132.2024.10752231

Natarajan, D. S., Subbaiah, B., Dhinakaran, D. P., Kumar, J. R., & Rajalakshmi, M. (2024). AI-powered strategies for talent management optimization. *Journal of Informatics Education and Research*, *4*(2). Advance online publication. DOI: 10.5281/zenodo.10537251

Nawaz, M., Abid, G., Arya, B., Bhatti, G. A., & Farooqi, S. (2018). Understanding employee thriving: The role of workplace context, personality and individual resources. *Total Quality Management & Business Excellence*. Advance online publication. DOI: 10.1080/14783363.2018.1482209

Nawaz, N. (2019). How far have we come with the study of artificial intelligence for recruitment process. *International Journal of Scientific & Technology Research, 8*(7), 488–493.

Nel, D. M., & Van Niekerk, A. (2023). Gain or loss: A conceptual framework of employee well-being during change. *Journal of Contemporary Management, 20*(1), 83–103. DOI: 10.35683/jcman1004.186

Nigam, K., Limaye, M., & Simon, L. (2025, March). The impact of artificial intelligence on talent acquisition and performance management. In *International Conference of Economics, Finance and Accounting Studies* (Vol. 14, pp. 193–201).

Nørskov, S., Damholdt, M. F., Ulhøi, J. P., Jensen, M. B., Mathiasen, M. K., Ess, C. M., & Seibt, J. (2022). Employers' and applicants' fairness perceptions in job interviews: Using a teleoperated robot as a fair proxy. *Technological Forecasting and Social Change, 179*, 121641. DOI: 10.1016/j.techfore.2022.121641

Nunoo, J., Darfor, K. N., Koomson, I., & Arthur, A. (2018). Employment security and workers' moonlighting behaviour in Ghana. *Journal of Economic Studies (Glasgow, Scotland), 45*(1), 144–155. DOI: 10.1108/JES-04-2016-0074

OECD. (2023). *Mental Health and Employment: Global Trends*. (accessed on 26th April, 25)

Ordanini, A., & Silvestri, G. (2008). Recruitment and selection services: Efficiency and competitive reasons in the outsourcing of HR practices. *International Journal of Human Resource Management, 19*(2), 372–391. DOI: 10.1080/09585190701799960

Ore, O., & Sposato, M. (2022). Opportunities and risks of artificial intelligence in recruitment and selection. *The International Journal of Organizational Analysis, 30*(6), 1771–1782. DOI: 10.1108/IJOA-07-2020-2291

Ostroff, C., Kinicki, A. J., & Muhammad, R. S. (2012). Organizational culture and climate. In I. Weiner (Ed.), Handbook of psychology, (2nd ed.). Wiley. . hop-212024DOI: 10.1002/9781118133880.hop212024

Otani, N., Bhutani, N., & Hruschka, E. (2024). *Natural Language Processing for Human Resources: A Survey* (No. arXiv:2410.16498). arXiv. https://doi.org//arXiv.2410.16498DOI: 10.48550

Ozkan, A. H. (2022). The effect of burnout and its dimensions on turnover intention among nurses: A meta-analytic review. *Journal of Nursing Management*, *30*(3), 660–669. DOI: 10.1111/jonm.13525 PMID: 34837289

Özkurt Id, C. (2024). Comparative Analysis of State-of-the-Art Q&A Models: BERT, RoBERTa, DistilBERT, and ALBERT on SQuAD v2 Dataset. *Chaos and Fractals*, *1*(1), 19–30. DOI: 10.69882/ADBA.CHF.2024073

Padhi, A., Mitra, A., & Paul, S. (2020). A Study on the Analysis of Training and Retention Strategies in some selected IT sectors at Odisha. *2020 International Conference on Computer Science, Engineering and Applications, ICCSEA 2020*. DOI: 10.1109/ICCSEA49143.2020.9132885

Page, L. C., Gehlbach, H., & Gill, B. (2019). How an artificially intelligent virtual assistant helps students navigate the road to college. *EDRE Working Paper No. 2019-10*. https://doi.org/DOI: 10.2139/ssrn.3333109

Paigude, S., Pangarkar, S. C., Hundekari, S., Mali, M., Wanjale, K., & Dongre, Y. (2023). Potential of Artificial Intelligence in Boosting Employee Retention in the Human Resource Industry. *International Journal on Recent and Innovation Trends in Computing and Communication*, *11*(3s), 1–10. DOI: 10.17762/ijritcc.v11i3s.6149

Palshikar, G. K., Apte, M., Pawar, S., & Ramrakhiyani, N. (2017). HiSPEED: A system for mining performance appraisal data and text. *Proceedings - 2017 International Conference on Data Science and Advanced Analytics, DSAA 2017, 2018-Janua*, 477 – 486. DOI: 10.1109/DSAA.2017.45

Palshikar, G. K., Apte, M., Pawar, S., & Ramrakhiyani, N. (2019). HiSPEED: A system for mining performance appraisal data and text. *International Journal of Data Science and Analytics*, *8*(1), 95–111. DOI: 10.1007/s41060-018-0142-x

Pandey, S., & Mehta, J. (2022). HRPA: Human Resource Prediction Analytics. *Proceedings of the 2022 3rd International Conference on Intelligent Computing, Instrumentation and Control Technologies: Computational Intelligence for Smart Systems, ICICICT 2022*, 721 – 726. DOI: 10.1109/ICICICT54557.2022.9917576

Pandey, S., & Sharma, V. (2016). Understanding work-related stress, job conditions, work culture and workaholism phenomenon as predictors of HR crisis: An empirical study of the indian IT sector. *International Journal of Human Capital and Information Technology Professionals*, *7*(2), 68–80. DOI: 10.4018/IJHCITP.2016040105

Pang, B., & Lee, L. (2008). *Opinion Mining and Sentiment Analysis*, now, 2008, .DOI: 10.1561/1500000011

Pan, Y., Froese, F. J., Liu, N., Hu, Y., & Ye, M. (2021). The adoption of artificial intelligence in employee recruitment: The influence of contextual factors. *International Journal of Human Resource Management*, •••, 1–23. DOI: 10.1080/09585192.2021.2007975

Papaevangelou, O., Syndoukas, D., Kalogiannidis, S., & Chatzitheodoridis, F. (2024). Efficacy of embedding IT in human resources (HR) practices in education management. *Journal of Infrastructure. Policy and Development*, *8*(1). Advance online publication. DOI: 10.24294/jipd.v8i1.2371

Paramita, D., Okwir, S., & Nuur, C. (2024). Artificial intelligence in talent acquisition: Exploring organisational and operational dimensions. *The International Journal of Organizational Analysis*, *32*(11), 108–131. DOI: 10.1108/IJOA-09-2023-3992

Parimi, S., & Chakraborty, S. (2019). Antecedents to employee attrition behavior in Indian IT/ITES sector. *International Journal of Engineering and Advanced Technology*, *9*(1), 1132–1142. DOI: 10.35940/ijeat.A9502.109119

Parker, K., Stroud, D., & McMahan, T. (2019). Candidate experience and the impact of AI in recruitment processes. *Human Resource Management Journal*, *29*(4), 13–27. DOI: 10.1111/1748-8583.12234

Patel, R., Gupta, A., Qin, X., & Brickner, C. (2024). A Generative AI and NLP-Based Research Prototype for Call Resolutions and Automation: The Case of a Healthcare Contact Center. *Proceedings of the 2024 Pre-ICIS SIGDSA Symposium, SIGDSA*, 12–2024. https://aisel.aisnet.org/sigdsa2024/16

Pathak, A., Tewari, V., & Shankar, S. (2018). Impact of Emotional Intelligence on employability of IT professionals. *Management Insight*, *14*(1), 14–21. DOI: 10.21844/mijia.14.01.4

Patterson, M. G., West, M. A., Shackleton, V. J., Dawson, J. F., Lawthom, R., Maitlis, S., Robinson, D. L., & Wallace, A. M. (2005). Validating the organizational climate measure: Links to managerial practices, productivity and innovation. *Journal of Organizational Behavior*, *26*(4), 379–408. DOI: 10.1002/job.312

Pattnaik, D., Kumar, S., & Burton, B. (2021, June). Thirty years of the Australian accounting review: A bibliometric analysis. *Australian Accounting Review*, *31*(2), 150–164. DOI: 10.1111/auar.12332

Pattnaik, D., Kumar, S., & Vashishtha, A. (2020, October 24). Research on trade credit–a systematic review and bibliometric analysis. *Qualitative Research in Financial Markets.*, *12*(4), 367–390. DOI: 10.1108/QRFM-09-2019-0103

Penz, D., Almeida, M. P. D., Amorim, B. C., Cembranel, P., & Rolt, C. R. D. (2023). Crowdsourced employer branding: An analysis from the platform glassdoor. *Revista de Administração da UFSM*, *16*(1), e7. DOI: 10.5902/1983465966608

Permatasari, D. A., & Maharani, D. A. (2021). Combination of Natural Language Understanding and Reinforcement Learning for Booking Bot. *Journal of Electrical, Electronic, Information, and Communication Technology*, *3*(1), 12. DOI: 10.20961/jeeict.3.1.49818

Peterson, K. D. (2000). *Teacher evaluation: A comprehensive guide to new directions and practices*. Corwin Press.

Peterson, R. A., & Comeaux, P. (1990). Evaluating faculty performance using student feedback: A reliability analysis. *Educational Measurement Journal*, *18*(3), 67–85.

Pico-Saltos, R., Carrión-Mero, P., Montalván-Burbano, N., Garzás, J., & Redchuk, A. (2021). Research trends in career success: A bibliometric review. *Sustainability (Basel)*, *13*(9), 4625. DOI: 10.3390/su13094625

Pillai, R., Ghanghorkar, Y., Sivathanu, B., Algharabat, R., & Rana, N. P. (2024). Adoption of artificial intelligence (AI) based employee experience (EEX) chatbots. *Information Technology & People*, *37*(1), 449–478. DOI: 10.1108/ITP-04-2022-0287

Pillai, R., & Sivathanu, B. (2020). Adoption of AI-based chatbots for hospitality and tourism. *International Journal of Contemporary Hospitality Management*, *32*(10), 3199–3226. DOI: 10.1108/IJCHM-04-2020-0259

Pipera, M., & Fragouli, E. (2021). Employee wellbeing, employee performance & positive mindset in a crisis. *The Business & Management Review*, *12*(2), 1–15.

Plimmer, G., Berman, E. M., Malinen, S., Franken, E., Naswall, K., Kuntz, J., & Löfgren, K. (2022). Resilience in public sector managers. *Review of Public Personnel Administration*, *42*(2), 338–367. DOI: 10.1177/0734371X20985105

Polyakova, A., Kolmakov, V., & Pokamestov, I. (2020). Data-driven HR analytics in a quality management system. *Quality - Access to Success*, *21*(176), 74–80. https://www.scopus.com/inward/record.uri?eid=2-s2.0-85086146828&partnerID=40&md5=bc478ab18646a70fb0551dc7fbde011c

Ponti, E. M., Vulić, I., Glavaš, G., Reichart, R., & Riedel, S. (2020). XCOPA: A multilingual dataset for causal commonsense reasoning. *Proceedings of the 2020 Conference on Empirical Methods in Natural Language Processing (EMNLP)*, 2362–2376. DOI: 10.18653/v1/2020.emnlp-main.185

Popescu, A. M., & Etzioni, O. (2017). Contextual NLP challenges in automated feedback analysis. *Journal of Artificial Intelligence in Education*, *12*(1), 45–60.

Pritchard A. (1969). Statistical Bibliography; An Interim Bibliography.

Putka, D. J., Oswald, F. L., Landers, R. N., Beatty, A. S., McCloy, R. A., & Yu, M. C. (2023). Evaluating a Natural Language Processing Approach to Estimating KSA and Interest Job Analysis Ratings. *Journal of Business and Psychology*, *38*(2), 385–410. DOI: 10.1007/s10869-022-09824-0

Putra, F. S. U., & Puspitasari, I. (2023). Implementation of Sentiment Analysis in HR Management and Development Planning Using Topic Modelling on Employee Review. *Kontigensi: Jurnal Ilmiah Manajemen*, *11*(2), 409–417. DOI: 10.56457/jimk.v11i2.358

Qualtrics, X. M. Institute. (2023). *Employee experience trends 2024: EMEA insights report.* Qualtrics. https://www.qualtrics.com/m/www.xminstitute.com/wp-content/uploads/2023/10/XMI_RR_DS_EXTrends2024-EMEA-2.pdf

Rabuana, N. K. D. N., & Yanuar, Y. (2023). The influence of work environment and work engagement on employee performance mediated by employee well-being. *Munaddhomah: Jurnal Manajemen Pendidikan Islam*, *4*(3), 541–557. DOI: 10.31538/munaddhomah.v4i3.523

Rachel, J. J. L., Bhuvaneswari, A., & Kumudha, M. (2024). Topic Modeling Based Clustering of Disaster Tweets Using BERTopic. *2024 MIT Art, Design and Technology School of Computing International Conference, MITADTSoCiCon 2024*. https://doi.org/DOI: 10.1109/MITADTSOCICON60330.2024.10575555

Rahman, Z. T., Lal, R., & Rena, R. (2025). Industry, Innovation, and Infrastructure: Contribution of SMEs in the Developing Economies. In Entrepreneurship in the BRICS (pp. 218-248). Routledge.

Rahman, Z. T., Lal, R., & Ratna, R. (2022). An Analytical Study on the Significance of Folk and Fairytales on the Psychology of Young Children. *International Journal of Early Childhood Special Education*, *14*(5).

Rahman, Z. T., Lal, R., & Rena, R. (2024). Challenges of Communication with Gen-Z in the Era of Artificial Intelligence-Interceded Digital Economy. In *AI-Oriented Competency Framework for Talent Management in the Digital Economy* (pp. 76–94). CRC Press. DOI: 10.1201/9781003440901-5

Rahman, Z. T., Lal, R., & Rena, R. (2024). Innovative and Futuristic Approach to the Agricultural Sector in China. In *Innovation and Development of Agricultural Systems: Cases from Brazil, Russia, India, China and South Africa (BRICS)* (pp. 257–285). Springer Nature Singapore. DOI: 10.1007/978-981-97-2926-5_12

Raiaan, M. A. K., Mukta, M., Fatema, K., Fahad, N. M., Sakib, S., Mim, M. M. J., Ahmad, J., Ali, M. E., & Azam, S. (2024). A Review on Large Language Models: Architectures, Applications, Taxonomies, Open Issues and Challenges. *IEEE Access : Practical Innovations, Open Solutions*, *12*, 26839–26874. DOI: 10.1109/ACCESS.2024.3365742

Rajesh, S., Kandaswamy, M. U., & Rakesh, M. A. (2018). The impact of Artificial Intelligence in Talent Acquisition Lifecycle of organizations: A global perspective. *International Journal of Engineering Development and Research*, *6*(2), 709–717.

Raji, I. D., & Buolamwini, J. (2019). Actionable auditing: Investigating the impact of publicly naming biased performance results of commercial AI products. *In Proceedings of the AAAI/ACM Conference on AI, Ethics, and Society* (pp. 429–435). DOI: 10.1145/3306618.3314244

Raji, I. D., Kumar, I. E., Horowitz, A., & Selbst, A. (2022, June). The fallacy of AI functionality. *In Proceedings of the 2022 ACM Conference on Fairness, Accountability, and Transparency* (pp. 959–972). ACM. DOI: 10.1145/3531146.3533158

Rajput, Q., & Anwar, S. (2016). Lexicon-based sentiment analysis of student feedback in higher education. *Journal of Educational Technology and Innovation*, *9*(2), 33–48.

Ramachandaran, S. D., Doraisingam, P., Nuraini, R., & Chaudhery, U. (2024). Examining the impact of digital transformation on HRM practices in Morocco's IT sector. *Humanities and Social Sciences Letters*, *12*(4), 811–830. DOI: 10.18488/73.v12i4.3903

Rana, R., Kapoor, S., & Gupta, S. K. (2021). Impact of HR practices on corporate image building in the Indian IT sector. *Problems and Perspectives in Management*, *19*(2), 528–535. DOI: 10.21511/ppm.19(2).2021.42

Rao, T. V. N., Patel, G. S., Bhavana, S., & Swetha, C. (2025). AI-Driven Decision Support System for Workplace Wellbeing. In Insights on Wellbeing and Happiness in the Workplace (pp. 1-18). IGI Global Scientific Publishing.

Ravichandran, N., Inaganti, A. C., & Muppalaneni, R. (2023). AI-Driven Sentiment Analysis for Employee Engagement and Retention. *Journal of Computing Innovations and Applications*, *1*(01), 1–9.

Raviprolu, A. (2017). Role of artificial intelligence in recruitment. *IACSIT International Journal of Engineering and Technology*, *5*(4), 94–98.

Rayhan, A., Kinzler, R., & Rayhan, R. (2023). *NATURAL LANGUAGE PROCESSING: TRANSFORMING HOW MACHINES UNDERSTAND HUMAN LANGUAGE*. DOI: 10.13140/RG.2.2.34900.99200

Reddy Yanamala, K. K. (2024). Integrating Machine Learning and Human Feedback for Employee Performance Evaluation. *Journal of Advanced Computing Systems*, *2*(1), 1–10. DOI: 10.69987/JACS.2022.20101

Reworked. (2024). Sentiment Analysis and Employee Mental Wellness: Opportunities and Guardrails. Retrieved from https://www.reworked.co/employee-experience/sentiment-analysis-can-help-mental-wellness-initiatives-given-the-proper-guardrails/accessed on 25/04/25

Rink, L., Meijdam, J., & Graus, D. (2024). Aspect-Based Sentiment Analysis for Open-Ended HR Survey Responses. *arXiv preprint arXiv:2402.04812*.

Rodgers, W., Murray, J. M., Stefanidis, A., Degbey, W. Y., & Tarba, S. Y. (2023). An artificial intelligence algorithmic approach to ethical decision-making in human resource management processes. *Human Resource Management Review*, *33*(1), 100925. DOI: 10.1016/j.hrmr.2022.100925

Ryan, A. M., & Derous, E. (2016). Highlighting tensions in recruitment and selection research and practice. *International Journal of Selection and Assessment*, *24*(1), 54–62. DOI: 10.1111/ijsa.12129

Saadati, H., & Hakimi, A. (2024). Optimizing the Ticket Response Process in Customer Support Systems Using Data-Driven and Machine Learning Methods: A Case Study of IFDA. *Optimality*, *1*(2), 188–204. DOI: 10.22105/OPT.V1I2.57

Sabbah, J., & Li, F. (2025). When humans and large language models collaborate, problem-finding illuminates. *Innovation (North Sydney, N.S.W.)*, •••, 1–34. DOI: 10.1080/14479338.2025.2504428

Saks, A. M. (2019). Social media and recruitment: The role of employer branding. *The Journal of Applied Psychology*, *104*(3), 256–273. DOI: 10.1037/apl0000365

Salas-Vallina, A., Alegre, J., & López-Cabrales, Á. (2021). The challenge of increasing employees' well-being and performance: How human resource management practices and engaging leadership work together toward reaching this goal. *Human Resource Management*, *60*(3), 333–347. DOI: 10.1002/hrm.22021

Salovey, P., & Mayer, J. D. (1990). Emotional intelligence. *Imagination, Cognition and Personality*, *9*(3), 185–211. DOI: 10.2190/DUGG-P24E-52WK-6CDG

Samal, A., Sharma, P., Naveen, S., Chethan Kumar, K., Kotehal, P. U., & Thirulogasundaram, V. P. (2024). Exploring the Role of HR Analytics in Enhancing Talent Acquisition Strategies. *South Eastern European Journal of Public Health*, *23*(3), 612–618. DOI: 10.70135/seejph.vi.1357

Sandu, A., Cotfas, L. A., Stănescu, A., & Delcea, C. (2024). A Bibliometric Analysis of Text Mining: Exploring the Use of Natural Language Processing in Social Media Research. *Applied Sciences 2024, Vol. 14, Page 3144*, *14*(8), 3144. https://doi.org/DOI: 10.3390/APP14083144

Saravanabhavan, N., Subashini, R., & Velmurugan, G. (2024). HRM Practices and Knowledge Sharing in IT Sector – A Study in Coimbatore, Tamil Nadu. *International Research Journal of Multidisciplinary Scope*, *5*(1), 607–620. DOI: 10.47857/irjms.2024.v05i01.0289

Sarker, I. H. (2021). Data Science and Analytics: An Overview from Data-Driven Smart Computing, Decision-Making and Applications Perspective. In *SN Computer Science* (Vol. 2, Issue 5). https://doi.org/DOI: 10.1007/s42979-021-00765-8

Sarker, I. H. (2021). Machine Learning: Algorithms, Real-World Applications and Research Directions. *SN Computer Science*, *2*(3), 160. DOI: 10.1007/s42979-021-00592-x

Sar, S., Mohanty, A. K., & Dash, M. (2017). An empirical study on critical issues of work life balance: A study of IT sector. *International Journal of Economic Research*, *14*(14), 275–284. https://www.scopus.com/inward/record.uri?eid=2-s2.0-85034663201&partnerID=40&md5=9cb6595e105e6e61cf10855ec413d911

Sarwar, H., Ishaq, M. I., Amin, A., & Ahmed, R. (2020). Ethical leadership, work engagement, employees' well-being, and performance: A cross-cultural comparison. *Journal of Sustainable Tourism*, *28*(12), 2008–2026. DOI: 10.1080/09669582.2020.1788039

Satpal, S. R., & Dhillon, M. (2019). Impact of factors affecting employee retention on turnover intentions: In Indian IT sector. *International Journal on Emerging Technologies, 10*(4), 273 – 282. https://www.scopus.com/inward/record.uri?eid=2-s2.0-85077690213&partnerID=40&md5=a31976cea09c6372a1da70f8e9c6f4a2

Sattu, R., Das, S., & Jena, L. K. (2024). Should I adopt AI during talent acquisition? Evidence from HR professionals of Indian IT organisations. *Journal of Organizational Effectiveness: People and Performance*, *11*(4), 1005–1022. DOI: 10.1108/JOEPP-05-2023-0186

Sawalha, M., Al-Shargi, F., Yagi, S., AlShdaifat, A. T., Hammo, B., Belajeed, M., & Al-Ogaili, L. R. (2025). Morphologically-analyzed and syntactically-annotated Quran dataset. *Data in Brief*, *58*, 111211. DOI: 10.1016/J.DIB.2024.111211 PMID: 39830618

Sawicki, J., Ganzha, M., & Paprzycki, M. (2023). The State of the Art of Natural Language Processing—A Systematic Automated Review of NLP Literature Using NLP Techniques. *Data Intelligence*, *5*(3). Advance online publication. DOI: 10.1162/dint_a_00213

Saxena, C., Kumar, P., Sarvaiya, R., & Khatri, B. (2023). Attitude, Behavioral Intention and Adoption of AI Driven Chatbots in the Banking Sector. *2023 IEEE IAS Global Conference on Emerging Technologies, GlobConET 2023*. DOI: 10.1109/GlobConET56651.2023.10150155

Schaufeli, W. B. (2017). Applying the Job Demands-Resources Model: A "How to" Guide to Measuring and Tackling Work Engagement and Burnout. *Organizational Dynamics*, *46*(2), 120–132. DOI: 10.1016/j.orgdyn.2017.04.008

Schaufeli, W. B., Salanova, M., González-Romá, V., & Bakker, A. B. (2002). The measurement of engagement and burnout: A two sample confirmatory factor analytic approach. *Journal of Happiness Studies*, *3*(1), 71–92. DOI: 10.1023/A:1015630930326

Scholz, T. M. (2017). Big data in organizations and the role of human resource management: A complex systems theory-based conceptualization. Frankfurt a. M.: Peter Lang International Academic Publishers. DOI: 10.3726/b10907

Sengar, S. S. (2023). From pixels to policies: Analysing the provisions and navigating the complexities of the Digital Personal Data Protection Act, 2023. *Available at SSRN*. https://ssrn.com/abstract=4547842 DOI: 10.2139/ssrn.4536795

Shah, I. A., & Mishra, S. (2024). Artificial intelligence in advancing occupational health and safety: An encapsulation of developments. *Journal of Occupational Health*, *66*(1), uiad017. DOI: 10.1093/joccuh/uiad017 PMID: 38334203

Shahzad, M. F., Xu, S., Lim, W. M., Yang, X., & Khan, Q. R. (2024). Artificial intelligence and social media on academic performance and mental well-being: Student perceptions of positive impact in the age of smart learning. *Heliyon*, *10*(8), e29523. DOI: 10.1016/j.heliyon.2024.e29523 PMID: 38665566

Shaikh, M., & Kasatt, R. (2020). E-governance in faculty evaluations: AI-based performance assessment methods. *Journal of Digital Governance in Education, 15*(3), 112–128.

Shakeel, A., & Siddiqui, D. A. (2021). The effect of Technological, Organizational, Environmental, and Task Technology fit on the Adoption and usage of artificial intelligence (AI) for talent acquisition (TA): Evidence from the Pakistani banking sector. *Organizational, Environmental, and Task Technology fit on the Adoption and usage of artificial intelligence (AI) for talent acquisition (TA): Evidence from the Pakistani banking sector.(October 15, 2021).*

Shaman, M. A. M., Samarasinghe, S. M., Tharinda, D., Gamage, D. C., & Gamage, A. (2022). Pre-Interview Reviewer Using Natural Language Processing for Software Engineers in The IT Industry : Pre-interview reviewer. In S. V., S. V., S. M., S. M., & S. J. (Eds.), *Proceedings - 2022 4th International Conference on Advances in Computing, Communication Control and Networking, ICAC3N 2022* (pp. 2300 – 2305). Institute of Electrical and Electronics Engineers Inc. DOI: 10.1109/ICAC3N56670.2022.10074186

Shamshiri, A., Ryu, K. R., & Park, J. Y. (2024). Text mining and natural language processing in construction. *Automation in Construction, 158*, 105200. DOI: 10.1016/J.AUTCON.2023.105200

Shankar, S., Anagh, G. S., & Vaish, A. (2017). Spirituality and skill for leadership towards Sustainable Management. *Purushartha - A Journal of Management, Ethics, and Spirituality, 10*(02).

Shankar, S., & Tewari, V. (2021). Understanding the emotional intelligence discourse on social media: Insights from the analysis of Twitter. *Journal of Intelligence, 9*(4), 56. DOI: 10.3390/jintelligence9040056 PMID: 34842754

Shankar, S., & Tewari, V. (2023). Impact of collective intelligence and collective emotional intelligence on the psychological safety of the organizations. *Vision (Basel), 27*(4), 458–473. DOI: 10.1177/09722629211012256

Shankar, S., & Tewari, V. (2025). *Investigating leadership discussion on social media: A NLP and machine learning perspective*. Technology in Society, Online First.

Shankar, S., Vyas, R., & Tewari, V. (2024). Applying machine learning algorithms to determine and predict the reasons and models for employee turnover. *International Journal of Information Technology and Management, 23*(1), 48–63. DOI: 10.1504/IJITM.2024.136187

Shankman, M. L., Allen, S. J., & Haber-Curran, P. (2015). *Emotionally intelligent leader-ship: A guide for college students* (2nd ed.). Jossey-Bass.

Shanmugam, R., & Giri Babu, N. (2016). Assessment of employee attrition among IT employees. *International Journal of Applied Engineering Research: IJAER, 11*(5), 3449–3453. https://www.scopus.com/inward/record.uri?eid=2-s2.0-84964043865&partnerID=40&md5=eed6b5e216649c702d31df6bac9e672c

Shannaq, B. (2024). The Role of AI in University Course Registration in the Middle East: AI and Machine Learning Approaches to Improve Academic Performance. *2024 2nd International Conference on Computing and Data Analytics (ICCDA)*, 1–6. DOI: 10.1109/ICCDA64887.2024.10867316

Shannaq, B., & Alabri, A. (2025). EVALUATING THE IMPACT OF CHATGPT IMPLEMENTATION ON HR PERFORMANCE SKILLS: A CASE STUDY OF ACADEMIC INSTITUTIONS IN OMAN. *Bangladesh Journal of Multidisciplinary Scientific Research, 10*(1), 11–21. DOI: 10.46281/bjmsr.v10i1.2281

Sharma, R., & Dhingra, L. (2024). Advancing Human Resource Strategies with Deep Learning: Predictive Analytics for Improving Employee Retention Rates. *2024 2nd World Conference on Communication and Computing, WCONF 2024*. DOI: 10.1109/WCONF61366.2024.10692087

Sharma, A., & Sharma, T. (2017). HR analytics and performance appraisal system: A conceptual framework for employee performance improvement. *Management Research Review, 40*(6), 684–697. DOI: 10.1108/MRR-04-2016-0084

Sharma, E., & Ahmad, J. (2022). Technology adoption model for HRM practices. *International Journal of Technology Enhanced Learning, 14*(1), 101–124. DOI: 10.1504/IJTEL.2022.120563

Sharma, N., Khatri, B., & Khan, S. A. (2024). Exploring the past and identifying the future research agenda for social media and tourist behavior: A bibliometric analysis. In *Social Media Strategies for Tourism Interactivity*. IGI Global., DOI: 10.4018/979-8-3693-0960-5.ch011

Sharma, N., Khatri, B., Khan, S. A., & Shamsi, M. S. (2023). Extending the UTAUT Model to Examine the Influence of Social Media on Tourists' Destination Selection. *Indian Journal of Marketing, 53*(4), 47–64. DOI: 10.17010/ijom/2023/v53/i4/172689

Sharma, R., Agarwal, P., & Arya, A. (2022). Natural Language Processing and Big Data: A Strapping Combination. In Sharma, R., & Sharma, D. (Eds.), *New Trends and Applications in Internet of Things (IoT) and Big Data Analytics* (Vol. 221, pp. 255–271). Springer International Publishing., DOI: 10.1007/978-3-030-99329-0_16

Sharma, S., Vashisht, M., & Kumar, V. (2024). Enhanced Customer Insights: Multimodal NLP Feedback System. *2024 IEEE International Students' Conference on Electrical, Electronics and Computer Science, SCEECS 2024*. https://doi.org/DOI: 10.1109/SCEECS61402.2024.10481937

Shirom, A., Nirel, N., & Vinokur, A. D. (2010). Work hours and caseload as predictors of physician burnout: The mediating effects by perceived workload and by autonomy. *Applied Psychology*, *59*(4), 539–565. DOI: 10.1111/j.1464-0597.2009.00411.x

Showkat, S., Shajan, K., & Pathak, V. K. (2019). Strategic human resource management and organizational performance: Mediating role of employee well-being in the Indian IT industry. *Journal of Critical Reviews*, *6*(6), 75–83. DOI: 10.22159/jcr.06.06.11

Silva, R. F., Gomes, A. C., & Pereira, L. M. (2022). Sentiment analysis of student evaluations: A case study from a Brazilian public university. *Education and Information Technologies*, *27*(5), 6943–6962. DOI: 10.1007/s10639-021-10858-1

Simmons & Simmons. (2020, October 5). Fine issued against H&M for data protection violations. Accessed on 26/04/25 https://www.simmons-simmons.com/en/publications/ckh3lyk2b14oj0917lz7sc9uf/fine-issued-against-h-m-for-data-protection-violations

Singh, A., Shukla, T., & Dwivedi, N. (2010). Innovation advancement. In Garg, P., Routray, S., & Gupta, M. (Eds.), *Innovation Advancement* (pp. 377–385). MACMILLAN.

Singh, M., Srivastava, S. P., Srivastava, S., & Singhal, T. (2024). Unlocking Predictive Insights for Employee Retention and Engagement: Harnessing Machine Learning and Big Data Analytics in HR Practices. *Smart Innovation. Systems and Technologies*, *390*, 497–505. DOI: 10.1007/978-981-97-2716-2_44

Singh, S., & Mahmood, A. (2021). The NLP Cookbook: Modern Recipes for Transformer Based Deep Learning Architectures. *IEEE Access : Practical Innovations, Open Solutions*, *9*. Advance online publication. DOI: 10.1109/ACCESS.2021.3077350

Singh, S., Pradhan, R., Panigrahy, N., & Jena, L. (2019). Self-efficacy and workplace well-being: Moderating role of sustainability practices. *Benchmarking*, *26*(6), 1692–1708. Advance online publication. DOI: 10.1108/BIJ-07-2018-0219

Singh, T., & Malhotra, S. (2020). Workforce analytics: Increasing managerial efficiency in human resource. *International Journal of Scientific and Technology Research*, *9*(1), 3260–3266. https://www.scopus.com/inward/record.uri?eid=2-s2.0-85078732809&partnerID=40&md5=ed78adc5c489b10eadc59bcfdf002089

Singh, V. (2023). Exploring the role of large language model (LLM)-based chatbots for human resources [The University of Texas at Austin; Application/pdf]. DOI: 10.26153/TSW/51146

Small, H. (1973, July). Co-citation in the scientific literature: A new measure of the relationship between two documents. *Journal of the American Society for Information Science*, *24*(4), 265–269. DOI: 10.1002/asi.4630240406

Smith, A. (2021). *8 trends that altered the recruitment industry forever*. https://recruitee.com/articles/recruitment-industry

Smylie, M. (2014). Teacher effectiveness and student satisfaction: Insights from higher education research. *Journal of Educational Policy and Leadership*, *21*(2), 78–101.

Solaiman, I., Talat, Z., Agnew, W., Ahmad, L., & Zhang, M. (2023). Evaluating the social impact of generative AI systems in systems and society. *arXiv Preprint*, arXiv:2306.05949. https://arxiv.org/abs/2306.05949

Soleimani, M., Intezari, A., Arrowsmith, J., Pauleen, D. J., & Taskin, N. (2025). Reducing AI bias in recruitment and selection: An integrative grounded approach. *International Journal of Human Resource Management*, •••, 1–36. DOI: 10.1080/09585192.2025.2480617

Sonmez, B., & Yildirim, A. (2018). The mediating role ofautonomy in the effect of pro-innovation climate and supervisor supportiveness on innovative behavior of nurses. *European Journal of Innovation Management*, *22*(1), 41–58. DOI: 10.1108/EJIM-05-2018-0088

Sood, I., & Kaushal, S. L. (2018). Emotional intelligence and leadership styles: A study of educational leaders in Himachal Pradesh. *Asian Journal of Management*, *9*(1), 419–426. DOI: 10.5958/2321-5763.2018.00064.1

Sousa, M. J. (2018). HR analytics models for effective decision-making. In de Waal B.M.E. & R. P. (Eds.), *Proceedings of the 14th European Conference on Management, Leadership and Governance, ECMLG 2018* (pp. 256 – 263). Academic Conferences and Publishing International Limited. https://www.scopus.com/inward/record.uri?eid=2-s2.0-85073779394&partnerID=40&md5=5d7f440d5d2caa4fce7152af7016e170

Sposato, M. (2021). Remote working in the time of COVID-19: Developing a web-based community. *International Journal of Web Based Communities*, *17*(1), 1–8. DOI: 10.1504/IJWBC.2021.112862

Springworks. (2023). *How to use ChatGPT for recruitment in 2023*. NASSCOM Community. https://community.nasscom.in/communities/ai/how-usechatgpt-recruitment-2023

Srivastava, G., Muneeswari, S., Venkataraman, R., Kavitha, V., & Parthiban, N. (2022). A review of the state of the art in business intelligence software. In *Enterprise Information Systems* (Vol. 16, Issue 1). https://doi.org/DOI: 10.1080/17517575.2021.1872107

Staffordshire University. (2019). Beacon: The digital assistant for students. https://www.staffs.ac.uk/news/beacon-digital-assistant

Sternberg, R. J. (1997). The concept of intelligence and its role in lifelong learning and success. *The American Psychologist*, *52*(10), 1030–1037. DOI: 10.1037/0003-066X.52.10.1030 PMID: 9329294

Stetler, K. L., & Magnusson, M. (2015). Exploring the tension between clarity and ambiguity in goal setting for innovation. *Creativity and Innovation Management*, *24*(2), 231–246. DOI: 10.1111/caim.12102

Steyvers, M., Tejeda, H., Kumar, A., Belem, C., Karny, S., Hu, X., Mayer, L. W., & Smyth, P. (2025). What large language models know and what people think they know. *Nature Machine Intelligence*, *7*(2), 221–231. DOI: 10.1038/s42256-024-00976-7

Subrahmanyam, S. (2025). The Integration of Artificial Intelligence and Machine Learning in Performance Evaluation. In Marcão, R., & Santos, V. (Eds.), (pp. 603–626). Advances in Human Resources Management and Organizational Development. IGI Global., DOI: 10.4018/979-8-3373-0149-5.ch028

Sun, J. (2024). Research on the Application of Large Language Models in Human Resource Management Practices. *International Journal of Emerging Technologies and Advanced Applications*, *1*(8), 1–8. DOI: 10.62677/IJETAA.2408125

Supraveen, U. J., Ali, S. S., Babu, K. S., Rao, V. R., & Bandi, G. N. S. (2022). HR Analytics - The Measurement of HR Processes using a Methodical Approach. *2022 International Conference on Computer Communication and Informatics, ICCCI 2022*. DOI: 10.1109/ICCCI54379.2022.9740999

Suresh, N., Antony Alphonnse Ligori, T., Khan, S. A., & Thoudam, P. (2019). Predicting financial distress of Bhutan telecom limited. *International Journal of Innovative Technology and Exploring Engineering*, *8*(8 SpecialIssue 3), 94 – 99. https://www.scopus.com/inward/record.uri?eid=2-s2.0-85070022376&partnerID=40&md5=df0e9d60b3abf123a9e72d40606132b5

Suri, N., & Lakhanpal, P. (2024). People Analytics Enabling HR Strategic Partnership: A Review. *SA Journal of Human Resource Management*, *11*(1), 130–164. DOI: 10.1177/23220937221119599

Taiminen, H. (2025). Organisational listening as a means to create more citizen-centric well-being public policies. *International Journal of Strategic Communication*, *19*(1), 105–117. DOI: 10.1080/1553118X.2024.2395406

Tan, K. L., Lee, C. P., & Lim, K. M. (2023). A Survey of Sentiment Analysis: Approaches, Datasets, and Future Research. In *Applied Sciences (Switzerland)* (Vol. 13, Issue 7). https://doi.org/DOI: 10.3390/app13074550

Tasneem, N. S., & Hemalatha, R. (2025). Real-Time Sentiment Analysis of Customer Feedback Using Neural Networks and NLP Methods. *2024 International Conference on IT Innovation and Knowledge Discovery (ITIKD)*, 1–6. https://doi.org/DOI: 10.1109/ITIKD63574.2025.11004792

Taunk, A. (2022). A Study On The Causes And Effects Of Moonlighting In The IT Sector. *Journal of Pharmaceutical Negative Results*, •••, 6698–6705.

Taut, S., & Sun, Y. (2014). The national teacher evaluation system in Chile: A case study in AI-driven faculty appraisal frameworks. *Journal of Educational Assessment*, *22*(1), 44–67.

Thurow, L. C. (1999). *Building wealth: The new rules for individuals, companies, and nations in a knowledge-based economy*. HarperCollins.

Torres-Samuel, M., Vásquez, C. L., Luna, M., Bucci, N., Viloria, A., Crissien, T., & Manosalva, J. (2020). Performance of education and research in Latin American countries through data envelopment analysis (DEA). *Procedia Computer Science*, *170*, 1023–1028. DOI: 10.1016/j.procs.2020.03.079

Town, P., & Thabtah, F. (2019). Data Analytics Tools: A User Perspective. In *Journal of Information and Knowledge Management* (Vol. 18, Issue 1). https://doi.org/DOI: 10.1142/S0219649219500023

Trajanoska, M., Stojanov, R., & Trajanov, D. (2023). *Enhancing Knowledge Graph Construction Using Large Language Models* (Version 1). arXiv. DOI: 10.48550/ARXIV.2305.04676

Tripathi, M. A., Madhavi, K., Kandi, V. S. P., Nassa, V. K., Mallik, B., & Chakravarthi, M. K. (2023). Machine learning models for evaluating the benefits of business intelligence systems. *The Journal of High Technology Management Research*, *34*(2). Advance online publication. DOI: 10.1016/j.hitech.2023.100470

Truic , C.-O., & Barnoschi, A. (2014). Innovating HR using an expert system for recruiting IT specialists - ESRIT. *Vision 2020: Sustainable Growth, Economic Development, and Global Competitiveness - Proceedings of the 23rd International Business Information Management Association Conference, IBIMA 2014, 1*, 1671 – 1680. https://www.scopus.com/inward/record.uri?eid=2-s2.0-84906265128&partnerID=40&md5=0d637b74184c03738046c5b2be006c96

Trust Insights. (n.d.). Case study: Employee sentiment. Trust Insights. Retrieved April 25, 2025, from https://www.trustinsights.ai/expertise/case-studies/case-study-employee-sentiment/

Tushman, M. L., & O'Reilly, C. A. (1996). Ambidextrous organizations: Managing evolutionary and revolutionary change. California Management Review, 38(4), 8–29. https://journals.sagepub.com/doi/10.2307/ 41165852

Tyagi, D. M., & Pandita, D. (2022). Artificial Intelligence and People Analytics-A Key to Employee Engagement. *2022 International Conference on Sustainable Islamic Business and Finance, SIBF 2022*, 224 – 228. DOI: 10.1109/SIBF56821.2022.9940118

Udahemuka, G., Djouani, K., & Kurien, A. M. (2024). Multimodal Emotion Recognition using visual, vocal and Physiological Signals: A review. *Applied Sciences (Basel, Switzerland), 14*(17), 8071. DOI: 10.3390/app14178071

Ullah, S., Ahmad, R., Namoun, A., Muhammad, S., Ullah, K., Hussain, I., & Ibrahim, I. A. (2024). A Deep Learning-Based Approach for Part of Speech (PoS) Tagging in the Pashto Language. *IEEE Access : Practical Innovations, Open Solutions, 12*, 86355–86364. DOI: 10.1109/ACCESS.2024.3412175

Upadhyay, A. K., & Khandelwal, K. (2018). Applying artificial intelligence: Implications for recruitment. *Strategic HR Review, 17*(5), 255–258. DOI: 10.1108/SHR-07-2018-0051

Upadhyay, P., Agarwal, R., Dhiman, S., Sarkar, A., & Chaturvedi, S. (2024). A comprehensive survey on answer generation methods using NLP. *Natural Language Processing Journal, 8*, 100088. DOI: 10.1016/J.NLP.2024.100088

Urbano, J., Couto, M., Rocha, G., & Lopes Cardoso, H. (2021). Inconsistency Detection in Job Postings [Application/pdf]. *OASIcs, Volume 93, LDK 2021, 93*, 25:1-25:16. DOI: 10.4230/OASICS.LDK.2021.25

Urwick, J., & Kisa, S. (2014). Science teacher shortage and the moonlighting culture: The pathology of the teacher labour market in Uganda. *International Journal of Educational Development, 36*, 72–80. DOI: 10.1016/j.ijedudev.2013.11.004

Uzoka, A., Cadet, E., & Ojukwu, P. U. (2024). Leveraging AI-Powered chatbots to enhance customer service efficiency and future opportunities in automated support. *Computer Science & IT Research Journal, 5*(10), 2485–2510. DOI: 10.51594/csitrj.v5i10.1676

Vadithe, R. N., & Kesari, B. (2024). Impact of Human Resource Analytics Adoption on Organizational Agility and Operational Performance: Examining TOIE Model. *SN Computer Science, 5*(7), 909. Advance online publication. DOI: 10.1007/s42979-024-03269-3

Van Esch, P., Black, J. S., & Ferolie, J. (2019). Marketing AI recruitment: The next phase in job application and selection. *Computers in Human Behavior, 90*, 215–224. DOI: 10.1016/j.chb.2018.09.009

Vashishth, T. K., Sharma, V., Tomer, T., Kumar, A., Kaushik, S., & Singh, B. (2025). AI in HRM: Transforming Employee Engagement and Satisfaction Amidst Challenges and Opportunities. In Ara, A. (Ed.), (pp. 157–188). Advances in Human Resources Management and Organizational Development. IGI Global., DOI: 10.4018/979-8-3693-7693-5.ch006

Vedapradha, R., Hariharan, R., & Shivakami, R. (2019). Artificial intelligence: A technological prototype in recruitment. *Journal of Service Science and Management, 12*(3), 382–390. DOI: 10.4236/jssm.2019.123026

Venkatesh, V., Morris, M. G., Davis, G. B., & Davis, F. D. (2003). User acceptance of information technology: Toward a unified view. *Management Information Systems Quarterly, 27*(3), 425–478. DOI: 10.2307/30036540

Venugopal, M., Madhavan, V., Prasad, R., & Raman, R. (2024). Transformative AI in human resource management: Enhancing workforce planning with topic modeling. *Cogent Business & Management, 11*(1), 2432550. DOI: 10.1080/23311975.2024.2432550

Vidhya, K. (2025). Harnessing AI and Digital Transformation for Strategic HRM Enhancing International Competitiveness. In Innovative Approaches for International Competitiveness Through Human Resource Management (pp. 35-70). IGI Global Scientific Publishing. DOI: 10.4018/979-8-3373-1005-3.ch002

Vishwanath, B., & Vaddepalli, S. (2023). The future of work: Implications of artificial intelligence on hr practices. Tuijin Jishu/Journal of Propulsion Technology, 44(3), 1711-1724.

Visser, M., Van Eck, N. J., & Waltman, L. (2021). Large-scale comparison of bibliographic data sources: Scopus, Web of Science, Dimensions, Crossref, and Microsoft Academic. *Quantitative Science Studies*, *2*(1), 20–41. DOI: 10.1162/qss_a_00112

Vorobeva, D., Costa Pinto, D., António, N., & Mattila, A. S. (2024). The augmentation effect of artificial intelligence: Can AI framing shape customer acceptance of AI-based services? *Current Issues in Tourism*, *27*(10), 1551–1571. DOI: 10.1080/13683500.2023.2214353

Vygotsky, L. S. (1978). *Mind in society: The development of higher psychological processes* (Cole, M., John-Steiner, V., Scribner, S., & Souberman, E., Eds. & Trans.). Harvard University Press.

Walther, C. C. (2024). *Human Leadership for Humane Technology: The New AI: Agency Ignited* (1st ed. 2024). Springer Nature Switzerland., DOI: 10.1007/978-3-031-67823-3

Wang, A. X., Chukova, S. S., Simpson, C. R., & Nguyen, B. P. (2024). Challenges and opportunities of generative models on tabular data. *Applied Soft Computing*, *166*, 112223. DOI: 10.1016/J.ASOC.2024.112223

Wang, B., Liu, Y., Qian, J., & Parker, S. K. (2022). Achieving effective remote working during the COVID-19 pandemic: A work design perspective. *Applied Psychology*, *71*(1), 16–59. DOI: 10.1111/apps.12290 PMID: 33230359

Wang, Y., Li, J., & Harper, M. (2024). Evaluating large language models for coding student feedback in health-professions education. *Medical Education*, *58*(2), 143–154. DOI: 10.1111/medu.15001

Warning, A., Weber, E., & Püffel, A. (2022). On the Impact of Digitalization and Artificial Intelligence on Employers' Flexibility Requirements in Occupations—Empirical Evidence for Germany. *Frontiers in Artificial Intelligence*, *5*, 868789. DOI: 10.3389/frai.2022.868789 PMID: 35592650

Weber, M. (1922). *Economy and Society*. Univ. of California Press.

Weber, M., & Eisenstadt, S. N. (1968). *On charisma and institution building: Selected papers*. University of Chicago P.

Wei, G., & Jin, Y. (2021). Human resource management model based on three-layer BP neural network and machine learning. *Journal of Intelligent & Fuzzy Systems*, *40*(2), 2289–2300. DOI: 10.3233/JIFS-189226

Wieneke, K. C., Berkland, B. E., Kruse, G. C., Priestley, M. R., Teal, D. M., & West, C. P. (2025, March). Charting a new path forward in addressing employee well-being in health care. [). Elsevier.]. *Mayo Clinic Proceedings*, *100*(3), 501–513. DOI: 10.1016/j.mayocp.2024.11.018 PMID: 40044362

Williams, L. J., Hartman, N., & Cavazotte, F. (2010). Method variance and marker variables: A review and comprehensive CFA marker technique. *Organizational Research Methods*, *13*(3), 477–514. DOI: 10.1177/1094428110366036

Williams, L. J., & O'Boyle, E. H. (2015). Ideal, nonideal, and no-marker variables: The confirmatory factor analysis (CFA) marker technique works when it matters. *The Journal of Applied Psychology*, *100*(5), 1579–1602. DOI: 10.1037/a0038855 PMID: 25822071

Williamson, B., & Piattoeva, N. (2020). Education governance and datafication. *Learning, Media and Technology*, *45*(1), 1–5. DOI: 10.1080/17439884.2020.1707100

Wolff, S. (2005). *Emotional Competence Inventory: Technical manual*. The Hay Group.

Wong, C.-S., & Law, K. S. (2002). *Wong and Law Emotional Intelligence Scale (WLEIS)* [Database record]. APA PsycTests., DOI: 10.1037/t07398-000

Workday. (2023). *Real-Time Employee Sentiment Dashboards: Peakon Insights Report*.

World Health Organization. (2022). *Mental health at work*. World Health Organization. https://www.who.int/news-room/fact-sheets/detail/mental-health-at-work (accessed April 25, 2025).

Wright, J., & Atkinson, D. (2019). *The impact of artificial intelligence within the recruitment industry: Defining a new way of recruiting*. Keele Management School, Keele University.

Wu, L., Qiu, Z., Zheng, Z., Zhu, H., & Chen, E. (2024). Exploring Large Language Model for Graph Data Understanding in Online Job Recommendations. *Proceedings of the AAAI Conference on Artificial Intelligence*, *38*(8), 9178–9186. DOI: 10.1609/aaai.v38i8.28769

Wu, T. J., Pan, Q., Zhang, K., & Zhang, R. X. (2024). Flexible working on employees' quality of work life: The role of locus of control through psychological perspective. *Current Psychology (New Brunswick, N.J.)*, *43*(43), 1–16. DOI: 10.1007/s12144-024-06848-y

Xiao, Q., Yan, J., & Bamber, G. J. (2025). How does AI-enabled HR analytics influence employee resilience: Job crafting as a mediator and HRM system strength as a moderator. *Personnel Review*, *54*(3), 824–843. DOI: 10.1108/PR-03-2023-0198

Yadav, U. S., Sood, K., Tripathi, R., Kumar, A., & Khan, S. A. (2024). Proficiency in the handicraft sector business in a volatile, uncertain, complex, and ambiguous environment. In *VUCA and Other Analytics in Business Resilience*. Emerald Group Publishing Ltd., DOI: 10.1108/978-1-83753-902-420241009

Yamashita, M., Shen, J. T., Tran, T., Ekhtiari, H., & Lee, D. (2023). JAMES: Normalizing Job Titles with Multi-Aspect Graph Embeddings and Reasoning. *2023 IEEE 10th International Conference on Data Science and Advanced Analytics (DSAA)*, 1–10. DOI: 10.1109/DSAA60987.2023.10302559

Yoon, S. W., Han, S.-H., & Chae, C. (2024). People Analytics and Human Resource Development – Research Landscape and Future Needs Based on Bibliometrics and Scoping Review. *Human Resource Development Review*, *23*(1), 30–57. DOI: 10.1177/15344843231209362

Yordanova, S., & Kabakchieva, D. (2022). *Employee turnover reduction by analyzing textual data with SPARK*. 040019. DOI: 10.1063/5.0099629

You, Y., Hu, Z., Li, J., Wang, Y., & Xu, M. (2022). The effect of organizational innovation climate on employee innovative behavior: The role of psychological ownership and task interdependence. *Frontiers in Psychology*, *13*, 856407. DOI: 10.3389/fpsyg.2022.856407 PMID: 35800933

Yuan, M., Bao, P., Yuan, J., Shen, Y., Chen, Z., Xie, Y., Zhao, J., Li, Q., Chen, Y., Zhang, L., Shen, L., & Dong, B. (2024). Large language models illuminate a progressive pathway to artificial intelligent healthcare assistant. *Medicine Plus*, *1*(2), 100030. DOI: 10.1016/j.medp.2024.100030

Yu, D., Li, L., Su, H., & Fuoli, M. (2024). Assessing the potential of LLM-assisted annotation for corpus-based pragmatics and discourse analysis: The case of apology. *International Journal of Corpus Linguistics*, *29*(4), 534–561. DOI: 10.1075/IJCL.23087.YU

Zagenczyk, T. J., Liao, H., & Gentry, W. A. (2020). AI-powered recruitment: Social media and the future of talent acquisition. *Personnel Psychology*, *73*(1), 33–54. DOI: 10.1111/peps.12336

Zawacki-Richter, O., Marín, V. I., Bond, M., & Gouverneur, F. (2019). Systematic review of research on artificial intelligence applications in higher education – where are the educators? *International Journal of Educational Technology in Higher Education*, *16*(1), 39. DOI: 10.1186/s41239-019-0171-0

Zhang, Z., Lu, J., & Wang, Q. (2025). The financial impact of human resources configuration: A quantitative analysis based on modified single candidate optimizer. *Egyptian Informatics Journal*, *29*, 100584. Advance online publication. DOI: 10.1016/j.eij.2024.100584

Zhou, S., Yi, N., Rasiah, R., Zhao, H., & Mo, Z. (2024). An empirical study on the dark side of service employees' AI awareness: Behavioral responses, emotional mechanisms, and mitigating factors. *Journal of Retailing and Consumer Services*, *79*, 103869. DOI: 10.1016/j.jretconser.2024.103869

Zhu, J., & Hudelot, C. (2022). *Towards Job-Transition-Tag Graph for a Better Job Title Representation Learning* (Version 1). arXiv. DOI: 10.18653/v1/2022.findings-naacl.164

Zhu, X. D., & Liu, J. (2020). Education in and after Covid-19: Immediate Responses and Long-Term Visions. *Postdigital Science and Education*, *1-5*(3), 695–699. Advance online publication. DOI: 10.1007/s42438-020-00126-3 PMID: 40476967

Zunic, A., Corcoran, P., & Spasic, I. (2020). Sentiment analysis in health and well-being: Systematic review. In *JMIR Medical Informatics* (Vol. 8, Issue 1). https://doi.org/DOI: 10.2196/16023

Zupic, I., & Čater, T. (2015, July). Bibliometric methods in management and organization. *Organizational Research Methods*, *18*(3), 429–472. DOI: 10.1177/1094428114562629

About the Contributors

Shad Ahmad Khan, an Associate Professor, School of Business, American University of Phnom Penh, Cambodia, stands as a beacon of excellence in academia. With over 14 years of teaching experience, Dr. Khan has established himself as a distinguished researcher specializing in green practices, online business management, individual loyalty, and higher education institutions. He is among the top 2% scientists in the world. He is part of several editorial boards of repute including being an Associate Editor of International Journal of Pluralism and Economics Education (Indexed in Scopus). His scholarly contributions, comprising 70+ Scopus indexed publications, along with a plethora of books, research articles, and book chapters, exemplify his dedication to advancing knowledge in his field. Dr. Khan's expertise extends beyond research, as evidenced by his involvement in funded projects, consultancy endeavors, editorial roles in esteemed journals, and active participation in academic conferences, where he often assumes roles as a session chair and delivers keynote addresses. His extensive engagement in organizing major events and conducting workshops underscores his commitment to fostering learning and professional development. Dr. Khan's multifaceted contributions to academia, coupled with his passion for teaching and research, render him an invaluable resource person poised to inspire and guide the next generation of scholars and professionals in their academic and professional pursuits. He is also associated with INTI International University, Malaysia as a Research Fellow, and Rushford Business School, Switzerland as Supervisor of Doctoral Programs in Business Administration.

Ayben Koy, born in 1980, graduated from Istanbul University's Faculty of Economics in 2004. She is currently a Professor of Finance at Fenerbahce University. Dr. Koy's she earned her Master's degree in Business Administration from Yıldız Technical University and later secured her Ph.D. in Finance from Istanbul University in 2016. Her doctoral research delved into the intricate realm of Derivative Markets, a topic of profound significance within finance. Dr. Koy is the author of three seminal books on derivative markets and has co-authored a significant work in financial econometrics. Her scholarly endeavors are particularly concentrated in the domains of finance, including derivative markets and capital markets.

Chandni Rani is currently an Assistant Professor at the University School of Business, Chandigarh University, Mohali, (Punjab) India. With over three years of teaching experience, her research interests span Human Resources, HR analytics, Organizational behavior, green HRM, and the application of artificial intelligence and virtual reality in HR and the healthcare sector. She is a lifetime member of the International Teachers Association. She is an avid researcher and presented papers at various national and international conferences. Dr. Rani has also played a pivotal role in curriculum development and pedagogy design, enhancing the learning experience at Chandigarh University.

Pooja Kansra is presently working as a Professor and Head of Economics at Mittal School of Business, Lovely Professional University, Phagwara, Punjab (India). She has a teaching experience of fifteen years and research experience of eleven years. Her areas of research include health economics, labor economics, gender economics, insurance and informal sector, digitalization. She is an avid researcher and presented papers in various national and international conferences. She is the recipient of several best paper awards from reputed institutions such MAIMS, IBS, NIT Srinagar, Delhi University and Lovely Professional University. She has to her credit various research papers published in Scopus Indexed Journals including Journal of Consumer Behavior (Wiley, ABDC A category), Economic and Political Weekly (EPW), Journal of Health Management (Sage Publications). Global Business Review (Sage Publications), International Journal of Diabetes in Developing Countries (Springer Publications), Health and Population: Perspectives and Issues (MOHFW) etc. She has the convener of three conferences organized in Lovely Professional University.

Tanveer Kajla is an engineering graduate with doctorate in Tourism Analytics, presently working in NALSAR University of Law, Hyderabad, India. He worked as Assistant Professor with Lovely Professional university. Prior to that he also worked as Research Associate under the ICSSR-IMPRESS Major Project at Punjabi University, Patiala (IN). He has published and presented papers in globally acclaimed conferences and Journals. He has been instrumental delivering expert talks on subjects like Business Analytics, Big Data Analytics, Microsoft Excel, R and Hadoop in academic institutions. His area of research includes Social Network Analysis, Sentiment Analysis, Twitter and Facebook analysis, Text Classification.

***

Munir Ahmad is a seasoned professional in the realm of Spatial Data Infrastructure (SDI), Geo-Information Productions, Information Systems, and Information Governance, boasting over 25 years of dedicated experience in the field. With a PhD in Computer Science, Dr. Ahmad's expertise spans Spatial Data Production, Management, Processing, Analysis, Visualization, and Quality Control. Throughout his career, Dr. Ahmad has been deeply involved in the development and deployment of SDI systems specially in the context of Pakistan, leveraging his proficiency in Spatial Database Design, Web, Mobile & Desktop GIS, and Geo Web Services Architecture. His contributions to Volunteered Geographic Information (VGI) and Open Source Geoportal & Metadata Portal have significantly enriched the geospatial community. As a trainer and researcher, Dr. Ahmad has authored over 50 publications, advancing the industry's knowledge base and fostering innovation in Geo-Tech, Data Governance, and Information Infrastructure, and Emerging Technologies. His commitment to Research and Development (R&D) is evident in his role as a dedicated educator and mentor in the field.

Rubel Amin is the Head of Supply Chain Management at Standard MH Group Limited. He is also an Adjunct Faculty at International University of Business Agriculture and Technology and International Standard University. He is also a Research Associate at the School of Business, Woxsen University, Hyderabad, India. He was an Instructor at USB, Chandigarh University. He has pursued his PhD at Chandigarh University, Punjab, India. He has more than 11 years of corporate experience in supply chain management and four years of teaching and research experience. He is also a certified supply chain manager from ISCEA, America. He has 21 publications in the field of supply chain management and is in Scopus, ABDC, and Web of Science-indexed international journals. More than three articles are under review. He has presented articles in 6 international conferences. He has reviewed and edited almost 50 articles. He is an official reviewer of Science PG, IGI Global, Emerald, and Springer Publisher. He is an editorial team member of Maroon Journal De Management. He has also published five articles in leading Bangladeshi newspapers. A certified researcher with a track record of contributing valuable insights and strategies in academia and industry. He has also started to attend in TV Channel's Program.

Zeeshan Asim is a distinguished academic and researcher with a focus on sustainable supply chains, blockchain technologies, and international business strategies. He has contributed significantly to understanding the intersection of digital innovations and global supply chain management, particularly within emerging markets. His work includes exploring the role of blockchain in enhancing transparency, resilience, and sustainability in large-scale manufacturing sectors

Shivani Dhand is an Associate Professor (14+ years of experience),a Certified SHRM (Society for Human Resource Management)faculty in the department of Mittal School of Business of Lovely Professional University.She is NLP(Neuro Linguistics Programming) Practioner She is also a member of the Indian Society for Training and Development (ISTD) and the Indian Society of Labour Economics. She is also a core committee member and Mentor of an NGO(Shalini Fellowship) Shivani Dhand has worked in an IT company as an HR. She has published 15 research papers in various journals which include Scopus-indexed, UGC care and peer-reviewed journals. She is a certified POSH trainer. She has worked with CPSC (Columbo Plan Staff College) Manila Philippines, and trained the faculty and Principals of various Institutions in Bhutan (2015). In 2016, She worked on one of the projects," Austria as an Innovation leader in EU in Austria and was awarded as best presentation and Excellent paper. Her research is situated in the field of Startups, HR Practices Human Resource Management, Entrepreneurship, and social entrepreneurship with a special focus on academic entrepreneurship.

Shahla Gahramanova is a senior lecturer at the department of "Economics and Business Administration" of Azerbaijan State University of Economics. She teaches "Business Ethics and Corporate Governance", "Corporate Social Responsibility", "Human Resource Management", "Business Communication / Business Correspondence" and other relevant disciplines related to management and business administration. In 1997 she graduated from Azerbaijan University of Languages majoring in "English-French", and in 2003 from the Ukrainian Diplomatic Academy under the Ministry of Foreign Affairs of Ukraine with a master's degree in "International Relations". More than 20 years of teaching/training experience along with research experience in business ethics, corporate social responsibility and sustainable development. Along with teaching Shahla Gahramanova has long held responsible positions in international organizations.

Gagandeep Kaur Gulati is a Professor at University School of Business, Chandigarh University. She did her Doctorate in Management from University Business School, Panjab University, Chandigarh. She has vast experience of 20 years of teaching and corporate. She has contributed research papers to numerous Journals and Books. Her specialization area includes: Entrepreneurship, Human Resource Management, Marketing Management, Women Empowerment and Values & Ethics. She is also a passionate entrepreneur herself and is trying to promote the handicrafts primariy- Phulkari. This is the Embroidery Art of Punjab. She has various rural female artisans in her team. She also possesses a Design Patent. She likes to research on women entrepreneurship specially thise who are further empowering more women.

Isha Jaryal is a dedicated individual with a passion for learning, personal growth, and sharing valuable insights. Known for her keen eye for detail and strong commitment to excellence, she consistently strives to deliver meaningful work that informs, inspires, and engages. Her focus lies in making a positive impact through well-researched insights, effective communication, and a steadfast commitment to lifelong learning.

Sara Kamal has worked as an assistant professor in ACN College, Mangalayatan University as well as AL Barkaat Institute of Management Science, Aligarh, India. She obtained her PhD from Aligarh Muslim University (AMU), Aligarh in 2020. Believing that job stress is spreading like epidemic, she conducted her dissertation research on "Role Stress and its relationship with Emotional Intelligence". She completed her MBA with specialization in Human Resources Management from AMU in 2010. She successfully qualified the UGC NET (2012) and UGC JRF (2013). Dr Kamal has to her credit five research papers published in national and international refereed journals.

Arvinder Kaur is an Assistant Professor in Global School of Finance and Accounting. She has a vast experience of 9 years in teaching Finance subjects. She has authored various research paper in Q1 and Q2 journals and has presented research papers in many prestigious national and international conferences.

Bhanupriya Khatri is an Associate Professor in the University School of Business at Chandigarh University, Mohali, India. She holds a Ph.D. and has over a decade of academic and research experience in organizational behavior, human resource management, and leadership development. In recognition of her innovative teaching methods, Dr. Khatri received the 'E-Guru Award' from Chandigarh University for her effective use of educational technologies in blended learning.

N Mahesh Kumar is working as Deputy Registrar at Narsee Monjee Institute of Management Studies, (NMIMS), Hyderabad. He is a doctorate in Commerce from the Jayoti Vidyapeeth Women's University, Rajasthan. He completed his Master's in Commerce at Osmania University, Hyderabad. He served Gedu College of Business Studies, Royal University of Bhutan as Assistant Professor.

Suresh N. served as an Assistant Professor at the Gedu College of Business Studies, Royal University of Bhutan. He obtained his Master's in Commerce from the

Osmania University India. He is currently a Research Scholar of Jayoti Vidyapeeth Women's University, Rajasthan

Abhishek Kumar Ojha is a dedicated student at University School of Business (USB), Chandigarh University. He is pursuing his degree with a keen interest in business management and emerging industry trends. Abhishek is known for his analytical mindset, teamwork skills, and active participation in academic and co-curricular activities. He aspires to build a successful career in the corporate world through continuous learning and innovation.

Shardul Shankar is a Ph.D. from Indian Institute of Information Technology, Allahabad; and Assistant Professor at Fortune Institute of International Business, New Delhi. He has received B.Tech. (Electronics and Communication Engineering) from Bhagwant University, Ajmer, PGDM (Marketing and HR) from School of Management Sciences, Varanasi and MBA from IIIT Allahabad. His areas of interest include Emotional Intelligence, Leadership, Human Resources, Cognitive Behavior, Computations, and Analytics etc. He has several papers, book chapters, book reviews, patents and commentaries published in National and International Journals of repute.

Heru Susanto is a researcher and academic at the School of Business, Universiti Teknologi Brunei. His work focuses on entrepreneurship,, innovation, and digital transformation in business. With over 2600 citations, and an h-index of 26

Shahina Barayil Thayipurath received her Masters in Business Administration from the Department of Management Studies Palayad, Kannur University in 2014. In 2022 She was hired as Lecturer at University Of West London RAK Branch Campus UAE. She secured Fellowship of higher education on 2024 and currently working on Senior Fellowship application. She writes and attend conferences on various management related topics Such as talent management, Digital consumerism, employee motivation. She is pursuing doctoral degree in management since 2023.

Asokan Vasudevan an Associate Professor at Inti International University, specializes in Operations Management, focusing on optimizing business processes and improving operational efficiency

Abhishek Kumar Yadav is a focused and enthusiastic student at the University School of Business (USB), Chandigarh University. He is pursuing his studies in business with a strong interest in management principles and strategic thinking. Abhishek actively engages in classroom discussions and team projects, showcasing leadership and problem-solving skills. He aims to excel in the corporate sector by applying his knowledge and creativity.

Farah Zahidi is an Assistant Professor at The Emirates Academy of Hospitality Management, Dubai. With over nine years of academic experience across the UAE and India, she specializes in digital marketing, human resource management, and data analytics. Her teaching portfolio spans undergraduate, postgraduate, and executive education programs, and she has mentored diverse cohorts ranging from young students to senior professionals. Farah holds a Ph.D. in Management and is an active researcher with published work in peer-reviewed journals and edited volumes. Her research interests include sentiment analysis, sustainable tourism, consumer behavior, and technology integration in hospitality. She is particularly passionate about blending academic insights with industry relevance to drive impact in the areas of hospitality and responsible business practices. Farah is also a certified trainer and regularly conducts workshops focused on strategic thinking, leadership, and data-driven decision-making.

Index

U

V

W